# IN SPITE OF THE GODS

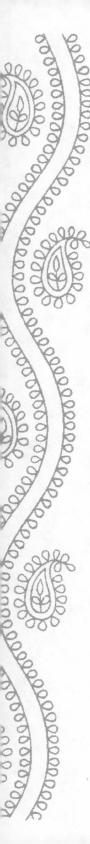

# IN SPITE OF THE GODS

## The Strange Rise of Modern India

EDWARD LUCE

DOUBLEDAY

New York London Toronto Sydney Auckland

Library of Congress Cataloging-in-Publication Data
Luce, Edward, 1968–
In spite of the gods : the strange rise of modern India / by Edward Luce.—1st ed.
    p. cm.
  Includes bibliographical references and index.
  1. India—Econominc conditions—21st century. 2. India—Civilization. I. Title.
  HC435.3.L83 2007
  954.05'3—dc22

                              2006014227

ISBN: 978-0-385-51474-3

# contents

# preface

This book is not about a love affair with the culture and antiquities of India. I have read too many paeans to India by foreigners to have any thoughts of adding to that extensive list. It is about the changing political economy and society of a country whose future will increasingly affect the rest of the world. When reporting on India for the *Financial Times* I usually adhered to the detached and impersonal style that journalists follow. But a book is different, and much of what follows is in the first person. Some of what is contained in these pages is of a critical nature, occasionally very critical. It is hard to observe and chronicle the workings of India's political, economic, and legal systems without sometimes feeling outrage at the squandering of life opportunities for the hundreds of millions of

Indians who still live in poverty. Their opportunities are improving, albeit not rapidly enough—but improving nevertheless. It is hard, too, not to feel frustration with the large numbers of foreigners and Indians who are still wont to see India through a purely spiritual lens. A lot is written about American and French exceptionalism (neither of which sanctifies poverty, it should be added). A lot more could still be written on the Indian variety.

Yet without my deep affection for—and fascination by—India I would never have written this book. Over the years and in the most unexpected ways India has taught me as much about humanity in general as it has about itself. Although occasionally mystifying, India has always opened its doors to me and other inquiring outsiders. With amazingly few exceptions, Indians have been unreservedly kind, open, hospitable, and tolerant of the interrogations of an intrusive foreigner. Quite without meaning to do so, India has also taught me how inhospitable we in the West—and especially in Britain—can often be. I hope the reader will recognize that there is no contradiction between criticism and affection. That way the reader will more easily chime with the book's anticipation of India's rise to a much more significant global role in the first few decades of the twenty-first century.

In five years of traveling around India, observing events and interviewing people—four years as bureau chief for the *Financial Times* and one working on this book—I can think of only a handful of occasions when I was denied access to somebody or to some information that I was seeking. Since I have interviewed many hundreds of Indians, some of them on many occasions, it would take a chapter simply to list them. So I will confine mention to a few people who have been consistently helpful, many of whom have become firm friends. With a few exceptions, I have omitted the names of politicians and businessmen, since availability to journalists is a normal part of their professional lives. I would like to express my profound thanks to Shankar Acharya, Swami Agnivesh, Montek and Isher Ahluwalia, Mani Shankar Aiyar, M. J. Akbar, Sohail Akbar (and his delightful parents in Allahabad), Anil Ambani, Kanti Bajpai, Sanjaya Baru, Rahul Bedi, Jagdish Bhagwati, Surjit Bhalla, Uday Bhaskar, Kiran Bhatty and Aslam Khan ("Karen and Islam"), Farhan Bokhari, Michael and Jenny Carter, Ram Chandra ("Golu"), Vikram Chandra, Vijay Chautiawale, Ashok Chowgule, Stephen P. Cohen, Tarun Das, Nikhil Dey, Jean Dreze, Gordon Duguid, Verghese George, Sagarika Ghosh, Omkar Goswami, Dipankar and Mala Gupta, Shekhar Gupta, Swapan Das Gupta, Husain Haqqani, David Housego, Tony Jesudasan, Prem Shankar Jha, Vijay Kelkar, Sunil Khilnani, Sudheendra Kulkarni, Hanif Lakdawala, Kamal M, Ram Madhav, Moni Malhoutra, Harsh Mander, Ashok Mehta, Pratap Bhanu Mehta, Vinod Mehta, Murli Menon, Khozem Merchant and Malavika Sanghvi, Anjali Mody, Jayaprakash Narain, Sunita Narain, Kishan Negi, Nandan Nilekani, T. N. Ninan, Udit Raj, N. and Mariam Ram, Mahesh Rangarajan, Aruna Roy, Raman Roy, Rajdeep Sardesai, Navtej Sarna, Tesi Schaffer, Suhel Seth, Jyotirmaya Sharma, Ajai and Sonia Shukla, Arun Singh, Mala and Tejbir Singh, N. K. Singh, Ashley Tellis, Karan Thapar, Ashutosh Varshney, and George Verghese.

I would like to underline my thanks to the following people who very kindly took the time to read this manuscript in full and correct errors of fact, judgment, and grammar. These were Michael Arthur, Suman Bery, Ramachandra Guha, Andrew Davis and Jackie Shorey, and Krishna Guha. Throughout the process of writing and researching this book, the help, expertise, and encouragement of Natasha Fairweather, my agent at A. P. Watt, was always indispensable. It was also a great pleasure and an intellectual stimulation to work with Kris Puopolo, my editor at Doubleday in New York, and Tim Whiting, my editor at Little, Brown in London. In addition, I would like to express my gratitude to the *Financial Times*, which, apart from allowing me a year's leave of absence to research and write this book, is the ideal employer for a foreign correspondent. No other newspaper permits its reporters such autonomy and latitude in pursuing their interests. The space it makes available for serious stories about

India continues to distinguish it from most other publications. Not once did the *FT* attempt to impose any preconceptions on what I wrote. Of very few other newspapers would this description consistently hold true.

My acknowledgments conclude with Aparna and Prahlad Basu, my parents-in-law, whose encouragement of my interest in India was equaled only by the insights and experience they were always ready to share. Aparna is a historian and was a professor at Delhi University for many years. Prahlad was—and is—a senior civil servant in New Delhi. Not many foreign correspondents (or sons-in-law) get this kind of assistance. I would also like to thank my own parents, Rose and Richard, who bear the heroic distinction of having read everything I have ever written, including—I subsequently found out—the diaries that I had clearly marked DO NOT READ which I kept as a teenager. Their unquestioning support is one of the reasons I am doing what I want to do in life. This book is dedicated partly to them. The other half of the dedication is to Priya, my wife, whose patience with my eccentric behavior during the course of my working on this book only snapped once or twice, but whose love has always been unwavering. Although she does not agree with all of my views, discussing them with Priya has helped me to clarify and enrich them. She is my victim and occasionally my culprit. Priya is also in many ways a cause of this book.

# IN SPITE OF THE GODS

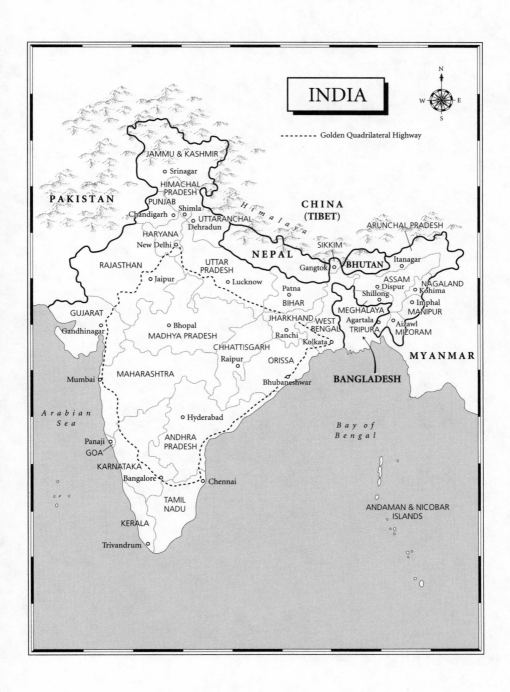

# INTRODUCTION

*To a western observer our civilization appears as all metaphysics,*
*as to a deaf man piano playing appears to be mere movements of*
*fingers and no music.*

RABINDRANATH TAGORE, perhaps India's
greatest poet, who won the Nobel Prize for
Literature in 1913

I had been living in India more than four years when I met André, a sixty-three-year-old Frenchman with a graying ponytail and a passion for Vedantic philosophy. But it felt as though we had met on many previous occasions. I was on a short visit to Auroville, a town in south India founded in 1968 by Mira Alfassa, a nonagenarian Frenchwoman whom everybody calls Mother. She had named the town after Sri Aurobindo, one of India's most celebrated spiritual leaders, whose life's journey, from student years at Cambridge to underground activism against British colonial rule and finally incarnating as a teacher-savant in a charming corner of peninsular India, merits a book or two in itself. Mother, André told me, had "departed her body" in 1973, twenty-three years after Sri Aurobindo, but, fortunately for the questing Frenchman, several months after he had arrived in Auroville.

Since André had moved to Auroville, the town—really an extended ashram—had grown to include several thousand people, most of whom, like the Frenchman, were Westerners who had come in search of the elixir of Indian philosophy. Most of them accepted, like André, that India was special among nations. It possessed a moral and spiritual force that was unique. India, he said, was the key to the survival of the human race. I had come to Auroville to find out what it was about India that gave rise to such faith. "When you are living in the West, in Europe, you feel completely lost," said André, who had welcomed me into his spacious whitewashed home. We were sipping hibiscus juice. "In the West you have to belong to society and follow a certain pattern. You are supposed to get a house, a career, and the whole of life is oriented toward money. India is not like that. India is a unique country," he emphasized, to the agreement of the others present. "Without India, the world is doomed to the poverty of materialism."

André was born during the Second World War and lived an unexceptional early life apart from an unpleasant stint as a soldier in Algeria during the insurgency against French rule. Then one afternoon in Paris he heard there was a conference on Auroville. Having already picked up a copy of the Bhagavad Gita, probably the most widely cited book in Hinduism, André already had some idea of what Indian philosophy might entail. Soon afterward he left for India. Up to this stage André's account was straightforward. But he had not explained what it was that drew him to the Gita or India in the first place. "It seems to me obvious why—I do not see why anybody should have difficulty understanding it," André said, although not unkindly. "India has thousands and thousands of years of practice at harmonizing differences and penetrating to the unity beyond. There is an essence to India that other countries do not have, which tells you that behind the diversity of life there is a spiritual reality called unity." I must have seemed nonplussed, since André saw the need to reinforce his point. "The human race today is in a global crisis that only India can solve by showing the way to superconsciousness, by explaining reincarnation and the unity of all things," he said. "No other country would accept Auroville. It would never survive in the West—they would turn it into a cult."

Mother wanted Auroville to be much more than a cult. But it is hard to get beyond all the hagiographical accounts to a sense of what she was like. She left behind a lifetime's worth of Delphic utterances. Born in Paris in 1878 to a Turkish father and an Egyptian mother, Mira Alfassa had as a child demonstrated a tendency to "commune with nature." Unlike other children, she had been able to leap great distances. She could also "talk with fairies and beings from the world hidden behind ours."[1] As a young woman, Alfassa embarked on a restless journey across different countries and many cultures in search of the key to understanding human existence. Finally in 1916, she moved to India and met Sri Aurobindo, who provided her with the answers. Together they launched a new spiritual movement. Its objective was to teach people that India would be the vehicle that would move the human race to a higher consciousness. They called this "supramentalism." There were other such movements in India, and other Mother-type figures. But the Aurobindo ashram struck deeper roots.

Before meeting André, I had visited the Matrimandir (Mother Temple), a vast elevated globe, about 150 feet in diameter and covered in petal-like golden discs. It was a peculiar sight that prompted thoughts of a spaceship that had been made in Hollywood but had somehow landed in the tropics. In the large clearing around the temple there must have been twenty or thirty people, spread out at polite distances from each other, doing an assortment of yogic stretches under a large banyan tree in the fading light of the day. Most of them were white. One or two might even have been from Los Angeles. Auroville's two or three thousand inhabitants, most of whom live in similar style to André, come from all over the world, as a brief glance at its telephone book made clear—names from Russia, South Korea,

Latin America, Japan, and Europe were there in strength. My guide, Manob Tagore, a soft-spoken Bengali and one of the most delightful people one could hope to meet, told me there were fewer Indians than you might deduce from leafing through the directory, since many of the Westerners had adopted Indian names. Manob told me that as a child he would be taken to see Mother. "She always seemed very calm and that made me feel calm," he said. "That is what I most remember."

André asked me to explain who I was and what I wanted to ask him. I said I was a British journalist who had lived in India for several years and that my wife, Priya, was Indian. I wanted to know why India exerted such a powerful spiritual pull on so many foreigners, since it had not had that effect on me. What I did not say was that I felt India had labored too long under the burden of spiritual greatness that Westerners have for centuries thrust upon it and which Indians had themselves got into the habit of picking up and sending back (with a cherry on top). Over the centuries, and particularly during the era of British colonial rule and its aftermath, many Indians endorsed in one form or another the view that India was a uniquely metaphysical civilization. To most Indians this self-image was certainly preferable to the belittlement that was doled out by many, although not all, of India's colonial rulers. Lord Macaulay, who authored India's first national penal code, infamously wrote that the entire corpus of Indian philosophy and literature was not worth a single bookshelf of Western writing. Worse, but sadly not untypical, Winston Churchill said that India "was a beastly country with a beastly religion" and that it was "no more a country than the Equator."[2]

Conversely, and from an equally emphatic but more deeply rooted tradition, André Malraux, the French novelist, wrote: "Remote from ourselves in dream and in time, India belongs to the Ancient Orient of our soul."[3] Again not untypically, Arthur Schopenhauer, the German philosopher, said the Christian New Testament must have come from India since it had the gentlest civilization known to mankind.[4] Given a choice between Macaulay and Malraux, or between Churchill and

Schopenhauer, one would naturally choose Malraux and Schopenhauer. And although the West has also produced many balanced and scholarly assessments of India over the past 250 years, the views of most ordinary Westerners has been tinged with either the dismissive or the romantic (as many still are). Much of India latched onto the romantic. Amartya Sen, India's Nobel Prize–winning economist, wrote: "The European exoticists' interpretations and praise found in India an army of appreciative listeners, who were particularly welcoming given their badly damaged self-confidence resulting from colonial domination." Nor was such an approach confined to Europeans or to the distant past. On arriving at Harvard University in the late 1980s, Sen found that every single book on India in the famous Harvard Coop bookstore was kept in the section titled "Religions."[5]

André would have approved of this. But the question I most wanted to ask him was whether his spiritual view of India was qualified by the existence of so much poverty in India. No visitor to India can fail to notice the juxtaposition of great human deprivation with its deeply religious culture. In India the sacred and the profane always seem to be linked. Some Indian philosophers have justified poverty as a consequence of the actions the poor committed in their past lives. The doctrine of reincarnation, it seems, makes it easier to overlook the squalor of the here and now. For some it even provides a moral underpinning to poverty. Did André not feel affected by the poverty he saw all around him? He looked at me with mild exasperation. "India is an unbelievably wealthy country because India alone understands the futility of materialism," he pronounced. He emphasized this point again. He must have guessed what I was thinking. Nowadays in India, there is also an increasingly visible cult of wealth. Half the country seems to be in pursuit of it. "If India is now acquiring all the TV channels and the mobile phones and trappings of modern living, then it will not misuse them or become intoxicated," he said. "It does not worry me. This is India."

What André put forward could not be dismissed as the eccentric musings of a hippie or the ravings of a cult follower. The Frenchman, who had clearly engaged with the complexities of the Rig Veda, the Upanishads, and much else besides in the multistory library of Hinduism, was neither a hippie nor—in the sense most Westerners would understand it—did he belong to a "cult," with its undertones of fanaticism, days of judgment, and orgiastic misjudgments. Most Aurovillians, as they call themselves, neither drink alcohol nor smoke marijuana. Equally, they are not required to sign on to any defined set of beliefs or creed. What they would all agree on, and what large numbers of educated and uneducated Indians alike would also affirm, is the unique philosophical and moral importance of India to the future of the world.

Although Auroville is mostly populated by foreigners their sentiments are common in contemporary India. By the same token, large chunks of what André said, particularly regarding India's otherworldliness, would pass uncontroversially at many a dinner party in Notting Hill, Montparnasse, or Beverly Hills. In short, a spirit of romance continues to guide the perceptions both of outsiders and of many Indians themselves. Indeed, so deeply embedded is otherworldliness in our conventional images, symbols, and vocabulary of India that those who consciously reject it are sometimes its unwitting promoters.

When we were leaving, André put his arm around me and said that in spite of my nationality he still liked me. Most British he disliked, he said apologetically, because of what they had done to India, because they always did things differently, like driving on the left and refusing to join European monetary union, and because they always acted so superior. "India will take the world to a higher plane," he said. "Everybody should understand that—even the British." I could not help liking him.

•  •  •

Powerful new images have emerged of India in the last ten or so years, fed mostly by its success in information technology and offshore call centers, the growing reach of Bollywood abroad—popularized in part by the increasing wealth and visibility of Indian communities in the United States, the United Kingdom, and elsewhere—and by India's much-analyzed nuclear weapons program, which was first openly declared in 1998. In the same way that viewing India through a purely religious lens often distorts one's view of the country—and can lead to a basic misreading of what is happening—these new images can also mislead. India's economy is changing rapidly by past standards. But the nature and scope of the changes are sometimes exaggerated. Indians themselves have gotten into a habit of counting their chickens before they are hatched. In recent years it has become commonplace in India to talk of the country as being on the verge of superpower status.

There is another way of viewing India that is perhaps more representative—and certainly more illuminating—which is through its deep-seated and dynamic culture of politics. In the late 1990s Rupert Murdoch, the international media tycoon, visited India to explore launching satellite and cable joint venture operations in the country's growing English-language market. After meeting all the government ministers in New Delhi, India's capital, he flew to Mumbai, India's commercial capital, to meet Dhirubhai Ambani, the (late) owner of Reliance Industries, India's largest private sector company. Ambani, who had a reputation as the shrewdest Indian businessman of his generation, asked Murdoch which people he had met in Delhi. Murdoch said he had seen the prime minister, the finance minister, and others. "Ah, you've met all the right people," said Ambani. "But if you want to get anywhere in India you must meet all the wrong people."[6] By this he meant the corrupt politicians (and probably their counterparts in the bureaucracy as well). In India if you are the wrong sort of person there is a reasonable chance you will end up in politics. But sometimes, perhaps a little less frequently, the right people do as well. In much the same way that Bill Clinton kept reminding himself that it was "the economy, stupid" in the 1992 U.S. presidential elections, in India it is more often a case of "the politics, stupid." Changes to India's economic and religious character cannot be fully grasped without an appreciation of its all-enveloping political culture and the role of the state.

My aim in this book is to provide an unsentimental evaluation of contemporary India against the backdrop of its widely expected ascent to great power status in the twenty-first century. The first chapter deals with the country's booming but peculiarly lopsided economy. Subsequent chapters evaluate India's ubiquitous state and portray India's main political movements. An evaluation of India's volatile relations with Pakistan and with its own Muslim minority is followed by an assessment of India's triangular dance with the United States and China that will come to shape the world in the twenty-first century. Finally, the book looks at India's experience of modernity and urbanization, in which the country's religious values are proving versatile at reinventing themselves in contemporary form. I conclude by looking at the challenges India faces in sustaining its much-anticipated emergence over the coming years.

More than two generations have passed since India gained freedom from British rule "at the stroke of midnight" on August 15, 1947. More than two generations have also passed since Mohandas Gandhi, who was the spiritual and strategic leader of India's Congress Party–led freedom struggle, was assassinated en route to his evening prayers in New Delhi by Nathuram Godse, a right-wing Hindu fanatic, on January 30, 1948.

Gandhi, whose success in maintaining a mostly nonviolent struggle against the British was an extraordinary feat of personal magnetism, continues both to divide Indians and to haunt their dreams. Great attention is still lavished on the transformative—and in some ways magical—effect that he had on ordinary people, in his capacity alone to bring the freedom struggle to the unlettered masses and to inspire their participation. It was Gandhi's ability to speak in the demotic idiom that converted the freedom struggle from a club of London-educated lawyers in three-piece suits seeking "English rule without the English" to a mass-based movement of all Indians.

Gandhi's role as a master of political strategy and tactics is well understood. Less attention has been devoted to the influence of Gandhi's antimaterialist philosophy on India's development since 1947. In many ways this influence lingers on, and not just through people like our friend André. Societies are in some ways like human beings. Things that have happened to them in their formative years have a tendency to shape their decisions and character long after those events have lost their context. Yet if Gandhi returned to India today he would be surprised by much of what he found.

India in the early twenty-first century is an increasingly self-confident, materialistic, and globalized place. In 1991 India abruptly changed economic course when it dismantled the tight system of controls and permits known as the "License Raj" that it had adopted after independence. Since then, India has clearly been on the economic ascent. The country is capturing an ever-greater share of software markets in the United States and Europe and starting to develop a manufacturing sector that can compete in world markets. India has also acquired the military trappings of an aspiring superpower. India's elites openly debate when—not whether—the country will develop intercontinental nuclear missiles. It is also a country whose urban and English-speaking middle classes are soaking up consumer brand culture as if it were a new religion. If Gandhi had not been cremated, he would be turning in his grave.

At the same time India in the twenty-first century remains home to more than a third of the world's chronically malnourished children as defined by the United Nations, and has an average life expectancy and literacy rate that lag pitifully behind many developing countries, most glaringly China. Roughly 750 million of India's 1.1 billion people continue to live in villages, almost half of which lack access to all-weather roads, and countless numbers of which (India has 680,000 villages) are not within reach of effective primary health-care centers or well-functioning elementary schools. Almost half of India's women do not know how to read and write, and a large proportion of those who are technically literate can do little more than sign their name.

It is also a country where much of the elite continue to subscribe to Gandhi's belief—enunciated in the context of a freedom struggle that was seeking to broaden its appeal—that the village should remain the main building block of Indian society. Many, including Jawaharlal Nehru, India's first prime minister and Gandhi's protégé, argued against him. The argument continues today. India is slowly urbanizing, and it is hard to imagine what could stop the continuing expansion of India's cities. But Gandhians continue to believe the village should occupy a holy space at the center of Indian nationhood. Their influence continues to undermine attempts to provide better planning for India's cities.

This is what Gandhi wrote of the village in a letter to Nehru: "I am convinced that if India is to attain true freedom, and through India the world also, then sooner or later the fact must be recognized that people will have to live in villages, not towns; in huts, not in palaces. Crores [tens of millions] of people will never be able to live in peace with each other in towns and palaces. They will then have no recourse but to resort to both violence and untruth."[7] In *Hind Swaraj* (Self-Rule for India), Gandhi's most important book and probably the most widely cited today, he wrote: "Remove his [the villager's] chronic poverty and his illiteracy and you have the finest specimen of what a cultural, cultivated free citizen should be. . . . To observe morality is to attain mastery over our minds and passions. So doing, we know ourselves. If that definition be correct, then India, as so many writers have shown, has nothing to learn from anybody else."

An element of Gandhi's cultural pride and some of his profound disdain for modernism should be seen in historical context as an effective tactical riposte to the insults that were often hurled at "benighted India" by the colonialists, and as a way of raising the self-esteem of the masses. Gandhi was brilliantly equipped to do so. Born in the western Indian state of Gujarat, Gandhi qualified as a barrister in London in the 1890s. Before he returned to India in 1913, Gandhi had already come to the world's attention in South

Africa where he had opposed the racial pass laws, and had suffered imprisonment in the process. It was in South Africa that he developed the strategy of nonviolent civil disobedience that he was to use to such good effect in India.

Gandhianism was not merely a tactic to bolster the freedom struggle. It was also a philosophy of how society should be organized and how people should live. It continues to influence the conscious and unconscious thoughts of much of India's intelligentsia today. To cite an enduring example: without an appreciation of Gandhi's impact on economic thinking, it is hard to explain why India has so badly inhibited the ability of its textile sector to grow to a size more fitting with its potential. As any student of development knows, textile production has played a critical role in the industrialization of most societies, from Britain in the eighteenth century to China in the twenty-first. Gandhi's legacy can be seen in India's continued tariff bias against synthetic fabrics in favor of cotton* (when the bulk of export demand is for the former), and in regulations that provide disincentives for textile companies to grow beyond a certain "cottage industry" size, which penalizes commercial success and protects failure.

Some of these policies have been relaxed since India changed economic course in 1991. And many of those now resisting any further relaxation in these regulations are doing so not on Gandhian grounds but because they represent vested interests that benefit from the status quo. But India's competitors, notably China, which in 2005 shipped out four times the value of India's textile exports and which provided equivalently larger numbers of jobs, do not have to wrestle with the legacy of someone who in many ways is a modern saint. It has been cited many times over the years, yet it is impossible to resist repeating what Sarojini Naidu, an Indian freedom fighter,

---

*Gandhi's use of the simple spinning wheel as a device to popularize knowledge of Britain's exploitative imperial tariff system served India's freedom struggle brilliantly. But as Amartya Sen has pointed out, it made no sense as an economic policy after independence.

once said of the Mahatma: "It costs us a lot to keep Gandhiji in poverty," she said. That meter is still running. Yet there are important lessons from Gandhi about respect for the natural environment that India would do well to rediscover, as I shall argue later in the book.

Bhimrao Ambedkar is much less well known outside India than is Gandhi. Yet to millions of Indians he is a more important figure than Gandhi. Ambedkar's bespectacled statues can be found in villages the length and breadth of this densely populated subcontinent. Unlike Gandhi, with whom he clashed repeatedly and often bitterly, Ambedkar saw no contradiction between accepting modern science and technology and opposing imperial rule. But as the first recognized leader of the caste that was formerly known as untouchable and which is now called "Dalit"—meaning "oppressed," or "broken to pieces"—Ambedkar gave India's most marginalized and atrophied human beings their first real hope of transcending their hereditary social condition.*

Ambedkar saw the caste system as India's greatest social evil, since it treated millions of people as subhumans by the fact of their birth. The hope that Ambedkar gave to Dalits may not yet have been redeemed in full measure or even substantially, to paraphrase the poetic address Nehru gave at independence. But there are enough among India's estimated 200 million Dalits who have tasted freedom and mobility since 1947 for it to be unimaginable that they would retreat to the mind-set of deference, acquiescence, and even invisibility that had been required of them for so long.

Ambedkar, who was India's first untouchable to be educated abroad, undertaking his postgraduate studies at Columbia University in New York and then qualifying as a barrister in London in 1916, was also the principal author of India's 1950 constitution, which enshrines the equality of individuals before the law and gives all adult

*Ambedkar rejected as patronizing the name *Harijan*—literally "children of God"—that Gandhi used for untouchables.

Indians the right to vote, regardless of caste or any other identity. The blue-suited lawyer had the last laugh over his Gandhian opponents during the drafting process when he used his superior knowledge of the law to neutralize upper-caste Hindu demands. Ambedkar succeeded in shifting several clauses, which, for example, called for the banning of cow slaughter, the prohibition of alcohol, and the social primacy of the village, out of the "Fundamental Rights" section of the constitution, which had legal teeth, and into the innocuous "Directives Principles" section, which was a nonbinding wish list.

Ambedkar's view of the village stemmed from his own experience, in which the humiliations he had suffered as a child, when barbers refused to cut his hair and wayside cafés had denied him entrance, were at least partially atoned for by the opportunities that an education in Bombay had provided him. With apologies to Indian readers, many of whom will have memorized these words, this is what Ambedkar thought of the Indian village: "The love of the intellectual Indian for the village community is of course infinite, if not pathetic. . . . What is the village but a sink of localism, a den of ignorance, narrow mindedness and communalism?"*8

Ambedkar, whose statue even today—in fact, especially today—can trigger a backlash wherever it is erected, described caste hierarchy "as an ascending scale of hatred and a descending scale of contempt." Megasthenes, who was the Greek ambassador to the court of Pataliputra, then India's leading power, in 300 BC, observed of India's caste rules: "No-one is allowed to marry outside his caste or exercise any calling or art except his own."9 This held good for more than two thousand years. But it does not serve as an accurate description anymore.

From Ambedkar's writings it is clear he hoped democracy would help dissolve the caste system. That has not happened, or at least not

---

*Communalism in India is taken to mean allegiance to one's own ethnic group, rather than to society, usually in terms of religion but also caste. The normal Western usage of the term communal, meaning "common living or sharing," is not intended anywhere in this book.

in the way he would have hoped. Caste has indeed been severed from its ritualistic and economic roots, but in terms of political identity caste is alive and kicking in today's India. Doubtless the Dalit lawyer would be horrified by some of the larceny and thinly disguised mafia rule that passes as lower-caste politics in much of India today, particularly in the densely populated and least advanced states of northern India. He would also be disappointed to observe that many of India's lower-caste parties today seek not to abolish caste but simply to improve their position vis-à-vis other castes, whether it is agitating to raise their respective government job quotas, or building more monuments to their leaders, gods, and symbols. Caste has not, as many had expected, given way to class in terms of political loyalties. As the joke goes, "In India you do not cast your vote, you vote your caste."

Nevertheless, caste as a hereditary determinant of occupation has gradually been eroded. Urban Indians, and many even in the villages, are no longer forced to perform hereditary functions, although many still do out of necessity. For example, upper-caste Brahmins can be found in the leather trade, a previously taboo occupation, and there are Dalits who cook food for people of other castes—again, until recently, something that would have been unthinkable. Caste intermarriage is also rising, although it is still extremely rare in the villages where more than two-thirds of Indians continue to reside. Ambedkar's hopes for a caste-free India are uncompleted. But it is tempting to believe that history is on his side.

Perhaps the largest ghost stalking today's India is that of Jawaharlal Nehru, whose legacy is as divisive as that of Gandhi or Ambedkar but whose role in shaping India's modern character, whether the state, democracy, or civil society, exceeds that of the other two. Nehru was prime minister between 1947 and 1964, and no other Indian leader, except his own daughter, Indira Gandhi, who held the job for fourteen years, has come close to Nehru's political longevity at the top.

Some of the apparent and bewildering contradictions of today's

India can be traced to Nehru. Although a strong believer in modernity, Nehru towers over the closest thing India has to a feudal royal family, the Nehru-Gandhi dynasty.* In fact Jawaharlal was in retrospect the second of the dynasty since his father, Motilal Nehru, had been president of the Congress Party and one of its earliest members after that body was founded in 1885.

After Gandhi was murdered, Nehru became India's foremost nationalist. Yet he only half-jokingly referred to himself as "the last Englishman to rule India." Educated at Harrow, one of Britain's most rarefied public schools, and Cambridge University before qualifying as a barrister in London, Nehru and his father were typical of the anglicized lawyers who dominated the Congress Party before Gandhi dressed the party in homespun cotton. While in Paris on "vac" from Cambridge, Nehru wrote to his father about a Shakespearean drama he had seen performed in French: "I don't think the actors were quite sure whether it was a pantomime or a tragedy!"[10] Although he accepted Gandhi's logic of dressing and behaving like an Indian, Nehru never lost the demeanor of an Edwardian gentleman. On the many occasions when Nehru was arrested by the British and imprisoned, he would, as a rule, eat cornflakes, fried eggs, bacon, and fried tomatoes, before submitting to his captors. Gandhi would have a drop of lime juice and some goat's milk.

But Nehru's anglophilia stretched much further than his private tastes. As prime minister in 1947 he made the decision to retain the services of India's elite imperial civil servants, roughly half of whom were Indian. In an era when imperial collaborators in other newly independent colonies were being executed, sent to labor camps, fleeing into exile, or at the very least losing their jobs, Nehru was having them round to tea and reading their briefing papers. He even pre-

---

*It was a coincidence that led Indira to marry Feroze Gandhi, a philandering journalist from north India who was no relation to the Mahatma. Feroze, who died young from a heart attack, belonged to the Parsi community of Persian Zoroastrians.

vailed upon Lord Mountbatten, Britain's last viceroy of India, to remain for a year as India's first head of state.*

The legacy of Nehru's Englishness—for want of a better word—is visible in every corner of early-twenty-first-century India, in the little-altered system of district collectors, who continue to combine both executive and judicial sway over the country's subprovincial units. This system is a source of both strength and weakness for India. It is a strength because the Indian Administrative Service (IAS) provides the glue that helps to keep a mind-bogglingly heterogeneous country together. But it is a weakness because IAS is staffed by an unsackable elite, for whom democracy is something of a rival. The uneasy, and at times bizarre, relationship between the IAS and India's elected but often semieducated provincial leaders is a recurrent theme in this book.

Nehru's Edwardian stamp is also visible in the continued cult of the omnipresent state, which he shared with many left-wing upper-class Englishmen of that era—notably the Fabians, who believed that socialism could be implemented peacefully through the state by a qualified class of "Platonic" technocrats. That Nehru was more influenced by the Fabians than by the Russian Bolsheviks, Indians can be thankful. But traces of Nehru's economic model, in which the state would lead the country's drive to industrialize at the expense of both consumption, which he saw as frivolous, and effective land reform, which he felt unable fully to accomplish in a democracy, are still visible in spite of the decision in 1991 to begin dismantling his notorious "License Raj" of extensive state regulation of the economy.

There are still strong echoes today of the distaste Nehru felt for private business and the pursuit of moneymaking, although they have grown fainter since 1991. Although he was a Brahmin, who, in spite of his sincere aversion to the caste system, was still known as Pandit Nehru (an honorific indicating his caste origin), traces of

---

*Nehru enjoyed an intimate friendship with Edwina Mountbatten, the last viceroy's wife, which could have been an added incentive.

Nehru's personal complexities are easy to recognize in the attitudes of many modern upper-caste Indians. Nehru wrote disparagingly of *"bania* civilization" and said socialism would lead to the end of the "acquisitive society." *Banias* are petty traders and moneylenders who are much lower in the caste pecking order than Brahmins. Contemporary India has a deeply ambivalent view of money and moneymaking that owes much to Nehru.

But Nehru's most important legacy, and one that remains mostly intact, was his secularism and his strong disdain for communalism. Nehru was a self-confessed atheist with an ill-concealed dislike of religiosity and all its ritual habits. The tendency, again, common among upper-class Englishmen of his time, to distrust spiritual or theological fervor sometimes spilled over into frustration with Gandhi, at whose feet he figuratively and sometimes literally sat.

"Religion as practised in India," Nehru wrote, "has become the old man of the sea for us and it has not only broken our backs but stifled and almost killed all originality of thought or mind." For the most part Nehru tolerated and even admired Gandhi's ability to speak in the language of the masses, but when the Mahatma talked of doing God's will, Nehru sometimes snapped: "His [Gandhi's] frequent references to God—God has made him do this, God even indicated the dates of that fast—were most irritating," he wrote.[11]

To the despair of almost all Indians, including Nehru, the country was partitioned in 1947 to create a separate homeland for India's Muslims, sparking riots that killed up to a million people and triggering the movement of twelve million people across the newly drawn borders. Nehru's insistence that Muslims be given equal rights in a secular independent India earned him the undying hatred of right-wing Hindu revivalists. Yet unlike Gandhi, Nehru died peacefully in his bed.

However, Nehru's secular legacy has suffered repeated and partially successful assaults from a resurgent Hindu right wing since the mid-1980s. It is revealing that India's Hindu revivalist movement, whose political party, the Bharatiya Janata Party (India People's

Party), headed the coalition government that took India into the twenty-first century, has co-opted the names and images of almost every national icon—including those of Gandhi and Ambedkar. But Nehru remains hate figure number one to the Hindu Right more than forty years after his death. The feeling was entirely mutual: "It is said," wrote Nehru, "that there are 52 lakh (5.2 million) sadhus [wandering ascetics] and beggars in India. Possibly some of them are honest. But there is no doubt that most of them are completely useless people, who wish to dupe others and live on their earnings without working themselves."[12] There is no estimate of how many sadhus India has today, although the country's population has more than tripled since Nehru made that remark.

The title of this book, *In Spite of the Gods: The Strange Rise of Modern India,* is inspired to some extent by Nehru's contention that India's greatest strengths are not exclusively, or even necessarily, located in its religious traditions. India's advantages are found in its vibrant democracy, which has confounded expectations by not only surviving but also entrenching itself deep within India's culture. They are also to be found in its traditions of pluralism, which have given the country hundreds of years of practice at managing social conflict without automatic resort to violence. It is true that the partition of the country along religious grounds and the subsequent aftershocks led to great bloodshed. But there is nothing in India's history that could approximate the mass killing Europe has suffered. India's strengths are also to be found in its deep well of intellectual capital and technological prowess, which finally today are helping to propel the country toward a global role more befitting the country's size.

But, as the subtitle of this book suggests, the character of India's rise is also strange, or unusual. That India is finally emerging as an important economic and political force on the world stage while remaining an intensely religious, spiritual, and, in some ways, superstitious society is unusual by the standards of many countries. Likewise, the fact that India, alone among large nations, embraced full democracy before it had a sizable middle class or anything close to majority literacy among its voters was unique at the time and remains so on this scale.

India's economy is now expanding rapidly without having gone through a broad-based industrial revolution—again, unusually so. The vast bulk of India's workforce remains in the villages. India's economic engine is powered not principally by its factories or by the manufacture of physical products but by its competitive service sector. This situation might gradually be correcting itself. But for the time being India's service sector has an economic weighting that gives it more in common with mature developed economies, such as the United States or Britain.

India's rise is also strange because of the volatile and sometimes harsh character of its politics. No other democracy has to operate with twenty-four-party coalitions. Deeply fragmented and often incoherent government is likely to be the norm in India for the foreseeable future. By most expectations, the corruption and administrative cynicism that are the result of this situation ought to be slowing India's development—and to some extent they are. Yet, much like Italy, where, so the joke goes, "the economy grows at night, while the government is sleeping," India over the last twenty years has been expanding at a rate exceeded only by China.

Finally, the character of India's rise is unusual because it is explicitly desired—and to some extent assisted—by other countries, most notably the United States, as we shall see later in the book. Rightly or wrongly, many countries around the world fear the rise and growing military reach of China in the coming decades and have concluded that India is the only country large and like-minded enough to act as a counterweight to its giant and growing neighbor across the Himalayas. India sometimes bristles at the suggestion that it could play such a role. Whether it likes it or not—and in spite of appearances, India does enjoy the attention—India's role as a potential counterbalance to China is a key element in the calculations of policy makers in the West and elsewhere. Perhaps the most important Indian piece on the geopolitical chessboard is the country's expanding nuclear arsenal.

•   •   •

In India things happen when you least expect them. And vice versa. This trait is a constant source of both delight and frustration with living in India. I had requested an interview with A. P. J. Abdul Kalam, the president of India, about plans for a vast engineering project to link up India's rivers. Opponents of the scheme, which at the time of writing in 2006 had yet to get off the ground, called it "Pharaonic." Supporters said it would solve India's timeless drought and flood problems once and for all.

The president, whose powers are strictly limited in India's Westminster-style parliamentary system, was a supporter of the rivers project. I was looking forward to hearing his views. "There is absolutely no possibility of an interview with the president—presidents of India don't give interviews," his private secretary told me over the telephone. I felt crestfallen and was about to hang up when he continued: "But the president would be very happy to invite you for a cup of tea and a little chitchat."

An engineer and scientist by profession, Abdul Kalam is known as the "father of the nuclear missile," since he was in charge of India's missile development program for many years. He was also the head of India's defense research and development organization when India first openly* tested nuclear warheads in May 1998. To the disquiet of some in India—but not many—Kalam greeted the successful tests, which had been carried out underground in the deserts of Rajasthan in western India, with the following words: "I heard the earth thundering below our feet and rising above us in terror. It was a beautiful sight."

*India conducted an oxymoronic "Peaceful Nuclear Test" in 1974.

The three tests were greeted with street parties and ceremonial distribution of sweets around India, causing great disquiet in Washington and around the world. Pakistan followed suit a few days later,
sparking even greater celebrations there. Since then, and in spite of
attempts by India and Pakistan to "normalize" relations and resolve
their long-simmering dispute over the Himalayan state of Kashmir,
the Indian subcontinent has frequently been labeled the "most dangerous nuclear flashpoint in the world"—a phrase first used by President Clinton. It was only under the Bush administration, after 2001,
that the United States began to modify and ultimately change its
judgment about India's nuclear status.

It is hard, in spite of the risks of accident or misunderstanding, for
someone living in the region to imagine nuclear war taking place—
not because of Pakistan, which is usually controlled by the army and
which views its nuclear arsenal as a genuine military tool; but because of India, which sees its nuclear deterrent as a purely hypothetical symbol that will win it recognition as a great power.

"Oh no, we don't talk about nuclear weapons," said the diminutive septuagenarian president, with his trademark mop of hair.
"Would you like a biscuit?" I had quickly got bored of rivers, on
which the president had said nothing startlingly new and it was anyway an off-the-record conversation so what he said could not be put
to much use. As a reporter I felt it would be remiss not to steer the
conversation onto more fissile terrain. To no avail.

The next time I saw the president was at some distance at India's
annual Republic Day Parade, which takes place on January 26, the
date on which, in 1930, Gandhi, Nehru, and the other leading lights
of the Congress Party first unfurled the Indian tricolor flag in defi-
ance of the British. Seventy-five years later I caught a glimpse of Abdul Kalam sitting in his presidential enclave with a visiting dignitary
and other luminaries observing the parade.

A grand tableau of tanks, airplanes, artillery, and nuclear-capable
missiles was cruising down the broad and long avenue that links the
presidential palace to the India Gate. "And this," proclaimed a soupy

voice over the speaker system, in a tone more suitable for a beauty pageant, "is the Agni II class nuclear-capable missile, which has a range of up to 1,500 kilometers." I could not see the president's expression. But I imagine it was happy.

Indian nationalism has evolved considerably since Gandhi elevated nonviolence and noncooperation into a badge of identity for his emerging nation. Gandhi would surely not have been pleased to discover that India had developed nuclear weapons or that its missiles were named after ancient Hindu gods—Agni is the Vedic god of fire. But in spite of this, today's India would not be unrecognizable to Gandhi. Nor would it be unrecognizable to Ambedkar or Nehru.

Although this book is not so rash as to predict the future, there are one or two things that can be suggested. Most Indians will remain proud of their nuclear status, since it proves they can accomplish technological feats without much help or encouragement from outside. In contrast, most of Pakistan's nuclear technology comes straight from China. Nuclear status also puts India in the same league as the major powers, a misplaced vanity according to some Indian and foreign critics, but one that should not be confused with aggression. Unlike many other countries in the neighborhood, India has no unfinished business, neither seeking nor claiming new territory. As the diplomats say, "India is a status quo power."

To go a little further, India's emergence as a stronger economic and military power over the next generation is much likelier to add to, rather than subtract from, global stability. This, admittedly, strays close to prediction, an art form I would normally leave to André, Mother, and others. But whatever India's vulnerabilities or faults, and this book grapples with some of the major ones, territorial expansion can almost certainly be removed from the checklist. As we have seen, spiritual expansion is quite another matter.

# 1. GLOBAL AND MEDIEVAL

India's Schizophrenic Economy

*Its stupendous population consists of farm laborers. India is one vast farm—one almost interminable stretch of fields with mud fences between. Think of the above facts: and consider what an incredible aggregate of poverty they place before you.*

MARK TWAIN, *Following the Equator*, 1897[1]

It took a long time. But finally in the late 1990s India started to build roads that could get you from A to B at something better than a canter. Until then, India's most significant highway was the Grand Trunk Road that bisects the country from north to south. Laid at various stages by the late medieval Mughal dynasty, then upgraded and extended by the British in the nineteenth century and popularized by Rudyard Kipling in his novel *Kim*, most of the "GT Road," as it is known, got acquainted with asphalt only after independence. But it is a single lane and one can rarely exceed an average of thirty miles an hour. So the relative novelty of India's double-lane expressways still generates a buzz. By 2006, India had all but completed the 3,000-mile "Golden Quadrilateral" expressway linking the country's four largest cities: Delhi to Mumbai (formerly known as Bombay) to Chennai (formerly known as Madras) to Kolkata (formerly known as Calcutta)* to Delhi. Average speeds on the better stretches are closer to sixty miles an hour.

For some, the expressways have heralded a modern era of speed, punctuality, and hygienic roadside bathrooms. For others, they represent a brash intrusion on the more lackadaisical world they cut through. To me, the new expressways provide an intriguing juxtaposition of India's multispeed economics. Curiosity—and an instinct of self-preservation—means I occasionally move into the slow lane. One of the best ways of observing India's galloping new economy is to count the number of car brands that whir past you in the fast lane. You tend to lose count at thirty or forty. In the early 1990s, as India was starting to relax import and investment restrictions on foreign manufacturers, you would at best have counted six or seven makes of car. More than 90 percent of them would have been Ambassadors, the stately but desperately uncomfortable colonial-era vehicles that are still used by VIPs, and Marutis, the cramped family passenger car, still manufactured under a joint venture between Suzuki of Japan and the Indian government. Nowadays you have little time to register the tinted and reflector windows of the Toyotas, Fiats, Hondas, Tatas, Fords, Volkswagens, and Mercedes-Benz, as they flash past.

But your speed is never quite what it should be. Coming far too frequently from the opposite direction, but on your side of the road, you encounter decrepit scooters, bicycles, and even camel-drawn carts, whose drivers appear blissfully unfazed by the fact that they are breaking all known rules of traffic and common sense. Once or twice, on the two-hundred-mile Delhi expressway to Jaipur, a city in the neighboring state of Rajasthan, my journey has been brought to a halt by a herd of goats. Even without the local fauna, the absence of lane discipline means you are mostly on the edge of your seat.

---

*The earlier names of all three cities were associated with the era of British rule, but only changed in the 1990s.

But it is at the side of the expressways in the glaring billboards advertising cell phones, iPods, and holiday villas and the shiny gas stations with their air-conditioned mini-supermarkets that India's schizophrenic economy reveals itself. Behind them, around them, and beyond them is the unending vista of rural India, of yoked bullocks plowing the fields in the same manner they have for three thousand years and the primitive brick kilns that dot the endless patchwork of fields of rice, wheat, pulse, and oilseed. There are growing pockets of rural India that are mechanizing and becoming more prosperous. But they are still islands. It is in this almost continuous contrast that you observe the two most striking features of India's early-twenty-first-century economy: its modern and booming service sector in a sea of indifferent farmland. It would be tempting, as you cruise happily toward your destination with a reasonable chance of being on time, to believe these features are from different worlds. Along the way, you might also glimpse an occasional factory and an assembly plant or two for vehicles or washing machines. But evidence of manufacturing in India is far thinner on the ground than it is in neighboring China.

•    •    •

By the time of independence, Nehru had already helped to forge a consensus in which the country would aim for complete economic self-sufficiency and the state would lead the effort by building up heavy industry, with an emphasis on steel plants and large dams. It has become fashionable since 1991 to write off Nehru as a hopeless idealist who tied the country up in socialist red tape for forty years. Much of the criticism is fair,* since India failed to achieve the high

---

*India's average growth rate of just 3.2 percent between 1950 and 1980 was subsequently labeled the "Hindu rate of growth" since it was barely higher than population growth (thus doing little to raise per capita living standards). But it was a sharp improvement on the average 1 percent annual growth in the first half of the century under the British.

economic growth rates that were seen at the time in Japan and later in South Korea, Taiwan, Thailand, and Malaysia. But in the late 1940s and 1950s Nehru's economic strategy was perfectly in step with worldwide economic fashion. It came with the blessings of a team from the Massachusetts Institute of Technology in Cambridge, which advised New Delhi on the country's early five-year development plans. India was also advised by Gosplan, the Soviet Union's economic planning agency.

The idea, which combined India's critique of the imperial economic system with a widespread global distrust of free trade following the disasters that had resulted in Europe and elsewhere during the "hungry thirties," was to give the state a primary role in an economy aiming for self-reliance, or *swadeshi*—the second most important rallying cry of India's freedom movement after *swaraj*, or self-rule. Of great importance in kick-starting this model were a series of large projects that stimulated further economic activity—much as the widely admired Tennessee Valley Authority had in the United States. Nehru liked to call such projects "temples of concrete."

Nehru's plans for a closed economy dominated by the state also came with the blessings of Britain's postwar Labour government, which had agreed to Indian independence, and which carried out its own nationalization of private sector industries to a far greater degree than did Nehru's India. Many of the Labour government's Fabian advisers were accorded a warm welcome in Nehru's New Delhi. Indeed, it was not until fifteen to twenty years after India's independence that international praise of the country's economic model was outweighed by rising concerns about its effectiveness. Until then India's trajectory was uncontroversial and relatively unexceptional.

Yet, in retrospect and in comparison to other developing economies in Asia, Nehru's economic policies served India poorly. In 1950 South Korea, which was yet to emerge from its war with Communist North Korea, had the same living standards as India (roughly

$50 annually per capita in 2005 prices). Fifty years later, South Korea's per capita income was above $10,000, which was more than ten times higher than that of India. More or less similar contrasts can be found between India and most of the countries of east and Southeast Asia. Even China, which devoted much of the first thirty years of its revolution to countrywide terror, now has double India's per capita income, having started at about the same level at the time of its revolution in 1949.

Why did Nehru's approach fail? In the answers can also be found the explanations for why India's economy today is developing in such a curiously lopsided way. At independence, India was an overwhelmingly rural, agricultural, and impoverished country. Almost nine out of ten Indians lived in villages and depended on the meager yields of farming, mostly subsistence farming, to live from day to day. In 1951, when India conducted its first census after independence, the country had a literacy rate of only 16 percent—which means little more than one in seven of its 320 million people could even sign his or her name. Average life expectancy was just thirty-two years, an extraordinary but credible figure that gives a fair picture of the abysmal quality of life for most of India's villagers. Common descriptions at the time talked of emaciated peasants with visible rib cages, "coolies" half bent from a (short) lifetime of manual labor, and children with potbellies from protein deficiency.

India at independence was a country desperately in need of rural land reform and measures that would drastically boost crop yields so it could feed its people and build a launch pad for future growth. What it got instead was public steel plants and aluminum smelters, which not only were, for the most part, heavily loss-making but also ate up India's precious foreign exchange resources. The Indian farmer needed local irrigation projects to help insulate him against the vagaries of India's wildly erratic annual monsoon. Instead Nehru unveiled grand dams, most of which are now crumbling and some of which were never completed. The average Indian also needed to learn how to read and write and have access to antibiotics and antimalaria drugs, without which it was virtually impossible to escape poverty. Instead, Nehru's Congress Party governments poured resources into universities for the urban middle classes and into new public hospitals in the cities.

Hindsight makes it easy to dismiss as hopelessly optimistic Nehru's belief that devoting most of India's scarce financial resources to grand projects would propel the country to industrial status within a generation. Yet even at the time there were skeptical voices who questioned whether higher education should receive the same budgetary allocation as elementary education, in a country where 84 percent of people were illiterate.[2] There were also a few critics who wondered whether the amount New Delhi spent on agriculture should be as low as a third of the total spending in India's first five-year plan, which was launched in 1952, plummeting to less than a fifth of spending in the second plan in 1957, when more than four-fifths of people depended on farming to survive.[3] But their voices were drowned in a sea of utopian rectitude. The disparity between the Indian policy elite's dreams for tomorrow and what most Indians needed at the time was stark.

To be fair, Nehru had tried land reform and to some extent succeeded in getting rid of the most feudal end of the spectrum. The notorious zamindari system that had been set up by the British in most of northern India, under which large landholders, the zamindars, were responsible for collecting taxes for the British from a penurious peasantry, had virtually been abolished by the end of the 1950s. But in most parts of India, Nehru's land reforms were either watered down or sabotaged altogether by the local Congress Party elites, who, to Nehru's growing frustration, were drawn disproportionately from the ranks of upper-caste landowners and notables. Nehru also tried and failed to set up cooperatives among the smaller farmers, whose plots were too small for mechanization and fertilizers to be affordable. Nehru's cooperative reforms, which were influenced by China's policies of the same era, were also shot down by Congress Party bigwigs at the local level—where they mattered. An impeccable democrat, Nehru at times expressed envy of China's ability to push through whatever it wished, whether the people wanted it or not. But he never gave any hint of a tendency to authoritarianism. "Let there be no doubt," Nehru told India's parliament in 1959, "I shall go from field to field and peasant to peasant begging them to agree to it [cooperative farming], knowing that if they do not agree, I cannot put it into operation."[4] But even if he had succeeded, it is doubtful cooperative farming would have made much of a difference in a country where caste divisions are most bitterly experienced at the grassroots.

The failure of Nehru's overall model became apparent at two different moments, a generation apart from each other. The first was in 1967, when Indira Gandhi, who had taken over as prime minister in 1966, two years after her father's death, was forced to devalue the Indian rupee under pressure from the United States and the International Monetary Fund (IMF). India's relative neglect of agriculture had been compounded by the incomplete success of Nehru's land reforms—large numbers of Indians remained landless. In exchange for increased international aid to enable India to import food following a succession of poor harvests, Indira Gandhi was compelled to swallow some unwelcome economic medicine. In devaluing the currency, the aim was to prevent future payment crises by stimulating greater exports and thus earning more foreign exchange.* But it marked a symbolic defeat for *swadeshi,* or self-reliance, the centerpiece of Nehru's master plan for India.

Worse, the devaluation followed several years of humiliation in which India's malnourished poor were kept alive by fleets of ships from the United States carrying surplus grain in food aid. The joke was that India was living from "ship to mouth." But Indira Gandhi, who, unlike her father, did harbor dictatorial tendencies, which were

---

*In addition to mounting food imports, India, ironically, was importing more and more capital goods to sustain its heavy industry in spite of the fact that the policy was known as "import substitution."

revealed in 1975 when she suspended democracy for nineteen months amid mounting protests over her failure to "remove poverty" (as she had promised in the previous election), remained committed to *swadeshi*. She also had a less subtle grasp of what her father had meant by socialism: "The public sector was conceived as the base of Indian industry so that the country might have more machines, more steel," she said two years after the 1967 devaluation of the rupee.[5] "It also ensured India's freedom. To the extent India depended on imports its independence was compromised."

The second and even more dramatic moment came in 1991, when India's economy went into a tailspin after its foreign exchange reserves dropped almost to zero in the aftermath of the Gulf War, which had triggered a steep rise in oil prices that technically bankrupted India.* Iraq's decision to put a torch to the oil fields in Kuwait before it retreated from advancing U.S.-led forces was the straw that broke the camel's back for India's economy, which was already living beyond its means. Unlike in 1967, when the lives of tens of millions of Indians depended on foreign aid, by 1991 India was more than self-sufficient in food production, having roughly doubled its agricultural yields in the "green revolution" of the 1970s and 1980s. Scientists from India and abroad had developed much better yielding varieties of rice and particularly of wheat, the two principal staples of the Indian diet; these advances had boosted output dramatically. But the very real successes of the green revolution were no comfort in 1991, when the final death knell sounded for India's *swadeshi* hopes. In exchange for emergency balance of payments assistance from the IMF, India again devalued its currency and was required to move much of its gold as collateral to London. Nehru's socialist dream of creating an economy that would be immune from the influence of the former colonial powers had culminated in bankruptcy,

---

*India's reserves fell to just US $1 billion, covering less than one month's worth of imports. Economists say financial reserves should cover at least six months of balance of payments needs, preferably a year.

and worse, a bankruptcy in which it was London that played the symbolic role of pawnbroker in saving India from collapse.

•    •    •

Like almost everyone in his circle, Alok Kejriwal went to an English-language school in the 1980s in Mumbai. Nehru had done his best to move India away from Britain's economic influence (at least until the Fabians came along). But with the English language, which he once described as the "glue of India," and which he ensured remained the principal medium of government and courts after independence, Nehru's love affair was lifelong. At school in the 1980s, Alok might have been introduced to *The Discovery of India,* Nehru's *Autobiography and Glimpses of History*—books in English that Nehru wrote mostly during his long years of incarceration by the British. Some of Nehru's prose is exquisite.

But India's great statesman would have been puzzled by Alok Kejriwal and the tens of thousands like him who are thriving in today's India. At thirty-six, Alok is a dollar millionaire, in large measure because of India's facility with the mother tongue of its former imperial rulers. The fact that India's middle classes speak fluent English has given India a huge competitive advantage over China in the service sector, where the ability to converse in the world's business language makes a large difference. Nehru also bequeathed another legacy with consequences as unintended as his championing of English: his governments created five elite universities of engineering, the Indian Institutes of Technology, or IITs, many of whose graduates are playing a leading role in the software markets of Silicon Valley, California. These were the country's top-notch engineers who were supposed to lead India to *swadeshi* by building heavy industries. There are several thousand Indian millionaires in Silicon Valley, many of them "IITans."

Coming from a traditional business family that makes socks,

called Hindustan Hosieries Ltd., Alok did not attend an IIT. But Alok found sock making and dealing with unionized shop-floor workers too predictable. So, to the horror and deep skepticism of his father, he struck out alone. Bathed in primary colors and adorned by retro-posters of early Bollywood films, the cheerful walls of Alok's company offices radiate the signature décor of India's new economy. Situated in midtown Mumbai in a district that was formerly dominated by textile mills, most of which went bankrupt in the 1980s, Alok's surroundings reminded me of Clerkenwell in London, or Haight-Ashbury in San Francisco. The décor is what some people call postmodern. I spent a lot of time talking to Alok and some of his sixty employees at C2W.com—contest-to-win.com—an outfit that markets brands through the Internet, mobile phones, interactive TV shows, and other new technology.

Alok's principal clients are global multinationals that are desperate for converts among India's rising class of spenders. India's consumers, said Alok, are tired of crude television commercials and other traditional marketing ploys. They want their marketing to be savvy and lateral. His diagnosis, which must be right since Alok is very rich, reminded me of Coca-Cola's ill-fated return to India in the early 1990s (having been kicked out in the 1970s): "We're back!" proclaimed Coca-Cola's campaign. Indians shrugged and carried on drinking Thums Up, Coke's local imitator, which never went away in the first place.

Alok, whose start-up capital came from Citibank and Rupert Murdoch's News Corporation, gave me an example of his methods. Garnier, the French shampoo company, wanted to introduce Indians to the use of hair conditioner, a habit that was confined to a tiny traveling elite. So Alok created a game that was linked on Garnier's India Web site in which contestants are awarded a year's free supply of L'Oréal if they win. In this interactive contest you attempt to climb up the long hair of Rapunzel, the fairy-tale princess, who is locked in a tower. If her hair is either too dry or too oily you fail.

Another game that C2W developed for Jockey, the underwear

maker, involves removing the knickers and shorts of lots of models who are dressed in the brand's underwear. A cackle of electronic laughter greets those who succeed. In a third game created for Yamaha motorbikes you attempt to pick up your girlfriend by negotiating steep turns on narrow roads. "Some curves demand attention" reads the slogan, once you have collected your animated girlfriend. It is all slightly risqué in a country much of which still outwardly pays homage to Gandhi's values. But C2W is a wild commercial success that is shaping the new horizons of marketing in India. Stanford University has even done a business study on C2W's mobile phone marketing strategy.

I asked Alok whether he was deliberately needling the Gandhian values of his elders. "I don't really care about Gandhi—Gandhi is retrograde," said Alok, over an espresso in his open-plan office. "Most of these people protesting against short skirts and foreign influences are hypocrites. Half of them send their children to English-language private schools and go abroad if they need a medical operation. These people are retrograde." Alok engages in conversation with an intensity he presumably uses on potential clients, peppering his remarks with the terminology of a world that consists of "ecosystems," "last miles," "mindshare," and "optimum space." When I asked for the bathroom I was pointed to a door with a placard that says "gentstogo.com." And when I asked him whether this work is intellectually challenging enough for him, Alok replied: "Wow! That is an awesome question!" He never really answered it.

Yet the world of which Alok is a part (admittedly a relatively privileged part)—of the Internet, of information technology, of software maintenance, and of call centers, back-office processing units, and research and development hubs—is in other respects very serious. The success of India's IT companies in attracting ever more impressive flows of offshore business from the United States and Europe has reverberations way beyond the air-conditioned offices of IT companies in Bangalore, Hyderabad, Delhi, or Mumbai. That success has convinced skeptics across India, who were raised in a culture of what economists called "export pessimism"—a consequence of Nehru's *swadeshi* philosophy—that Indian companies can, after all, compete and make profits in the global markets. This demonstration effect is increasingly visible in India's manufacturing sector and among businesses that have no connection to IT or to the service industry.

India's software prowess has also helped revolutionize the country's foreign exchange situation, which in 1991 had almost broken the country's economy. Then India's reserves were less than US $1 billion. By 2006 they had climbed to US $140 billion, as good a barometer as any of India's newfound spirit of confidence. India's software sector clocked up a milestone in 2003 when it earned more dollars that year than India spent to import oil—the erratic energy bill that has haunted the country's economy for decades. Rising prices from the deteriorating situation in Iraq following the U.S.-led invasion sent India's oil bill shooting upward again in 2004 and 2005. But it had minimal impact on India's balance of payments situation.

Having kept a straight face in the late 1990s while it profited from the West's paranoia about the Y2K computer bug, which provided the liftoff for India's software companies, India's IT and IT-enabled sector also reached a visibility that was changing the face of the country's urban economy. The employment of hundreds of thousands of young engineers, scientists, and economics and English graduates, on pay scales that often exceeded those of their parents nearing retirement age, created a new generation of consumers with little time for India's traditional pace of life. They were also impatient with the time-honored verities of their parents: be polite to your boss, work your way up the hierarchy, don't spend more than you earn, and so on.

Alok said his employees, most of whom are dressed such that they would blend in with their counterparts in San Francisco, never talk about money in cash terms. They measure their pay in EMIs, or equal monthly installments. These are monthly deductions from your bank account that continue for years, enabling you to pay off the car, motorbike, microwave, freezer, air-conditioning units, and flats that you have not yet earned. You can even take an EMI holiday. Most go to Thailand or the Maldives. "Holiday now, pay later," says the commercial. Alok also provides stock options, as an incentive for employees to stick around until the company is listed on the stock market, in a world where people are constantly job hopping—another novelty for India where a secure job is conventionally something you cling to for life. But stock options are not much incentive for an employee who slices up his or her (almost half of Alok's employees are female) income into exact bytes of EMI. "Saving is the last thing on these guys' [his employees] minds," Alok said.

The rapid ascent to affluence of Alok's employees and those like them across metropolitan India explains why the country so quickly became a destination that Western and Asian exporters could no longer ignore, no matter how much bureaucratic torture they had been subjected to during previous forays into the Indian market. One of the first things I read when I arrived in India was an agonized article in one of the leading English-language dailies about the small size of India's cell phone market. In 2000 India had a grand total of just 3 million mobile phone users, the precise number that neighboring China was adding to its subscriber base every month. By the end of 2005, India was adding 2.5 million users a month and had exceeded a total base of 100 million. Retail explosions like this do not happen very often.

But to the frustration of many foreign retail companies, such as Wal-Mart, which has spent years quietly lobbying to enter the Indian market, New Delhi has kept the doors shut to direct foreign investment in the Indian retail sector. With more than 15 million retail outlets—compared to 900,000 in the United States[6]—and an economy where consumption accounts for almost two-thirds of gross domestic product (compared to 42 percent in China), the Indian market is probably the most lucrative final frontier for America's retail giants. Yet India remains deeply suspicious of the impact that operators such as Wal-Mart would have on the millions of "mom and pop" stores that line the streets. In practice, India is likely to liberalize its market slowly, having in 2005 permitted "single-brand" retailers, such as

Nike or Nokia, to own outlets in India. Operators like Wal-Mart will probably have to wait longer, especially while New Delhi's coalition government depends on the backing of India's Communist parties to remain in power. Lacking any alternative, the foreign retailers will nevertheless wait.

Judging India as a whole, its commercial potential looks less dramatic than its large population implies, given the fact that average annual incomes are still below $1,000. But the country's middle class, which, depending on how it is measured, amounts to between 50 and 300 million people, still exceeds the total population of most countries. In other sectors that New Delhi has opened up, such as banking, insurance, and consumer goods, Western companies such as Citibank, AIG, and Pepsi have quickly become market leaders in their segments. During my time in India I have often been amused by the foreign executives I have met who spend years occupying the same hotel rooms while they await the green light for their company to invest in India so that they can set up a permanent office. The fact that they are prepared to wait so long is an indication of how important the Indian market is to the global strategy of most U.S. and European corporations. In 2005 GE, which kick-started India's offshore boom in the late 1980s when it set up its first Indian call center near Delhi, launched an Indian bank. GE said it anticipated "indefinite" double-digit growth in the Indian banking market over the coming decades. No one blinked. The fact that India has so far to travel makes it an especially attractive long-term prospect to many foreign investors.

In Alok—and the many entrepreneurs like him in booming urban India—the global multinationals have an energetic ally. His unabashed aim in life is to make as much money as possible. "My ambition is to make C2W a billion-dollar company," said Alok. "I am greedy, I have no trouble admitting to that." We had returned to his flat on Pedder Road, one of Mumbai's smartest addresses. The walls of Alok's flat were adorned with contemporary Indian art. Modern art is the abiding passion of Chhavi, Alok's wife, who works at C2W in the mornings. "It is a relaxed setup," said Alok. "Chhavai doesn't have any KRA [Key Responsibility Area]." Their two charming young daughters were playing in the living room. One of them wore a T-shirt that said "Miss Behave."

I suggested Alok's real role in life was to sell globalization to Indians: G2I, perhaps. "People live brands and eat brands—if you can understand them and what people see in them, then you are in the right place," he said. "In today's world brands are the new religion." I told him that before he had said this I thought I was an agnostic. Alok had left me nowhere to go but atheism. Alok laughed. "You know, at thirty-seven, Ed, you're just out of reach of our target age bracket [seventeen to thirty-five]." Twenty years ago Alok's overt pursuit of money, and his honest admission of it, would have marked him as tasteless or unusual, even in Mumbai, which has been India's financial capital since the Victorian era, and is home to the oldest stock market in Asia. But India has changed, in some respects quite radically, since 1991. "You know, I have some friends from Tamil Nadu [India's southernmost state] where the culture still frowns on you if you talk about money," said Alok. "But they are the unusual ones nowadays." I told Alok it was interview2end.time and he laughed, although this time politely, because I was beginning to repeat the joke.

•   •   •

India, as many Indians like to remind you, is a unique country. But what makes it particularly unusual, especially in comparison to China, is the character of its economy. In spite of much breast-beating in the West, China is developing in the same sequence as most Western economies have done. China began with agricultural reform, moved to low-cost manufacturing, is now climbing up the value-added chain, and probably, at some stage in the next ten to twenty years, will break into internationally tradeable services on a larger scale. India is growing from the other end.

India's service sector accounted for significantly more than half of its economy in 2006, with agriculture and industry accounting for roughly equal shares of what remained. This allotment resembles how an economy at the middle-income stage of its development should look, such as Greece or Portugal. But Greece and Portugal do not have to worry about a vast reserve army of 470 million laborers in their hinterlands. India's problem, and its peculiar way of addressing it, presents the country with a daunting challenge. The cure may be economic. But the headache is social.

When India started to liberalize its economy in 1991, there was effectively only one television channel on offer: Doordarshan, the state broadcaster, which, much like the word *television*, literally means "sight (or vision) from afar." By 2006 there were more than 150 channels and three or four new ones were being added every month. In 1991, Doordarshan reached only a small minority of homes. Such is the electricity situation in much of rural India that even those villages that had a TV set would only intermittently get good access. India's general election of 2004 marked the first national poll in which the majority of the electorate could watch the spectacle on television. Roughly a third of these people, or more than 150 million people, had multichannel cable television piped into their homes.

What today's villagers and small-town dwellers in India see seductively paraded before them as they crowd around their nearest TV screens are things most of them have little chance of getting in the near future: the cars, foreign holidays, smart medical services, and electronic gadgets that dominate the TV commercials. Most of these products are not meant for them at all but are targeted at—and often by—people like Alok. Such items are beyond the reach of the majority in a country where the average per capita income in 2006 was still below $1,000. Sooner or later if you are unable to get what you are repeatedly told you should want, something has to give. India's more farsighted policy makers frequently remind themselves that if the country is to forestall a social backlash, rising crime, and further lawlessness, which blights life in many of its poorer states, they must make sure that economic growth keeps accelerating. On every occasion that I have interviewed Manmohan Singh, the quiet bespectacled Sikh who was India's finance minister in 1991, when the country began to loosen its regulatory stranglehold on the economy, and who became prime minister in 2004, he emphasized the same argument: "The best cure for poverty is growth." Judging by India's own record, it is hard to dispute this.

India's economy has on average expanded at 6 percent a year since 1991, roughly double the "Hindu rate of growth" it experienced in its first four decades after independence. The sharp economic acceleration has coincided with a steady fall in the rate of India's population growth, so the relative growth of individual incomes is even better than the economic growth numbers would suggest. Put vividly: the difference between India's abysmal decade that began in 1972 and the more impressive decade that began in 1995 is the difference between countrywide unrest, which led Indira Gandhi to declare the state of emergency—in which she suspended democracy amid an epidemic of national strikes, protests, and rising violence—and the relatively normal functioning of democracy associated with the more recent decade after Manmohan Singh ushered in economic reform. In the first decade, India's economy grew by 3.5 percent a year while its population grew by 2.3 percent a year, leaving an average annual increase in personal income of 1.2 percent. In the second decade, India's economy grew by 6 percent a year while its population growth fell to 2 percent a year, so per capita incomes grew by 4 percent every year. It would have taken fifty-seven years for an Indian family to double its income in Indira Gandhi's decade. In Singh's decade, it would take just fifteen years.[7] In an age when you can watch exactly how the other half lives on your flickering screen, it is the difference between anarchy and stability.

Yet, on its own, faster growth is not enough: Growth, as economists say, is a necessary but not sufficient condition for removing poverty. What also matters is the quality of growth—whether it is capital-intensive, as it has been in India, in which case it will not employ many people, or labor-intensive, which, as in the case of China, will give much larger sections of the television-viewing population a stake in the growth they see dangled in front of them. Before he became prime minister, I used to talk to Manmohan Singh quite regularly. Because of his preeminent role in India's policy-making history—he has, since the late 1960s, held almost every important economic post in New Delhi—it is worth reproducing his diagnosis of India's economic situation. After he became prime minister, he measured his words more carefully.

"For the first forty or fifty years of India's independence we were plagued by two shortages: a shortage of food and a shortage of foreign exchange. These were the twin problems that dominated everything," Singh said, in his barely audible voice. "Now we have solved both, the first through the green revolution and the second through higher export earnings and a more liberal trade regime. Today we have plenty of food and plenty of foreign exchange. Today our key problems are quite different. But there is an old mind-set that refuses to face up to them and is still fighting yesterday's battles. Our biggest single problem is the lack of jobs for ordinary people. We need employment for the semiskilled on a large scale, and it is not happening to anything like the degree we are witnessing in China. We need to industrialize to provide jobs for people with fewer skills. Why is it not happening on the scale we would hope? Because we are not as single-minded as China in pursuing our goals in a clear manner."

Manmohan Singh was outlining India's twin economic challenges of today: the need to modernize agriculture and the related objective of providing more manufacturing jobs for India's underemployed peasantry. In his characteristically polite way, Singh referred to "mind-set problems" that were making it more difficult to reach these goals. Perhaps the biggest mental hurdle to both is the Indian elite's continuing love affair with the village. It has become popular for journalists and academics in India to write off Gandhi's philosophy as officially dead. Certainly, as a political ideology, Gandhianism in today's India is an orphan. None of India's large array of political parties officially endorses the Mahatma's philosophy of the village. But as a social attitude Gandhi's view of the village lives on very noticeably in much of India's civil service, it can be heard coming from the mouths of many of India's senior diplomats and judges, and it is still mainstream among India's nongovernmental organizations, the tens of thousands of charities that in many parts of rural India provide the village schools, basic medicines, and the arts and crafts livelihoods that the Indian state often fails to deliver.

Gandhi can also be taken as shorthand for an even more deeply rooted attitude that is quite common among privileged and upper-caste Indians, who, at many levels view the brash new world of metropolitan India as a challenge to their traditional domination of culture and society. This attitude is also a continuing echo of the anticolonial struggle against the British, in which the village and the home was seen as that part of Indian culture that was least touched by colonial influence. Even those who argued with much of Gandhi's philosophy, such as Rabindranath Tagore, the great Bengali writer, poet, and educator, still attributed to the Indian village an almost holy status—an attitude that is not quite as noticeable among those Indians who live in villages. "We have started in India, the work of village reconstruction. Its mission is to retard the process of racial suicide," said Tagore. And again: "The villages are the cradle of [Indian] life, and if we do not give them what is due to them, then we commit suicide."[8]

Devdoongri is a tiny hamlet in a drought-prone corner of Rajasthan, the state in India's northwest that borders Pakistan and the state of Gujarat. Since much of it is covered by desert, Rajasthan is also by land area the largest of India's twenty-nine states. But its population, most of whom are dependent on the unpredictable annual monsoon to feed their crops, is relatively small at just 52 million people. Parts of Rajasthan, particularly the eastern parts that are closer to New Delhi, are quite well irrigated. But the districts around Devdoongri, which are home to the western section of the arid but strikingly beautiful Aravalli range of hills, are lucky to get good rains every three years. Government provides very little in the way of reliable irrigation to make up the difference. When I visited in July 2005, the long-suffering villages of this area were praying for good rains. Their prayers were partially answered.

I had come to stay with Aruna Roy, one of India's most admired and effective social activists who made Devdoongri her home in the late 1980s. Although from a privileged and anglophone upper-caste family background, and although she joined the Indian Administrative Service in 1969, Roy abandoned all this for a life among the people. Roy is a Gandhian to the tips of her fingers. Her saris are always made of cotton. She is a vegetarian. She lives ascetically among the villagers. She uses the occasional hunger strike and more frequently the dharna, or sit-down protest, to pressure the authorities—both tactics Gandhi pioneered against the British. And although she concedes that escaping your caste identity is much more difficult in the village than in the town, she sees the village as the key to India's future.

Coming from an air-conditioned residence in New Delhi was not the best preparation for a stay with Roy. Her base is a collection of small mud huts that, until a few months earlier, had home-baked tiles for a roof. The roofing had been replaced with manufactured tiles since, as she told me only half jokingly, the cobras would occasionally drop onto the ground during the night while stalking rats across the thatch. But because of the heat, which is always most oppressive before the break of the monsoon, we all slept outside in a row on the ground and on charpoys—the traditional wooden beds held together by a maze of woven jute thread, on which farmers like to take their afternoon siesta. My addition to the group was a bonus for the mosquitoes. Each meal was a nutritious vegetarian mix of rice, roti (Indian bread), dal (lentils), and a variation of potatoes, eggplant, and ladyfingers, with a glass of buttermilk. Afterward we rinsed our hands and plates in a parsimonious trickle of water, which, owing to continuous shortages, is strictly conserved. We sat cross-legged on the ground and ate with our hands.

Aruna's "left-hand man" is Nikhil Dey, an intelligent and articulate man in his early forties who has been with her since the move to Devdoongri, and who comes from an equally privileged background in the city. Nikhil's father was second in command in India's air force. There were many others, in what seemed like a tightly knit but ever-extending family. Aruna's followers greet each other with a clenched fist and say *Zindabad!*, meaning "Long Live!" in place of *Namaste* or *Salaam Alekum,* the more conventional Indian hellos (for Hindus and Muslims respectively). In spite of the crushing heat, I found being among them quite energizing. Aruna's group, the Mazdoor Kisan Shakti Sangathan, or MKSS (which means the Organization for the Empowerment of Workers and Peasants), agitates to secure the basic rights of ordinary villages from an often impervious bureaucracy.

I was curious to understand what motivated Aruna since I thought this would help explain her attitude toward the village. "I have had long conversations with my friends about whether it is politicians or civil servants who are more corrupt," said Aruna, who is in her fifties but has the zest and intensity of a much younger woman. Occasionally her stern, headmistressy expression gives way to infectious laughter. One of her followers had earlier read out a sycophantic letter from a small-town academic in which the correspondent begged Aruna, cringingly so, for permission to write her biography. "These *chamchas* [hangers-on]," she said. "Where do they come from?" Aruna said she thought that civil servants should be blamed more for corruption, since they usually came from more privileged backgrounds than do the politicians. "That's why I left," she said. "I couldn't take it anymore. I wanted to live among and work with villages to join them in their struggles for change."

Nikhil took me to Sohangarh, a typical Rajasthani village, in the same district as Devdoongri. The MKSS had conducted a survey of the income and living standards of the eight hundred village residents, information that gives a fairly accurate picture of how a villager lives in most of north India. Like many such villages, Sohangarh is centered on a small and dusty public square through which the occasional sacred cow wanders on its afternoon rounds. The village is dotted with modest shrines to Hindu gods. A few of the richer peasants have electricity, but at best for only three to four hours a day. Most villagers make do with their own hurricane lamps to negotiate the dark. There is, of course, very little water, so people can change their clothes only every few days.

Like anywhere in India, you see adults washing themselves decorously while fully dressed in their white tunics, for the men, or more colorful saris for the women. The average landholding is just half an acre, barely enough to feed the family and very rarely enough to produce a surplus for the market. The average plot size will become progressively smaller as the land is divided up among the sons of the next generation. There is little prospect, on any commonsense assessment, that such a small area of farmland could bring material security let alone prosperity to the growing population of the village in the future. Unless there is significant migration to the city, which would enable the consolidation of farm holdings through voluntary sales, the further subdivision of the plots down the generations will only make the situation worse.

What little income the villagers receive is mostly earned from outside in the form of weekly cash payments from menial and casual jobs in Beawar, a local town, or Jaipur, the capital of Rajasthan, or in larger cities outside the state. Contrary to the image of an India in which villages rely wholly on the soil for their survival, men are escaping the village because it cannot sustain their families. By 2001 more than a third of India's rural households depended on nonfarm income for their livelihoods.[9] This suggests a pent-up demand to migrate to the city. According to Aruna's survey, the village of Sohangarh had as a whole earned Rs 5.1 million (about US $120,000) the previous year, at an average of $150 per person. The average daily surplus to spend on extra food supplies was 6 rupees (about 10 cents) per person and 3 rupees on what Nikhil smilingly referred to as the un-Gandhian habits of tea and bidis, the popular hand-rolled cigarettes of the poor.

Nikhil gathered a group of the local men to tell us about their lives. The village women held back at a polite distance, although curious to eavesdrop on the exchange. Most of the men were wearing the striking red turbans and sporting the handlebar mustaches that are the trademarks of the Rajasthani peasant. At Nikhil's request, one by one they stood up and announced their profession. It was a roll call of agricultural failure. The first was a well digger who travels from village to village. Another worked as a security guard for Reliance Industries, one of India's largest companies, in Delhi. The next was a cloth worker who had lost his job in the city. The fourth had been trying for years without success to join the army. The next two were menial workers at a hotel in the city of Ahmedabad in the neighboring state of Gujarat. And so on. Barely any of the men stay behind in the village because farming is not enough to make ends meet. While they are away, their women and children tend to the family cow and the small plot. Very few of the men can find secure jobs in the city. The nature of city employment is not enough, either in terms of a secure contract or a decent income, to persuade them to sell their land and migrate. The men of Sohangarh, and those living in hundreds of thousands of villages like it, naturally hold onto the plot because it is the best insurance they have.

I asked Nikhil whether he believed the village—Sohangarh or any other—could provide an economic future to all its inhabitants. Like Aruna, Nikhil is one of those self-sacrificing activists who keep emerging from urban India. Gandhians might be nonviolent, but some are as tough as leather. "It is funny," said Nikhil, "but even when I was a teenager living in my parents' house in Delhi leading a consumer lifestyle with all the mod cons [modern conveniences] I wanted to live in a village and do something like this. I did not find the move to the village in the slightest bit difficult. In fact when I go back to stay with my parents that is a much harder adjustment to make. I don't want air-conditioning or electricity or the other elements of the affluent lifestyle," he said. But if the villagers decided to move to the city, I asked, would they be sacrificing their culture? Nikhil took some time to reply. "That would be too simplistic," he said. "But I believe we should not risk losing all of this [pointing to the village]. We can make the village work through better farming and cottage industries. If people leave the villages then they also lose the rootedness that comes with living where you are from, and the strength you draw from your natural surroundings."

The more I talked to Aruna and Nikhil, the less I could escape the feeling that although they care deeply for the welfare of the villagers and have done as much as anyone to give them the courage to fight for their rights, their work was also about something larger. They have a vision of society in which the land will sustain the majority of the population although with profound social reform at the grassroots level. Perhaps *swadeshi*—self-reliance—would best sum up their point of view. They want India to buck the universal trend in which society urbanizes as it develops. "In some respects we are Gandhian and in other respects we are Marxist," said Nikhil. "But we prefer to avoid being labeled." It would be hard to imagine any one of these villagers voluntarily turning down the opportunity to have electricity or any other comforts of a "consumer lifestyle." Nor is it easy to imagine an economic model that could sustain 700 million Indian villagers in economic security and in a condition of social enlightenment, which is what Nikhil and Aruna are fighting for. Indians will continue to move to the city. Many more would move if there were secure jobs to be found.

A hundred years ago, France was predominantly rural. Now it is predominantly urban. But French culture lives on and so do its villages. Aruna and Nikhil's view of today's world is that it consists of multinational companies that wish to exploit India's people and resources for hit-and-run profits. In essence, these companies are modern versions of the East India Company, the British outfit that used its royal charter to colonize India in the eighteenth century. They see a "neoliberal" dystopia that profits from the entrapment and immiseration of the developing world's poor—and in which moving to the city in today's India happens not voluntarily but because you have been brutally uprooted by new technology and the profit motive. This new globalized form of capitalism forces people to migrate to the city by replacing their skills and traditions with the work of large machines. Once in the city, they will be slotted in as microscopic cogs in the giant apparatus of globalization. In short, it is a view that harbors many more fears than hopes about economic liberalization and urbanization.

•   •   •

Less than 10 percent of India's dauntingly large labor force is employed in the formal economy, which Indians call the "organized sector." That means that fewer than 40 million people, out of a total of 470 million workers, have job security in any meaningful sense. It means that only about 35 million Indians pay any kind of income tax, a low proportion by the standards of other developing countries. The rest, in more senses than one, are in the "unorganized economy." They are milking the family cow; making up the seasonal armies of mobile casual farmworkers; running small shops or street-side stalls; making incense sticks and bidis; driving rickshaws, working as maids, gardeners, and nightwatchmen; and bashing metal as mechanics in small-town repair shops.

Of the roughly 35 million Indians with formal sector jobs, which are, to some extent or other, registered, monitored, measured, and audited, 21 million are direct employees of the government. These are the civil servants, the teachers, the postal workers, the tea makers and sweepers, the oil sector workers, the soldiers, the coal miners, and the ticket collectors of the Indian government's lumbering network of offices, railway stations, factories, and schools.

This leaves just 14 million people working in the private "organized" sector. Of these, fewer than 1 million—that is, less than a quarter of 1 percent of India's total pool of labor—are employed in information technology, software, back-office processing, and call centers. Software is clearly helping to transform India's self-confidence and the health of its balance of payments situation with the rest of the world. But India's IT sector is not, and is never likely to be, an answer to the hopes of the majority of India's job-hungry masses. Nor do foreign companies employ large numbers of Indians—estimates vary between 1 and 2 million people, depending on the definition of a foreign company. The remainder in the organized sector are employees of Indian private sector companies.

Understanding the difference between organized and unorganized India is the key to understanding why India's economy is so peculiar: at once confident and booming yet unable to provide secure employment to the majority of its people. Contrary to much of conventional wisdom in the West, which often, quite wrongly, sees Indian employees of foreign multinationals as exploited sweatshop labor, the 14 million who work either for Indian or foreign private companies are the privileged few—India's aristocracy of labor. In 1983, as India was entering the twilight of its *swadeshi* phase, the average labor productivity of the worker in the private organized sector was six times that of his counterpart in the unorganized sector. By 2000 that gap had risen to nine times.[10] The gap in earnings was similar. This is a world of difference. Crossing from one world to the other takes good education and skills, or a huge dose of luck. It does not happen often enough.

India's ability to provide a better bridge between the old world and the new depends a great deal on the extent to which it can provide jobs for low and semiskilled employees in its manufacturing sector. In terms of scale, India can only be measured against China. In 2005 India employed just 7 million people in the formal manufacturing sector, compared to more than 100 million in China. Given the large investment flows and the priority that Nehru gave to industrialization, many people find it puzzling that sixty years after independence India's manufacturing sector remains so small in terms of the number of people it employs. That is because Nehru's strategy was essentially capital-intensive—its priority was to develop India's technological capacity, rather than to employ the maximum number of people. But it does not follow that Indian manufacturing is correspondingly weak or uncompetitive. Measured by quality, if not quantity, many of India's homegrown private sector manufacturers are considerably more impressive than their counterparts in China. Again, India finds itself higher up on the ladder than one would expect it to be. It is just that most of its people are still sitting at the bottom.

This very Indian paradox is everywhere visible. But one of the best places to see it is in the impeccably maintained and clean-swept company town of Jamshedpur in the eastern state of Jharkhand, close to the isolated Himalayan kingdom of Nepal. Jamshedpur is almost a museum of India's industrial history from its nationalist beginnings in the late nineteenth century long before the British departed, to the India of the early twenty-first century that exports galvanized steel to China and auto components to America and Japan.

The town was established in 1902 by Sir Jamshed Tata, founder of the Tata Group, India's largest private sector company. At the beautifully kept park in the center of the town, fourth- and fifth-generation menial employees of the company can be seen leaving rice or flowers or offering *puja* (small prayers) beneath the imposing bearded statue of Jamshedji,* as he is still known. The sight reminded me of Rudyard Kipling's description of lower-caste Hindus and Muslims worshiping at "each other's wayside shrines with beautiful impartiality." But the prayers are well deserved. For the poor, a job with Tata is a job worth having. With it comes access to high-

---

*"Ji" is an honorific suffix that is given as a mark of respect. If you want to get something done in India, and all else has failed, adding "ji" to the end of the person's name often has an open-sesame effect.

quality company medical care, pukka (quality) housing with clean and drinkable tap water, and good schools in which to educate your children. But there are fewer and fewer jobs.

Like many large Indian manufacturing companies, Tata's balance sheet has gone from respectable in 1991, when a new world was opened up by Manmohan Singh's abolition of the industrial licensing system, to world-class today. Yet the company's payroll count has gone in the opposite direction. In 1991 the imposing steel mill in Jamshedpur turned out just 1 million tons of steel a year and employed 85,000 people. Now, in 2005, it is making 5 million tons a year and employs 44,000 people. Tata Steel's turnover has risen from $800 million to $4 billion over the same period. "We could probably get the labor force down to 20,000 and move up to a production of 10 million tons," said one of the Tata executives assigned to show me around.

Tata Steel's story, in which it transformed itself from a labor-intensive company that supplied low-cost steel to the domestic market in 1991 to a capital-intensive company that supplies world-beating automobile steel to Japan's shiniest car companies today, parallels that of other successful Indian manufacturers. Up until 1991, Tata Steel made everything it possibly could in its own backyard, since it was always too much of a struggle to import spare parts or new machinery under India's "import substitution" regime. Naturally this need for bureaucratic approval was a distraction from what the company was supposed to be doing and added greatly to its labor force. The company also employed large numbers of lobbyists and "gofers" who spent their time hanging around ministries and petitioning bureaucrats.

It was yet another questionable legacy of the well-meaning society Nehru wanted to build. Nehru gave India some of the strictest labor laws in the world, making it virtually impossible to sack an employee, even if the person you wanted to fire was a chronic absentee. Nehru gave India an industrial licensing system in which companies such as Tata needed the permission of bureaucrats for even the smallest investment decisions on what they could produce, when they should produce it, and where they should produce it.

Some parts of Nehru's model, such as the Orwellian "License Raj," have been dismantled. But some, such as the absurdly strict labor laws (which were made even stricter by Indira Gandhi in 1976), remain. This means that companies are reluctant to hire large numbers of people even when they are expanding since they fear being stuck with boom-era payrolls during the next recession, which would push them into bankruptcy and endanger everyone's job. But it also means companies prefer to outsource as much as possible of their work to small, unaudited outfits in the "unorganized sector," so they can escape the labor laws, which are unenforceable in India's labyrinthine informal economy. There are other legacies that have yet to be abolished, including the "Inspector Raj" of constant inspections that plagues much of Indian business. As Gurcharan Das, former head of Procter & Gamble's India operations, wrote, "In my thirty years in active business in India, I did not meet a single bureaucrat who really understood my business, yet he had the power to ruin it."[11]

There are also unintended consequences to another of Nehru's critical policies: the decision to pour as much money into English-language universities for the middle classes as he did into primary schools for the villages. The elite Indian IIT engineering graduates, some of whom are doing so well in Silicon Valley and Massachusetts, are also working for companies like Tata Steel and Reliance Industries. Because of its strong and large university system, India's scientific and technical capacity is ranked third in the world,[12] behind the United States and Japan but ahead of China. In contrast to India, China has spent a much higher share of its budget on elementary schools for people at the bottom of the ladder. India produces about 1 million engineering graduates every year, compared to fewer than 100,000 in both the United States and Europe. Yet India's literacy rate is only 65 percent. China's is almost 90 percent.[13] "We have some of the best engineering graduates in the world working for us," the Tata executive told me, after leading a tour of the company's state-of-the art production line for cold-rolled steel. "And they come much cheaper than engineers in Japan."

The fortunes of Dinesh Hinduja, who owns Gokaldas Exports, one of India's most successful garment makers, which stocks the shelves of Marks and Spencer's in the United Kingdom and Banana Republic in America, illustrate India's paradox even more vividly. Businessmen such as Hinduja in India and China are the reason that so many in the West fear the economic resurgence of Asia's two giant neighbors. Situated in Bangalore, the booming capital of the south Indian state of Karnataka, Gokaldas Exports turns out two million garment pieces every month for twenty-six brand labels around the world. Prominent clients include The Gap, Pierre Cardin, and Abercrombie. They even put the bar code and the price tag onto the garments before they ship them out of India.

Hinduja's highly trained workforce can turn out clothes in nine hundred different styles, switching production techniques as fast as youth fashion changes in the West. They embroider and print posh fabrics for the older generation, and batter and tear their jeans for the young. Watching the bemusement of Hinduja's employees as they jump all over the jeans to give them that couldn't-care-less effect turned my tour into one of the more entertaining factory visits I have made. "They find it very hard to understand why they should make such a nice pair of jeans and then kick them around afterward," he said. Hinduja picked up a sensible cotton shirt that already had its £85 price clipped onto it and the Marks and Spencer label. "If this had been made in the UK, it would have cost three or four hundred pounds," he said. "The moment your competitor shifts production to India or China, you have no choice but to follow, otherwise you would go out of business."

By the standards of other developing countries, including China, Hinduja's outfit is defined as "complex manufacturing." India's garment exports are not made in the large labor-intensive ware-houses you find in China, which employ millions of people, but in small units like those of Gokaldas Exports, which employ tens of thousands. Hinduja employs 33,000 people. If he could operate in China's environment, in which there are millions of literate workers, his workforce would be closer to 200,000, he says. We walk around one of his factories. It is staffed mostly by women. There is a medical center and a day-care facility. "We try not to hire men, because they are less reliable," he said. "We had one case of a man who was a drunkard and we fired him. He appealed and it took us fifteen years and huge amounts of management time before we won the appeal."

Hinduja's competitive edge in complex manufacturing is an almost perfect illustration of India's economic paradox. He can hire any number of highly qualified graduates who will be instantly at home with fashion software so they can design the clothes on computers. Since they are also fluent in English they can then market the clothes at the grand garment fairs in Paris, New York, London, and Milan. Hinduja probably makes more money than his counterpart in China. But he makes sure not to expand his payroll count too much, since labor in India is a sunk cost. Hiring workers in India is a decision that you can reverse only if you have great patience for dharnas, and deep pockets for litigation. "When I expand, it is always in a capital-intensive and not a labor-intensive direction," he said.

There is another idiosyncrasy to Hinduja's operations, which can also be found across India's textile sector. Small-scale cottage industries receive big financial and regulatory incentives for remaining small, which is an effective disincentive to growing larger. So Hinduja has broken up his production lines across lots of smaller units in different parts of Bangalore. He must also pay much higher excise and tariff duties than his Chinese counterparts on all of his fabrics, except for cotton, which remains a talisman of India's national identity. Since his competitors in China do not pay such duties on any of their raw material and do not need to fragment their production lines, Hinduja has no choice but to produce luxury garments, which means using more complex techniques. He has to go higher up the economic value-added chain. "We compete because we have a better pick of highly educated English-speaking graduates than China," he said. "We couldn't possibly compete on price with China by making the cheaper garments."

The second most entertaining visit to an Indian garment factory was to a site near Chennai, the capital of Tamil Nadu, India's southernmost state, which faces the island of Sri Lanka. The company makes underwear for Victoria's Secret, America's popular lingerie chain for women. Again, almost all the employees are female. Their company dress is as conservative and decorous as the Madonna bras and crotchless knickers they make are not. As in Hinduja's company, the employees of Intimate Fashions, a part German, part Sri Lankan company, have to switch techniques at a moment's notice. And they have to import most of their material, including lace from France and microfiber from Germany. "We have Valentine's Day, then the summer collection, then the winter collection—all the time the orders are changing," said the manager. Unlike in India's northern states, almost all of Tamil Nadu's workforce is literate. It is a much better governed state. The government of Tamil Nadu has also managed to relax some of the national labor laws in the state, since India's federal constitution gives considerable leeway to the provincial capitals. So Intimate Fashions has expanded its workforce more rapidly than it might have. But to the evident puzzlement of many of its well-proportioned seamstresses, the underwear they make keeps getting smaller and smaller.

India's growing manufacturing reach is also visible in its pharmaceutical and biotechnology sector, which again draws strength from the country's serried ranks of science, engineering, and technical graduates. In the cite of Pune, formerly known as Poona, in western India, the Serum Institute, which is owned by the Poonawallah Group, supplies almost half the United Nations' annual supply of vaccines. With just a few hundred employees, almost all of them college graduates, the Serum Institute supplies the triple vaccines that inoculate tens of millions of children every year in the developing world. The company began as an offshoot of the Poonawallah family's horse-breeding concern and is situated next to the town's race-track. Horses naturally produce the serum to inoculate humans against tetanus. Today, every other child in the developing world is inoculated with one or other of the institute's products—shots for meningitis, polio, measles, rubella, and tetanus. India's advantage in medicines and drugs is no longer just about making cheaper generic drugs than the West. Indian drug companies have more applications for patents pending with the U.S. Food and Drug Administration than do drug companies in any other country.[14]

Bharat Forge, India's largest auto-components manufacturer, is located just a few miles from the Serum Institute. The company, which exports engine components and chassis parts to Europe, China, and the United States, bases its advantage on the software and engineering talents of its workforce. The average shop-floor worker in China is paid less and produces more than his or her Indian counterpart: China's unit labor costs for basic manufacturing are much lower. But like Gokaldas, Bharat Forge has moved to higher-skilled production in order to get an advantage. It is competitive because it uses information technology and engineering skills to design more sophisticated vehicle components. India's auto-components exports are expected to surge from about $3 billion in 2006 to over $20 billion by 2012.[15] But the industry is capital-intensive. Bharat Forge proves that India can compete on the world markets. It does not yet prove that India can lift its masses out of poverty.

India has a highly unusual economy. Its complex steel plants are helping put their Japanese and American counterparts out of business. Its elite private hospitals conduct brain surgery on rich Arab clients and do hip replacements for elderly British "medical tourists" (who are frustrated by the long queues at Britain's National Health Service). Employees at India's call centers are empowered by telephone or computer to accept or reject insurance claims of up to $100,000 from American policyholders half a world away. And its drugs sector is on the cusp of producing new products from India's indigenous research and development skills. Yet large numbers of India's farmers still subsist at African standards of living. Fewer than one million Indians produce annually more in IT and software export revenues than several hundred million farmers earn from agricultural exports.

It is true that India's higher economic growth rates in the last fifteen to twenty years have helped lift more people out of poverty than in previous decades. According to the government of India, the proportion of Indians living in absolute poverty dropped from 35 percent to just over 25 percent between 1991 and 2001. The ratio is likely to have dropped further since then. Some parts of India, particularly in its southern states and in the western part of the country, where the system of administration is widely regarded to be of a higher quality, have generated many more jobs than before, in both the organized and unorganized services and the manufacturing sectors. As is so often the case in India, the picture cannot be reduced to one simple snapshot. Yet contrary to what demographers would expect and what has happened in other developing economies, India's rate of urbanization has actually *slowed* over the same period that its economic growth has accelerated. In 1981, 23.7 percent of India was urban. In 2001 it had only risen to 27.8 percent.[16] Of course, the absolute numbers of people moving to the city is still large by the standards of other countries. Seventy million Indian villagers moved to the city between 1991 and 2001. "The surprise is that just when the urbanization process was expected to accelerate, it slowed down," writes Rakesh Mohan, the deputy governor of India's central bank, and one of the country's leading economists. "This has been caused by both faulty national economic policies that have discouraged urban employment growth, particularly industrial employment, and by rigidities that have inhibited urban infrastructure investment."[17]

Some of India's business leaders believe the economic gap between rural and urban India cannot persist without eventually provoking a backlash. In 2004, Manmohan Singh asked Nandan Nilekani, the chief executive of Infosys, one of India's most successful information technology companies, to join a task force on urbanization. Unusually among Indian leaders, Manmohan believed more rapid urbanization and a stronger manufacturing sector was essential to India's future success. Nilekani, who had put $1 million of his own money into a project to improve urban governance in Bangalore, where Infosys is based, accepted the offer without hesitation.

"Much of the elite in India still attach great importance to the village, even though none of them actually lives in one," said Nilekani, over a cup of tea in his office at the Infosys campus. "In my view they are dangerously wrong. India must urbanize much more rapidly and much better than we have done so far. This is what is happening in China. And this is what has happened in every developed country on the planet. India cannot buck this trend. And even if it could, why should we want to? There are fundamental problems with the Indian village. The village is unable to give its people jobs and it never will, because reform of agriculture will mean mechanization of farming and fewer jobs. The village is a trap for the lower castes. It is a kind of prison. We cannot modernize the Indian economy—or Indian society—unless we urbanize more rapidly and urbanize better than we have done so far."

Many people who visit India are struck by the squalor of the urban slums that assault their senses almost immediately after they leave the airport. They find it hard to understand why so many Indians would voluntarily want to live in such conditions, when they could be milking the family cow back in the village. But most of the migrants have voted with their feet (some have been involuntarily displaced by natural disasters or dams). In their view even the most squalid slum is better than living in the village. In spite of the inadequacies of India's urban planning and the absence of secure employment, the city offers economic and social opportunities to the poor and to the lower castes that would be inconceivable in most of rural India. India has more than 100 million rural people who do not own any land. Many more are likely to move to the cities in the years ahead, whether slum conditions have improved or not.

"The answer is not to send people back to the village, which anyway you can't do in a democracy," says Nilekani. "It is to improve the quality of urban governance and to provide the poor with real jobs. The urban elites feather their nests with the best of comforts. Then they want to pull up the ladder and deprive everyone else of the same opportunities. Unless we start to provide the masses with jobs and increase the rate of economic growth, then everybody's security will be threatened. We have to embrace the future."

India's economy offers a schizophrenic glimpse of a high-tech twenty-first-century future amid a distressingly medieval past. But to me what is more perplexing is that it is among India's elites—those who have been the largest beneficiaries of the liberalization of the economy since 1991—that you find the most robust defenders of an old mind-set that could be described as modernity for the privileged, feudalism for the peasantry. It would be unfair to Aruna and Nikhil in Devdoongri, whose vision for India's villagers is centered on grass-roots "participatory democracy," to class them as defenders of feudalism. They are at the progressive end of a wide spectrum that includes every type of village romantic, from upper-caste civil servants who block attempts at better urban planning, to colleagues of Nilekani in the IT industry who sometimes appear to believe that if only the digital revolution could be extended to the villages then people would not want to move (this is a widespread sentiment).* Meanwhile, most of the evidence suggests that the peasantry—including in north India—does not necessarily acquiesce in this view. Many poor farmers get informal jobs in the city that enable them to remit income to their families back in the village. Because the jobs are not secure,

---

*Given the lack of water, electricity, and paved roads in many, if not most, of India's villages, the idea that India's principal social and economic gulf is the digital divide does seem strange. It gives the impression that some of the urban leaders are insufficiently acquainted with the economic realities of rural India.

their families remain behind. This is one reason why India's official measured rate of urbanization has not accelerated.

• • •

Accompanied by my mother-in-law, Aparna, an academic who was head of the history department at Delhi University before she retired, I was visiting a village in Uttar Pradesh, India's most populous state with 170 million people, crammed densely into the plains around the Ganges, India's holiest river. The suggestion for the visit had come from Virender Singh, Aparna's driver, who like many of Uttar Pradesh's peasantry helps to sustain his family by working as a menial in New Delhi. Virender had been asking me for years to come and see what his village was like.

The village is about a three-hour drive from Delhi, along potholed roads that are chock-a-block with scooters, bicycles, donkey carts, and antique tractors that have been reincarnated, bizarrely, as what must be the slowest taxi service in the world. You often see twenty or thirty people crammed onto the back of a tractor and stuck to each other like glue, chugging along patiently at fifteen miles an hour. As the region is across most of the Gangetic Plain, which dominates northern India, the landscape is flat and monotonous. The villages seem infinite. It is hard to recall a view in which humans do not dominate both foreground and background. Every few miles you see the Dickensian silhouette of an ailing sugar factory, supplied from the unending sugarcane fields of western Uttar Pradesh. During the harvest season, traffic can stop for miles around as the sugarcane farmers queue for as long as two or three days in their tractors and on their donkey-drawn carts to get their cane weighed at the mill. That the millowners do not open more queues and provide more weighing machines, and that the farmers appear to be calmly suffering this trial of patience, is testimony enough to the balance of power in rural Uttar Pradesh. To the outsider, the Indian farmer seems to display an almost limitless tolerance, honed presumably by generations of practice. But there are strong new undercurrents beneath the still surface.

Virender's family home is like any other in the villages of Uttar Pradesh. Six buffaloes are kept within the small family compound, which is flanked by mud walls and covered by a straw roof. The dung of the buffaloes is put to multiple uses—as building material for cementing the house, as fuel for cooking, and as antiseptic flooring in the rooms. Cow dung is even used as an antiseptic in childbirth, which in families like Virender's still takes place at home. Maternal mortality in Uttar Pradesh, which is home to 8 percent of the world's poorest people,[18] is among the highest in India.

My mother-in-law and I were asked to sit on the family's only charpoy while Virender boiled some buffalo milk for us to drink. The roof and walls of the small kitchen, which also doubles as a sleeping area for eight people, were blackened to charcoal with the soot of the family hearth. The tubercular hacking cough is as common a sound in the north Indian village as the lowing of the cattle and the ringing of the temple bell. Virender said he was the only member of his family to work in Delhi out of four brothers. Virender's small monthly salary accounts for 90 percent of the family's income. The two-acre family plot, on which the brothers mostly grow jawar, a north Indian gram, or pulse, is just enough for the family's subsistence. The same story applied, in varying degrees, to all the neighbors in the village, he said. At least one member of each family remits income from the city.

We decided to visit the largest house and one of the few pukka constructions, located at the other end of the village near the main road. As with many unannounced intrusions I have made in India, the family was quite happy to welcome strangers into their home without explanation. They were the Thakurs, or upper-caste landholders, of the village. They said they had fifteen acres, some of which they rented out. But this would still barely account for their stupendous home, which flanks a large marble-paved courtyard in the center of which sits a garish fountain. They said their family land had shrunk to about a third its size following Nehru's land reforms in the 1950s and 1960s.

In another wing of the house they had constructed a small private temple to Sai Baba, a medieval savant who has a large following across the country. The ceilings of their living room were bordered with bright blue and white alabaster floral motifs, which reminded me of a stately ballroom in Regency England. Unlike most of the rest of the village, which makes do with kerosene lamps, the house was fully electrified and air-conditioned. But like the rest of the village this Thakur family depended upon the remittances of one family member to keep them afloat. When I had asked how they had built their inimitable home, the mother of the house responded, "My son works for MTNL in New Delhi," as if no other explanation were needed. Mahanagar Telephone Nigam Limited is the main urban state-owned telecom company in India. Its pay scales would be dictated by civil service norms—an executive would receive a salary of between $500 and $1,000 a month, cushioned by plenty of noncash benefits, such as free or subsidized housing, electricity, and telephone calls. Although it is a princely sum by the standards of the rest of village, even this salary could not possibly account for the family's opulent style of life.

But then almost nobody who has had dealings with MTNL or any other public utility in India would believe that the majority of its officers subsist on their salary alone. The paycheck is mere pocket money. The real earnings come from a well-defined and universally acknowledged system of bribery, in which the customer variously coughs up to get a new telephone line installed, to get an extortionate and unitemized bill reduced, to reinstate a line that has arbitrarily been cut, and so on.

For all but the anglophone elites, who have opened up new opportunities for themselves since 1991, a job with the government is the most coveted there is. "Government job," said Virender, when I asked what job he most wanted. "Government job," said his nephews and nieces, who seemed surprised I needed to ask. "Government job," said every villager to which Nikhil and Aruna had introduced me in Sohangarh a few months earlier. For the overwhelming majority of Indians, having a government job is not merely a question of security, although the fact that you cannot be sacked is a large incentive. Nor is it just a question of gaining a higher social status, though this is also a big attraction to most people. To the majority of Indian villagers, a government job is in the first place an instant leapfrog into a much higher standard of living. One might say it is the difference between a rickety hut built with buffalo dung and a house that is furnished with the finest marble from Rajasthan.

# 2. THE *BURRA SAHIBS*
## The Long Tentacles of India's State

*Just as it is impossible to know when a swimming fish is drinking water, so it is impossible to find out when a government servant is stealing money.*

From KAUTILYA's *Arthashastra* (Science of Wealth),
India's classical political text, written around 300 BC

From the imperial corridors of New Delhi's loftiest ministry to the sleepiest rural magistrate's court, India's government offices and courtrooms share a number of instantly recognizable characteristics. These are the trademarks of a state that is never absent from your life, except when you actually need it. If you were to assess India's economic situation by walking its corridors of power, it would be impossible to guess the country was going through a software revolution. Instead of computers you have armies of men shuffling paper. Instead of vacuum cleaners you have lower-caste sweepers carefully reshuffling the dust beneath your feet. As a substitute for a specific appointment, you are told: "Just come." Yes, but at what time? "Don't worry. Just come." In place of waiting rooms you have queues of supplicants spilling over into the corridors and the courtyards outside, each hoping to snatch a moment with the VIP whose mere word or signature can put an end to a hundred sleepless nights and a thousand wasted phone calls. Instead of servants—civil or otherwise—you have masters.

Which is why, when I visited the offices of V. J. Kurian, a senior IAS officer who heads the highways department in the southern state of Kerala, I had to ask at least twice before I was sure I was in the right place. I had come to talk to Kurian about his much-admired feat of building an international airport for Cochin, a colonial-era port toward the southernmost tip of India. The moment we walked into his department I was certain we had been misdirected. There were no peons clutching dusty files tied with string. In place of the noisy antique telex machines there were sleek wide-screened computers. And there were no petitioners lurking outside the office of the *burra sahib* (big boss), in the hope of a chance encounter. My confusion was both solved and compounded when Kurian came out of his office and said: "I'm sorry I've kept you waiting. Do please come in and sit down." The appointment had begun two minutes late. Fortunately for me, Kurian was happy for the time to run well past schedule. Fortunately also, Kurian, like so many people in India, found it almost impossible to be reticent when talking to a foreign journalist. It is a trait in which I have constantly delighted.

Building an airport, or undertaking any public project in India, is a relatively straightforward matter if you are not squeamish about corruption and do not mind too much about the quality of the end product. In this respect Kurian, who took charge of Cochin airport in 1992, was—and is—an eccentric. As a result of his obdurate refusal to play by the usual rules of the game, Cochin has a clean and efficient new international airport. Unlike most other airports in India, this one also makes a profit. But Kurian had to negotiate an obstacle course of hurdles to get there. "The most difficult moment was when I was called by the chief minister," said Kurian, as we munched banana chips and drank the sugary office tea. Under India's federal system, a chief minister is like a prime minister of a province. The role is more powerful than that of a governor in the United States. "The chief minister [I was asked to omit his name] said he wanted me to choose the second lowest bidder for the contract to build the airport runway and that I should discard the lowest bidder. When I said I would not break the rules, he said there was one *crore* [Rs ten million, or about $200,000] in it for me. I stood my ground. The chief minister did not know what to say."

Shortly afterward, and to nobody's surprise, Kurian was transferred to an obscure job with little appeal or glamour. In India, it is almost impossible to sack a civil servant, so if the carrot fails then politicians usually transfer the offending official to an isolated district or a marginal department. But within two years, a new chief minister recalled Kurian because the airport was suffering heavy losses. By 2005 it was achieving profit margins of 70 percent, principally because of contracting out the retail services, most profitably the duty-free outlets, to private companies for hefty fees. Arriving at Cochin airport is as disorienting as pitching up at Kurian's office. It is clean, modern, sleek, and, unlike its counterparts in Delhi or Mumbai, which provide the first view of India to most arriving foreigners, the foyer does not appear to need twenty-four-hour crowd control. Yet in spite of the airport's having a reputation for being professionally managed, Kurian continues to be plagued by "requests" from ministers and other civil servants. "On one occasion the minister for corporations and electricity lost his temper with me because I refused to hire two hundred of his people as airport laborers. I told him that I had contracted out almost every single job to the private sector and so I had no control over who was hired or fired." On another occasion the airport project was almost torpedoed when Air India, the state-owned carrier, said it would refuse to fly to Cochin unless it was given the contract to manage the ground-handling operations—a traditional source of patronage and moneymaking. On this occasion, Kurian had no choice but to concede. But elsewhere he has prevailed. "If you stand firm and you don't mind where you get transferred to, then usually there's nothing they can do to you," he said.

But Kurian remains a relatively unusual person—a senior bureaucrat who has consciously minimized his own discretionary powers and those of his colleagues so that he can do his job better. I reminded him of a widely cited equation for corruption in India: M + D = C, Monopoly plus Discretion equals Corruption. For the youthful forty-five-year-old, who earns Rs 42,000 a month (about $1,000), a fraction of some of the offers he has received from the private sector, mention of this Einsteinesque formula was a cue to open up. As with many impressive people in India, Kurian invoked the divine. "I can only explain my luck and survival by fate and by divine providence—I have been blessed," he said. I nudged him back onto the fact that he had also made an earthly decision to take anything they could throw at him. Why did so few other IAS officers do so? "It is hard to say," said Kurian. "The honest IAS officers deal with corruption by not doing anything—if you don't do anything then you are not corrupt. The problem with this is that there is so much to do." Kurian said that in Kerala, one of India's better-governed states, some people even admire corrupt officials. "They say if you're not making money you must be really stupid." Keralites have a word for honest officials—pavangal—which means "a highly moral person of good intentions," but which also means "naïve" and "gullible." Likewise, those who know how to offer bribes are described as buddhi, which means "cunning" and implies the "power of discrimination that distinguishes adults from children."[1] It is a revealing vocabulary.

Kurian said most people misunderstood how difficult it was to clean up India's system of administration. "When I talk to left-wing friends I tell them they have got it so wrong: 'The true exploiter class in India is the bureaucracy. About 1 or 2 percent of the population work for the government and they live off the people. These are your exploiters.' If you look at the new recruits to the IAS they are worse than my generation. They want money straightaway. They want to be wined and dined in the most exotic holiday resorts and they make no disguise of their love of money. Nowadays they can see how much money their friends and peers are making in the private sector. That is why it is getting worse."

As if to keep his conscience dancing, Kurian was constantly interrupted by telephone calls during our conversation. One caller was an official from another department who wanted Kurian to use his influence to get him upgraded to a business-class seat for his flight that afternoon. Another was an official from the notorious customs and excise department who wanted free parking for himself and his colleagues for an evening reception at the airport. Kurian complied with their requests. "What can you do?" he asked me sheepishly. "These are little, little things. There is no harm." I laughed both at the relevance of the interruptions and at Kurian's honesty. If he had to pull "little, little" strings, at least he was transparent about it.

And yet our conversation also prompted thoughts of how difficult it is in India to tame a creature that in many ways remains out of control, in spite of the drastic curtailment of many of the central government's powers since 1991 when Manmohan Singh began to dismantle the License Raj. It also reminded me of a comment by Arun Shourie, who was minister for administrative reform in New Delhi from 1999 to 2002. Talking about his efforts to reform the bureaucracy, Shourie said, "It is as if we were to start hacking a path through the Amazon forest. By the time we have proceeded a hundred yards, the undergrowth takes over again."

Shourie also provided an example of the farce that sometimes results from efforts to reform a system that will go to great lengths to thwart even the smallest of changes.[2] In April 1999, India's ministry for steel submitted a formal query to Shourie's ministry for administrative reforms. The grave matter, which would take almost a year to resolve and would consume the valuable time of some of India's most senior officials, was about whether civil servants should be allowed to use green or red ink, as opposed to the blue or black normally used to annotate documents.

After several weeks of meetings, consultations, and memoranda, the IAS officers in Shourie's department concluded that the matter could be resolved only by officials at the bureau of printing. Another three weeks of learned deliberation ensued before the bureau of printing returned the file to the department of administrative reform, but with the recommendation that the ministry of training and personnel be consulted. It took another three weeks for the file to reach the ministry of training, since the diligent mandarins at administrative reform needed time to consider the expertly phrased deliberations of the bureau of printing.

And so this question of state meandered for weeks and months, in meeting after meeting through ministry after ministry, before the following Solomonic compromise was struck: "Initial drafting will be done in black or blue ink. Modifications in the draft at the subsequent levels may be made in green or red ink by the offices so as to distinguish the corrections made," said the new order. Hierarchy also had to be specified: "Only an officer of the level of joint secretary and above may use green or red ink in rare cases [duly set out, with appropriate caveats]." As Shourie noted: "A good bureaucratic solution: discretion allowed but circumscribed!" If Franz Kafka had inserted such a story into one of his novels, critics would have accused him of going too far.

As for Kurian, he has received handsome offers to join prominent companies in India's private sector. So far he has not felt tempted. "It might sound naïve in this day and age to say I am motivated by public service. But it is true," Kurian said, as I was finally leaving. For a moment I wondered whether I might ask Kurian to arrange an upgrade for my flight back to Delhi the following day. The moment passed.

●    ●    ●

India has had more time than most parts of the world to get used to the state. Historians estimate that states began to form in India from at least the sixth century BC, at the time when Buddha was emerging in north India as the great philosophical skeptic of early history. *Arthashastra,* or the Science of Wealth, which is quoted at the start of this chapter, was written sometime between 300 and 200 BC for the Mauryan dynasty, whose most acclaimed scion, the Buddhist emperor Ashoka, is seen as perhaps India's greatest ruler. In his potted history of the world, H. G. Wells, the British writer, said: "Amidst the tens of thousands of names of monarchs that crowd the columns of history the name of Ashoka shines, and shines almost alone, a star."* Scholars have estimated that Pataliputra, Ashoka's capital, whose ruins are beneath the modern-day city of Patna in northern India, had a population at least as large as that of imperial Rome. At a time when the Roman Empire had yet to be born and northern Europeans were not even at the stage where Romans would call them barbarians, Ashoka could draw upon the *Arthashastra,* a manual of governance that scholars consider the equal in sophistication and subtlety of Machiavelli's *The Prince* written more than seventeen hundred years later.

The tome, penned by Kautilya, of whom little is known, can still evoke a shiver of recognition in early-twenty-first-century India.[3] We are introduced in it to the idea of *mandala,* in which the kingdom views its diplomatic interests through ever-widening circles, always allying itself with the next circle but one to unite against the circle in between. This is probably the earliest formal exposition of the doctrine of "the enemy of my enemy is my friend." Kautilya also lists the duties of each caste in minute detail. His description of the Vaishya, or merchant caste, as "thieves that are not called by the name of thief," is one that can still be detected in some public attitudes. At

---

*The deciphering, by British archeologists in the nineteenth century, of the famous Ashokan edicts, which were carved onto pillars the length and breadth of India, brought to life a figure that time had virtually forgotten. Strictly Buddhist, Ashoka's edicts exhort his subjects to be kind to animals, to refrain from violence, and to provide shelter to travelers. These are perhaps the earliest example of public service announcements.

another point Kautilya elegantly suggests that the king's tax policy should resemble a bee's extraction of honey from a flower: nothing should be taxed more than once, so that the enterprise can flourish and profit to be taxed again another day (this idea evokes slightly less recognition in contemporary India). He also recommends detailed rules of order for the bureaucracy. All departments of state should be headed by more than one person, to prevent their capture by selfish interests. Officials should be transferred frequently for the same reason. And no decision should be made by any official before he consults a network of superiors. More famously, Kautilya lists forty different ways that a bureaucrat can cheat a king of his revenues.

Many ages have passed since Kautilya penned his curiously bloodless vision of how a good government should operate. And it would, at the very least, be odd to project sentiments from India's ancient manuals onto the nation's modern character if only because so much time has elapsed. Yet there is a cultural—rather than a political—continuity to India that can be found in few other places except China. When A. L. Basham, the British classical historian, wrote his still widely admired book *The Wonder That Was India* in 1954, he tried to persuade his American publishers to make a minor alteration in the title.[4] The book was part of a series that featured the Aztecs, the Greeks, the Mayas, the ancient Egyptians, and so on. Professor Basham said that in India's case the "was" should be changed to "is," since the country's civilizational story was unbroken. Although his publishers would not concede the change, it was a good argument.

In contrast, the story of the state in India after Ashoka's empire had broken up is one of almost continual fragmentation, warfare, and dissolution until the Mughal dynasty swept into north India from central Asia in the early sixteenth century. It was only when Emperor Akbar took the throne in 1550s, holding it until his death in 1605—a reign almost exactly corresponding to that of Queen Elizabeth I of England—that most of what is present-day India was again united under one dynasty covering roughly the same expanse of territory Ashoka had ruled. The contrast with China, which was governed from the center for most of the last twenty-five hundred years, with only brief interludes of breakup or civil war, is stark. So too is the historical contrast between the Indian and Chinese systems of bureaucracy. China had a nationwide system of competitive examinations in which even a lowly peasant could on merit become a mandarin. Until the British colonized India in the eighteenth and nineteenth centuries, positions in the Indian government were almost all hereditary and were mostly held by upper-caste Brahmins.

Today the most prominent lingering influence on India's state is British—with some traces of the Mughals. Remote from the people and Olympian in its self-image, the British colonial administration aimed to be "minutely just and inflexibly upright."[5] It has become fashionable since India's independence for historians in the West and India to dismiss the Indian Civil Service of the Victorian era as racially aloof and overtly imperialist. But this is to overlook the progressive and in many respects radical impact on the Indian mind-set of a service that professed equality before the law and the impartial administration of justice. Although Indian judges were almost never allowed to try British defendants, British rule marked the first time in India's history that Indians were defined as equal to each other in the eyes of the law. The fact that in early-twenty-first-century India there is still a debating society of lower-caste Hindus named after Lord Macaulay, the imperialist who authored the still-existing Indian Penal Code, is testimony to this. Nor is it surprising that B. R. Ambedkar, the lower-caste leader who framed India's constitution, hinted at times that he was more fearful of an independent India ruled by upper-caste Hindus than he was of continuing British rule.

For more than two hundred years, Britain's cadre of district collectors saw themselves as "Platonic Guardians,"[6] an elite who remained deliberately aloof from the masses but that governed in their interests. This suited imperial purposes well since it was an efficient way of collecting taxes and of maintaining law and order. But it left a tradition of detachment and of paternalism that remains evident today.

To most Indian villagers the following description of late-nineteenth-century India by a celebrated Indian writer looking back on his childhood might fit quite well today. "Overhead there appeared to be, coinciding with the sky, an immutable sphere of justice and order, brooding sleeplessly over what happened below."[7] Others have detected in today's India a popular attitude that thinks of the state "like the monsoon, as an aspect of nature."[8] Few people believe they can fight nature.

I have visited many of the colonial whitewashed bungalows inhabited by district collectors across India and wandered into numerous district "collectorates"—the local headquarters where the official presides both as the local magistrate and as the local arm of the executive. Although the portrait hanging in the collector's office is of Mohandas Gandhi and not of King George IV, a British colonial official would feel immediately at home. The collector is surrounded by a beehive of peons and never moves anywhere within the district without a phalanx of sidekicks. At every village he (and increasingly she) will be garlanded like a film star with carnations, jasmine, or marigolds. Since the average population of each Indian district is almost two million people—larger than many of the member states of the United Nations—the village will only rarely, if at all, play host to the collector. So the village leaders will do their utmost to impress the *burra sahib* in the fleeting time they have. Even the collector's mode of transport, a colonial white Ambassador with the insistent red light flashing on top, is unchanged from the latter motorized days of the Raj.

Many of today's IAS officers are of high caliber and are motivated by the desire to uplift the lives of ordinary people. But very few succeed in keeping hold of the idealism with which they started their careers. I have lost count of the number of district collectors who have described their job to me as a losing battle to fend off an ever-rising tide of petitioners, supplicants, complainants, plaintiffs, and sycophants. Like King Canute, they cannot stem the tide. Like their British predecessors, they usually come from elsewhere and are far

removed from their friends and peers. They work all day and sometimes all night, since there is little else to do in *mofussil* (small-town
rural) India.

But many IAS officers, especially since the 1970s, when corruption
appears to have become widely accepted as normal in India,* have
themselves become corrupt. Many even accept cheating as a legitimate part of the job. Since these bureaucrats are unsackable there is
almost nothing local people can do about a corrupt IAS officer, assuming they believe the official is doing anything wrong in the first
place. In the last chapter we met Aruna Roy and Nikhil Dey, whose
group, the MKSS, fights against corruption in some of the poorest
districts of India. Their campaign to hold the Indian civil service to
account is one of the most impressive challenges so far to a cadre that
owes much of its ethos to an imperial era that took its curtain call
more than two generations ago.

I accompanied Aruna and Nikhil to the main public square in
Beawar, the district capital in their corner of Rajasthan, where they
had spent forty days staging a dharna, or sit-down protest, to embar-
rass the local authorities into providing information on public spending. The exercise, which caught the nation's attention, was far from
academic. In a part of the country where public relief programs are
sometimes the only difference between starvation and living, tens of
thousands of men and women had been denied the daily minimum
wage of Rs 73 ($1.75) after performing weeks and months of back-
breaking manual labor. Others found that their names had been included on the government's "muster rolls" although they had not
provided their labor at all. Corrupt officials were pocketing the
wages of these "ghost workers" for labor on relief projects, such as
filling in potholes or building small "check dams," that were themselves often fictional. Having forced the authorities to publish details

*Indira Gandhi, who was prime minister for most of the 1970s, famously said of
corruption: "What can you do about it? It is a global phenomenon." India consistently ranks among the worst countries in the annual index of corruption carried
out by Transparency International, a nonprofit group in Germany.

of how much they had spent on what, the MKSS then set about verifying the state's own information. They discovered in one administrative subunit covering a group of villages that Rs 4.5 million out of a total of Rs 6.5 million of public spending was entirely fictional. The name of the *panchayat,* the local council, is Janawad.

"It was high comedy," said Nikhil. "The government officials took us to a check dam that we knew had been registered as four different dams on their spending accounts. Then they took us to the same check dam three more times by three different routes hoping we wouldn't notice it was the same one. We weren't even angry. We were laughing too much." Aruna and Nikhil's inquiry yielded fictional muster rolls, imaginary health clinics, schools that did not exist, and tens of thousands of people who had never been paid for their work. Embarrassed by all the media attention, the Rajasthan government reluctantly conceded to make an inquiry into the allegations. Although the inquiry upheld the MKSS's findings, not one civil servant was fired, let alone convicted. Nevertheless, the case of Janawad has become a symbol in Rajasthan of how to combat bureaucratic venality. "We never despair because we are making real progress," said Aruna. "It is becoming more difficult for the bureaucrats to be corrupt in the future. We have raised the cost of corruption."

During MKSS's regular protests and agitations Shankar Singh, the group's puppet-wielding and folk-singing mascot, keeps thousands of peasants entertained with compositions that are now well known across many villages in Rajasthan. "They [the officials] are as fat as watermelons," Shankar sings to the protestors in Hindi. "Their faces are as red as tomatoes. All they know how to do is give false assurances. Cut the noses off these high-nosed characters! They fed false names onto the muster rolls and they stole our money for development. Cut the noses off these high-nosed characters!" Shankar's show, conducted under the noses they want to cut off, causes hilarity among the villagers. It is a humorous and irreverent display of Indian democracy in action. In India, the more local you get, the worse the corruption seems to be and the more control civil servants have over people's lives. This is reflected in voter turnout, which shows an ascending scale of participation the lower down you get, with national elections evincing the least interest. Voter turnout for the *panchayat,* which covers a handful of villages, is often higher than for national polls. When I visited the home of Virender, my mother-in-law's driver, in a village in Uttar Pradesh, I was surprised to discover that nobody knew the name of their member of parliament. But almost everyone knew the name of their representative in the state legislative assembly.

Nikhil took me to the offices of a nearby *panchayat,* called Vijay-pura, where the elected head, Kalu Ram, was from the MKSS and was not affiliated with any of the established political parties. Ram, who belonged to a Dalit (untouchable) caste, told me he visited the district collector only if he was accompanied by a group. His office contained a few plastic chairs and one temperamental fan. We were plied with a continuous flow of milky tea in small metal containers. Ram told me: "When I started this job I went alone to see the collector to ask for the money that is supposed to be spent on the *panchayat.* He said: 'Let's negotiate.' I realized it was not worth going alone. If you go in a group to see any officials they cannot deny later on what he has agreed to."

Outside Ram's office, which he will inhabit for four years, there was a bright yellow board that listed all the local public works projects, which included spending on road repairs, maternity clinics, new wells, and recreational centers. Each item stated the amount spent and the date on which the project would be completed. There were also large muster rolls painted on the walls so that people could check whether their names had been included and whether the wages they received were accurate. All of this was the result of the MKSS's right-to-information (RTI) campaign, which had forced the Rajasthan government to enact a law in the late 1990s. The Rajasthan law quickly gained recognition in other states. In 2005 New Delhi passed a right-to-information act to cover all of India. Arun Shourie, the former minister for administrative reform in New Delhi, must have been amused to learn that New Delhi excluded from the act some of the annotations written in the margins of official documents—regardless of ink color. Aruna and Nikhil were not so amused. Skullduggery often flourishes in the margins.

"It is very hard to get people out of the habit of paying for what is theirs by right," said Ram. For example, people often want a copy of their birth certificate so they can provide the documentation to get a food rationing card—something they should get for free. But along with their request these people would still try to slip in three or four hundred rupees. Similarly a widow might want her husband's death certificate so she could qualify for assistance. As I spoke to Ram two panic-stricken men in white turbans rushed in looking desperate for his help. They were petty local officials who feared the police would file charges against them because they had misplaced public property. The property in question was a long piece of paper containing the names of those on the next muster roll. It had been eaten, they claimed, by the next-door neighbor's goat. I found it hard to contain my amusement at what seemed to be the Indian equivalent of "The dog ate my homework." But everyone else appeared to believe the story. "The neighbor's goat could well have eaten their muster rolls," said Nikhil. "At this time of year before the monsoon there is no grass, so goats eat anything, including paper." I decided it was the wrong moment to crack a joke about scapegoats.

Having reassured the two men that the goat would indeed take the blame, Ram was then approached by an old lady who was spitting with so much anger her veil kept falling from her face. It took several minutes to calm the lady down and understand what had so enraged her. She showed us her food ration book and said the manager of the local "Fair Price" shop, where people who are classified as below the poverty line receive subsidized wheat and rice, had ripped out four coupons in exchange for only one coupon's worth of grain. Ram started taking notes. "While you are worried about your stupid formalities," the lady yelled, "what about my stomach?" We stood up and marched down the road with her to the Fair Price shop. At first Ganga Singh, the food dealer in question, strenuously denied having stolen the lady's coupons. Then, when he realized we were not going to disappear, his demeanor transformed and he smilingly handed over another three portions of wheat to the old lady. But the wheat was of such poor quality that even the local camels would have thought twice before eating it. Like many such food dealers, Ganga Singh had sold off the good-quality government-supplied wheat on the black market and replaced it with inedible chaff. To this allegation also, after more elaborate discussion, Ganga Singh cheerfully admitted in the full knowledge that nobody present could do anything to remove his license. Eventually the lady departed with four rations of good wheat. It was a normal day in a normal village in Rajasthan. "This is what life is like for the poor in India," said Nikhil. "The government does not behave well toward them."

• • •

In the Soviet Union there used to be a joke about people who were employed by the state: "You pretend to work and we pretend to pay you." In India the joke should come with a slight variation: "You pretend to work and we will pay you handsomely." It is true that India's elite IAS officers are underpaid relative to their increasingly well remunerated counterparts in the private sector. But, unlike most private sector employees, they are entitled to many non-salary benefits, including free housing, telephone, electricity, first-class travel, and other perks. More than 90 percent of India's 21 million public sector employees are in the Class III or Class IV category of civil servants— junior officials, teachers, government drivers, peons, and so on. They are paid almost three times the salary of their peers doing equivalent jobs in the private sector. Only Ghana and Côte d'Ivoire in Africa have a higher ratio than this.[9] And that is just the salary. In addition to all the other benefits, public employees have cast-iron job security. Under the curiously drafted Article 311 of India's constitution, it is virtually impossible to demote a corrupt civil servant, let alone to sack him.[10]

But probably the biggest non-salary benefit for many civil servants is the opportunity to make money on the side. Rajiv Gandhi, who took over as prime minister from his mother, Indira, in 1984 after she was assassinated, was among the biggest critics of corruption (before he was himself assassinated in 1991). He estimated that 85 percent of all development spending in India was pocketed by bureaucrats. Some accused Rajiv of exaggerating, others of misleadingly precise guesswork. But Rajiv's diagnosis is not challenged by those who are best acquainted with the system—the civil servants themselves. "Corruption has reached such proportions in India that I sometimes wonder how much longer we can bear it," Naresh Chandra, a former cabinet secretary, the most senior civil service job in India, told me in an interview. Another former cabinet secretary, T. S. R. Subramaniam, told me: "Many people, especially foreigners, do not appreciate the extent of corruption in India. They think it is an additional nuisance to the system. What they do not realize is that in many respects and in many parts of India *it is* the system." Perhaps the best description comes from Pratap Bhanu Mehta, one of India's most respected political scientists, who heads a prominent think tank in New Delhi. "At almost every point where citizens are governed, at every transaction where they are noted, registered, taxed, stamped, licensed, authorised or assessed, the impression of being open for negotiation is given," he wrote.[11]

One reason that such corruption does not provoke greater outrage is because most of India's middle class and the country's larger private businesses were liberated from the worst excesses of state interference when the License Raj was abolished in 1991. Those in the elite, who control the media and who shape public opinion, are least affected by it. Many believe corruption is therefore on the retreat. What is less appreciated is the extent to which India's License Raj of quotas, permits, and hair-splitting regulations continues to exist outside the "organized" economy. Beyond the manicured lawns of middle-class India, the tentacles of the License Raj continue to reach into the lives of vast numbers of Indians. Most of them tend to be poor. And much of this is carried on beneath the noses of India's elite.

For example, in New Delhi there are 500,000 people who operate bicycle rickshaws, yet there is a ceiling of just 99,000 permits to operate a rickshaw. Rickshaw drivers are some of the poorest slum dwellers in India. Rather than raise the ceiling for the rickshaw permits or abolish the quota altogether, the state ensures that more than 400,000 people continue to operate illegally. The illegal rickshaw drivers have to pay regular bribes to the police each month to keep operating.[12] Worse, a Delhi bylaw specifies that the owner of the rickshaw must also be its driver. This means that budding entrepreneurs from the slums usually remain in the slums since they are forbidden from buying more than one rickshaw and employing others. Naturally, those who do own more than one rickshaw pay the police handsomely to turn a blind eye.

For the same reason, New Delhi's 600,000 street hawkers are deliberately kept in a state of legal limbo. Many of New Delhi's middle classes complain that the hawkers are occupying public space for free. In fact, they pay between Rs 800 and Rs 1,000 a month each in bribes.[13] In spite of losing up to a third of their meager earnings this way, the hawkers are often raided by the police or by the excise department. Their goods—the fruit juice, the dark glasses, the steaming Samosas, the imported cigarettes, and the T-shirts of which tourists and local residents so often avail themselves—are "confiscated." They almost never get them back. These are some of the benefits-in-kind of working as a policeman or as an inspector in the customs and excise department. Life can be very cruel to the poor in India.

India has managed to avoid famine since independence chiefly because it is a democracy, as economist Amartya Sen has demonstrated. At times of acute shortage or crop failure, electoral pressure and the free media provide the state with an incentive to ensure the rapid and well-targeted distribution of emergency relief. The country's last instance of mass starvation occurred in the early 1940s under the

British before India had democracy, and millions died of hunger. India's avoidance of famine since independence is in striking contrast to China's record—up to 30 million perished during Mao Zedong's "Great Leap Forward" in the late 1950s. But India's democracy has a much less impressive record than authoritarian China for protecting its poor from other afflictions such as illiteracy, tuberculosis, and malnutrition. One of the Indian state's most important functions, which was spelled out in the country's 1950 constitution, is to eliminate hunger and provide all with access to clean drinking water. New Delhi's failure to accomplish this goal is less glaring now than it was twenty or thirty years ago. Higher rates of economic growth have contributed to a steady reduction in poverty: the proportion of Indians living below the official poverty line fell from more than 40 percent of the population in the 1980s to just under 26 percent by 2001. But that still means that in 2006 almost 300 million Indians can never be sure where their next meal will come from. They also live with the probability that more than one of their children will die from an easily preventable waterborne disease. Almost a million Indian infants die of diarrhea every year.

India's failings have nothing to do with a lack of resources. Poorer countries, such as Bangladesh and Botswana, have better human development indicators than does India.[14] New Delhi has enough financial capital not just to develop and maintain an arsenal of nuclear warheads but also to embark on a race with China to send an unmanned space mission to the moon—something that both countries hope to achieve by 2010.

Yet India's state seems stubbornly unable to provide even the most basic of amenities to many of its poor, such as public toilets for the urban slums, chalk for primary school teachers in the countryside, or clean syringes for its doctors in the country's *mofussil* health clinics. In light of the growing threat of an HIV-AIDS pandemic in India, which we will look at in the final chapter, the poor quality of most of India's rural health clinics is particularly worrisome. India spends less on primary health care as a proportion of gross domestic product than does almost any other developing country.[15]

Chief among the Indian state's failings is its system of food subsidies for those living below the poverty line. As Sen predicted, food distribution is highly effective in India when there is a threat of famine. Yet at the same time 47 percent of India's children who are under five years old are "chronically malnourished" by United Nations standards.[16] A malnourished child is likely to be stunted both mentally and physically for the remainder of her life—the majority of malnourished children are girls. When she becomes an adult she will pass on many of her mineral deficiencies to her children.

How can a state that achieves feats of genuine technological prowess fail in such a basic objective? Observing the workings of India's food subsidy system in greater detail brings us close to an answer. It is not about lack of food. India's grain production has more than quadrupled since independence, whereas its population has merely tripled. The Indian government also holds vast food surpluses. At one stage in 2003, India was storing more than 60 million tons of grain in its public warehouses, enough to provide a ton of rice or wheat to every single family living below the poverty line. It also comprised more than a fifth of world grain stocks at the time. Nor does the answer lie in spending limits. India spends almost as much on defense as on all its antipoverty programs put together. The answer, unfortunately, is more likely to be found in changing the mentality of India's civil servants and in translating the general public's inability to communicate its frustration with the bureaucracy into genuine reform of the system through the ballot box. It is a complex problem. But India's ability to find better solutions will have serious implications, for good or for ill, way beyond its national borders.

One of the most disturbing experiences I have ever had was visiting the slum of Sunder Nagri, which ironically means "beautiful town," in New Delhi. Situated just a few miles from the beautiful and imposing buildings of political New Delhi, which were designed by Edwin Lutyens, the British architect, in the 1920s, Sunder Nagri is home to tens of thousands of people living in conditions that ought to have disappeared from India long ago. I was accompanied by members of a group called Parivartan, which means "renewal," who cause as much nuisance to officials in India's capital as Aruna Roy's people do to the bureaucrats of Rajasthan. They took me to see a group of local women in a small hall off one of the slum's narrow but cheerfully decorated side streets. There was a large sign in Hindi hanging in the center of the hall that said SILENCE IS DEATH.

Each of the women had experienced unimaginable horrors. One had visited the police station to register a case of rape. She was taken to one of the cells and raped by those to whom she had turned for help. Another woman had lost a child who was playing outside on the street when he fell into a culvert and drowned in the sewage. The local member of New Delhi's legislative assembly had promised to inquire into the matter, but she never heard from him again. Another, a widow, had been trying and failing for years to get a certificate proving her husband had died so that she could benefit from a small state pension. But she could not afford to pay the bribe to get the certificate. These were isolated horrors. And I do not want to give the impression that the lives of India's poor consist of nothing but torturous endurance. Like many other visitors, I am always struck by the sense of community, color, and laughter that one often sees in India's slums. And I am always humbled by the generosity of the inhabitants both to outsiders and to each other.

Many of the women to whom I spoke and many of the poor Indians whom I have met in villages and slums across the country have been deprived of their right to subsidized food. India's system of government can be negligent and callous. But the state's army of statisticians regularly churns out reports that supply incriminating evidence of its own guilt, as do a library's worth of independent studies.[17] The documents vary in their details but all point to a glaring and massive "diversion" of public food grains from those to whom they are supposed to be targeted. Rates of theft vary widely from state to state in India with the better states, such as Kerala and Tamil Nadu, getting more than 80 percent of subsidized government food to their poor. Meanwhile in the northern state of Bihar, India's second poorest with a population of 75 million, more than 80 percent of the food is stolen. The all-India average varies between a quarter and half of all food being stolen, depending on the survey. The evidence conveys a pattern of routine larceny at all levels at the state.

One of the women at Sunder Nagri described how she had tried and failed to secure a BPL (below poverty line) card so she could get hold of the subsidized grain, kerosene, and sugar to which she and her family were entitled. The same government surveys show that up to 40 percent of those who possess BPL cards are not themselves poor. They have acquired the cards through bribery. So between a quarter and a half of India's subsidized food is stolen and nearly half of those who get access to the food that is not stolen do so fraudulently. "They would not even give me the correct application form unless I bribed them," said the lady, who was an immigrant to New Delhi from the state of Bihar. "Then when I bribed them, they gave me a form in English, which I do not understand. So I had to pay somebody sitting outside the office to write out my application." Having finally received the card at great expense, the lady then went to visit the local Fair Price shop. It was almost never open. When it was, all that was available was mildewed old wheat grain. The women showed me a sample. It was crawling with insects. The food dealer who runs the outlet had evidently sold the quality government grain on the black market. To do so he would have needed the cooperation of a network of government officials.

On this occasion I forgot to ask what jobs the women would like to see their children get when they were older. But I have little doubt that most of them would have wanted their children to work for the government. It is hard to argue with so common an inspiration even though the aspirants themselves are implicitly condoning the corruption of which they are so often victims. Pratap Bhanu Mehta, the political scientist, describes the ambivalence of Indians toward the state as a "civil war within our souls." He continues: "In a society that does not often acknowledge the worth and value of individuals, where the visible means of proving one's worth through substantial achievement are open only to a few, corruption is a way of saying you are somebody."[18] A job with the government confers status, money, and opportunity. For those who live in slums such as Sunder Nagri, a government job is the most obvious way of moving up to a better class. To the poor the state is both an enemy and a friend. It tantalizes them with a ladder that promises to lift them out of poverty but it habitually kicks them in the teeth when they turn to it for help. It inspires both fear and promise. To India's poor the state is like an abusive father whom you can never abandon. It is through you that his sins are likely to live on.

•   •   •

I was having a quiet lunch with Sanjoy Dasgupta, a senior IAS officer, in the south Indian city of Bangalore when something unusual happened: Dasgupta burst into tears and remained in this state for several minutes. We were dining at the Bangalore Club, a traditional members-only institution founded during the Raj. The club prominently displays a framed copy of a large unpaid bill in the name of Winston Churchill, who was stationed here as a military officer in the 1890s. Perhaps because of the club's starchy traditions, nobody appeared to notice Dasgupta's discomfort. The civil servant had been telling me about Captain Thomas Mun, a British district collector, who in the late nineteenth century had apparently transformed the lives of hundreds of parched villages in a district nearby. Riding on horseback almost continually for a period of years, the district collector had covered vast tracts of the south Indian countryside in search of the right places to sink wells. Even today, over a century later, the local villagers still celebrate the official's legacy by leaving small offerings at the walls that he sunk. In the late 1990s Dasgupta took the same job that Captain Mun had as district collector of Kolar in what is now the southern state of Karnataka. So moved was Dasgupta by the affection with which the long-dead official was still held, he set about finding Mun's abandoned gravestone. Having cleaned it up, he invited Captain Mun's descendants and a representative from his former military regiment in Britain to a small commemoration in Bangalore. "The love and dedication that one man showed to poor voiceless villagers should be an inspiration to us all," Dasgupta told me. "He died serving them." And then he started to cry.

Decades from now the inhabitants of Kolar, a ruggedly beautiful but impoverished district that suffers from very sporadic rainfall, might well see Dasgupta in a similar light. Motivated by a sense of public service, Dasgupta has made use of the latest technology to improve the water situation for villagers in the area. Whereas the Victorian Mun used his own amateur (but effective) knowledge of geology to locate the right spots to dig for underground water, Dasgupta has commissioned satellite imagery from the Indian Space Research Organization (ISRO), which is based in Bangalore. ISRO's remote sensory images revealed more than 4,000 ancient "tanks," or small reservoirs, that had fallen into disuse and become hopelessly silted up. These were the lifeblood of a once-efficient system of irrigation for the farmers. Dasgupta set about restoring them.

I visited one of the villages that was benefiting from his efforts. They told me that before Dasgupta had begun his tank restoration project only wealthy farmers could count on regular irrigation for their crops, since only the wealthy could afford to install the electrical connections and buy the equipment to sink the bore wells that are needed to pump water from the ground. As a result, the area's water table had dropped from just 40 feet in the 1960s to more than 600 feet by the early twenty-first century. The natural wells on which the poorer farmers rely were useless at such depths. The ancient habit of harvesting rainwater as it falls from the skies and feeding it through hundreds of channels into tanks had disappeared. The tanks and their feeder channels were maintained by a family in the village, whose specific task was hereditary. But after independence in 1947, the government said it would take charge of all irrigation to bring development to the people. It is a story that is repeated across India—and only small pockets of the country are so far benefiting from the type of project Dasgupta had launched. In the name of the poor, the state provides free electricity to farmers so they can pump water from the ground. But it is only the rich farmers who can make use of the electricity to pump out the water. Their modern pumps suck out the groundwater that had once been available to all, plunging the water table to ever-lower depths. Since the rich pay nothing for the electricity, their pumps are constantly in use. "If you give something for free then people will always overuse it," said Dasgupta. As is so often the case, the gap between the Indian state's rhetoric and its actions is vast. In the name of the poor, the poor are deprived of water.

Yet as Dasgupta discovered with ISRO, there are arms of the Indian state that are almost as efficient and impressive as their counterparts in the developed world. The space agency, which was set up in the 1960s by Vikram Sarabhai, an inspirational figure from an old industrialist family in the western state of Gujarat, is in charge of a satellite program that is considered as good as any in the developing world, if not better. Other countries, such as Malaysia and Thailand, rent India's satellites for meteorological purposes. As do UN scientists studying global warming. As did Dasgupta.*

Some countries, including the United States, have long alleged that the science behind ISRO's satellite-launch vehicles is supplied directly to India's military establishment for its nuclear missile program, which requires similar launch technology. ISRO denies the charges and insists its mission is wholly separate. "It is like asking: 'Have you stopped beating your wife?'" said S. K. Das, the senior civil servant at ISRO. "We cannot prove a negative." What ISRO does prove is

*I was very saddened to learn that Sanjoy Dasgupta died suddenly of a heart attack in late 2005.

that the Indian state is perfectly capable of being efficient and accountable when it wants to be. For example, India's Election Commission, which organizes and monitors fully computerized national polls involving more than 600 million voters, presides over free and fair elections that Western observers say "stand comparison with any third world and most first world countries."[19] Each successive Indian general election is by definition the largest democratic exercise in history. Nobody has ever alleged the overall result was hijacked. Likewise, the policing and sanitation for India's grand Kumbh Mela, a Hindu religious gathering which takes place every twelve years at the confluence of the Ganges and Jamuna rivers, is unparalleled. Somehow the state manages to ensure the safety and health of more than ten million people who are camped on the banks of the rivers. It is a very impressive logistical feat.

Evidently India's problems with governance have more to do with the state's priorities than with its capabilities. Das believes ISRO owes its efficiency to the fact that it was granted independence of action. "ISRO is accountable only to the prime minister, so we don't have all these ministries interfering with our day-to-day operations. Because we are treated well and given autonomy, people very rarely leave," he said. Likewise, India's Election Commission has statutory powers giving it independence, and civil servants who work there cannot be transferred if they displease the politicians. This does not apply to bureaucrats working in normal government departments. Immunity from transfer gives the election commissioners the confidence to make tough decisions and to ignore the pressure of those who want to stuff the ballot boxes. In ISRO's case, there is an additional reason: "Launching satellites is such a difficult and precise technology and it is so hard to get it right, that if there was even one percent corruption the satellite would come crashing down to earth," said Das. "We cannot afford to be corrupt. It is a national priority." As indeed are free and fair elections.

Contrast this with the notorious inefficiency of the highway department in Uttar Pradesh, India's most populous state. Uttar

Pradesh has among the worst highways in India. So potholed are they that most of the state's villages cannot get their farm surplus to market. *Kutcha* (substandard) roads are one of the main reasons that only 2 percent of India's farm output has any value added to it beyond being harvested, or milked. More than a third of India's vegetables and fruit rot before arriving at market. It is no use blaming lack of manpower. The highway department employs one person for every 1.25 miles of road, which is among the highest ratios of worker-to-road in the world.[20] Many of these employees do not bother to turn up for work since they cannot be sacked. Any attempt to offer voluntary layoff to public sector workers prompts an outcry about abuse of worker rights. There is little such outrage about what happens every day to the produce of Uttar Pradesh's far poorer and far more numerous farmers. But even if the state's road maintenance crews did regularly report for duty, the government in Lucknow, the historic capital of Uttar Pradesh, would still be unable to equip them with enough tools for the job, such as steamrollers and tarmac, because it already spends most of its road budget on salaries. The employees of the UP highway department are paid more than three times the market's going rate.

The same pattern is visible in numerous public sector departments across much of India. Perhaps uncoincidentally, this inefficiency is particularly visible in the poorest states of the north. In their development programs[21] India's poorest states have a ratio of 70 cents of direct spending to every $1 spent on salaries. This is before accounting for what is euphemistically described as the cost of "leakage," otherwise known as corruption. To put it starkly, the amount spent on the salaries of a few million employees is far greater than what is directly spent on all antipoverty measures for hundreds of millions of people.

There is an even bigger item of fraudulent accounting on India's books: public subsidies. We have observed what happens to food subsidies. The same applies to fertilizer subsidies, the second largest subsidy item in New Delhi's annual budget. If all of India's "pro-poor" subsidies are added together and evaluated, two-thirds of subsidy spending is "non-merit"[22] in the felicitous words of the Indian government itself. This means the subsidies go to the nonpoor, and often to the rich.

Most of the rest of India's annual budget is spent on interest payments to service the government's debt, on salaries and pensions for its employees, or on the military. As a result India's central government and its states have a combined budget deficit of almost 10 percent of gross domestic product. Since the state borrows so heavily to fund expenditure, which it mostly lavishes on itself, there is a continual shortage of capital for everyone else. And so the cost of borrowing increases, which sharply lowers the overall level of investment in the Indian economy, costing millions of potential jobs. Furthermore, after spending so much money on itself, the state has very little left over to spend on better infrastructure, which would create many new jobs directly, and indirectly even more. Better roads, electricity, railways, and ports would stimulate higher investment by private businesses, which would expand overall employment. The difference between these vicious and virtuous circles is the difference between lifting hundreds of millions out of poverty within a generation, or leaving the majority as they are to watch their vegetables rot and hope their children have better luck.

At a certain stage, anyone trying to write about the gap between what the Indian state says it does and what it actually does starts running out of appropriate vocabulary. Hypocrisy is too mild a word to describe those who defend this system in the name of the poor. More diplomatically, Amartya Sen has compared the outcomes of the Indian state's policies to "friendly fire,"[23] when soldiers accidentally shoot their own men. Sen best illustrates this "lethal confusion" in his appraisal of India's price support system for farmers, which is designed to reduce poverty. Under the policy, the government buys wheat and rice from farmers, giving them a higher price than the market would pay in order to increase their incomes. The "minimum support price" system sounds reasonable in theory.* But in practice it is a maximum support price system. A small proportion of wealthy farmers in the well-irrigated states of Punjab and Haryana corner almost all the subsidy, because they produce much higher surpluses of grain than other states and because they operate a ruthlessly effective lobbying system in New Delhi. The government's intervention sharply raises the purchasing price of food, thus inflating its selling price. Higher food prices hit everybody, but they hit the poorest the hardest, since they spend most or all of their incomes on food. In theory, the Fair Price shops should shield the poorest from higher prices by supplying them with cheaper food. But we have seen how the subsidized food outlets work in practice. As Sen's "friendly fire" quip suggests, India's food policy is aimed at an enemy called poverty. Instead it shoots the poor. By the same token, India's judicial system, which we turn to in the next section, is supposedly blind. But it often has eyes for the rich and powerful.

·   ·   ·

It was one of those beautiful Indian dawns in which you savor every drop of mist before the heat of the day forces you back indoors. I was at the Madras Club in the south Indian city of Chennai having breakfast with Shriram Panchu, a senior advocate at the High Court, who was giving me his views on the Indian legal system. We were seated outside on the verandah between neoclassical stone pillars and beneath the lazy whirring of a giant ceiling fan. On the river across from the club, you could spot the occasional fully crewed boat flitting through the mist and the flash of early-morning sunlight on their oars.

*It reminds me of a joke: Someone tries to convince a bureaucrat of the merits of a policy and ends by exclaiming: "And it works in practice." The bureaucrat replies: "That's all very well, but does it work in theory?"

I had been introduced to Panchu the previous weekend up in the Nilgiris (Blue Mountains) in the small town of Coonoor, a former colonial summer retreat, surrounded by tea gardens. We were with the family of a mutual friend, Ramachandra Guha, one of India's best-known historians, and his talented wife, Sujata, who owns her own design company. We had met for lunch at the club in Ooty, another colonial "hill station," which, like Coonoor, has become a favorite weekend escape of the middle classes of both Chennai and Bangalore. All of us had been amused by the portraits of red-jacketed colonial fox hunters and their bloodhounds that covered every available square inch of the club's yellowing walls. It was in the Ooty Club that the game of snooker was invented by what I presume were extremely bored British military officers. "Does all of this make you feel nostalgic for home?" Panchu asked kindly. "No," I said truthfully, through a mouthful of heavily boiled peas and carrots.

Over breakfast at the Madras Club, Panchu and I had agreed that India has preserved aspects of traditional British culture in far greater detail than has Britain itself. One such aspect was the mania among India's anglophone elites for belonging to exclusive clubs. Another was the lifestyle to which India's judges are still accustomed. "Most Indian judges live a very genteel life," said Panchu. For a judge the normal day in court begins at 10 a.m. and winds up at 4:15 p.m., with at least one hour for lunch. The judge's holiday leave is extensive and in addition most Indian courtrooms adjourn for all of India's religious days. India has more religious holidays than any country in the world. Apart from the mainstream Hindu and Muslim festivals, there are days commemorating key moments of the national freedom struggle, and then there are the festivals for Sikhs, Christians, Buddhists, Jains, and Parsis. Many of the religious holidays are voluntary. But Indian judges seem to be compulsively ecumenical. "There are some judges who take every available holiday," said Panchu.

The Indian judicial system's leisurely approach to life is made worse by the fact that so many judicial appointments are unfilled at any time. In addition to the fact that India already has one of the lowest ratios of judges to population in the world, the senior judiciary appears to be in little hurry to fill the large number of vacancies below them. In some parts of India, one quarter of all judgeships are empty. Panchu blamed this on a culture of intense lobbying or *maska,* which he loosely translated as "buttering up." "The collegium [which decides on appointments] is subjected to so much lobbying, gift-giving, and garlanding by aspiring judges that it takes its own sweet time in coming to decisions," he said. "The collegium is also afraid of being accused of corruption, or bias or incompetence in whom they appoint. There is no risk to the judges in leaving a vacancy unfilled. The risk is all in the reaction to whom they appoint to fill that vacancy."

It is important to underline that just as there are many self-sacrificing officers in the IAS, there are also many Indian judges with a strong reputation for integrity. And there are some, particularly in the senior appeals courts, who hand down rulings that are both timely and courageous, which regularly check the powers of an executive that has lost its sense of balance. India has reasons to be thankful for having a legal system that often attracts people of quality. China has much reason to envy India for its independent judiciary.

But like the IAS, which, since the early 1990s, has had ever-greater difficulties in attracting qualified people because there is so much money to be made in the private sector, the best-quality (and best-paid) Indian lawyers are increasingly reluctant to apply for judgeships. A judge in India gets an Ambassador car with a chauffeur and a siren, an official residence with gardeners and cooks, a full waiver from utility charges, and a large amount of kudos. But the judge's formal salary looks smaller and smaller as the years go by. At around Rs 30,000 a month (about $700), a high court judge in the autumn of his career is paid the same as a twenty-five-year-old engineer in the software industry or a young graduate in the media or in advertising. "The lifestyle is great. But if you want to send your children to a good university abroad or even in India, the judge's salary is next to useless," said Panchu. "The pension is linked to the salary. So once you have retired and given up your official residence and your chauffeur, you have to think of other sources of income."

Inevitably, many judges are corrupt. Panchu reels off a lengthy and disorienting list of examples of corrupt judges in Chennai, none of whose names I can print. But as I discovered in conversation with others, the judges in question are well-known outside the legal world to be partial to "doing deals." Many of the judges are quite openly available for hire to fix cases in exchange for cash in the knowledge that it is almost impossible to dislodge them from their posts. Indian judges have as much immunity—and impunity—as their counterparts in the bureaucracy. To remove a judge from the Supreme Court, you need a two-thirds majority of votes in parliament, the same margin as needed to amend the constitution. It has never happened. Panchu mentioned one judge who has a menu of fixed prices. You pay $x$ thousand rupees to get bail if you are standing trial for a narcotics offense, $y$ thousand for manslaughter, and so on. He also mentioned a number of judges who run such operations like a family business. "Many corrupt judges use their sons or sons-in-laws to complete the transaction," said Panchu. "It is quite widespread." It is also revealing: if you were doing something of which you were ashamed, your first thought would be to conceal it from your family.

But perhaps the biggest problem is the gigantic backlog of suits in India, which in 2006 amounted to 27 million cases. At the current rate at which India's courts wade through proceedings, it would take more than three hundred years to clear the judicial backlog.[24] "The motto of our judiciary really ought to be 'justice delayed is justice denied,'" said Panchu. It is hardly a new problem for India. There were similar complaints about the slow wheels of justice during the era of the British, many of whose laws, like their social clubs, are unchanged. But complaints about slow justice stretch back much further than the British. One of India's ancient texts[25] warns its readers of a legendary King Nrga, who was reborn as a lizard because he kept two litigants waiting for too long over a cow dispute. If King Nrga were ruling today, there would be many a lizard presiding over India's courtrooms.

The cost to Indian society of its sclerotic legal system is steep. Although the higher courts, and particularly the Supreme Court, allow important cases to jump the queue, it takes as long as fifteen years for some murder trials to be heard. By this point many of the witnesses are dead and most of the rest cannot remember much that would be admissible in court. A very low proportion of criminals is convicted. There is also an economic cost to India's slow-moving courts. Almost $75 billion in capital is tied up in legal disputes.[26] This would amount to roughly 10 percent of India's gross domestic product in 2006. The capital that is tied up is money that could be invested in jobs and growth.

Perhaps unsurprisingly, legal disputes between different arms of government, or between one ministry and the next, account for a large share of the 27 million cases that are in the pipeline. India's state has a knack for clogging itself up. But the largest backlog of cases is civil suits within families, such as disputes over inheritance, family property, divorce, and custody. Here there is greater prospect for reform. Panchu had recently set up India's first mediation center, which is inspired by a similar system in parts of the United States, and which he hopes will take hundreds of thousands of civil cases out of the Indian legal system.

Another, increasingly important, innovation in India's legal system is for courts to accept petitions from any member of the public to hear cases of public interest—so-called PILs, public interest litigation. India's Supreme Court has said it will even accept petitions on a postcard from somebody in prison. Such cases tend to jump the queue. And they provide important redress to a bureaucracy and a political system that is often deaf to questions of public importance. The PIL has grown in importance since the 1980s, partly because India has moved from one-party majorities to a seemingly permanent condition of coalition government. This has fragmented the legislature and enhanced the political power of the courts to intrude on the terrain of the executive. The Supreme Court has ruled on PILs ranging from the right to clean drinking water to the state's alleged complicity in communal riots and the removal or demolition of illegal structures in cities. In spite of the many inadequacies of India's legal system, the PIL offers a real alternative when citizens feel that the other arms of the state have become deaf to their rights.

But the PIL's growing popularity has clogged up the judicial system even further. India needs many more civil mediation centers if it wants to provide anything approaching timely justice. "We are persuading people that they will save hugely both on cost and time if they go to a mediator and avoid the courts," said Panchu. "Civil cases account for up to a fifth of the judicial backlog. So if we can succeed in persuading people of the merits of mediation, it would be a big help." I could only wish him luck. By this stage the sun had risen and a searing heat was starting to intrude.* We retreated to our vehicles.

A couple of weeks later at a very different kind of meeting, I was given a jolting reminder of Panchu's views on the price India often pays for its slow-moving legal system. I was in Dadar, a nondescript district of midtown Mumbai, drinking coffee with a senior policeman in a seedy hotel. The police officer, who was head of the crime unit for a zone covering about a quarter of this vast metropolis of sixteen million people, had recently been suspended pending an investigation into his role in an extrajudicial killing of a terrorist suspect. The policeman, whose name, for obvious reasons, I promised to withhold, had the standard Indian policeman's mustache. His thinning hair was oiled and brushed carefully over a bald patch. He wanted to talk. "They have given me six months paid leave. I have plenty of time on my hands," he said. Like a small number of other senior policemen in Mumbai, he was an encounter specialist, an of-

---

*So intense is the summer heat in most of India that at one dinner party our hostess said, in full seriousness: "Please sit down to eat or the soup will get hot."

ficer who kills criminals in "fake encounters." Indian newspapers often describe the criminal as having tried to "flee the scene." Sometimes there is "an intense shoot-out." The incidents usually result in dead criminals and unscathed policemen. Often the bullet holes are to be found in the back of the corpse.

My interlocutor was happy to explain the way encounter specialists operated. He was very candid about his own role in killing suspects whom he believed the courts would either absolve or forget. He flatly denied any involvement in the killing of the alleged terrorist, a man who had been detained for questioning after a bloody incident in 2003 that involved two car bombs that were detonated near Mumbai's seafront, killing fifty-seven bystanders. The Indian government said the bombing was facilitated by Pakistan's Inter-Services Intelligence Agency, Islamabad's equivalent of the CIA. But the case remains unresolved.

"It is ironic that the one time I didn't actually kill the person in question, I get suspended," the policeman said. "Why would I want to kill a key witness who could have led us to the organizing network behind the bombs?" I did not have an answer to this one. But I felt it would be wise to agree with whatever he said. I asked how many encounter killings he had carried out. "About fifty," he said, "which compared to X [the man who heads the anticrime unit in another zone of Mumbai] is not very many. He has been involved in about eighty." My goodness, I replied, that is many more than you. "I always have to be 100 percent certain before I agree to anything," he said. Did he have to get approval beforehand? He gave me a patient look. "It is very rare that you get a freelance encounter killing," he said. "I have never been involved in a killing that hasn't either been approved or requested by the senior commissioner of police. We do not break the chain of command."

I found this insight both reassuring and unsettling. Although the encounter system has been widely chronicled in the Indian media and elsewhere, and although I have spoken to other policemen about the phenomenon, I had not fully understood how organized and hierar-

chical it could be. He then explained to me that the killing of the alleged terrorist suspect—for which he had been suspended—had been
carried out not by himself, but by a senior policeman in Mumbai's
antiterrorist unit who had been bribed to kill the witness. The policeman claimed he was being framed, which he said was also part of the
deal that was struck by the officer who had been bribed. "He [the
antiterrorist officer] paid a lot of money to get transferred to the job
in the antiterrorist unit, which is highly coveted and very prestigious," he said. "Naturally he has to find ways of repaying his
debts." Something in the officer's manner and his way of speaking
made me believe him. But it was a baseless hunch. Dnyanesh Jathar,
a veteran Mumbai-based journalist who had arranged the meeting,
told me the case against our interlocutor would probably fizzle out.

And what were the ground rules for agreeing to an encounter
killing? The suspended policeman gave me an example of the type of
case that might result in an order to kill the suspect. It involved a very
grisly murder that had taken place more than thirteen years earlier
in 1992 in which he was the chief investigating officer. He said he
had assembled a clear-cut case against the alleged culprit. But the
trial was postponed for a couple of years. And the defendant got bail.
Before the new trial date approached, some of the key witnesses
"turned hostile"—they changed or withdrew their testimony. Another key witness was killed in a car accident. Only now was the case
coming to court. But it was no use. "It is a waste of time and it is
damaging to our morale," he said. "All the defendant needs to do is
find a corrupt judge to buy him time and he will do the rest. If you
see the nature of some of these murders, if you see how these *goondas* [thugs] terrorize people in the slums, then you would want to do
the same. Even if the judge is honest, the case usually takes too long
to come to trial. We end up with useless witnesses who can't remember anything of value."

The day-to-day lives of Mumbai's senior police are bound up with
the city's notorious mafia gangs. The city's best-known mafia don is
Dawood Ibrahim, who has an Interpol arrest warrant against him

and is alleged by New Delhi to be living in Karachi, Pakistan. There is also Chhota Rajan, a rival of Ibrahim, who, like most celebrity dons, is often spotted in Dubai, in the United Arab Emirates, but who is unlikely ever to be brought to justice in India. Most of the bigger dons who have fled Mumbai control proxy dons from exile. But their power is declining. They made their money in the 1970s and 1980s smuggling goods that were easily available in other countries but that were closely regulated under India's strict regime of import controls. "The mafia dons were making most of their money from smuggling gold and electronic goods," said the policeman. "Since the 1990s restrictions have been lifted so there is much less money to be made in smuggling. They still have protection rackets and prostitution rings, but they are not as lucrative."

In the last few years, the Indian government has relaxed the rules governing the financing of the film industry, which means that Bollywood film producers can tap mainstream sources of financing much more easily nowadays and do not so often have to rely on backing from the underworld. As the anti-Prohibitionists argued in America in the 1930s, the simplest way to get rid of crime is to get rid of the controls on things people want. "Ten years ago, we would have two or three gang killings every day," said the policeman. "Now it is a few each month. It has definitely improved." He said the work of Mumbai's police was now increasingly absorbed in tackling the two new frontiers of organized crime in the city: contracts from Islamist terrorist groups (which we will look at in a later chapter), and battles for control of Mumbai's most expensive real estate. Although India has dismantled many of its trade restrictions, the country maintains a very detailed system of property market controls in its largest cities, particularly in Mumbai, which has some of the highest land values in the world. In the past people talked of the "Bollywood mafia." Now they talk of Mumbai's "land mafia."

The only time the policeman's bonhomie gave way to anger was when I asked him about the entry of mafia dons and *goondas* into mainstream politics. By standing for election, criminals hope to gain respectability and to protect themselves from possible encounter killings by the police. But these strongmen also fill a gap that is left by the state. Many of Mumbai's slum dwellers, who account for a majority of the city's population, receive next to nothing from the state. So they turn to strongmen. We talked about Arun Gawli, one alleged mafia don, who is now a member of the state assembly of Maharashtra (the state of which Mumbai is capital) and with whom I had spent the previous evening. Gawli, whose constituency is in midtown Mumbai, had denied ever having been involved in a murder. I related this to the policeman. He and the junior police assistant who had accompanied him but who had remained silent until this point of the conversation both erupted in laughter. They then began to enumerate each of the multiple cases "pending" against Gawli, most of them involving alleged murder. I asked why they had not arranged an encounter with Gawli, since they clearly believed him to be guilty. The policemen exchanged glances. "So far we have not had a good opportunity," said the senior one.

I thought a great deal in the following days about this unusual conversation, and I shared its contents with other people who were better informed than me. In spite of having a Westminster-style system, in which employees of the state are required to be politically neutral, India is no stranger to partisan civil servants, biased judges, and pliable policemen. When a policeman crosses the line and becomes a vigilante, he often acquires a taste for it. It would take a strong character never to misuse the power of life and death over others. Later we will look at an incident that took place in the state of Gujarat in 2002 in which up to two thousand innocent Muslims were massacred by Hindu militants, while the local police stood by and watched, allegedly on the instructions of their political masters. It has happened before, even in Mumbai. I wondered how many years of incremental compromises and accumulated cynicism it would take before you could watch children and their mothers being burned alive without intervening.

Away from such horrors, in the everyday policing of rural and urban India, it is relatively common for the police chief to take orders from one local political faction or one ascendant rural caste leader or another. In the ranks below the elite Indian Police Service, which is a parallel stream to the IAS, India has hundreds of thousands of police constables who have minimal training, low average levels of education, and a weak sense of belonging to an institution. Unlike the Indian military, which instills a much greater esprit de corps in its recruits, the loyalties of India's police often appear to be open to negotiation. "Procedures [for bribery] are organized in networks that are built around key individuals," according to one account of life in rural Uttar Pradesh.[27]

Whatever your social standing, and from whichever corner of India you come, your experience of the Indian state is too often governed by which "key individual"—and not by which key institution—you are dealing with. In India men are still often stronger than laws. It would be hard to deny that most of the poor in today's India can only rarely expect to be treated with respect by the state, let alone in the same way as their social or economic superiors. India has been described as being a "rich-poor nation" with a "weak-strong state."[28] The writ of the state is visible almost everywhere you look in India; but it is also a state whose powers are easily hijacked by groups or individuals for their own private gain. Sometimes, as we discovered with Sen's point about "friendly fire," they even claim to be doing it for the benefit of the poor. The poor do not always take this literally. Often they sign away their allegiance to independent strongmen who operate their own private fiefdoms like parallel ministates. Such as Gawli.

•   •   •

"There is no pillow as soft as a clear conscience" said the poster with a picture of Mecca, the holy center of Islam, behind it. The picture was hanging on a wall in the waiting room of the five-story headquarters of Arun Gawli in the heart of Mumbai's textile district. Many of Gawli's supporters, who are mostly drawn from the working classes, see him as something of a hero. In the *chawls,* or working-class tenements, around his constituency, which is now dominated by the empty hulks of bankrupt garment factories, Gawli is seen as a benefactor. People call him "Daddy." At the back of his headquarters, there is a sprawling *chawl,* divided into blocks each of which is a warren of hundreds of apartments that measure ten feet by twelve. Families of up to ten people sleep side by side in a space that is probably smaller than the average American shoe closet.

The young men of the *chawl* take their exercise in a sweaty gym that Gawli donated to the community. In front of his headquarters, which also doubles as his residence, he maintains a medical dispensary that gives free antibiotics and other drugs to anyone who walks in off the street. In front of the dispensary is a Shiva temple, whose bells ring for prayers every hour or two. Gawli also maintains a small *gau shala,* or cow shelter. The smell that wafts up from below is a mix of cow dung, temple incense, cut flowers, traffic fumes, and a mouthwatering hint of baking bread.

We were shown up to the top story where Gawli sleeps and prays. On the terrace outside there was an artificial garden whose flower beds were arranged around a depiction of Mount Kailash, the Himalayan home of the god Shiva, that dispensed a small waterfall into a pond below it. Inside the terrace rooms, the walls were covered with representations of Krishna, Shiva, Lakshmi, and other gods. There were also pictures of large mosques. If someone had not tapped me on the shoulder and pointed out that Gawli had arrived, I would have mistaken him for a tea boy or a sweeper. A small man in his fifties, he was wearing a white tunic and seemed completely unprepossessing.

"That is all in the past," said Gawli when I asked him about his mafia role. So how did you make all this money? I asked. "My father used to own a large cattle pen. Then cattle were banned from Bombay and he made a lot of money from selling the land. We built this on a portion of the land," he said. Even his flunkeys, who were seated with us on the terrace, looked a little surprised to hear such an eccentric declaration about the source of Gawli's income. Gawli then told me he had twice been falsely imprisoned for life and twice been acquitted on appeal. He spent a very long time explaining which mafia don had been in and which mafia don had been out, and who killed whom and when and why. I quickly lost track of all the details. There were too many names. But the gist of the story was plain enough.

Strongmen like Gawli came into their own in the 1980s and 1990s when Bombay's textile industry started to crumble. The mill owners, who had been cornered by a fatal combination of excessive regulation and militant trade unions, used people like Gawli to break strikes and recruit *badli*—or casual laborer—replacements. In the West they would have been called "scabs." Behind India's privileged working classes—those who have formal sector jobs—lies a vast reserve army of unemployed laborers who are willing to step in with few preconditions. India's social divisions make it easy for large employers to split the unions. But this is a double-edged sword. The unions themselves keep splitting of their own accord, which can cause confusion and add to indiscipline in the mill. There are few workplaces in India where there is genuine labor solidarity. Balasaheb Ambedkar, leader of the untouchable, or Dalit, community, used to complain that the left-wing-dominated trade unions that controlled the shop floors of the textile mills in the 1930s refused to work alongside Dalits. This was because the work involved the use of saliva on the threads, and other castes considered Dalit saliva too polluting.

The political space vacated by an easily fragmented working class was mostly filled by the Shiv Sena, the army of Shivaji,* a right-wing Hindu chauvinist party whose rallying cry is "Mumbai for the Mum-

---

*Shivaji was a seventeenth-century Maratha general who fought and frequently defeated the encroaching Mughal empire. The name also coincides with the popular god Shiva.

baikars." The rest was filled by people like Gawli: strongmen from the underworld who spoke the slang of the working classes, but whose goal was amassing money and power. After the textile industry collapsed, the mill owners wanted to sell their land, which is situated in prime zones of central Mumbai, and is valued at huge amounts. Mumbai's powerful class of property developers needed people like Gawli with the muscle and credibility to help them get around the city's network of regulations governing the redevelopment of land. Gawli would step in to "persuade" slum dwellers to move so that land could be redeveloped for more lucrative uses. Yet in the *chawls,* Gawli is still a working-class hero. "They are my people. I give them free power and water and medicine because the state gives them nothing," he said. "I am the friend of the Hindus, the Muslims, and all the working classes." But did he go into politics to protect himself from any more criminal cases? "The poor are ignorant but they suffer terribly," he said. "They need someone to speak for them in politics. All these bureaucrats are just in it to line their own pockets."

On the street below us, the temple bells started to ring. It was sunset. Gawli politely asked if I could excuse him while he attended evening *arti,* or prayers. He disappeared and within a few minutes the terrace was engulfed in the scented smoke of sandalwood, which is traditionally burned for Hindu ceremonies. From the terrace I watched the sunset bleed slowly across Mumbai's crowded horizon. In the foreground there were the sprawling slums and sleek high-rises that give this city its unsettling but pulsating quality. The temple bells were joined by the sudden eruption of Muslim calls to prayer from the minarets of a dozen mosques around us. The noises merged into a strange cacophony that was surprisingly haunting against the crimson sunset. It was a blend you find only in India.

"I owe my life and my success to the blessings of Shiva," said Gawli on his return from prayer. It struck me that I had rarely met a politician or a strongman in India who did not claim divinity was on his side. Gawli also delivers God to the doorsteps of his constituents, making sure always to make generous donations to the local mosques for Eid ul-Fitr, the feast that comes at the end of Ramadan, the month of fasting, and money for the Ganapati procession, in which the elephant-headed Ganesh is paraded through the streets. "The people want it," he said. "Religion is important to them." Then two large suited men arrived carrying briefcases and desiring to talk to Gawli. He introduced me to them as his lawyers. They help Gawli to keep the state at arm's length. "In my line of work you need lots of lawyers," he said. "Everything is paperwork."

The lingering sandalwood smoke was suddenly replaced by industrial quantities of insect repellent, which small vehicles below were pumping out into the streets. Mumbai had just suffered one of its worst floods in decades after receiving a record thirty-seven inches of rainfall in one day. The authorities, who had wasted valuable years failing to upgrade the city's sanitation systems, feared an epidemic and were taking no chances. As ever, the state was waking up too late to a problem about which activists and the media had long since warned. We were quickly enshrouded in a cloud of fumes and were forced to retreat indoors. After the air outside had cleared, Gawli took me to his elevator and clasped his hands together in the conventional Indian good-bye. "It has been a pleasure and an honor. May you take the blessings of Shiva," he said, as the elevator doors were closing. The gods may or may not be in sympathy with Gawli. But there are policemen in Mumbai who are certainly not.

# 3. BATTLES OF THE RIGHTEOUS

## The Rise of India's Lower Castes

*The liberation of spirit that has come to India [since 1947] could not come as release alone. In India, with its layer below layer of distress and cruelty, it had to come as disturbance. It had to come as rage and revolt. India was now a country of a million little mutinies.*

V. S. NAIPAUL[1]

There is a Sanskrit word, *dharma*, that appears frequently in India's ancient Hindu texts. It is usually translated as "duty" or "religion." Someone who is dharmic is "righteous." But the word has many layers of meaning.[2] The ancient texts talk of a dharma of life, in which the individual should always be truthful, respectful of elders, obey the law, and live generously and selflessly. There is also a dharma of governing, in which the king should uphold harmony and stability. And there is a dharma of the universe, which underlines the unity and spirituality of all things.

But it is the dharma of castes that perhaps gives us the best insight into how India's traditional society saw itself. Each caste possessed a different dharma, which specified separate duties and abilities depending on the caste into which you were born. At the summit was the dharma of the priestly Brahmin caste, which granted these people control over all spiritual and religious aspects of society. They also possessed the "sacred power" of the word, and were the only caste permitted to read and write. Next there was the warrior Kshatriya caste, whose dharma was to command the military and to rule the secular world as kings. If a new dynasty emerged from the wrong caste background, then the Brahmin priests would invent the necessary Kshatriya family tree for it: "Whoever rules is a Kshatriya," say the texts.[3] The merchant Vaishya caste follows in the traditional ranking. As we have seen, the Vaishyas were viewed by some of their betters as a caste of "thieves who are not called by the name of thief."[4] But they had an important dharma to take care of the material needs of society. One of their original roles was to look after the principal currency of ancient India, which was cattle. The cow gradually evolved into a holy animal. Fourth, there is the Sudra caste, who were the farmers, the servants, and sometimes the foot soldiers at the bottom of society. They kept their distance from other castes and were not even permitted to hear the recitation of the sacred Vedic texts. The ancient laws of Manu, which set down caste duties in detail, teach that each caste must rigidly stick to its own dharma: "It is better to do one's own duty badly than another man's well."

Beyond these rankings, and outside of the pale of society, were the outcastes or untouchables, who had no caste name. The texts only mention them in the context of pollution: no other caste should have contact with them. It was forbidden to eat food prepared by an untouchable. Their role was to perform tasks that no other human would consider, such as removing human waste, usually referred to as "night soil," making leather from the carcass of a cow (that had died of natural causes), or sweeping the streets. So polluted were the outcastes that in some parts of India they were required to forewarn others of their approach by clapping two blocks of wood together. Fa Hsien, a Chinese Buddhist traveler to India in the fifth century AD, recorded his observations of the "pollution on approach" of untouchables. He also wrote that only the untouchables and the other lower orders were permitted to eat meat.[5] India's texts also prescribed different punishments for the same crime depending on your caste. For example, a Sudra who insulted a Brahmin faced death, whereas a Brahmin who killed a Sudra was awarded the same light penalty—usually a fine—as he could expect for killing a cat or a dog. One text states that a Sudra who "arrogantly teaches Brahmins their duty shall have boiling oil poured into his mouth and ears."[6]

Such are the conventional accounts of the origins of traditional Indian society. However, more recent scholarship has shown that the ancient texts should not always be taken literally. There is historical evidence to show that in practice, as opposed to what is described in the pages of the manuals, ancient India was less rigid than many supposed, and that castes could and did change their ranking through either luck or alliance. For example, the great Mauryan dynasty, which was headed by Emperor Ashoka, is believed to have originally been Sudra. But caste as a system was rarely transcended, even if groups or individuals could occasionally improve on their particular ranking. Thus, the Mauryas were reclassified as Kshatriya (in spite of the fact the Mauryas were Buddhist and a rejected caste). The gradual spread of Islam and its militant sense of equality after the eighth and nineth centuries AD inspired a wave of anti-caste movements within Hinduism during what is called India's medieval period. These breakaway cults were known as bhakti, or devotional, movements, which stressed worship of a particular deity and equality of all before God. They generated great fervor and attracted followings from all castes. But over time the anti-caste bhakti movements gradually morphed into new castes themselves and were quietly slotted into the traditional hierarchy. Hinduism has a way of pacifying and absorbing its challengers. It is both rigid and flexible. Modern Indian society is similar. India's lower orders have been struggling for decades to achieve equality of respect and recognition. That struggle still has a long way to go.

•   •   •

In many respects the town of Aurangabad, in an arid corner of Maharashtra, India's second largest state, is unexceptional. Aurangabad's dilapidated old town, which dates from the days when it was ruled by the princely state of Hyderabad, several hundred miles to the south, is surrounded by the nondescript sprawl that characterizes so much of contemporary India. Its narrow waterways are choked with rubbish. Flies proliferate in the searing dry heat of summer. A puff of wind can scald your skin. Traffic, mostly scooters and motorbikes, collects lazily at railway crossings and, now and then, is halted altogether by a noisy wedding procession. On the main commercial avenues you pass the provincial bank branches, roadside tea stalls, and chain sweet shops that are to be found all over small-town India. Then there are the sacred cows, feeding on piles of garbage and whatever else has been discarded on the streets. The town somehow manages to be both colorful and drab.

Aurangabad also happens to be a center of the Mahar community, populated by an untouchable, or Dalit, caste many of whose members were converted to Buddhism in 1956 by Bhimrao Ambedkar, the Dalit lawyer who framed India's constitution. Ambedkar, who established a college here in 1950, which was inaugurated by Jawaharlal Nehru, the prime minister at the time, was also a Mahar. The caste's duties included being porters, messengers, watchmen, and guides for their social betters. Although there were other Dalit groups* required to

---

*The term *Dalit* is generic. In practice India has hundreds of untouchable subcastes, including the Mahars, who traditionally lived separately from each other and did not intermarry. The same applies to the four *Varnas*—the traditional name for caste. Each Varna—the Brahmins, Kshatriyas, Vaishyas, and Sudras—has hundreds of *jatis,* or subcastes, who traditionally married only within their communities. In today's India, many *jatis* are now merging to form larger subcastes.

perform more humiliating tasks, the Mahars were never permitted to enter temples or to draw water from the same well as the rest of the village. Ambedkar helped them to reject the role to which they were born. Other lower-caste leaders were agitating, along with Mahatma Gandhi, for Dalits to be given access to temples and wells. But Ambedkar was dismissive of the chances of bringing about any real change in the mentality of upper-caste Hindus. He declared that he did not want to enter their temples at all. "I was born a Hindu," he said, "but I will not die a Hindu." It took Ambedkar many years of studying before he chose Buddhism, which he believed was the most egalitarian of the world's religions. Other virtues included the fact that Buddhism was Indian in origin, so he could not be accused of lack of patriotism, as might lower-caste converts to Islam and Christianity. And, importantly for Ambedkar, who rejected all forms of superstition and ritual, Buddhism was also the religion that came closest to atheism in his view. He based his sense of the religion on Buddha's original teachings—and not on subsequent interpretations—in which the philosopher had rejected the existence both of the soul and of the afterlife. Ambedkar converted to Buddhism in the town of Nagpur along with half a million fellow Mahars at what must have been one of the largest ceremonies of mass conversion in history. He died shortly afterward, a Buddhist.

Ambedkar's statue and likeness is visible all over Aurangabad and in countless other small towns across India. I visited Milind College, on the road that leads out of town toward the world-renowned Ellora Caves, which include some of the most enchanting and dramatic Hindu and Buddhist temple art in India. Ambedkar named the college after the legendary Greek king Milinda, who challenged any priest or scholar to beat him in philosophical debate. For years, nobody succeeded until a monk called Nagsen arrived on the scene. In their debate the Buddhist monk tied Milinda into knots. The king conceded defeat and gave up his throne to follow Nagsen for the remainder of his life. "For Ambedkar, King Milinda was a symbol of intellectual honesty, which was a virtue he felt was lacking in Hinduism," Indrajit Alte, the dean of Milind College, said to me.

Ambedkar was obsessed with education. A colonial survey in the early twentieth century found that only 0.13 percent of India's untouchables—about one in eight hundred—could read or write.[7] There are no updated numbers for today's India because caste-specific surveys were banned from the census after independence. But it is estimated that at least a third of Dalits in today's India are now literate. It would be safe to guess that a majority of Ambedkar's Mahar community can read and write. As a result, the community has captured a far larger share of white-collar jobs and government sinecures than has any other Dalit group. There is a sizable Mahar middle class, much of them living in Aurangabad, and also a Mahar working class in the town's factories and assembly lines. Most Mahars have left their villages never to return.

As a child, Indrajit Alte sat outside the temple in his village hoping in vain to be permitted entry. Then his family converted to Buddhism and they moved to the city. "In Aurangabad, or Bombay, or any town, you are treated with respect. You can walk down the street and nobody knows your caste," said Professor Alte, about half of whose 3,600 students are Dalits. "But when I return to my family village, people of other castes who cannot even read and write will not allow me into their homes, or even to share a cup of tea. This is how they treat the head of a college from the city. You cannot escape your caste in the village even if you have changed your religion."

Professor Alte took me to a room overlooking Milind College where Ambedkar used to sleep and study after he had resigned as minister for law from Nehru's government in 1951. He resigned partly in protest at the delay in passing the Hindu Civil Code bill, which he viewed as essential to promoting gender equality (such as giving daughters inheritance rights). The legislation was broken up into four bills, which were enacted in the mid-1950s. The room, which stands alone on the college roof and is shaped like a stupa, the steeple of the Buddhist temple, contained some of Ambedkar's belongings, including a long bamboo stave with eight notches, which represented Buddha's Eightfold Path of righteousness. There were

faded black-and-white photographs of Ambedkar wearing his trademark horn-rimmed spectacles and Western suits and talking to various other statesmen. On the walls, garlands of flowers were hung
over each of his monsoon-stained pictures. The professor told me a
story of an educated Mahar village boy who had apparently humiliated a group of orthodox village Brahmins in the area. The local
Brahmins hold an annual ritual to discover whether the coming monsoon will be a good one, which they divine by filling up a linga—a
phallic representation of the god Shiva—with water. The boy used
his scientific education to debunk the ritual. "This is what Ambedkar
meant by fighting against caste," said the professor. "It was also a
battle against superstition."

But the gulf between the lives of the Mahars who still live in villages and those who live in towns like Aurangabad is large. In the villages, Buddha has become just one more god to be placed alongside
the popular Hindu deities in the Mahar household, such as Shiva,
Krishna, Ram, and Vishnu. Some households even keep a small fig-
urine of Ambedkar among their pantheon of gods. When the women
are menstruating, they remove Ambedkar's likeness so as not to pollute him. It is hard to imagine the Dalit leader would have been flat-
tered by this. By the same token, village Mahars greet Hindu villagers
with the phrase *"Jai Bheem"* (Long Live Ambedkar), to indicate they
should no longer be seen as untouchables. But when Mahars greet
each other they say *"Ram Ram,"* the traditional Hindu greeting.[8]
Many of the Brahmin households claim Buddha is an incarnation of
the Hindu god Vishnu. Some of the Mahars appear to agree. Converting to Buddhism seems to have changed very little in the lives of
village Mahars.

The city is a world apart. We visited the neighborhood of Amit Sudarkar, a young activist, in a Mahar area of Aurangabad. Although
this was a poor area, I was immediately struck by the cleanliness of
the streets compared to other parts of town. Everything was neatly
swept and washed. Above each house fluttered the multicolored flag
of international Buddhism and the blue flag depicting the Ashokan

wheel, named after the great Buddhist emperor of India's early history. Inside the homes there were pictures of film stars and cricketers. I did not see any gods: only small framed pictures of Ambedkar and Buddha. Like many urban Dalit neighborhoods in other parts of India, the Mahars lived next to a Muslim locality. "We get along much better with the Muslims than the caste Hindus because we look out for each other," said Sudarkar. "Before we converted to Buddhism we used to eat beef with the Muslims." I was in Aurangabad with Sohail Akbar, a Delhi-based photographer and friend, who has accompanied me on several trips. Both of us were struck by the self-confidence of the Mahars we met. Some of them were teachers, one owned her own beauty parlor, a third was a mechanic. These were literate people. Almost everyone we met was either the first or second generation of educated Mahars, and they radiated self-confidence. It is hard to overstate just how radical a change this represents for people whose parents, grandparents, and ancestors stretching back hundreds—perhaps thousands—of years were born to a lifetime of bowing and scraping.

A crowd gathered, as so often happens when outsiders are in the vicinity. They dragged us to their local temple. All it contained was blue walls and paintings of Buddha and Ambedkar. I was amused that Ambedkar's portrait always depicts him with rosy thick lips, much like those of Buddha. But there was no incense, no bells, and no candles. "We do not pray to Buddha, because we believe he was a human being—not a god," said Sudarkar. "We pray for peace, or else we just meditate. Sometimes we just come here to read." Then the people wanted to introduce us to the local dentist, whose office was nearby. He was also a Mahar. The dental clinic was air-conditioned and spotlessly clean. "People from other castes come to me regularly for treatment," the dentist told me. The others, wishing to make sure I understood the full import of the fact that upper castes were now routinely permitting an untouchable to stick his fingers in their mouths, muttered: "Imagine that?" "Very good dentist," "Mahar dentist." Most of them spoke some English in addition to Hindi and Marathi, the principal language of Maharashtra. Sadarkar said: "There is still discrimination against us—we do not live in mixed communities and we go to our own schools. But we are free and we know our rights."

Once the proceedings were under way it was hard to resist the pressure to visit other sites that illustrated some accomplishment or other of these proud Mahars. Our tour was gathering a momentum of its own. The next stop was a museum devoted to Ambedkar's life. Half the books in the museum's library were about Malcolm X's Black Panthers in America. After Ambedkar died, his Republican Party of India broke up into squabbling factions. A group of Dalits inspired by Malcolm X set up the Dalit Panther movement, which still exists, although it never got very far. "We feel a lot of kinship with what blacks suffered in America before the civil rights movement and what blacks suffered in South Africa under apartheid," said the museum curator. But in some respects what untouchables have suffered—and still do—is worse. Even during apartheid, and in the deep recesses of the American South, white families would often employ black cooks and black wet nurses. "Upper-caste Hindus would rather have died than let an untouchable cook their food or suckle their babies," said the curator. "It would have been polluting." After the museum, we visited Ambedkar University, which until the early 1990s was called Aurangabad University. Even then, the change of name prompted riots by angry upper-caste Hindus, although they failed to overturn the decision.

Then we were taken to a small Buddhist seminary that was situated under one of the rocky hills that encircle the town. The monks, who were mostly young men in their twenties and thirties, appeared sterner than the Mahars we had met in town that day. They all wore maroon robes. They talked to us about why Buddhism had virtually disappeared from India, the land of its birth, when it continued to thrive in so many other parts of Asia to which it had spread. The monks said the great Indian Buddhist centers of Taxila and Nalanda (in modern-day Pakistan and Bihar, respectively) had been plundered by Brahmins, who feared that Buddha's egalitarian message would undermine their stranglehold on society.* "They destroyed Buddhism because it had no caste," said one militant young novice. "Where are the Brahmins without caste?" I asked why so few of India's other Dalit groups, such as the Chamars, who are the traditional leather workers, or the Valmikis, the scavenger caste who remove the excrement of other castes, had converted to Buddhism. The monks said that many of the other Dalit groups felt rivalry with the Mahars, though they still erect statues of Ambedkar. "The upper castes are experts at brainwashing and intimidating the lower castes into remaining within Hinduism," said the young novice. "Many lower-caste people do not understand that it is impossible to change Hinduism. Hinduism has no pope or Vatican. The Brahmins are too slippery."

It was an interesting diagnosis. And it was hard not to feel sympathy with their anger. My conversations with the monks and the other Mahars had also helped to clarify something that many foreigners, including me, find hard to understand: the fact that Dalits and other lower castes are often as bitterly divided against each other as they are against the Hindu upper castes. It was something Ambedkar had tried to overcome. Now, fifty years after his death, even his limited success in helping to unite some Dalit groups with each other and with other lower castes is open to question. India, as the writer V. S. Naipaul said, has become a land of a million mutinies: some are mutinies of lower orders against the upper orders; there are also mutinies of upper orders (and some lower orders) against Muslims; and there are mutinies of both lower orders against each other and upper orders against each other. But India is also a land of unexpected alliances: between enemies of enemies, between Muslims and lower castes, and between people who disdained each other yesterday and

*In fact, the great monastery of Nalanda was probably plundered by a Muslim dynasty. But there is plenty of evidence to show that Hindu dynasties in an earlier phase of India's history took steps to suppress Buddhism.

may tomorrow do so again. In one large Indian state there is even an alliance between Dalits and Brahmins (against almost everyone in between). Indian politics, like the shifting caste alliances below it, bubbles in a strange cauldron of its own, defying easy comparisons with anywhere else. And yet India's caste parties resemble each other in striking and important ways: they are centered on strong and charismatic leaders, who permit little internal party democracy or challenge to their authority; they defend a system of strong state regulation, since that enhances their ability to distribute jobs and contracts to their caste followers; and they are notably more efficient than other parties at organizing their supporters to turn out on polling day.

● ● ●

I was in Patna, the capital of Bihar in India's north, to observe an important state assembly election that would choose the next government of India's third largest state. I had just come from the buzzing city of Hyderabad in the southern state of Andhra Pradesh, which is a magnet for much of India's software investment. The contrast between the two cities could not be greater. In Hyderabad there are as many five-star hotels as you would find in any Western city. Most of them offer a seamless "wifi" service so you can connect to the Internet by laptop from anywhere in the building. At Patna's best hotel the crackle on the internal phone system was so noisy you could not communicate with the receptionist. "Hello, hello, is this a long-distance call?" No, I am calling from room 212. "Hello, hello? Do you have a reservation?" Naturally, Internet access was unthinkable. Likewise, although often clogged with traffic, Hyderabad's roads are paved and smooth. Meanwhile in Patna, a city of three million people, there is not a single functioning traffic light. Such is the reigning inertia, the city has not even changed the colonial names of its streets. I got a kick out of driving up and down Boring Road. It was named after a British official.

Patna is actually a very interesting place. Many people used to refer to it as the capital of "Laluland," so named after India's most celebrated and witty lower-caste leader, Lalu Prasad Yadav. Lalu and his wife, Rabri Devi, had been ruling the state since 1990 courtesy of a powerful electoral formula known as "MY"—or Muslim-Yadav, an alliance between the state's Muslims and the caste of Yadavs, from whom the leader takes his last name. The Yadavs are one of India's largest "Other Backward Classes," a government term that covers most of India's Sudra castes. Yadavs are the traditional cowherd caste of north India and are relatively low down on the traditional pecking order, but not as low as untouchable Mahars or Chamars. In a state that is probably more bitterly divided by caste than any other in India, the MY combination had delivered an impregnable 30 percent of the vote to Lalu in four successive elections. But in this election Lalu's alliance appeared to be fraying. Other caste alliances were beginning to pick off some of the wealthier Yadav and Muslim voters, who were getting tired of Lalu's caste-identity politics, which had come at the expense of economic growth and law and order.

The week I was visiting Patna, the news was dominated by the kidnapping of a young pupil from the town's elite English-language private school. It was the fifth kidnapping in as many months. Bihar's kidnapping industry is closely connected to the state's other large industry: politics. It is no coincidence that the number of kidnappings increases sharply when elections are on the horizon. Running an election in one of Bihar's 243 provincial constituencies costs between Rs 10 and Rs 50 million ($200,000 to $1 million),[9] an absurdly large sum for a state with an annual income of less than Rs 15,000 per person ($300). Apart from its annual output of succulent mangoes and lychees, which are exported to other parts of India, Bihar has virtually no industry. Bihar's principal sources of income are the grants it receives from New Delhi for its budget, and remittances from the millions of Bihari villagers who go to Delhi, Mumbai, or Punjab to do casual jobs in the informal sector. Most of Bihar's middle classes have fled.

"If I had known then what I know now I would never have returned to Bihar," said Dr. Ajay Kumar, who runs his own medical practice in Patna, and who had just stepped down as head of the Bihar Medical Council. Kumar had been working as a doctor in Britain's National Health Service in 1984 when he decided to return to Patna. It is a decision he bitterly regrets. Dressed in a blue boating jacket with gold buttons, Kumar looked out of place in a town where it is wise not to stand out. As a Bhumiyar, the caste of traditional Bihari landowners, and a qualified doctor, Kumar is both upper caste and middle class (the two do not always coincide: there are many poor Brahmins living in the villages). In the eyes of the lower castes, Kumar is "feudal." And in the eyes of the kidnappers he is a primary target. "I sleep with a gun under my pillow," Kumar said, as we chatted over tea at his clinic, while he kept a wary eye on the black-and-white closed-circuit TV that overlooks the entrance to his surgery. "All the time I am getting threats of abduction or extortion. It is desperate here. Most of my colleagues have left. They won't come back."

Kumar alleged that the kidnappers and the police were often one and the same. He also said that the police, as one or two senior Bihari policemen also attested, behave as though they are the personal staff members of their political masters. Earlier in the visit I had talked to D. P. Ojha, who had been head of the police for the entire state of 75 million people before he was shunted into early retirement. One of Ojha's transgressions had been to arrest Mohammed Shahabuddin, a member of parliament for Lalu's party, who faces multiple charges of murder, kidnapping, and extortion. In an interview on national television, Shahabuddin had casually threatened D. P. Ojha's life. Almost 100 of India's 545 members of parliament in New Delhi have "criminal backgrounds,"[10] which means they have been indicted for one or more crimes, but not convicted. Once they are elected, it is virtually impossible to convict them, which is one of their main incentives for entering politics in the first place. In turn, the wealth and muscle power of the mafia dons gives an incentive to political leaders, such as Lalu, to adopt them as electoral candidates. Of the almost one hundred alleged parliamentary criminals, Bihar and Uttar Pradesh account for by far the largest share. Anyone who gets in their way, such as D. P. Ojha, risks the consequences. Like Kumar, Ojha said he was too old to think of leaving his home state. So he runs a one-man show to combat political corruption. "We have excellent laws, even in Bihar. Our problem is the people who are supposed to be upholding these laws," the retired police commissioner told me. "When the gamekeepers are poachers in disguise, why should anyone else take the law seriously?"

It was a good question, which I thought was worth putting to Lalu Prasad Yadav. Lalu, as everyone calls him, is also a member of parliament in New Delhi. He was indicted in the late 1990s for alleged corruption in a fodder subsidy scandal. He was briefly imprisoned so he stepped down as Bihar's chief minister in favor of his wife, Rabri Devi, who has presided over the state ever since. But the indictment did not prevent Lalu from becoming India's minister for railways in 2004, a senior cabinet position in the government headed by Manmohan Singh. The strength of Lalu's party in New Delhi made him the second largest partner of Singh's multiparty coalition government after the Congress Party. The resulting cabinet was a curious mix of urbane technocrats, such as Manmohan, and earthy rural leaders, such as Lalu. Some despaired of its incoherence. Others were more philosophical. At a party shortly after the election, one of Manmohan's colleagues said to me: "I think we should all be studying the history of how corrupt American politics was in the early twentieth century. It proves that you can still rise to become a great power." The analogy was not unreasonable: India's economy has continued to grow at 7 percent a year since 2004.

However, the economy of Bihar has gone from bad to worse. It is India's most rural state with more than 90 percent of the people living in villages. For most Biharis, the countryside is far from a rural idyll. Fewer than one in ten Bihari households has electricity. Only one Bihari in twenty can afford a scooter. Life expectancy is the lowest in India. The average Bihari can expect to live fifteen fewer years than his counterpart in the state of Kerala, where most people have access to medicines, schooling, and electricity.[11] There are no real jobs in Bihar, and the economy is so anemic that it collects only 0.7 percent of India's national sales tax revenues, despite accounting for more than 7 percent of India's population. Fewer than one in forty Biharis possesses a television.[12] For entertainment, many rely on Lalu, whose public speeches can still draw crowds of several hundred thousand people. He can be very witty. During the election campaign, one reporter informed Lalu that Hema Malini, a glamorous Bollywood actress, had said she was a fan of his. "If she is my fan, then I'm her air-conditioner," Lalu shot back.

This was my second meeting with Lalu and I was a little nervous. After my first interview a couple of years earlier I had written an article that Lalu had publicly criticized. Lalu had been sitting in his garden with a large collection of cronies and it was nighttime. He was talking in a continuous banter that generated much laughter. I had written: "There was the unmistakable whiff of marijuana in the air."[13] I stand by the offending sentence, since the smell was hard to confuse and the person accompanying me had agreed. But Lalu had not taken kindly to the remark.* He told the local media and anyone else who cared to listen that Western journalists such as I were out to defame him: "They are in league with the Brahmins," he said.

On this occasion getting into Lalu's compound was difficult, although not because of my article. His residence was surrounded by hundreds of people shouting slogans. It was a winter evening and the air was thick with fog. Our car had to crawl myopically for fear of hitting someone. It was hard to make out what they were shouting about. I found Lalu amid a thicket of microphones and cameras giving a press conference in his garden. Once he had dismissed the me-

*Marijuana is legal in most parts of India, and in many states, including Bihar, it is sold at licensed government outlets. It is supposedly only meant for use during holy festivals.

dia, I joined him and his wife around a fire on his verandah. Lalu was sprawled on a rattan chair with a blanket around his shoulders, occasionally warming his hands by the fire. Rabri Devi served lemon tea and Bihari sweets. I asked Lalu what he thought he had achieved for Bihar in the last fifteen years. "Our two biggest achievements are social justice and communal harmony," he said. "We have given courage to the downtrodden. Dalits can now hold their heads up high. They are no longer oppressed by the Brahmins and by the landowners. And Muslims are safe. We have defeated the Hindu nationalists." Much of this was true. But Bihar had no rule of law. Lalu said: "Whenever anyone writes about Bihar they talk about law and order problems or they talk about caste violence. That is because we have an upper-caste media in India. Even foreigners are fooled by these things." Then Lalu said that two years earlier a journalist from the *Financial Times* of London had written that marijuana had been smoked in his presence. That was me, I told him. "No no, it definitely wasn't you," said Lalu, looking a little flustered. "He didn't look at all like you, he was, he was. . . ." But it *was* me, I insisted. "Oh, it doesn't matter," said Lalu, looking genuinely uncomfortable. "I am sure it was a cultural misunderstanding. It can happen very easily." I confess I was charmed by Lalu's embarrassment. Here was a man who is celebrated up and down India for his perfect one-line insults. During the 2004 national election campaign, Lalu suggested the poll be resolved by a running race between the leaders of the two main parties, Sonia Gandhi, the fifty-nine-year-old Italian widow of Rajiv (with whom Lalu is allied, and whom we will meet in chapter five), and Atal Behari Vajpayee, the septuagenarian Hindu nationalist prime minister (whom we will meet in the next chapter). Vajpayee had recently had operations on both of his knees. The prime minister could barely walk let alone undertake a running contest. But even Vajpayee's friends had laughed at Lalu's joke. We asked Lalu about the noisy slogan shouting outside his residence. "They are my people and they are shouting pro-Lalu slogans," he said. The crowd, it turned out, was packed with aspiring candidates for the Lalu party ticket in the forthcoming vote. "When I drive through the crowd," he said, to the merriment of those inside the compound, "I draw the window curtains so I don't have to look at their faces."

The interview then descended from banter into circus. Lalu insisted on showing me around his compound, which he had converted into a menagerie for his favorite animals, mostly cows, of which there were two hundred. There were also two white Arabian horses. During his spell in prison in the late 1990s, Lalu said he had a vision in which Lord Krishna, who is the god most beloved of Yadavs, had told him to become a vegetarian and to be kind to cows. Lalu had complied. "It sounds like you are trying to become a Brahmin," I said to him. Lalu was born into acute poverty in a Bihari village and spent his childhood in rags and without shoes tending the village herd. Lalu's nine children have all been educated at English-language schools. One of Lalu's daughters lives in Singapore and is married to a senior software executive. Lalu ignored my joke. We were inside the cow shelter and Lalu was introducing me to his favorites. Each had a name. Dozens of full-time attendants were assigned to look after the cows. "This is my favorite," said Lalu, patting its head lovingly. Then he put up both his hands in front of the cow's face and said: "This hand is for Lalu and this hand is for Ram Vilas Paswan [Lalu's fiercest electoral competitor]." The cow did not move when Lalu showed it the hand that represented Paswan. But then something peculiar happened. Lalu put his other hand up—the one that represented himself—and the cow slowly but emphatically nodded its head. I looked in vain for an attendant who might be pulling the cow's tail or tugging on a piece of string. But the trick was authentic. It must have taken Lalu hours and hours of practice.

A few months later Lalu's party was ejected from office in Bihar, although it retained its pivotal role in the national coalition. Lalu remained India's minister of railways. Many people hailed the 2005 election result as a vote for "good governance" following fifteen years of misrule by Lalu and his cronies. But the coalition of lower-

and upper-caste parties that defeated Lalu, which was led by Nitish Kumar, a former railway minister and a member of another lower caste called the Kurmis, was stitched together in much the same way and using much the same appeals to caste identity as Lalu had used. Lalu's opponents fielded a higher proportion of candidates with criminal backgrounds than Lalu did himself. Even in defeat, Lalu's logic lived on. I have little doubt that he will be back.

●   ●   ●

It has taken India's lower-caste leaders decades of practice to master the complexities of Indian democracy. Now they are better at it than anyone else. In Indian politics, lower-caste voters have an advantage that is of little help in other spheres of life: the sheer weight of numbers. About half of India's population is lower caste, in one form or other. If you add in India's 150 million Muslims and the tens of millions belonging to India's linguistic groups who are living outside their language area, more than half of India's population is officially classified as minority.[14] Lower-caste parties have another advantage: their non-caste competitors have to pitch their message as widely as possible. The Congress Party aims to appeal to everyone by stressing a secular and inclusive Indian nationalism and a centrist view of the economy. The Hindu nationalist Bharatiya Janata Party (BJP; the India People's Party) tries to appeal to almost every voter except for Muslims and Christians. Hindus make up 85 percent of India's population. But the lower-caste parties can ruthlessly target their message at their own narrow slices of the population. It means they are more efficient at garnering their respective "vote banks." But their strategy limits their overall electoral tally to their own caste population. If all the lower castes were to make common cause with each other and merge into one large lower-caste party, the new party would probably govern India in perpetuity. What prevents them?

A small clue might lie in Lalu's constant references to Lord

Krishna. Lalu's unique personality has often prompted contrasts with rebel leaders in other parts of the world. Unlike Lalu, very few of them—whether we look at the great Italian nationalist rebels of the nineteenth century, the Chinese revolutionaries of the first half of the twentieth century, the agitators of early Victorian England, or the Jeffersons and Madisons of the American Revolution—consulted astrologers or soothsayers, or gave much license to religious imagery. They were modern history's levelers, who sought to unite the people against the monarchy, the church, the landed aristocracy, or foreign rule. Their rhetoric was universal and they promised equality. The rhetoric of Lalu and the leaders of India's other six or seven nationally significant lower-caste parties is aimed at a specific category of people. It excludes or ignores others who live in the same kind of poverty. Some foreign and Indian observers describe India's lower-caste parties as left-wing because they stand for the underprivileged. This might be to miss the trees for the forest—to reverse the aphorism. Each lower-caste party stands for only one section of the underprivileged. Lower-caste politicians do not unite the lower orders by stressing what they have in common. Instead, they slice them up by focusing on what divides them. It is much closer to ethnic politics than it is to class politics.

Lalu's numerous caste of Yadavs is also quite visible in other parts of India, particularly the large states of Uttar Pradesh and Madhya Pradesh. His counterpart in Uttar Pradesh is Mulayam Singh Yadav, whose key right-hand man, Amar Singh, we will meet later on. Like Lalu, Mulayam Singh Yadav's party relies on the support of an alliance between millions of Yadav and Muslim voters who are united in antipathy to Brahmins and increasingly to Dalits. Mulayam's party has also garnered the votes of many Rajputs, a subcaste of the traditional warrior Kshatriya caste, to which Amar Singh belongs. His Yadav party is one of India's newfangled caste alliances.

Lalu and Mulayam are both members and former presidents of the All-India Yadav Mahasabha (assembly). The Mahasabha has developed an interesting ideology. It claims all Yadavs are descended from

Lord Krishna, the god who was also depicted in the epics as a cowherd, the traditional caste function of the Yadavs. According to this view, the genes of Yadavs are as pure as or even purer than those of the Brahmins. The Mahasabha has also pronounced both Mulayam and Lalu to be incarnations of Krishna. But it left unsaid any view it may have on the bloodlines of other lower castes, who presumably remain as polluted as they were before. This is what one of the speakers said at the Mahasabha's annual conference: "We have assembled here from different parts of the country. We speak different languages . . . our habits and customs are different but we feel oneness and brotherhood because the same blood is running in our veins."[15]

Like the originators of other caste origin myths, the Yadavs say they were denied by trickery or historical injustice their rightful place in the upper layers of the caste hierarchy among the righteous and should not be grouped among the polluting castes. Almost all of India's larger subcastes have constructed similarly proud mythologies of an elevated ancestry that was taken from them in the mists of time by scheming Brahmins or thieving Kshatriyas. With the notable exception of the Mahars, whose outlook remains heavily influenced by Ambedkar, most of the other untouchable castes, including the Chamars, also claim descent from some god or great saint. Perhaps the most intriguing claim is that of the Bedias, a caste of prostitutes who are shunned by everyone, at least during daylight hours. Bedia women say that caste identity comes from the bloodline of the father, and since most of their clients are Rajput men, they argue that their true caste is Rajput, which is relatively high up on the scale. The Bedias even hired the services of a Brahmin priest who pronounced, somewhat elliptically, that it is the seed that is sown on the field that matters and not the soil of the field—the soil being female, the seed male.[16] The Rajput men disagree. The opinion of their wives is not recorded.

In much of rural India caste discrimination is as rampant as ever and hundreds die every year from caste violence, some at the hands of the police. According to the Indian government, violence by the police against Dalits whom they have falsely arrested is still routine in the villages of India: "During interrogation, injuries sustained by the arrested person are so great that he usually dies."[17] Equally, Dalits are still often denied entry into temples. But what is more noteworthy is that so many Dalits want to enter the temples in the first place. Seventy years ago Ambedkar wrote: "Hindu society is a myth. The name *Hindu* is itself foreign. It was given by the Mohammedans to the natives for the purpose of distinguishing themselves. Each caste not only dines among itself and marries among itself but each caste also prescribes its own distinctive dress."[18] This may have been accurate at the time. But in today's India it would be hard to distinguish people's caste by what they wear or where they eat.

Beneath the radar, there have been fairly dramatic changes in the lifestyles of the lower castes over the last few decades. Ordinary Yadavs may or may not believe they are descended from Lord Krishna. But Yadavs and other lower castes do increasingly behave in their private habits and beliefs as though they were upper caste. Indian scholars call this "Sanskritization,"[19] in reference to the classical language that was the preserve of the Brahmins. The term describes a trend in which the lower orders are now copying the culture of the upper orders by following the same gods, attending the same temples, and celebrating the same festivals. In urban India, it is often only by the name that you can distinguish the caste of a person. Other attributes, such as dress or dietary habits, have become increasingly general to all castes. In their lifestyles, the wealthier among the lower castes—farmers who may have profited from the green revolution or those who have found secure jobs in the city—are reinventing themselves. If you enter an urban home in today's India, it would be hard to tell the caste of its occupants. The gods depicted in the small household shrine are the same. The people follow the same traditional upper-caste rituals.

But in the political world, India's lower castes move in the opposite direction from "Sanskritization," which many now follow in their personal lives. Instead of seeking to emulate their Brahmin role models as they do in their cultural and religious behavior, the lower castes use politics to play out their revenge against the upper castes and to extract compensation for their low social status. Usually they get what they want. India's affirmative action program is the largest in the world. It is far larger and more extensive than that of America. In India, half of all government jobs are reserved for three separate categories of underdog: Adivasis, who are Indians of tribal origin, making up almost 10 percent of the population; Dalits officially accounting for 12.5 percent of the population; and "Other Backward Classes," which include castes such as the Yadavs, accounting for 27 percent of the population. Together, about 50 percent of India's public sector jobs are allocated to these groups. In addition, each state has its own system of set-asides. In some states, including Rajasthan and Tamil Nadu, the quota for provincial government jobs is as much as two-thirds. Few of these positions are allocated by competitive examination. In practice many of the jobs are dispensed by the relevant caste leaders and their networks of hangers-on. Or else they are up for sale to the highest bidders.* It is arguably the most extensive system of patronage in the democratic world.

Expanding this system is the *only* serious item on the agenda of the lower-caste parties. None of the caste parties publishes manifestos at election times setting out policies on the economy, foreign policy, or defense. What the lower-caste parties offer their supporters is the ability to extract greater powers of patronage from the larger parties in exchange for making up the parliamentary numbers in multiparty coalitions. That is why Lalu, whose party helped bring Manmohan Singh's government to power in New Delhi, was given the ministry of railways, which oversees a workforce of almost 1.5 million people (second only to China's People's Liberation Army as the largest em-

---

*The *Financial Times* driver in Delhi once applied for a job as a government driver. He was told it would cost Rs 100,000 to get the position. Each job has a fixed price.

ployer in the world). Since they dispense few jobs, neither the foreign ministry nor the ministry of finance would have held the same appeal. Likewise, when Mulayam Singh Yadav's party helped prop up an earlier coalition government in New Delhi in the 1990s, he became minister of defense. Most of India's large defense industry is publicly owned. Neither Lalu nor Mulayam has submitted anything resembling a coherent plan on how to manage India's economy. But both are hostile to privatization of state enterprises since any reduction in the public sector would shrink their source of patronage. Both men also support extending the system of public job quotas to the private sector. This is still an unlikely prospect, in spite of anecdotal evidence that many of India's older private sector companies do practice caste and religious discrimination in their hiring policies. Mere mention of reserving jobs on grounds of caste rather than qualifications sends shudders of horror through India's company boardrooms.

•   •   •

What can be said about Lalu and Mulayam is true many times over for Mayawati, who is leader of India's largest untouchable party, the Bahujan Samaj Party (BSP, meaning Majority of the People). Like many Dalits, Mayawati has only one name. But in recognition of her status as their "tallest leader," many Dalits refer to her as Behenji Mayawati, "honored sister." Mayawati has thrice been chief minister of Uttar Pradesh, India's largest state. When she first took power in 1996, she was both the first woman and the first untouchable in India's history to take charge of the state. She quickly gained a reputation as someone who delighted in causing great discomfort to her upper-caste civil servants. Within the first year of her administration she ordered 1,400 transfers of IAS officers, which was—and remains—a clear record. Some of the senior IAS officers whom she most disliked had to change jobs every few weeks at great cost to their children's schooling. There was no logic to Mayawati's minirevolution other than to humiliate the Brahmins and also, according to some allegations, to raise money from IAS officers who were prepared to pay bribes to either stay put or move back to where they had been stationed before. "Mayawati likes to keep the Brahmins dancing," one of her advisers said to me. "Our people in the villages enjoy watching the spectacle very much." Other less sympathetic observers, including the World Bank, whose development projects in Uttar Pradesh were badly disrupted by Mayawati's game of musical chairs, were less amused.

Mayawati has never granted me an interview, since she has little interest in speaking to the English-language media, foreign or Indian. On one occasion I came close. There was a large Dalit rally in the north Indian town of Gaya near to the famous Bodhgaya temple, which was built on the spot where Buddha was reputed to have achieved enlightenment under a *peepul* tree. Her public meeting took place in a large *maidan,* or park, in the center of the town. It was attended by thousands of cheering supporters. After Mayawati had finished speaking she left the podium and moved toward a waiting Ambassador car, which would whisk her to a helicopter a couple of hundred yards away. Waving my press pass I managed to enter the enclosure and approach Mayawati. Before I could get any closer, I was barred by four men, whose standard-issue dark glasses and handguns identified them as political musclemen. I managed to shout my request to Mayawati, who glanced suspiciously at me for a couple of seconds before getting into the car. Then her cavalcade of vehicles proceeded for all of thirty seconds to the waiting helicopter, with her security men running alongside, brandishing their guns. Mayawati gave a brief imperious wave from the hovering chopper to the crowds below her. Then the helicopter nosed off into the distance to another rally at another *maidan* teeming with starstruck supporters.

Few, if any, leaders in today's India can bank on as much loyalty from their voters as Mayawati has. India's electoral analysts say

Mayawati's BSP party (not to be confused with the Hindu national-ist BJP) has the most disciplined vote bank of any party in India. Whatever the circumstances, and whatever her record in office, Mayawati's party can rely on the votes of one-fifth of the Uttar Pradesh electorate, which roughly corresponds to the proportion of Dalits among the state's 170 million people. Even after Mayawati was caught red-handed in 2003 awarding contracts to her favorite construction companies to build a large shopping complex around the resplendent and historic Taj Mahal, her voting tally did not fall. She was forced, however, to abandon her plans to bring Las Vegas to India's greatest monument.

Mayawati's overriding agenda is to bring more Dalits into govern-ment jobs. Her mentor, Kanshi Ram, founded the BSP in the 1980s af-ter he had been refused a day's leave from his government job on the occasion of Ambedkar's birthday, a public holiday. The incident trig-gered a pent-up frustration. Ram said Dalit civil servants were rou-tinely denied promotion and respect by their peers. His new party's agenda, said Ram, was to give Dalits self-respect and to create more government jobs for them: "Political power is the master-key with which you can open any lock," he said.[20] Mayawati uses power with a fury that makes Lalu and Mulayam seem like consensus politicians. Her campaign speeches often consist of a long list from which she reads out the caste origins of each of her candidates. She makes no at-tempt to present policies or opinions on more general subjects. In one closely studied campaign, Mayawati devoted 91 percent of her speeches to the issue of "social justice," which is code for government jobs for Dalits.[21] In contrast to most of her competitors, Mayawati did not once refer to issues such as "good governance," "nationalism," "prices," or "corruption."

Dalits list most of these themes as major issues of concern in their lives. Yet when it comes to casting their votes, their choice seems to boil down to the caste of the candidate. Essential services, such as roads, electricity, and jobs, are in short supply in the rural economy of Uttar Pradesh. So the voter, especially the lower-caste voter, needs access to the people who have control over them. Sharing a caste background with the politician helps. Evidence that you have voted for the politician helps even more. Kanchan Chandra, a scholar at MIT, who conducted these surveys, argues persuasively: "Elections in a patronage-based democracy [like India] are in essence covert auctions in which basic services, which should in principle be available to every citizen, are sold instead to the highest bidder."

Elections in Uttar Pradesh are also about muscle power. Both the Congress Party and the BJP have been virtually eclipsed in Uttar Pradesh, which is by far the most important among India's twenty-nine states, since, with 84 out of India's 543 constituencies, it is home to almost a sixth of India's parliamentary seats. Eight of India's thirteen prime ministers have come from Uttar Pradesh. Neither of the national parties can match the ruthlessness of the state's two principal lower-caste parties, or their ability to command such loyalty among their vote banks.

One of the most extraordinary pieces of Indian electioneering I have observed is the sight of Mulayam's Samajwadi (socialist) campaigners driving through the city of Allahabad in a cavalcade of about forty vehicles, consisting mostly of Mercedes and Toyota Safaris. Thickets of guns poked out of each vehicle. Doubtless voters were meant to be intimidated. But they would also have been impressed. The electioneering was for a by-election in Allahabad, a city of four million people that was an important metropolis for the Mughals and the British. Allahabad is an important north Indian city.

The election had been triggered by the assassination of Raju Pal, the BSP member of the legislative assembly who had been gunned down in the city's main commercial street opposite a car showroom at midday. The corpse was pumped with more than twenty bullets. Mayawati's party alleged that the murder had been carried out by Ashraf, the brother of Atiq Ahmed, who is the area's member of parliament in New Delhi for Mulayam's party. Ashraf was immediately imprisoned. But that did not stop him from standing in the by-election from jail. His opposing candidate was Puja Pal, the pretty twenty-five-year-old widow of the murdered BSP legislative representative. The contest boiled down to a young widow battling her husband's alleged murderer. It had all the makings of a Shakespearean tragedy.

The first to grant me an interview was Puja Pal. We drove out on dirt tracks at night to a village on the outskirts of town. Pal was dressed in white, the color of mourning. She had been married only a few weeks earlier. Fifty or sixty of her supporters crowded round us in the courtyard of the house to observe the interview. Every time I asked Pal a question, someone else would answer it for her. I requested that Pal answer directly. The Samajwadi had claimed that the BSP was running an Islamaphobic campaign, since her opposite number was a Muslim. They were also alleging that she was blaming the criminalization of politics in the city on the Muslims. Atiq Ahmed, the member of parliament who was campaigning against Pal on his imprisoned brother's behalf, was allegedly the most feared mafia don in Allahabad. Pal's late husband, according to the gossip, had been on Atiq's payroll many years earlier. But he had struck out alone.

I asked Pal whether she was running an anti-Muslim campaign. "Look around at all these people," said Pal, having finally been permitted to answer for herself. "He is a Muslim, he is a Muslim, and he is a Muslim. Ask them." They all nodded happily. Pal then said she had not been allowed to see her husband's body, since it had been burned by the police the same day he was killed, ostensibly to forestall a potentially riotous funeral procession. She claimed that Mulayam Yadav, the chief minister, had ordered the police to dispose of the corpse this way. She also mentioned lavish sums of money that had allegedly changed hands to bring about the murder of her husband. None of this was possible to verify. But I could not help admiring the courage of this young widow. She narrowly lost the election, which took place in June 2005. As I and the photographer Sohail Akbar departed, Pal's supporters hung garlands around us, as if it were we who were the politicians. It would have caused offense to refuse.

Getting to see Atiq Ahmed was much trickier. Everybody wants to see him. He is a right-hand man of Mulayam in New Delhi. He can also get things done for you in Allahabad. Access is closely regulated. After persistent telephone calls, I was eventually allowed inside his heavily guarded compound, which was opposite the local mosque in the densely populated Muslim quarter of Allahabad. There was a fleet of tinted-glass cars parked in front of the entrance to his mansion. Once inside, the first thing I saw was the household armory, with row upon row of guns stacked against the wall. As I waited for the appointed time, Atiq's octogenarian father sat and chatted with me. His beard was dyed red with henna. He had just completed his third and final hadj (pilgrimage) to Mecca. Neither Atiq nor Ashraf had yet been on the hadj. "They are both still children," said the father about his middle-aged sons. We were interrupted by a young man who said our interview with Ahmed would have to be postponed because he had to rush to join Mulayam who had landed by helicopter in the center of town to address an election rally.

I finally got to see Ahmed at his party headquarters in town later in the day. He was seated in a tiny room on a plastic chair and was shouting at someone on his cell phone. I was a little anxious about questioning him. But he waved a friendly hand toward some chairs and ordered tea and sweets. His face was dominated by heavy jowls, a thick mustache, and bulging eyes. His teeth were stained red with *paan,* an addictive mix of betel nut, lime, and tobacco leaf that you chew for hours. He was quick to laugh. I asked why he had alleged that the Dalit party was running a Hindu nationalist campaign. "Dalits are very simple people," he said. "They are nice people also. But you know some of them think that if they fall sick they can cure themselves just by tying a yellow string around a tree. In politics, they follow one leader in the morning and another in the afternoon. They are very easily misled. Mayawati is wooing the Brahmins because the Brahmins don't like the Muslims or the Yadavs. So this is what has happened."

I said most people thought the election was really a contest between two rival mafia gangs for control of the city. Politics was incidental. Ahmed looked surprised. Then he revealed a broad betel-stained smile. He seemed to appreciate the question. "Oh, that is all false propaganda spread by the Hindu nationalists," he said. "Pay them no attention. Such nonsense is talked." But what about all your guns? I asked. "They are not my private guns," he replied. "They belong to the intelligence agencies who have been assigned to protect me." I did not believe him. But there was no point in pursuing it. Then I said that people claimed he had done nothing to contribute to the development of his state. "It is very difficult to bring development to India," said Ahmed, looking suddenly thoughtful. "It is such a complicated and diverse country. If you drive in your car fifty miles south of Allahabad, you will find the customs change. Our customs are very diverse. We [the Samajwadi Party] are adding new castes to our political equation. We are not just Yadavs and Muslims but also Rajputs. The more castes we add the more we will be judged by voters on our performance and not on our identity."

Ahmed's prediction may or may not prove true in the coming years. Certainly, the tendency of lower-caste parties to woo one or another of the upper-caste groups is growing. It was an alliance such as this that proved to be Lalu's undoing in Bihar. In Uttar Pradesh, Mayawati is selecting Brahmin candidates in areas where upper castes are concentrated. But the logic behind her electoral arithmetic is unrelated to development. In their daily lives many Dalit farm laborers feel more oppressed by wealthy Yadav farmers than they do by distant Brahmin civil servants. Few Brahmins farm for a living: the caste's ancient dharma forbids the Brahmin to touch a plow. Most Yadavs continue to farm for a living. So Dalits and Brahmins both resent and fear Yadavs (Brahmins because they are losing their traditional domination of society). Any development agenda that might result from such an unholy alliance would be purely incidental.

But there was little time to probe Ahmed further and he seemed uninterested in the issue of economic development. He stood up and led us through his party headquarters to our waiting car outside. A hundred or more men who had been lounging outside Ahmed's small office immediately sprang to their feet. Many of them were armed. It felt like we were strolling through an army camp. Instead of a parliamentarian, it was a two-star general who was waving us off. I felt no surprise a few weeks later when I heard who had prevailed in the Allahabad campaign.

•   •   •

As a journalist, I had been inside the homes of very wealthy people before. But nothing compared to what I saw at 27 Lodhi Estate in central New Delhi. It was (and remains) the official residence of Amar Singh, a member of parliament for Mulayam Singh Yadav's Samajwadi Party. The airy bungalow, which is one of 204 similar residences in the capital allocated to the nation's most senior politicians and officials, is officially protected under New Delhi's heritage laws. It was designed, like much of the city, by the architect Edwin Lutyens. Amar Singh, who had agreed to allow me and a mutual acquaintance to look over the property, had generated controversy in the newspapers for having carried out extensive alterations to his bungalow. During our guided tour Amar Singh was keen to demonstrate that the changes he had made were in fact "improvements."

Although himself a Rajput, which is relatively high caste, Amar Singh is one of the two or three most powerful leaders among India's lower-caste parties. A portly man nearing fifty, and with the obligatory mustache, Amar Singh was accompanied by Jayaprada, a former Bollywood actress who had been recruited into politics in the 2004 election. In spite of being a member of parliament, Jayaprada at all times referred to Amar Singh as "sir." He said to us: "I was not very enthusiastic to show you my residence after what the media has been writing about me. They come here, eat my food and write what they like."

The same month, Mulayam Singh Yadav, the chief minister of Uttar Pradesh, had appointed as his chief secretary a person who had been voted by her colleagues (at an annual convention of civil servants) the second most corrupt civil servant in Uttar Pradesh. Her appointment caused a furor. Allegations against the Samajwadi Party include selling electoral tickets to the highest bidder, accepting bribes from civil servants to be moved to more comfortable postings, handing out industrial licenses in exchange for favors, and fixing supposedly blind lotteries to allocate prime urban land to friends.

Amar Singh is also the founder and head of the Uttar Pradesh Development Council, a group of politicians and businessmen whom the media has labeled "crony capitalist." Prominent members include Anil Ambani, who controls Reliance Infocomm and Reliance Energy, two of India's largest companies; and Subroto Roy, who owns the Sahara Group, a diversified private company with an airline, TV channels, and sprawling private residential estates. "If this is crony capitalism then we should all be crony capitalists," Singh said to me, pointing out that the Uttar Pradesh Development Council had brought in many new investments for his state. What about the corruption allegations against his party? "There might be a little corruption here and there," Singh said. "You cannot check everything."

Our guided tour began with the garden. Amar Singh took us along the outer perimeter, whose walls had been recast with white marble bas-reliefs of gamboling cherubs and nubile winged angels, a curious hybrid of classical Greek art and modern pornography. Next we entered a prefab annex Singh had erected, which contained a modern gym with the usual NordicTracks and cycle machines. In the adjoining room there was a large marble Jacuzzi with gold-plated taps. Singh then took us across to the main building, against the exterior of which he had constructed a sweeping *Gone With the Wind* staircase that took us up to the terrace of the bungalow, which had been converted into a roof garden with grass and rose beds. "Are you liking this?" asked Singh. Next we went inside. The main room was dominated by a vast portrait of Singh and his family. Next to it were gold and jewelry-studded depictions of the god Krishna. No corner of the walls or the floors remained unadorned by some trophy item or other: a silver *Ravissant* receptacle here, a priceless antique vase there. In each of the main rooms, Singh had given pride of place to one of the most expensive items of home entertainment in the world: the 60-inch plasma screen Bang & Olufsen TV. Each would retail for as much as $60,000.

But the grandest cut was reserved until last. Amar Singh, whose excitement had been mounting as the tour progressed, took us into the main dining room. At the side of the room he had demolished a portion of the wall to create a small alcove that jutted into the garden and was protected by a glass screen. Behind the screen was a small and illuminated marble basin out of which gurgled a soothing stream of water. Singh took out what looked to be a giant TV remote control and pointed it at the high ceiling above the dining table. I half expected another screen to pop out. He pressed the button and something started to happen to the heavy stone Lutyens ceiling. Slowly but noiselessly, it began to divide. It was impossible to guess what was about to be revealed. We were actually—I almost convinced myself—characters in one of those Bond films and Singh was about to feed us to birds of prey. After the ceiling had fully parted we were greeted with a dazzling view of the roof through the prism of a small glass pyramid that was clearly modeled on the structure that sits above the Louvre gallery in Paris. The shimmering glass refracted the verdant foliage of the terrace beyond. Everyone gasped, half of us in shock, the other half in admiration. "Now," said Amar Singh, turning toward us, beaming from ear to ear, "do you think these are improvements or just alterations?"

•    •    •

Most of this chapter has focused on the deep caste divisions of north India and the corruption that often goes with them. A majority of Indians live in the north, which gives the region a correspondingly larger impact on the character of national politics. Many who despair of the north's sometimes pathological caste relations glance longingly toward the south, for example, to the state of Tamil Nadu, which seems to have put the worst of caste conflict behind it. Caste still exists in Tamil Nadu. And much like in the north, Tamil Nadu's two principal political parties seem to sit up all night and day thinking of ways to break up their opponent's caste alliances. As in Uttar Pradesh, neither the Congress Party nor the BJP has much of a presence in Tamil Nadu, accounting for less than a fifth of its representation between them. Yet guns only very rarely spill over into Tamil Nadu politics and there are far fewer politicians with "criminal backgrounds" in its legislative assembly. The state provides basic services with a much higher degree of efficiency to most people. Things appear to function, at least to a minimum standard of acceptability. "We estimate that roughly 30 percent of public resources are diverted in Tamil Nadu compared to about 70 percent in the north," the chief secretary of Tamil Nadu told me. As a result, the state has paved highways, large inflows of private investment both foreign and domestic, and an economy that generates jobs on a significant scale. It is no coincidence that Tamil Nadu is the most urbanized state in India, with almost half of its people living in towns. Bihar is the least urbanized state, with fewer than 10 percent of its people living in towns.

Tamil Nadu, which was among the first regions in India to be ruled directly by the British in the eighteenth century, has a much longer experience than the north with lower-caste political agitation. As long ago as the 1880s, when the British were starting to classify Indians by caste for a census, the city of Madras was already a hive of lower-caste radicalism. The government of Madras, as Tamil Nadu was then known, conceded public sector job quotas to lower castes in the 1920s, thirty years before India allocated quotas to Dalits and almost seventy years before New Delhi extended national set-asides to "Other Backward Classes." Tamil Nadu holds the record in India for the highest proportion of set-asides, amounting to 69 percent of its government jobs. This has good and bad consequences. The bad part is that it is very hard to reform the state's bloated bureaucracy or instill a system of meritocracy. Most quotas are supposed to be temporary. But as the saying goes: "There is nothing as permanent as a temporary government measure." The good side is that the state's upper castes have had many decades to get accustomed to "social justice" as a normal part of politics, even if they do not particularly like it.

Another positive aspect is that almost 90 percent of Tamil Nadu's sixty million people are literate, compared to just half of the people in Bihar. This owes something to the fact that lower-caste agitation began in Tamil Nadu long before India got democracy, which meant that after independence lower-caste leaders had to focus on other arenas to empower their followers. As a result, there was a much greater emphasis on educating the masses as the most obvious way of raising their social status. Other reasons could be that Tamil Nadu, like neighboring Kerala, had far more extensive experience than the north of Christian missionary activity in the eighteenth and nineteenth centuries, so there were many more opportunities for the lower castes to attend schools. Bihar and Uttar Pradesh are deep in India's landlocked interior. Tamil Nadu is a coastal state so it was always more open to foreign influences. Tamil Nadu also has a relatively low proportion of Brahmins, amounting to just 3 percent of its population, compared to between 15 and 20 percent in the northern states. The state's unusual caste demography meant it was easier for everyone else to unite against the upper orders and release their stranglehold on society. Finally, Tamil Nadu has a completely different language and script and so it is linguistically shielded from many of the less savory trends that are visible in the "Hindi belt," a term commonly used for India's north.

Tamil Nadu gave the rest of the world an impressive display of its efficiency after the devastating tsunami of December 2004 struck. India is no stranger to large natural disasters. Thousands died in the coastal state of Orissa in 1999 when it was hit by a large cyclone. Earthquakes claimed thousands of lives in the western Indian state of

Gujarat in 2001 and in Kashmir in 2005. But none of the other states responded with anything like the degree of alacrity of Tamil Nadu, whose disaster was as devastating as anything India has seen in recent decades. Between 15,000 and 20,000 people were killed by the giant wave that hit the state's coastline.

I visited the district of Cuddalore, which is about a hundred miles south of Chennai. The district had suffered several hundred deaths from tsunami, and tens of thousands of people had been made homeless. Within a year of the disaster, the government had rehabilitated almost all of Cuddalore's displaced people in pukka accommodation. By contrast, in Orissa there were still people living in camps in 2006, people who had been made homeless seven years earlier by the cyclone. Most of the victims I met in Cuddalore were lower caste. But they were fully aware of their rights. "In Orissa the women were too afraid to come out of their huts and talk to me," said Joseph Williams, a Tamil doctor who had assisted in both disasters. "In Tamil Nadu it is difficult to get the women to stop talking."

In one village that was particularly badly hit, I was taken to the temporary shelters in which many of the 3,000 villagers were now housed. Dozens of people gathered to answer my questions. The shelters were rudimentary. But they were more impressive than the makeshift contraptions in which millions live permanently in the slums of Mumbai, Delhi, or Kolkata. The refugees had the use of toilets that were cleaned daily. During our conversation the women frequently interrupted the men. This is rare in the north. Literacy can do wonders for people's self-confidence. Some of the women had been cross-checking the assistance and financial compensation they had received against what had been announced in the newspapers. "Where is the 3,000 crores [about $750 million] that the World Bank pledged?" one woman asked me. Another said: "We have only been compensated for eighty-four boats but we lost ninety-six." I asked how many people who were present had lost a relative. Everyone raised their hand. Then I asked how many had received the Rs 200,000 compensation for their dead. Everyone raised their hand.

All had been allocated free housing in the new township that was under construction a few hundred yards inland.

Inevitably, the village was divided along caste lines. My guides, who were working for Action Aid, a nongovernmental relief organization, told me there was a "greater fishermen's" caste and a "lesser fishermen's" caste and that these two castes had lived in different parts of the village. But the new village was providing mixed housing. Unusually, the caste least affected by the disaster were the Dalits who were too low down in the pecking order to live near the sea. Those who were affected the worst were the "greater fishermen" who lived on the edge of the sea in the prime spots. Amid the swaying palms was an endless stretch of rubble from the devastated housing set against the azure backdrop of a becalmed sea. I asked the women how quickly they had received aid. In the Gujarat earthquake of 2001, much of the assistance was held up, sometimes fatally, by the eagerness of national VIPs to be photographed visiting the disaster zones. Their private planes clogged up the small airstrips that were also being used by relief agencies to bring in supplies. In addition, the relief effort was compromised by an unseemly competition between different aid agencies to get to the scene. The government of Gujarat had clearly lost its grip on the situation. In Tamil Nadu, however, the state government allocated different villages to different aid agencies and retained an iron coordinating grasp on the effort. There were no epidemics. "We got assistance quite quickly," the women agreed.

It is not just Tamil Nadu's disaster response system that is relatively efficient. The state also has one of the best records for delivering everyday services to the poor. One of the most important is the "midday meals" program, in which children are given an incentive to attend school by the availability of free cooked food. Mostly it works. In many other parts of India midday meals rarely arrive, partly because education is valued less highly than in the south but also because upper-caste families will not permit their children to eat food they suspect has been prepared by lower-caste cooks. In Tamil Nadu this no longer appears to be a problem. Marrying within your caste is still normal. But the majority of people, except for some among Tamil Nadu's small enclave of Brahmins, who have a reputation for being even more finicky about caste rules than others, have overcome the more offensive aspects of caste pollution rules. Much the same contrast applies to health centers. This is what Jean Dréze, one of India's leading economists (of Belgian origin), said in a survey of Tamil Nadu's rural clinics: "They were clean, lively, and well staffed. Patients streamed in and out, evidently at ease with the system. It was a joy to see this, in contrast with the bare, deserted, gloomy, hostile premises that pass for health centers in north India."[22]

It is not my aim to glorify Tamil Nadu. The state suffers from chronic problems, such as poor water supply in its cities and abysmal irrigation for its farmers. It also has a militant civil service that refuses to be reformed. It took the state's police more than twenty years to apprehend and then shoot Veerappan, Tamil Nadu's most celebrated criminal. Veerappan, whom some saw as a Tamil "Robin Hood," had plundered the state's beautiful tropical parks of wild elephants and sandalwood. His gang was alleged to have killed hundreds of innocent people over the years. He was reputed to have many police officers and local politicians on his payroll, which would explain why he eluded the law with such ease for so long. Eventually, in 2004 Veerappan was cornered and shot. Jayalalithaa, Tamil Nadu's chief minister and a politician who is as intimidating as Mayawati, handed out rewards to 752 policemen. After Veerappan was dispatched, each of the policemen was given Rs 300,000 rupees (about $7,000), a plot of land, and a promotion. More than 10,000 police in the neighboring state of Karnataka also claimed to have played a role in Veerappan's killing and demanded similar consideration, in spite of having "just missed" Veerappan on numerous occasions. In turning down their request, B. N. Alburquerque, Karnataka's chief of police, was the only senior figure in either state to show a sense of humor about this absurd demand. "If the operation had been botched up, no one would have claimed responsibility," said Alburquerque. "Success has many fathers, while failure is an orphan."[23]

But Tamil Nadu's problems pale in comparison to those of most of north India. Although the state has yet to confront the issues of a large administrative service that lacks accountability, it possesses something very valuable that is not evident in most of the north: a civic society. It is much more difficult to hijack public space in Tamil Nadu. Its large urbanized middle class accepts the need for rules that everyone should follow, even if they are not followed all of the time. At a trivial level it is evident in Chennai's enforcement of basic everyday regulations such as no-smoking zones, which in cities like New Delhi are honored mostly in the breach. More important, as we have seen, it is also evident in the routine provision of basic public services to people from all backgrounds. Tamil Nadu's civic culture may be hard to measure. But it is an invaluable asset that gives it a decisive economic edge over most of the north.

Many Indian modernizers hope that Tamil Nadu points the way that the north is heading—toward a more moderated and civilized clash between the castes in the field of politics and elsewhere. Tamil Nadu proves that caste sentiments can be diluted, especially in urban settings. But caste has far from disappeared in urban India. In a very detailed nationwide poll conducted in January 2006,[24] 74 percent of respondents said they did not approve of intercaste marriages. Among the educated—and overwhelmingly urban—respondents, 56 percent of graduates also disapproved of such marriages. Likewise, 72 percent of all respondents agreed that parents should have the final say in their children's choice of marriage partners. Among urban respondents, 59 percent agreed. Certainly in an urban setting it is easier to escape the traditional caste functions and taboos that are still likely to govern life in the villages. It is easier to be anonymous in the city. But that does not necessarily mean you transcend your caste. You are still likely to vote for your caste party, marry within your caste, and live in residential areas where your caste is congregated. It is true that you are much less likely to be born into a particular job or caste function, as would still be the case for most villagers. But in other respects—not least in the world of politics—caste in India shows few signs of withering away.

# 4. THE IMAGINARY HORSE

## The Continuing Threat of Hindu Nationalism

*Oh Rama be wise. There exists no other world but this. That is
certain.*

Advice given to Lord Ram by Javali, a skeptical priest,
in the Hindu epic the Ramayana[1]

I had never heard of "biofuturology" before. But for
two hours this strange science held me spellbound. I
was in the central Indian city of Nagpur at the spacious residence of a prosperous industrialist whose
company makes packaging materials. But it was his
friend and mentor, Dr. Ramachandra Tupkary, who
was doing most of the talking. A retired engineer, Tupkary was one of the leading intellectual thinkers of India's large "family" of Hindu nationalist groups. The
parent of the family is the Rashtriya Swayamsevak
Sangh (RSS)—the Organization of National Volunteers—which has between two and six million members depending on whom you ask (it does not publish
membership rolls). But even the lower number would
make the RSS the second largest political movement in

the world after the Chinese Communist Party. One of its offspring is the Hindu nationalist Bharatiya Janata Party (BJP), which led India's coalition government between 1998 and 2004.

A soft-spoken man, Tupkary had been both the editor of the RSS intellectual journal and the leader of its annual "officers training camp," a semimilitarized gathering of senior volunteers held in Nagpur every summer. Tupkary's views, I thought, might give me a better insight into the Hindu nationalist way of thinking.

It was one of the hottest days of the year in India's hottest city, and it took a while for my mind to regain its bearings after I had come in from what felt like a Turkish sauna on the streets outside. Tupkary started by defining biofuturology for me. It is a science, he said, that gives you an intellectual master key to understanding the development of the human race. He said the human brain is divided into two halves: the right side is equipped to deal with diversity and the left side with uniformity. The typical Indian has a "right-side brain" and the typical European has a "left-side brain," although he conceded there were plenty of exceptions to this rule. Cultures that have a strong right-side brain are good at dealing with complex thoughts and tend toward a democratic and decentralized society. Their minds are original but disorganized. People who have a strong left-side brain are more disciplined but tend toward autocratic and centralized societies. They are better at organizing but lack imagination. Hindus are right-side, Muslims are left-side. Polytheistic Indians are right-side, monotheistic Europeans are left-side. The software of human development comes from India. The hardware comes from the West. "Are you following?" asked Tupkary. I was indeed.

After independence, Tupkary continued, India had gone badly astray because it was run by people with overdeveloped left-side brains, who had been educated in Western ways. They had believed in simplistic notions such as a secular constitution and the industrial society. They had taken India farther away from itself. But now India was slowly moving back to its natural mental state, in which diversity, complexity, and—another new term—"demassification"[2] were again the ascendant forces. Demassification describes India's tradition of small cottage industries, which harnessed the creativity of "right-side" Indian people, as opposed to the regimentation of large factories, which corraled its victims into a mind-numbing "left-side" way of life. The global pendulum was now swinging back India's way.

"Many people in the West and even in India fail to realize this," said Tupkary. "India was a developed society long, long, long before it was colonized by Muslims and by Europeans. We had a developed economy thousands of years ago. We had demassified oil production; we had sophisticated medicine and science. We had a very high standard of living. Civilization was born in India at least ten thousand years ago and from India it spread to the rest of the world. Hindustan is a microcosm of the universe. It contains every contradiction and tendency. Now history has turned full circle. Once again India is in a position to help the world." I must have seemed out of sorts because Tupkary was looking at me indulgently. My head was beginning to throb on both its left and right side. "It is quite complicated to understand all in one go," he said to me gently. "Would you like another *nimbu panni* [lime juice with water]?"

India's cultural pedigree is indeed ancient. One of the world's earliest civilizations existed in the Indus Valley in what is now Pakistan between approximately 3100 and 1700 BC. It coincided with the other early city-state cultures of Mesopotamia, in what is today's Iraq, and the Yangtse Valley in China. Unlike in the other two ancient cultures, scholars have been unable to decipher the fragments of script engraved on the various Indus Valley pots and seals that have been uncovered at the main archeological sites of the Harappan civilization (the first site was discovered in Harappa near modern-day Lahore). The largest site, at Mohenjo-Daro, was discovered in the 1920s. The Harappan script remains elusive. But scholars have revealed some tantalizing characteristics about the civilization:

the Harappans maintained probably the most advanced system of sanitation and drainage known to the ancient world; they had a strikingly uniform culture across dozens of cities separated by hundreds of miles and many centuries; they were obsessive town planners, replicating their standard grid network of streets in each city; they maintained some kind of loose confederated republic with no apparent system of monarchy or dynasty; they buried their dead (*Mohenjo-Daro* means "mound of the dead"); and they were unfamiliar with the horse. The last two observations are particularly important.[3]

At some stage in the early part of the second millennium BC, the Harappans disappear from sight. Initially historians thought the Harappan cities had been ravaged by horse-riding Aryan invaders who swept down into the subcontinent from central Asia sometime between 2000 and 1500 BC. Some still argue that this is what happened—and there is evidence, in the form of mass sites containing smashed human bones, to show that the Harappans could have met a violent end. Other scholars say the Harappan civilization was already fizzling out at the time the Aryan-speaking peoples began to migrate peacefully into India early in the second millennium. Both accounts draw upon archeological evidence (coins, pots, bones, brickwork, and terra-cotta seals) and clues contained in later literature. Their dispute is about the details of the arrival of the Aryan-speaking peoples in India, not in the fact of their arrival, nor in the timing. There is substantial overlap between the two accounts. But the question of whether the Harappans were already fading out or whether they were pushed into oblivion by the incoming Aryans is unresolved. Perhaps it will never be answered conclusively. But academics are at least agreed on the rules of evidence for debating the question.

In 1998 the whole discipline was turned on its head when the Hindu nationalist BJP came to power. With little evidence but with very clear reasons, the intellectuals of the Hindu nationalist movement argued that the Aryan peoples had in fact come *from* India and

Slum residents fetch water in today's Mumbai *(Getty Images)*

Call center workers, Bangalore *(Getty Images)*

Nandan Nilekani, chief executive of Infosys, one of India's most successful
IT companies *(Getty Images)*

Social activist Aruna Roy and some of the Rajasthani villagers with whom she campaigns *(Sohail Akbar)*

A typical traffic scene in rural India *(Sohail Akbar)*

A passenger jet comes in to land over the slums of Mumbai *(Getty Images)*

Slum shacks among Mumbai's tower blocks *(Getty Images)*

Lalu Prasad Yadav, one of India's most celebrated and witty lower-caste leaders
*(Sohail Akbar)*

At prayer before Bhimrao Ambedkar, who gave hope to those marginalized
in Indian society *(Sohail Akbar)*

Villagers waiting to sign up for paid election work *(Sohail Akbar)*

Sri Sri Ravi Shankar, one of India's most successful gurus

*(Empics)*

Members of the Hindu nationalist Bajrang Dal train with bamboo staves *(Sohail Akbar)*

A Muslim man surrounded by Hindu rioters begs for his life during the Gujarat riots, March 2002

*(Reuters/Corbis)*

A Hindu activist armed with an iron bar, Gujarat, February 2002 *(Getty Images)*

migrated to the rest of the world. The Harappans must therefore have been Aryan. Furthermore, the Hindu nationalists argued that the Harappan era and the following Vedic era had been dated far too recently and ought to be pushed back a few thousand years. The objective was straightforward: to establish that India was the sole cradle of civilization, long predating the Greeks, Chinese, Babylonians, and others. India had exported civilization to the rest of the world through migration. If true, the theory would shoot to pieces not only all accepted scholarship on ancient India but also much of the foundations of classical archeology for the rest of the world. The theory was bold. But it lacked something important: the support of accredited and respected scholars.

Murli Manohar Joshi, who was the BJP's minister for education between 1998 and 2004, spent a lot of his budget on projects that he hoped would lend the theory more respectability. Joshi, who had been a professor of physics at Allahabad University before he went into politics and was a lifelong supporter of the RSS, packed the boards of New Delhi's various historical and social science bodies with people who agreed with him. Established scholars who refused to trim their sails to the new winds did not have their appointments renewed. Some, such as Romila Thapar, probably India's best-known classical historian, were subjected to a very personal hate campaign by the RSS, both in India and in the United States, when she spent a year as a visiting scholar. Expatriate Indians belonging to American chapters of the RSS tried to prevent her from speaking in public at all. "Almost all other research projects were sidelined," said Thapar. "Everything was crowded out by the drive to prove something that had no basis in empirical support."[4]

Although the Hindu nationalist account of India's history has so far failed to achieve any academic breakthroughs, the viewpoint has seeped into mainstream public opinion. India's school textbooks were rewritten to present the Aryan-Harappan theory as fact and were then distributed in thousands of schools across the country. The textbooks said new evidence had proved that the Harappans did after all possess horses, which meant the Indus Valley civilization was indeed Aryan. In support of the contention, the textbooks mentioned the recent discovery by two academics[5] of the unmistakable depiction of a horse on one of the Harappan terra-cotta wax seals. It did not seem to matter that in the year 2000 the discovery had been exposed as a simple case of fraud. Michael Witzel, professor of Sanskrit at Harvard University, showed how the two academics had manipulated computer-generated images of the seal to conjure up a horse. The textbooks were neither withdrawn nor amended.

The BJP's textbooks also put a new slant on more recent periods of Indian history. For example, they showed Islam as having come to India at the point of the sword during India's medieval period without reference to its peaceful spread through trading links in south India much earlier. Before the arrival of Muslims, Hindu society had been been contented and peaceful. There was no mention of what happened to Buddhism in India. Indian Christians, meanwhile, spent their time torturing people in the Inquisition. The word *caste* did not appear once in the textbook on history. In the section on modern Indian history, the assassination of Gandhi in 1948 by Nathuram Godse, a right-wing Hindu nationalist, was simply omitted. Taken together, the changes amounted to an overhaul of what was conveyed to children about their society and its history. The message was that India was Hindu and Hindu was India. There was no room for other identities. The experience of the lower castes was simply airbrushed out of the picture. Imaginary horses could fill only some of the blank spaces.

The BJP government also painted much of India's higher education in saffron (saffron is Hinduism's holy color and it is also the backdrop tone on the BJP's electoral logo). Joshi introduced courses in Vedic mathematics and Vedic science at Indian universities. Composed sometime between 1500 and 1000 BC, the Vedas were handed down orally from generation to generation until at some stage in the first millennium BC they were put down in writing. The Vedas are religious incantations. Some of the hymns are hauntingly poetic, others are intricately sophisticated and subtle in their theology. India produced some of the world's greatest astronomers between AD 100 and 900 and is credited with introducing the binary system, which is the basis of modern mathematics. But the discovery of the zero came many centuries after the Vedic era, which produced little of scientific value. "Despite the richness of the Vedas in many other respects, there is no sophisticated mathematics in them, nor anything that can be called rigorous science," wrote Amartya Sen.[6] Even if the Vedas had made great breakthroughs in knowledge, the rules of scientific evidence are universal. It makes no more sense to talk of science as Vedic than it would to label Newtonian physics as Christian.

The Hindu nationalist government invested a lot of capital in seeking both to shift the Vedas back to a much earlier stage of prehistory and to locate the earliest prototype of human learning within these incantations. So far the project has found no supporting evidence in scholarship. Many decades ago, A. L. Basham, the classical historian, said the Vedas offered romantic nationalists the perfect opportunity to indulge their fantasies. This was because so little could really be known about the Vedic era. "Around these phantoms later tradition draped glittering mantles of legend," he wrote. "But when the mantles are removed only vague shadows remain."[7]

•  •  •

The political scientist Benedict Anderson described nation-states as imagined communities: *"Imagined,"* he wrote, "because members of even the smallest nation will never know most of their fellow members, meet them, or even hear of them, yet in the mind of each lives the image of their communion."[8] Most people think of their nation as a natural entity awakened by history, oppression, or revolution. But this view overlooks the way in which nations seek to establish their identity by defining themselves against other nation-states. One of the principal tools of nation building is the selective rummaging through history for events that can provide rallying stories or myths. Every country, including the oldest nation-states, such as Britain and France, tailors its national holidays, educational systems, and public monuments to these ends (largely at the expense of other countries in the case of Britain and France). But India is unusual in that it retains two competing and very opposed ideas of the nation: the first, largely created by the Congress Party during the freedom struggle, stressed a plural, secular, and composite India (in contrast to Pakistan); the second, represented by the Hindu nationalist movement, pushes for a more exclusive and Hindu definition of India (in an unintentional echo of Pakistan). It is only in the last twenty years that the second view has provided a serious challenge to the first.

The 1990s were a turbulent and disorienting time in Indian politics and government. The sharp and rapid decline of the once-dominant Congress Party created space for a new kind of politics. But what emerged was far more fluid and less predictable than what it replaced. Between 1947 and 1989 India had six prime ministers. Between 1989 and 2004 it had seven. Some of the gap vacated by a declining Congress Party was filled by the emergence of a small platoon of lower-caste and regional parties as we saw in the last chapter. These groups have little idea of India beyond their own particular status within it. They do not challenge the Congress Party–dominated freedom movement's definition of Indian nationhood even though they present a strong electoral challenge to the Congress Party. The remaining gap was filled by Hindu nationalism, which is a much more coherent force. The main aim of the Sangh Parivar (the "family of the RSS," of which the BJP is the political arm) was—and is—to reconstruct India's national identity along Hindu lines. Rewriting India's history is a key plank in that project.

The RSS was founded in Nagpur in 1925 by K. B. Hedgewar, a medical practitioner. Whereas the Congress Party was dominated by lawyers and journalists, the RSS was dominated by people from a scientific background. Both groups were almost exclusively Brahmin in their formative years. Even today, the RSS and the BJP are dominated by the upper castes. Hedgewar was its first Sarsangchalak, or leader. Three out of four of Hedgewar's successors were also from scientific backgrounds: M. S. Golwalkar, perhaps the most influential Hindu nationalist of the twentieth century, was a zoologist; Balasaheb Deoras was a lawyer; Rajendra Singh was a physicist; and K. S. Sudarshan, the current head of the RSS, who took over in 1999, is an engineer. Unsurprisingly, the Hindu nationalist idea of India abounds with scientific imagery. Much like the German and French romantic nationalists of the late nineteenth century who influenced them, the leaders of the RSS see the nation as a living organism that is deeply rooted in the national soil. They reject the fictional "social contract" between individuals that underlies most Western ideas of the nation-state because it implies the individual has a choice in the matter. The way the RSS is organized was inspired by European fascism. The principal unit of the RSS is the *shakha,* which is a group of individuals who gather each morning to perform exercises and recite nationalist stories in tens of thousands of neighborhoods across India. Every day several hundred thousand, and possibly upward of a million, Indian men gather at their local *shakhas* for a dawn routine of martial training and indoctrination. The uniform they put on is a mix between the khaki outfit that was worn by the British colonial police and sartorial details taken from Mussolini's fascist Blackshirts, who were already an icon to Hindu nationalists when the RSS was founded in 1925. The *shakhas* are equivalent to the semimilitarized cells that formed the building block both of Mussolini's fascist movement and the Nazi Hitler Youth Movement in Germany.

Golwalkar, whose books *We or Our Nationhood Defined* and *Bunch of Thoughts* are the bibles of today's RSS volunteers, wrote: "The ultimate vision of our work . . . is a perfectly organised state of society wherein each individual has been moulded into a model of ideal Hindu manhood and made into a living limb of the corporate personality of society." He likened the *shakha* to a cell in the human body: "Each cell feels its identity with the entire body and is ever ready to sacrifice itself for the sake of the health and the growth of the body." The main aim would be to create a Hinduism that was masculine so that it could prevail against the muscular cultures of Islam and the West. This view sprang from the diagnosis that India and Hinduism had become too "effeminate" over the centuries. The frailty of the effeminate Hindu body had enabled outside powers to dominate the country with ease. The aim, therefore, was to copy the unity and organization of the monotheistic or "Semitic" cultures, the better to repel them. Christophe Jaffrelot, probably the best scholar of Hindu nationalism, describes the RSS strategy as "emulate then stigmatise."[9] In other words, copy the strengths of your enemies while also demonizing them. It explains why Gandhi, who in so many respects was an inspiring exemplar of Hinduism, was so hated by the Hindu militants. Gandhi stood for nonviolence, which they saw as effeminate. And Gandhi preached love of other religions, which made him a traitor.* Nathuram Godse, the man who shot Gandhi, came from an RSS family.

The main aim of the RSS is to create a Hindu society in its own image. Each cell in the body of Indian society would have to conform to the whole. In their imagined community, an Indian would be defined as someone who saw India not just as his fatherland, but also as his holy land. This would obviously exclude Indians who looked to Mecca or to Rome for their spiritual sustenance. "The foreign races in Hindustan must either adopt the Hindu culture and language, must learn to respect and hold in reverence Hindu religion, must entertain no ideals but those of glorification of the Hindu race and culture . . . or may stay in the country, wholly subordinated to

---

*Even Gandhi shared some of the stereotypes of the Hindu nationalists. Both took their cue from the British who liked to classify castes and religions. "The Hindu is by nature a coward," wrote Gandhi in 1924, "whereas the Muslim is a bully."

the Hindu nation, claiming nothing, deserving no privileges, far less any preferential treatment—not even citizen's rights," wrote Golwalkar.[10]

According to this view, Muslims and Christians were not just "foreign"; they also belonged to different "races." It is worth stressing here what might be obvious to most readers: India has an extraordinary hodgepodge of different races, languages, and cultures. Even the Aryans are nowadays described by scholars as a language group, rather than a race. But even if the Aryans were a race, they too came from elsewhere. Very few of India's Christians and Muslims are descended from Christian and Muslim immigrants to India. The overwhelming majority are descendants of lower-caste Hindus who converted in the (mostly forlorn) hope of escaping their low status. Christianity has been present in India since the first century AD, when large-scale conversions took place in the southern state of Kerala. Islam has been present in India since the eighth and ninth centuries AD, when it spread through south India ports that had trading ties with Arabia. Christianity's Indian pedigree significantly predates its arrival in most of Europe. And Islam's history in India begins several hundred years before Protestantism was born. However, the RSS still keeps a crack in the door open for India's religious minorities. Lal Krishna Advani, who was India's deputy prime minister during the BJP government and an RSS *swayamsevak* (part-time volunteer), said he approved of "Hindu Muslims" and "Hindu Christians," meaning those who accept, like most Hindus, that there are many paths to god. The RSS also runs a program called Ghar Vapasi—or "welcome back to Hinduism"—for Indian Muslims and Christians* who wish to reconvert to Hinduism.

---

*According to India's decennial census, Christians formed 2.8 percent of India's population in 1951 and just 2.3 percent by 2001. Yet the Hindu nationalists maintain that India is rife with Christian proselytization.

• • •

Interracting with members of the RSS is never quite what I expect it to be. Often they are very charming. I once caused some puzzlement while dining at the home of a very hospitable RSS sympathizer in Ahmedabad, capital of the state of Gujarat. His other guest was Manmohan Vaidya, the head *pracharak* (full-time volunteer) for Gujarat. The dinner had been arranged to educate me about the movement. Vaidya described to me what it was like to be a RSS *pracharak*. The *pracharak* takes a vow of celibacy that ensures he will remain married only to the movement. He sleeps in dormitories in the network of rest houses and centers the RSS maintains up and down the country. He cannot drink alcohol, smoke cigarettes, or eat meat. His whole existence is bound up with the cause. The life Vaidya described to me sounded tough and self-denying. Apart from vegetarianism, I said, you seem to have quite a lot in common with Islamic fundamentalists. Vaidya looked startled. Then he laughed: "We are very dedicated. I suppose you could say we have some things in common. But they are very superficial. We are Hindus." Just Hindus, I asked, or Hindu fundamentalists? "We are not fundamentalists, we are nationalists," he said. "There is a big difference."

Some months later I visited Nagpur, the headquarters of the RSS, to observe its annual "Officers Training Camp." The main RSS building, which is located in the heart of the industrial central Indian city, overlooks a large, dusty parade ground, which is where the RSS volunteers conduct their daily drills. It is a kind of giant *shakha* for the RSS national leadership lasting for thirty days. I was accompanied by Ram Madhav, the talkative and engaging national spokesman for the RSS. We observed 2,000 men of all ages marching up and down the parade ground, each wielding a *lathi*—a long bamboo stave also used by the police. They were dressed in the standard kit of the RSS volunteer, consisting of a plain white shirt, khaki shorts held up by a sturdy black belt, yellow socks, and black shoes. They wear the trademark RSS black cap, an inversion of the traditional white Congress Party cap. The RSS salute, which is frequently rendered, is unmistakably fascist: standing to attention, you swivel your right arm across your chest with the palm of your hand facing down. At dawn each day the trainees gather in front of the fluttering saffron flag of the RSS to salute it and then sing "Vande Mataram"—Hail Motherland—which is the Hindu nationalist anthem. The day begins at 4 a.m. and continues until 10 p.m. The routine consists of martial training and "character building," punctuated by discussion groups and traditional games such as Kabbadi,[11] which involves two teams breathlessly trying to catch each other while shouting "Kabbadi Kabbadi." Individual sports are discouraged, even those, such as chess, that originated in India. As a game of foreign origin, cricket is out of bounds.

Having observed the drill, my photographer friend and I were taken to the RSS official headquarters in the heart of Nagpur's old town. This is where the senior leadership lives. The head and deputy head of the RSS share a small suite. Their bedrooms, which both adjoin a small living room, are bare and monastic. Some people argue that the RSS is not technically fascist since fascist ideology is built around the personality cult of the leader. The RSS stresses collective leadership with the Sarsangchalak playing the role of "guide and adviser." Whether absence of a personality cult excludes the RSS from being fascist strikes me as a pedantic question. But certainly the RSS could be described as ascetic. I was fascinated by the Sarsangchalak's simple bed chamber. It seemed like the living quarters of a monastery abbot, or perhaps a very self-denying pope. "This is the bed the Sarsangchalak will probably die in," said my guide, a *pracharak*. Then we were taken to the family home of Hedgewar, the first Sarsangchalak of the RSS. It was a beautifully restored Chitpavan (Hedgewar's subcaste) Brahmin home, very typical of how the well-to-do Hindu classes used to live. Hedgewar's family had moved in the nineteenth century to Nagpur from Hyderabad, which was ruled by a

Muslim Nizam* who was intolerant of dissent. This family history must have had something to do with Hedgewar's Islamaphobia.

"Isn't it a beautiful house?" said our guide. I have always wondered why Hindu nationalists are so keen to win the approval of people who would be very unlikely to sympathize with their outlook. It is hard to reconcile the RSS's aggressive view of the world with the gentle courtesy of many of its members. They convey disdain for foreign ideas and culture and yet a desire to win the recognition and goodwill of foreigners. Theirs is a complex psychology—far more complex, perhaps, than their ideology. I was accompanied on the visit to Nagpur by Sohail Akbar, my Delhi-based photographer friend who also happens to be Muslim. Sohail was a little nervous about how the RSS would respond if they discovered his religious background. Luckily nobody did, or else if they did, they never let on.

It was particularly important to conceal Sohail's full name during our next visit. The most militant offshoot of the RSS is the Vishwa Hindu Parishad (VHP)—the World Council of Hinduism. The RSS is in charge of the overall reform of society. The BJP is its political arm. And the VHP is the arm that deals with reform of Hinduism as a religion. The VHP's youth wing, the Bajrang Dal, supplies the shock troops whenever there is a communal riot. Named after Hanuman, the monkey god who burned the island of Lanka with his tail in the classic Hindu epic the Ramayana, the Bajrang Dal consists of young men between the ages of fifteen and thirty. We visited a Bajrang Dal training session in Nagpur. Unlike in the RSS drills, the young men of the Bajrang Dal—some of whom had barely reached puberty— were training with swords and air guns, in addition to the *lathi*.

"This," said the trainer, wielding a *lathi* in slow motion, "is how you kill a man with a blow to the back of his head. It is very

---

*About a third of British India was ruled by separate princely states. Most of the five hundred or so principalities were too small to matter. But a number, such as Hyderabad and Kashmir, were significant enough to appear as though they were independent states in their own right. They were not.

simple." I asked some of the young men, most of whom wore fierce military mustaches, why they had signed up for this kind of training. One, a tribal teenager from an area of India where Christian missionaries are active, said: "The Christians are trying to proselytize our people. We need to defend ourselves." Another said: "In our town the Muslims kill cows and make a huge noise when we are trying to pray. We kill or get killed." All were very eager to display their skills to us. The Bajrang Dal claims to have trained between 300,000 and 400,000 people. The head trainer was equally friendly. "This is commando training for the defense of Hinduism," he said. "We have nothing to hide." The training session was taking place in full view of the passing traffic on the grounds of a college sports field in the center of Nagpur. "If they had known it was a Muslim taking their photographs God knows what they would have done," said a relieved Sohail after we had left. Sohail's apprehensions were perfectly reasonable. The Bajrang Dal played the leading role in two of India's three worst riots of the last quarter of a century, in 1992 and in 2002. The other major riot was directed by Congress Party supporters against the minority Sikh community following the assassination of Indira Gandhi by her Sikh bodyguards in October 1984.

The riots of 1992 were a direct outgrowth of the Hindu nationalist project to rewrite India's history. The 3,000 people who were butchered—mostly Muslims—were proof, if any were needed, of how lethal history can be when the identity of a multiethnic nation-state is under question. The violence was triggered when a large mob of Hindu militants demolished a mosque in the Hindu holy town of Ayodhya on December 6, 1992. Spearheaded by L. K. Advani, who became leader of the BJP in 2004 after it was defeated at the polls, the Hindu nationalists had in 1987 launched a national campaign to demolish the mosque. They claimed the Babri Masjid, or the Mosque of Babur, which was named after the first emperor of the Mughal dynasty, stood on the site of a temple that Babur had razed in 1528. They also claimed that the site was the birthplace of the lord Ram, after whom the Ramayana epic was named. There is no evidence of the existence of Ram, whom most educated Hindus take to be a mythical or legendary figure (Tagore thought the Ramayana was "a marvelous parable"[12]). Meanwhile, the holy texts date Ram's birth several hundred thousand years ago. Nor is there any clear proof that a temple had once stood on the site. The theory of Ram's birthplace and the missing temple only gathered momentum after India gained independence. A skeptic might see in the Ayodhya campaign a good example of what Benedict Anderson meant by the power of imagination. In 1984, before the Ram temple campaign had been launched, the BJP had just 2 seats in India's 545-strong parliament. By 1989, two years after the Ayodhya campaign was launched, the BJP's strength had risen to 84 seats. The peak of the BJP's popularity was in 1999, when it won 183 seats (the party's strength fell back to 138 seats in the 2004 election).

The 2002 riots in the state of Gujarat were directly related to the killings that had followed the demolition of the Ayodhya mosque a decade earlier. The Gujarat riots were triggered by the incineration of 58 Hindu train passengers in the town of Godhra on February 27, 2002. Godhra, which has a large Muslim population, is an important stop on the train journey that takes passengers from Gujarat to Uttar Pradesh, where the town of Ayodhya is situated. In the previous weeks the train had been full of VHP militants who were traveling to Ayodhya as part of a campaign to pressure the government to build a Ram temple on the ruins of the demolished mosque. The campaign has yet to achieve its aim (and, for once, India's judiciary should be forgiven for taking so long to hear an insoluble case to determine which religion should have legal entitlement to the site). Members of the Muslim community, many of whom work as hawkers and "coolies" at the Godhra railway station, claim the Hindu militants had been taunting them for weeks. Government inquiries into the incident failed to reach a firm conclusion about how the fire was started in the compartment where 58 people lost their lives. But all eyewitnesses agreed that a large and angry mob of local Muslims was present when the burning occurred.

The BJP state government of Gujarat, which was headed by Narendra Modi, an RSS *pracharak* who had become chief minister a few weeks earlier, declared a day of mourning on February 28 so that the funerals of the passengers could be held in the streets of Ahmedabad, Gujarat's largest city. It was a clear invitation to violence. The Muslim quarters of Ahmedabad and other cities in Gujarat turned into death traps as thousands of Hindu militants converged on them. As the rioting unfolded, Modi quoted Newton's third law: "Every action has an equal and opposite reaction," he said. Modi's words served as a green light for the killers. The reaction was substantially more than equal. In the wave of bloodletting that was unleashed, hundreds of separate incidents were chronicled by eyewitnesses and some of the killings were recorded by television cameras. The most disturbing feature of the riots was the treatment meted out to Muslim women and their children. Mobs gathered round and raped the women. Then they poured kerosene down their throats and the throats of their children and threw lighted matches onto them. Hundreds stood by and cheered these gruesome incinerations, which symbolized revenge for the burning of the train passengers in Godhra. The male family members were forced to watch their wives and children burn to death before they too were killed. The killings appear to have been planned. The rioters possessed electoral registers and were able to single out the homes of Muslims living in mixed communities, leaving the homes around them untouched. They were also able to pinpoint Muslim-owned businesses that had taken the precaution of having a Hindu business partner and adopting Hindu names on the shop front. Hundreds of Muslim shops were destroyed. There was a pattern and efficiency to the killings that implied some degree of premeditation.*

The second most disturbing feature of the riots was the role played by the Gujarat police, who stood by and watched the slaughter take

---

*History has a way of producing strange coincidences. February 27—the date of the Godhra burnings—was also the date of the notorious fire in the German Reichstag in 1933 that gave Hitler the opportunity to seize power.

place. In some instances they allegedly assisted the rioters by giving them directions to the addresses of local Muslims. In others they allegedly turned fleeing Muslims back into the arms of the mob. Numerous inquiries[13] into the riots that have been conducted by Indian and international human rights groups have produced evidence that the Gujarat police were under instructions not to interfere. "The mob caught my husband and hit him twice on his head with the sword,"[14] Jannat Sheikh, a Muslim housewife, testified to an independent legal inquiry. "They then threw petrol in his eyes and burned him. My sister-in-law was stripped and raped. She had a three-month-old baby in her lap. They threw petrol on her and the child was thrown in the fire. My mother-in-law was unable to climb the stairs so she was on the ground floor with her four-year-old grandson. She told them to take away all the money and jewelry but to spare the children. They took the money and jewelry then they burned the children. Unmarried girls from my street were stripped, raped, and burned. The police were on the spot but they were helping the mob." This was one of hundreds of corroborated eyewitness accounts taken by human rights groups. In almost every case, the police refused to record witness statements.

One BJP minister, Haren Pandya, a rival of Modi, had agreed to testify to a commission of inquiry in 2003 about the instructions that had been given to the police. Pandya was assassinated by an alleged Muslim terrorist shortly before he was due to testify. No trial has taken place for Pandya's murder. At the time of writing in 2006, only a handful of people have been convicted for murders during the Gujarat riots. More than 200 Muslims remain incarcerated without trial under India's antiterrorist laws for the killing of the train passengers in Godhra. Not one Hindu has been detained under these laws. The defeat of the national BJP-led government in 2004 did little to change the situation. Under India's federal constitution, law and order is principally a state subject. Narendra Modi's state government was reelected by a sweeping two-thirds majority in December 2002, nine months after the riots took place. Modi's campaign theme was the

"Pride of Gujarat." On the campaign trail, he equated Gujarat's Muslims to a "fifth column," an enemy within, whose loyalties were to Pakistan.

Another unsettling feature of the Gujarat riots was the response of the national government in New Delhi. Atal Behari Vajpayee, the prime minister at the time, did not visit the scene of the violence for a full month after it happened. According to people I spoke to in the prime minister's office, Vajpayee, who was generally seen as the moderate face of the BJP, attempted to sack Modi after the riots but was overruled by his colleagues. Having failed to do the right thing, Vajpayee chose to swim with the tide: "Let us not forget how the whole thing started: Who lit the fire? How did it spread?"[15] asked Vajpayee at a party conference in the beautiful beach resort state of Goa a few weeks later. "Wherever in the world Muslims live, they tend not to live peacefully with others. They want to spread their faith by resorting to terror and threats." Others openly celebrated the restoration of "Hindu pride" they believed the riots had brought about. The RSS hinted that any future incidents would result in equally bloody outcomes. M. G. Vaidya, who was the RSS spokesman at the time, issued the simple statement: "Let the Muslims understand that their real safety lies in the goodwill of the majority." Such statements were usually accompanied by the rider that Hindus, unlike Muslims, were a tolerant people. Most Indians I know, whether Hindu or Muslim, and in many cases friends of mine who reject any religious label, are strikingly tolerant. It is part of their national heritage. It would require a leap of imagination to place the RSS within that same heritage.

There was a final, equally upsetting, aspect to the Gujarat riots. That was its aftermath. More than 200,000 people were made homeless and ended up in refugee camps. The government provided little or nothing in the way of compensation for the loss of relatives, homes, or businesses. The state provided only a trickle of relief provisions to the camps. Most of the makeshift schools and shelters for the refugees were provided by the Islamiya Relief Committee, a charity run by an orthodox and relatively hard-line branch of Sunni Islam. Many of the Muslims who were targeted in the killings were either Bohra or Ismaili, which are esoteric sects from the minority Shia Muslim strand of Islam. Neither sect would remotely identify with Pakistan, which is a majority Sunni Muslim country in which the Shia minority are often treated as second-class citizens. Yet the Gujarat Muslims had been deserted by their police, the state's system of justice, and by the state's welfare officers. It was principally Islamic organizations that provided the help.* Many young and angry Muslim men, both Shia and Sunni, found in these organizations a new lodestar that had helped them when they needed it most. "It is bitterly ironic that young Muslim men who had no radical instincts before the riots, came out of the riots very radicalized," said Hanif Lakdawala, a Muslim based in Ahmedabad, who runs a charity for women who live in the slums. "If the state had done something for the Muslims—if it had shown any concern at all for their welfare or for the principles of justice—then they would have had something else to turn to." Imagined communities tend to beget other imagined communities. Then they draw strength from each other.

•   •   •

What can be said about imagined national histories can apply just as much to religious traditions. Just as Christians in medieval Europe imagined Jesus as a blond and embraced the concept of deicide (murder of God) when it suited commercial interests to persecute Jews, and just as liberal Muslims today scour the hadiths for evidence of equal opportunity rights for women, so Hindu revisionists reinvent the past for contemporary purposes. One such tool is the sacred cow. Mere mention of

*It is important to mention that thousands of young Indians, most of them Hindu, also went to Gujarat to volunteer their help for the victims in the aftermath of the riots. The many journalists, who took great risks to record what happened in the riots, were mostly Hindu.

this theme is enough to provoke great anger among Hindu nationalists, so I will be careful. I was once on a television panel in India sitting next to the BJP cabinet minister for information and broadcasting. It was election time in various states, as it almost invariably is in India. Inevitably the BJP had raised the campaign issue of banning cow slaughter. I said that most Indians I had spoken to worried much more about prices, jobs, and water supply. Issues such as cow slaughter or banning forcible religious conversions were red herrings dreamed up by electoral strategists to divert people's attention from the real problems. The minister's expression was incandescent. Wagging his finger at me, he said: "Do not disrespect the cow. It is a sacred animal. Are you disrespecting the cow?" Of course not, I said, fumbling for an adequate response. The minister succeeded in diverting the issue.

D. N. Jha, a historian at Delhi University, got it much worse. In 2001 Jha, a diminutive man in his early seventies, wrote a book, *The Myth of the Holy Cow,* which provided evidence that beef used to be eaten by large sections of Hindu society—including Brahmins—in the ancient past. I have no means to judge the authenticity of Jha's arguments. And it is true there is a strong tradition of Marxism in Indian scholarship, which often produces work of doubtful credibility. Many on India's Left have sought to portray India's Hindu-Muslim problems as an invention of the British, who maintained their rule by dividing Indians into artificial categories. Some have even claimed caste was invented during the colonial era.* Clearly, there is questionable scholarship on both the Left and the Right. But India has free speech and Jha was denied it. His book was immediately banned by the BJP government and has not resurfaced (I picked up my copy in London). For a while Jha was confined to his campus residence at Delhi University because youths from the Bajrang Dal and right-wing student activists were

---

*It is one thing to manipulate existing religious and caste divisions, which the British undoubtedly did. It is quite another to conjure them out of thin air. One unintentional effect of such scholarship is to rob Indians then—and now—of any role in making their own history. It also elevates the British into geniuses, an epithet with which few who study the imperial story in India would readily agree.

threatening to kill him. "Nobody stood up for me, not even the publishers," Jha said. "When you use the word 'cow' people lose all reason."

Cow protection movements emerged in the late nineteenth century in north India where there were large concentrations of Muslims. The Arya Samaj, a militant Hindu reformist sect, which could be compared in some ways to Calvinism, chose the supposedly endangered holy cow as an emotional tool to create a feeling of Hindu-ness among the masses. The sect's aim was to bring lower-caste Hindus into the fold, in an almost precise foreshadowing of the strategies of Hindu nationalism today. To further my research, I decided to visit the cow product research center near Nagpur. Run by the VHP, the center seeks to build on the five traditional village products of the cow: milk, ghee (clarified butter), butter, urine (for religious purposes), and dung for fuel. We were accompanied by Sunil Mansinghka, a senior VHP activist. The center, which draws on the research skills of dozens of young men with PhDs in medicine and biology, also runs a hostel and a school for the local tribal population that is named after Swami Vivekananda, a widely respected Hindu philosopher and social reformer. "Please remove your *chappals* [sandals]," said Mansinghka as we approached a vast cow shed. What, barefoot? I asked, with an eye on the puddles of cow urine and cow dung that covered the ground. "Yes, barefoot," he replied. "Cow dung is an antiseptic. If you have athlete's foot, you will be cured."

Outside the cow shelter there was a signboard that said: DO NOT TEASE THE COW, GIVE IT LOVE. SPITTING IS PROHIBITED INSIDE. GIVE ANY DONATIONS OR OFFERINGS TO THE WORKER NOT TO THE COW. I stepped gingerly into the shelter, trying not to slip. Mansinghka said: "These cows are the pure cow breeds of Hindustan. We have spent a long time separating the foreign cow breeds from the indigenous breeds, which are much superior in every way." He wheeled me face-to-face with a very fierce looking bull, whose vast dangling testicles were the size of cricket balls. I recoiled. "Do not worry," said Mansinghka, wheeling me back to face the bull, "it is a pure Indian breed. It cannot hurt you. Not like the bulls in the West." I was pushed eyeball to eyeball with the bull for a split second. Then I was somehow maneuvered through the two-inch layer of cow product to the middle of the herd. I was handed a silver tray with candles on it and also turmeric, rice, flowers, and red paste. I was instructed to circle the tray a few times above the head of one of the cows before smearing the paste on the cow's forehead and my own. "Now you are praying to the cow. She is my mother. She is your mother," said Mansinghka. Mother seemed unfazed by all the attention.

Then I was taken to the laboratories. The first room hit me about sixty feet before we arrived. It contained hundreds of bottles of cow's urine, stacked up, one upon the other. There were Bunsen burners and some of the urine was bubbling away in beakers. "This is an antioxidant that will cure cancer," said one of the lab researchers, waving a capsule under my nose. Then there were urine derivative products for curing bronchitis and obesity, one that produced energy, and another that purified blood. Next we were shown cow dung products. Cow dung, too, conceals an impressive range of world-beating cures. My favorite product was cow dung soap. There was also a cow dung shampoo for dandruff. Mansinghka said the center had submitted a number of cow derivative applications to the U.S. Patent and Trademark Office and other countries. "God lives in the cow dung," said Mansinghka. "All of these recipes are contained in the holy texts."

Mansinghka, a Rajasthani in his late thirties, told me that there was no medicine outside the Vedas that was worth using. It occurred to me that he was utterly sincere. Taken together, his beliefs amounted to textbook fundamentalism—a modern condition in which you take the beliefs that people in the past had on some level accepted as symbolic and hold them to be literally true, even scientifically demonstrable: God made the world in seven days, Eve came from Adam's rib, Ram was born on this precise spot, and so on. But the cow research center did have some impressive uses for cow's product, which Mansinghka also showed me. Outside we walked from tree to tree, each of which had been fertilized with specially enriched cow biomass, smelling the leaves. Each leaf gave off the striking odor of the fruit of the tree—mangoes, lemons, oranges, and other fruit. This seemed very pleasant. And for all the science I know perhaps cow's urine really can cure cancer.

At the end of the tour Mansinghka, who had been looking throughout for some sign that I had been converted to the merits of the holy cow's product, said: "When you write, please be kind to the cow. She is our mother." I was happy to promise not to disrespect cows. We had returned to Nagpur and were dropping Mansinghka off at the VHP offices. On the street just outside the entrance to the building, there was a cow with its head stuck in a large pile of rubbish, chewing through plastic and other waste. It was an everyday scene, even in Nagpur, the capital of the cow protection movement. Nobody seemed to mind the cow's abysmal diet.

On October 15, 2002, five Dalit men were lynched by a large mob of upper-caste Hindus in the town of Jhajjar quite near to New Delhi. The men had been found carrying the carcass of a dead cow, which they had purchased from someone in a nearby village. Although, as Chamars, leather work was part of their hereditary profession, someone alleged they had killed the cow before going to work on its skin. So they were strung up and left twisting in front of a large crowd. After the murders, the traumatized local Dalit community insisted the cow had already been dead when the men took possession of it. The overwhelming majority of Indians were horrified at the medieval cruelty of this rare incident. Giriraj Kishore, the VHP's national leader, had only this to say: "According to our *shastras* [holy texts] the life of a cow is very important."[16] By implication, it was more important than the lives of five lower-caste Hindus.

•   •   •

The hot and cold relationship between Hindu nationalism and India's lower castes is key to understanding the fortunes of the BJP. It explains why the BJP is unlikely to win an overall majority in India's national parliament until it finds an effective way of winning sustained support from lower-caste voters. Membership of the RSS and the BJP has always been overwhelmingly upper caste. In the 1990s some attempts were made to co-opt prominent lower-caste—and even Muslim—political figures into the BJP so the party could broaden its electoral base. The efforts met with limited success. As we saw in the last chapter, the narrower a party's social base in India, the more effective it is at targeting its vote bank. The BJP did not appear very credible when it suddenly started to promise all things to all people.

What propelled the BJP to national prominence was an upper-caste backlash against the growing trend in the 1980s (and ever since) to reserve government jobs for different categories of lower-caste people. In Ahmedabad, Gujarat, which is the capital of saffron politics in India, upper-caste men rioted in 1981 and 1985 against the Congress Party state government's extension of public sector job quotas to "Other Backward Classes." The move led to the unraveling of the Congress Party's traditional domination of Gujarati politics, in which, since independence, it had consistently relied on the support of the Gujarati upper castes to get reelected. That group's votes went to the BJP and have never returned. What happened in Gujarat was then played out on a national stage in 1990 when V. P. Singh, the prime minister of a short-lived minority coalition government, embraced the report of the Mandal Commission, which recommended the set-aside of 27 percent of all national government jobs for "Other Backward Classes." Singh's decision sparked riots in the streets of New Delhi and several upper-caste students immolated themselves in full view of the TV cameras.

More significantly, the decision led to a collapse of V. P. Singh's unwieldy coalition. His government consisted of all those parties that hated the Congress Party, which effectively meant everyone, including the BJP and the parties of both Lalu Yadav and Mulayam Yadav. Hatred of the Congress Party was the only sentiment that united them. After Singh had embraced the Mandal recommendations, the BJP withdrew its support from the coalition, prompting its disintegration. L. K. Advani, the BJP leader, then launched a national Rath

Yatra, or chariot procession, to Ayodhya that culminated in the demolition of the Babri Masjid two years later. The ostensible target was Islam. But the fuel that kept Advani's chariot on the road was uppercaste anger against lower-caste politics. Advani's strategy for overcoming the problem was to unite both sides of the divide under the banner of Hinduism behind the goal of building a Ram Mandir (Ram Temple) in Ayodhya. To some extent it worked. From 1990 onward, the twin poles of Indian politics were Mandal versus *Mandir*: lower-caste politics or Hindu nationalism. The Congress Party occupies an uneasy middle ground between the two.

I was passing through Mumbai in 1998 shortly after the BJP came to national office. Although the BJP was only one of twenty-four parties in the coalition, it dominated the government. Its grip on the coalition was tightened after it won fresh elections in 1999. The BJP-led coalition lost power at the polls in 2004. But those five years marked the first—and, to date, the last—time in India's modern history that a non–Congress Party government had governed for a full term. Atal Behari Vajpayee, the septuagenarian leader, was also the first Indian prime minister not to be either from the Congress Party or a former member of the Congress Party.

Many people I met in Mumbai back in 1998 were nervous about what the BJP would do now that it had finally reached office (barring a thirteen-day interlude in 1996, when Vajpayee had barely had a chance to get his feet under the desk). The BJP did not disappoint. Within a few weeks of coming to office in 1998, it tested five nuclear weapons under the Thar Desert of Rajasthan. Many Indians who had opposed nuclear weapons and cherished the moral foreign policy position that Nehru had fashioned after independence suddenly found themselves waving the Indian tricolor. I was at a party in Mumbai, talking to a novelist who described himself as a liberal. "I do not support the BJP, but this is a very special moment in Indian history," said the writer. "For the first time in more than a thousand years we have a Hindu government. And it had the courage to take on America with the nuclear tests."

On communalism, Vajpayee had soothed the worst fears of his coalition partners by agreeing to abandon, while in office, three of the BJP's most cherished goals: the creation of a common civil code, which would have meant the abolition of the separate personal laws that Nehru had conceded to Muslims; building a Ram Temple in Ayodhya on the site of the demolished mosque; and abolishing an article in the Indian constitution that gives a greater degree of autonomy to the state of Jammu and Kashmir*—the divided Himalayan state, all of which is claimed by Pakistan. The BJP honored its promise to put these three policies on ice while it was in office.

In 1998, there was another apprehension held by some of India's middle classes and by many foreign investors in India. Like every other political party in the country, the BJP has a strong emotional attachment to the independence movement's rallying cry of *swadeshi*—or economic self-reliance. Manmohan Singh, the Congress Party finance minister in 1991, had done away with the main elements of Nehru's economic framework. But the BJP and others still rallied to the old cause. *Swadeshi* was, and is, a strong element of RSS philosophy, which frequently describes foreign products as "polluting."

In 1995 the BJP government of New Delhi (the local city government) had closed the city's only branch of Kentucky Fried Chicken, the American fast-food chain, after health inspectors found a fly in the kitchen. Those familiar with standards of hygiene in the typical Delhi restaurant were a little skeptical about the BJP's pretext. The closure was anyway unnecessary since Indian consumers almost unanimously consider plain fried chicken to be the opposite of *finger lickin' good*. But the closure sent a clear political message. Likewise, in 1998 the BJP promised in its election manifesto that it would accept foreign investment but only in areas where new technology was needed: "Microchips not potato chips," said the slogan. So there was

*The state of Jammu and Kashmir consists of two principal parts—Jammu, which is predominantly Hindu, and the valley of Kashmir, which is mostly Muslim. A third part, Ladakh, is mostly Buddhist. From now on it is referred to simply as Kashmir.

some concern in 1998 that the BJP would set the clock back on Man-mohan Singh's economic reforms. This fear too was belied by events. Vajpayee's government took with increasing enthusiasm to liberal economic reforms, although it had better luck attracting investment in potato chips than microchips.

But the greatest hope of the BJP's electoral supporters—probably only a minority of whom could be described as genuine Hindu nation-alists—was that it would uphold its promise of being "The Party with a Difference." This very effective electoral slogan sent the clear message that the BJP would not succumb to the corruption that was enveloping so many areas of Indian public life. The slogan served as an effective way of differentiating the BJP both from the Congress Party, which cre-ated the system of corruption, and from the lower-caste parties, which had perfected it. People might not approve of the BJP's communal ha-treds. But they could still look forward to a period of clean government.

This hope proved optimistic. The BJP satisfied some of the blood-lust of its hard-core supporters, as we saw in Gujarat. And the RSS, which had been voicing mounting disaffection with the government's liberal economic agenda, was partly mollified by the BJP's decision to "saffronize" much of India's educational curricula. But in the day-to-day workings of government, the BJP proved as corrupt and as oppor-tunistic as any other party. The only real difference in "The Party with a Difference" was its open disdain for minorities. And even here, the leadership sent mixed signals. In 2004 Atal Behari Vajpayee could not resist appealing to the Muslim vote when elections loomed. The prime minister became the butt of many sardonic jokes during the campaign when he donned green ceremonial headgear to stage photo opportu-nities with Muslim dignitaries. Evidently the strategy failed. The BJP was thrown out of office. It was an unexpected end for a government that appeared to have gone from strength to strength.

Before I moved to India, a colleague at the *Financial Times* who is very familiar with the country said to me: "Remember, in India things are never as good or as bad as they seem." One of the most striking aspects of the 2004 elections was that *both* of India's national parties suffered a decline in their vote share. The BJP's vote share fell from 24 percent of India's voters in 1999 to 22 percent in 2004. The Congress Party's vote share fell from 28 percent to 26 percent.

The true victors in 2004 were the plethora of small lower-caste and regional parties, whose collective share of national representation continues to rise and rise and now exceeds half of all national votes. None of these parties has an economic program. Few are interested in foreign policy or peace initiatives with Pakistan (or war, for that matter). At moments of national crisis, the BJP has the ability to overcome caste differences and unite a large number of Hindus around their religious identity. But only at rare moments. When normality prevails, Hindus return to their narrower caste or linguistic identities. In the battle between Mandal and *Mandir,* Mandal appears to have the upper hand. "Fragmentation rules!" might be a good summary of India's political direction.

During the 2004 election campaign, I visited Gujarat to observe the fortunes of the BJP in its heartland. The party had decided to downplay Hindu nationalism and talk about the success of its economic reforms in the past few years. India had achieved an economic growth rate of 8.4 percent the previous year and was on target to emulate that number in 2004. In spite of the pogroms in 2002, Gujarat was one of the principal beneficiaries of India's liberal economic reform. Gujarat's standard of living is among the highest in India. It is also India's most globalized state. A large proportion of software entrepreneurs in Silicon Valley and the thriving Asian middle class in Britain are from Gujarat. Yet enthusiasm for the BJP's 2004 election slogan, "India Shining," was hard to find.

While in Gujarat during the 2004 election campaign I managed to locate Lal Krishna Advani, the deputy prime minister and the man who had thought up the Ram Mandir strategy that had propelled the BJP to national prominence in the 1980s and 1990s. Advani was sheltering from the midday heat in the spacious residence of a local businessman in Ahmedabad. A few weeks earlier I had visited the home of a VHP leader in the state of Uttar Pradesh, who had expressed bitterness about the moderate tone of the BJP's election campaign. The Ram Temple, he said, was still a pipedream. He felt particular resentment for Advani and Vajpayee. "Advani and Vajpayee rode to power on the chariot of Ram, but when they got to the throne they abandoned Ram," he said. It was a complaint that had been echoed increasingly by hard-line activists as the BJP's term in office wore on: Where was the Ram Temple?

In 2002, the Hindu nationalist hard-liners thought the government had finally found its soul when it rallied to the support of Narendra Modi, Gujarat's chief minister, and allowed him to call a snap election in which open hatred for Muslims was the sole theme. During the campaign, Ashok Singhal, a VHP leader, said: "What happened in Gujarat will be repeated all over the country."[17] The BJP won the Gujarat election hands down. But it was a moment of national crisis. The election took place against the tense backdrop of a military standoff between India and Pakistan. Gujarat is on the border with Pakistan. After 2002, tensions between Pakistan and India receded. Suddenly economic growth and regional stability became the main priorities. The BJP sent its attack dogs back to the kennel and tossed them the occasional bone.

I was quite fortunate to stumble across Lal Krishna Advani during the 2004 campaign. Unlike Vajpayee, who gave me several interviews, the deputy prime minister had avoided my requests. Seated in the corner of a large room, Advani looked as though he was attending a funeral wake. Arun Jaitley, the BJP's minister for law, and the man who did as much as any other cabinet minister to protect Narendra Modi from being sacked after the riots, was also present. Both parliamentarians represent Gujarat in New Delhi. "Please sit down," said Advani. "What did you want to ask me?" Advani was born in Karachi, which was then part of a united India ruled by the British. His life had been built around hatred of Pakistan and distrust of India's Muslim minorities. His symbolic chariot procession across India had left a trail of dead Muslims in every town through which it passed. Yet during the 2004 campaign even Advani, like Vajpayee, had donned Muslim headgear for the TV cameras.

I said to him that the RSS had been complaining that he had abandoned saffron politics. "Ever since I was a child, the RSS has influenced me and my philosophy," said Advani. "I will never abandon the *Sangh* [organization]. But our biggest achievement in the last six years has been to strengthen the system of federalism in India. We have proved that multiparty coalition government does work, it can provide stable government for India. That is our biggest achievement."

Advani refused to be drawn out on the question of whether he had abandoned Hindu nationalism. I quoted some of the rude things people in the RSS and the VHP were saying about him. Everyone was expecting the BJP to win the 2004 election. Furthermore, they were expecting Vajpayee, whose eightieth birthday was looming, to stand down in favor of Advani as prime minister. But the heir apparent, who at seventy-seven was only a little younger than the prime minister, looked exhausted. Either Advani had an inkling that all the opinion polls were inaccurate and that the BJP was going to lose, which is exactly what happened a few weeks later; or else the man who was (at least indirectly) responsible for the deaths of as many innocent Muslims as any other figure since India was partitioned could not muster any enthusiasm for the moderate election campaign he was running. "Not the RSS, I don't believe they said that about me," Advani protested weakly. "I don't believe they would say that. Maybe some people in the VHP would say that but not the RSS. It is a very disciplined organization." What Advani said was true. But during the 2004 election the RSS was disciplined only in its apathy. Very few of its hundreds of thousands of members in Gujarat volunteered to do election work for the BJP, a decisive source of strength for the party in earlier elections. The RSS wanted shock and awe. But the BJP confined its campaign message to economic growth rates and the soaring stock market index.

A few months after the BJP was defeated, one of the most powerful priests in orthodox Hinduism was arrested on suspicion of murder. Dubbed by the media (a little dramatically) as the "Hindu pope," the Shankaracharya of Kanchi was shown on TV screens up and down the country being bundled like a common criminal into a police van and taken to prison. Advani, who by this stage had become the leader of the opposition BJP, scented a perfect opportunity to revive the war cry of "Hinduism in danger." This tack would also help appease the RSS, whose members were still muttering bitterly about Advani's supposed betrayal of the Hindu nationalist cause. The Shankaracharya—an official title that means "wise teacher"—had allegedly arranged the murder of a temple official who was blackmailing him about an affair he was having with a young woman. He was also alleged to have laundered money from the accounts of his temple in Kanchi, a holy town in the south Indian state of Tamil Nadu.

There were suspicions that Jayalalithaa, the chief minister of Tamil Nadu, who had ordered the arrest, was inflating the allegations against the Shankaracharya for political reasons. Jayalalithaa's Tamil nationalist party had been allied to the BJP in the 2004 elections. Her party's representation in New Delhi had been wiped out. It was left with no seats out of the state's forty parliamentary constituencies. Since she is known as a ruthless political operator, many believed Jayalalithaa had deliberately engineered the high-profile humiliation of the Shankaracharya to signal her rejection of Hindu nationalism and the end of her alliance with the BJP. A few weeks earlier, Jayalalithaa had abolished a state anticonversion law (targeting Christian and Muslim proselytizers) that had been enacted only a year before. To add to the suspicion, Jayalalithaa ordered the arrest of the Shankaracharya on the eve of Divali, the festival of lights, which is probably the most holy day in the annual Hindu calendar. She could have chosen any other day. It was like waving a red flag at a (Western) bull.

Advani seized the opportunity to put the Hindu juggernaut back on the road. He and his colleagues went on a three-day hunger strike and staged a dharna, or sit-down, outside parliament in New Delhi to protest the humiliating treatment of the Shankaracharya. The BJP leader said that the patience of Hindus was close to a snapping point. He compared the Shankaracharya's arrest to Indira Gandhi's suspension of democracy in 1975. "The arrest is as significant in the history of the nation as the imposition of Emergency," said Advani.[18] "Even during British rule, Hindu leaders were not treated this way." The stage was set for a dramatic confrontation between the votaries of saffron politics and India's new secular government. But to the surprise even of his detractors, Advani's protest was a flop. Hardly anyone showed up. After a few hours even the TV camera crews went home.

The reluctance of most Hindus to express outrage over the arrest of their supposed pope was striking. Perhaps people felt there was some truth to the allegations against the Shankaracharya (the case had yet to come to trial at the time of writing, in 2006). Whether that was an explanation, the lack of popular feeling illustrated something more fundamental about Indian society: there is no such thing as a Hindu pope, because there is no such thing as a Hindu church. The Shankaracharya's temple in Kanchi is mostly frequented by Brahmins. All the priests are Brahmin and so are most of the temple staff and worshippers. The Shankaryacharya is merely a Brahmin pope. In contrast, as a rallying theme, building a temple to Ram had appealed to a broad cross-section of Hindus, since all castes are familiar with the Ramayana. In his rush to rouse the Hindu nationalist faithful, Advani had forgotten his most basic electoral arithmetic. In January 2006, Advani stepped down as leader of the BJP in favor of Rajnath Singh, an upper-caste leader from Uttar Pradesh. Although Singh is drawn from the traditional ranks of the BJP, he appointed a number of lower-caste leaders to senior positions in the party. The new leader, it seemed, had learned from some of his predecessor's mistakes.

* * *

I was still several miles from the ashram. But I could already make out its imposing meditation hall illuminated in shimmering blue and white light. I had come to visit Sri Sri Ravi Shankar (not to be confused with Ravi Shankar, the classical sitar player), who is perhaps the most prominent of a new breed of highly successful Hindu evangelists, at his Art of Living Foundation near Bangalore in south

India. It was evening and hundreds of devotees had already congregated for evening prayers. From close up, the meditation hall was even more striking. Rising to five stories, it had been built entirely from marble. The hall was shaped like a lotus. There were 1,008 marble petals covering the exterior of the building symbolizing the diversity of human consciousness. It was only a few years old. The funding for this extravagant construction had come from corporate donations—much of it from the software companies in nearby Bangalore—and revenues the foundation earns from its hugely popular courses in breathing techniques and meditation. "Come inside," said the polite young lady assigned to show me around. "You are just in time to watch the *guruji* take his evening questions."

The interior was even more striking, fashioned like a Roman amphitheater. We sat on polished white marble steps looking down at the stage in the center. I felt like I had stepped inside a large wedding cake. Above us the walls and ceilings were covered with pink lotuses. On the pillars that supported the dome around the central stage were the symbols of the world's main religions: the Islamic Crescent, the Star of David, and the Cross of Jesus. In the center, much larger than the other representations, was a depiction of Lakshmi, the Hindu goddess of wealth. Alone on the stage, on what looked to be a large throne, sat a man in flowing white robes with an equally flowing beard and silky locks of hair falling luxuriantly around his shoulders. It looked as if Jesus were shooting a shampoo advertisement. This was Sri Sri Ravi Shankar.

There was some chanting and clashing of cymbals. Then the prayers ended and a hush descended over the hall. It was time for the *guruji* to take questions. I was expecting people to ask about higher consciousness or metaphysics. But the questions consisted mostly of mundane queries about how to deal with recalcitrant teenagers, whether staying late in the office was a good thing, and how to choose a marriage partner. The *guruji* spoke in a quiet but sonorous voice. But his answers were more like those of an advice columnist than a prophet. Someone asked how she could truly know she was a good person. "You don't need to be sweetie-sweetie, goodie-goodie all the time," said the *guruji*. The audience broke into delighted laughter. Puzzled, I looked around to see hundreds of shining eyes and ecstatic expressions. The next question, which came by e-mail and was read out by one of the *guruji*'s followers, ended with: "I love you so much, *guruji*." Someone asked about whether it was always wrong to pay bribes. "You shouldn't be too idealistic all the time," said the *guruji*. "Sometimes you have to make little, little compromises." Again, the audience erupted in laughter. I was beginning to wonder about the Art of Living's breathing techniques.

After the Q&A session had ended, I was told it was now time for my "audience" with Sri Sri Ravi Shankar. It took a while for the interview to begin because throngs of people had surrounded the *guruji* seeking his blessing. Half of them were Westerners. "Can I have your blessing, *guruji*," shouted a blond woman as the *guruji* was finally entering the interview room. He turned slowly and placed his hands on the woman. Her young face was a study in beatific joy. Then he entered the room. After we had settled down, I asked Sri Sri Ravi Shankar what he thought about the arrest of the Shankaracharya of Kanchi. "It was a shock to me," he said. "It was also a shock to hear about all the financial inefficiency in the *mutt* [temple]. But I am not surprised at the lack of public reaction. The Hindus are a very docile people. We are a nonviolent people. But maybe it has also to do with the fact that the institution never really reaches out to people. Other sections of society don't feel any attachment to his temple."

In contrast to the Shankaracharya's temple in Kanchi, which is dirty, the Art of Living Foundation was spotlessly clean. Its meeting rooms looked like executive boardrooms. There were liquid crystal displays. People from all walks of life and religions are welcome at the Art of Living Foundation. All sorts of credit cards are also accepted. Sri Sri Ravi Shankar has a reputation for being a mystic and a liberal. What is less widely known is the *guruji*'s close attachment to the RSS. He has shared platforms with VHP leaders at public meetings. I asked him whether the Ram Temple should be built in Ayodhya. "Suppose," he said, "that it was the birthplace of Jesus or Mohammed. What would you have done? Would you have tolerated another structure on that site? Let us build a temple to Ram and let the Muslims make this gesture as an act of goodwill and then the temple will also belong to Allah and to all Muslims." To Allah? I asked. "Yes, as you must have seen, we accept all paths to God. Sometimes we wish other religions would do the same."

The *guruji*'s words reminded me of Advani's desire to see more "Hindu Muslims" and more "Hindu Christians." They also reminded me of an interview I had had with Narendra Modi in Gujarat. Modi had said: "We have nothing against people who are not Hindu. What we cannot accept is when people say, 'We are whiter than white. Our religion is better than yours.'" As we saw, Modi demonstrated his opinion of such people in more robust ways. I wondered whether the *guruji* really believed in all this. He seemed courteous and gentle—although I suspected he might also be suffering from a mild dose of narcissism. "Why do people want to convert people to other religions?" the *guruji* asked. "It is a great pity. We should protect the cultural diversity of the planet and not try to change it." I pointed out that the Art of Living Foundation was thriving in places such as California, London, and the Netherlands. "Yes, but we are not a religion. We do not try to convert anyone. There are many paths to God."

A few weeks later I received a telephone call from Ram Madhav, the national spokesman of the RSS. "I am calling about Sri Sri Ravi Shankar," said Madhav. "I was talking to him the other day and he said he was disappointed with your article in the *Financial Times*. You only quoted his views on politics and the Shankaracharya. He said he was hoping you would quote his views on tolerance and on spiritualism." It was true my article had lacked space to quote the *guruji*'s opinions on other matters. But I was surprised the *guruji* should have chosen the RSS—of all organizations—to convey his complaint. I promised that I would take the next opportunity to quote Sri Sri Ravi Shankar at greater length. Now I have fulfilled my promise.

I confess, I did not feel blessed by my meeting with the *guruji*. Yet he does possess knowledge of great importance, as do other Indian celebrity cult leaders, such as Deepak Chopra, Ramdev, and many more. In order to flourish again, the BJP and the RSS will need to take lessons from India's modern breed of businessmen-gurus, whose marketing and public relations skills can reach people from many different backgrounds. The Shankaracharya may or may not be guilty of criminal acts. But he can certainly be charged with declining relevance. Modern religious figures like Sri Sri Ravi Shankar, meanwhile, are becoming increasingly relevant. The BJP's challenge will be to learn from people like the *guruji*.

"It is very clear that the established Brahmanical order is incapable of rising to the challenge,"[19] wrote Swapan Dasgupta, India's best-known newspaper commentator on Hindu nationalism. "The conclusion is obvious. There is a thriving tradition of what can loosely be called evangelical Hinduism. They are the Pat Robertsons and Billy Grahams of modern Hinduism. The failure of organized Hindu nationalism lies in not being able to link up with the congregations of individual evangelists."

The era of Brahmin-dominated politics in India is dead. The upper-caste RSS's cult of material sacrifice and self-denial is losing relevance in a country where consumer values are spreading rapidly among all castes in the cities. People no longer associate Hinduism with poverty or celibacy. Whether Brahmin or Sudra, rural or urban, consumers are voting for a new kind of Hinduism with their wallets. Converting these wallets into electoral dividends will be the goal of the BJP in the coming years. Equally, the trend of Sanskritization, where lower castes adopt the lifestyles and markers of the upper castes, is a phenomenon that could play to the advantage of the Hindu right wing, by gradually reducing the sharper differences between Hindu castes. Hindu nationalism could well govern India again. It is much too soon to write its obituary.

# 5. LONG LIVE THE SYCOPHANTS!

## The Congress Party's Continuing Love Affair with the Nehru-Gandhi Dynasty

*Power has never attracted me, nor has position been my goal. I was always certain that if I ever found myself in the position that I am in today, I would follow my own inner voice. Today that voice tells me that I must humbly decline this post [prime minister]. I appeal to you to accept the force of my conviction and to recognise I will not reverse this decision.*

SONIA GANDHI turning down the prime minister's job
on May 18, 2004, following her party's election victory

Few individuals in today's India—perhaps none—excite as much adulation and hatred as Sonia Gandhi. There is little about the shy and reticent character of Sonia Gandhi that could justify either sentiment. She was born in a small north Italian town in 1945. At Cambridge in the 1960s, Sonia met and fell instantly in love with Rajiv Gandhi, the son of Indira and grandson of Jawaharlal Nehru. Rajiv was studying engineering and she was learning English. They were married in 1968 and moved to New Delhi to live in the house of Indira, her mother-in-law, who was prime minister at the time. Both she and Rajiv, who became a full-time pilot for India Airlines, kept a strict distance from politics. Then, in the first of many tragedies to befall the family, Sanjay Gandhi, Rajiv's younger brother, who was the heir apparent to Indira, died in a plane crash in 1980. Dynastic duty called. Sonia wrote that she "fought like a tigress"[1] to dissuade her husband from getting involved in politics, so afraid was she of the consequences, but without success. Rajiv was inducted into the cabinet.

In 1984 Sonia's mother-in-law, Indira, was assassinated by her bodyguards, and it was Sonia who cradled the dying prime minister in her arms as she was rushed to the hospital. To Sonia's alarm and despair, Rajiv was sworn in as prime minister after his mother had been pronounced dead. Her forebodings were justified. Seven years later, while on the election campaign trail in south India, Rajiv was assassinated by a Tamil nationalist suicide bomber. Sonia was not with him. "I watched him, peeping from behind the curtain, until he disappeared from view, this time forever,"[2] Sonia wrote of the last time she had seen her husband. For seven years Sonia ignored the pleading of Congress Party loyalists to join politics in her husband's stead. At least once she turned down the offer to become prime minister. Then in 1998 Sonia finally caved in to the relentless tide of flattery, cajolery, and pleading to become president of the opposition Congress Party. Six years and two elections of relatively undistinguished leadership ensued before, to the surprise of most people, the crown was suddenly hers for the taking again. Against all odds and almost every opinion poll, the Congress Party–led alliance had ejected the BJP-led government from office. It was Sonia, and to some extent her children, Rahul and Priyanka (whose political debuts were made in the campaign), who took the credit. In the eyes of many people, Sonia's position could no longer be written off solely as an inheritance. She had earned the job of prime minister. It was an extraordinary outcome in a life that had largely been spent in disdain of politics. But she had gradually warmed to the role. India, meanwhile, was blowing hot or cold—and not much in between.

There was a time, during the run-up to the 2004 election, when mere mention of Sonia Gandhi's name could enliven a dull dinner party, splitting the guests between those who admired the Italian-born Congress Party leader and those who felt contempt. I always felt baffled by the strength of feeling on either side. In some cases Sonia Gandhi would evoke both sentiments in the same person. I can think of two senior Congress Party parliamentarians who had despaired in private before the election about having an "uneducated Italian housewife" as their leader. The same men stood up publicly in front of the nation and the world on May 18, 2004, and tearfully pleaded with Sonia Gandhi to become prime minister following her renunciation of the job. Suddenly she was no longer an uneducated housewife. She was their "friend, philosopher, guide" and the savior of the nation. It took the breath away. It was not mere sycophancy. What they conveyed was an acknowledgment of the Congress Party's sole remaining organizing principle: the Nehru-Gandhi dynasty. Both (highly educated) men became cabinet ministers.

The venom reserved for Sonia Gandhi by her opponents was—and is—as potent as the adulation conveyed by her supporters. During the election campaign, Narendra Modi, the BJP chief minister of Gujarat, called Sonia Gandhi "a half-bred Jersey cow" and "that Italian bitch." He said that Sonia's two children, Rahul and Priyanka, were not fit to drive his car or to clean his shoes. Other less rabid BJP figures despaired that a country of a billion people could choose a foreign-born person as its leader. In the days following the defeat of the BJP-led coalition, Sushma Swaraj, a former cabinet minister, threatened to shave her head and become a *sanyasin* (someone who renounces the material world) unless Sonia Gandhi rejected the job. The BJP had planned a nationwide campaign led by a senior Hindu religious figure to protest against the insult of suffering a "foreign woman" as prime minister. In the event, they were outmaneuvered by Sonia Gandhi, who got her (very Hindu) act of renunciation in first. She appointed Manmohan Singh as prime minister in her stead. Her decision showed judgment of character. Singh had never uttered an embarrassing word of fulsome praise for Sonia Gandhi in public. Yet he had always been polite about her in private.

In the photographs of Sonia Gandhi taken before her husband was killed in 1991, she comes across as a smiling, radiant, and attractive woman, often dressed in the finest Gucci or Prada outfits. In the pictures, Sonia is often gazing adoringly at Rajiv. She seemed deeply in love with her husband. After 1991, Sonia always looks glum and funereal. Her occasional smile is lifeless and diplomatic. But her dress sense has altered. She is only caught on camera wearing a sari. On May 20, 2004, Sonia Gandhi and Manmohan Singh emerged from the presidential palace in Delhi to announce the latter's appointment as prime minister. "The nation will be safe in Dr. Singh's hands," said Sonia. Then it was Manmohan's turn to speak. But my gaze, like everyone else's, was riveted to Sonia. Her smile was oceanic. No matter what questions the reporters fired at her, it simply would not go away.

•   •   •   •

The author Salman Rushdie once described the Nehru-Gandhi family as a "dynasty to beat *Dynasty* in a Delhi to rival *Dallas*."[3] That was in the 1980s. At an earlier stage the Nehru family could have perhaps been likened to Evelyn Waugh's *Brideshead Revisited*. The traditional Nehru family home in the city of Allahabad is the closest thing in India to the heritage properties that punctuate much of the British countryside. The architecture of Anand Bhavan (House of Joy), the larger family building, is Islamicate. But the interior is a hybrid between the traditional Brahmin household and the most aristocratic of British residences. The property was bought in 1902 by Motilal Nehru, Jawaharlal's father, who was making a fortune as a barrister in the courts. Although Motilal was a leading member of the Congress Party, which had been established in 1885, his style and manner were those of a pukka English gentleman. Tradition held no appeal for Motilal. He was expelled from his caste for refusing to undergo a ceremony of purification on his return from England.[4] Crossing the "black waters" was considered polluting. Motilal shrugged off the excommunication. He was far too busy enjoying the lavish proceeds of his earnings. Motilal was the first person in Allahabad to purchase a motorcar. His consumption of champagne was legendary. It was rumored, falsely, that he sent his linen to Paris to be laundered. He was accurately reputed to wear only suits that had been tailored in Savile Row.[5] Anand Bhavan had more than one hundred servants. It was a royal lifestyle. Many years later in 1928 when the Nehrus had switched their dress to *khadi*—homespun cotton—Motilal wrote to Gandhi saying he wished the "crown" (presidency of the Congress Party) for Jawaharlal. Motilal, who had held the post himself, was already talking in the language of dynasty.

Touring through Anand Bhavan, which is now a national museum, is a disorienting experience. Outside on the bustling streets of Allahabad, a city of four million people, there are the usual bodice-ripping posters advertising Bollywood films. Inside, you find yourself perusing a world that has almost completely vanished. You see the Edwardian waistcoats, pith helmets, and traveling kits of irons, toasters, and early electric shavers to which father and son were accustomed. Their reading habits were those of the English gentry. Books by Lewis Carroll and Thackeray pack the shelves. On his birthday every year, the young Jawaharlal would be weighed against a pile of wheat that would be given away to the poor.[6] The young Nehru is pictured dressed in the snooty outfits of Lord Fauntleroy. This was a family that, as Lord Macaulay had famously wished for Indians almost a century earlier, was "brown in colour, but English in taste, morals and intellect."

As you move through the upholstered rooms, a change starts to occur. In place of the matching silk ties and handkerchiefs, you see simple homespun outfits. During the 1920s and 1930s, Anand Bhavan became an informal meeting place for Congress Party leaders. Gandhi would hold strategic meetings here and sit outside on the verandah in between sessions, spinning cotton at his wheel. There is a framed letter from the Anglo-Irish playwright George Bernard Shaw, addressed, somewhat presumptuously, "from one Mahatma [Great Soul] to another," in which *Gandhi* is misspelled as "Ghandi." The Indians touring through the mansion, which was donated to the nation by Indira Gandhi in the 1970s, seemed spellbound. It contains a mixture of dynasty and sainthood and a world that no longer exists. This is an advantage for royalty. It should have a touch of the foreign and it should excite the imagination.

Motilal died a couple of years after his son had first become president of the Congress Party in 1928. Nehru was in prison for agitating against British rule when his father died. He was also in prison when his mother, Swarup Rani, and his wife, Kamala, died. On each occasion he was either given leave to visit them on their deathbeds or to attend their funerals before returning to his cell. From prison, he wrote endlessly to Indira, his only child, who was being raised by governesses, stern aunts, and at boarding schools. Nehru's letters of historical instruction to Indira were later collated into *Glimpses of World History*. There has been much debate about whether Nehru deliberately groomed his daughter to succeed him as prime minister. The evidence is weak. As a widower, Nehru requested that the young Indira be his hostess and household manager when he was prime minister in the 1950s. Naturally Indira got to know everything that was happening and everyone who was doing it. This awkward and shy young woman gradually became an operator in her own right. By 1959, Indira was president (for one year) of the Congress Party. Her son Sanjay rose to prominence in the 1970s by leading the Congress Youth wing.

When Nehru died in 1964, Indira was invited into the cabinet by Lal Bahadur Shastri, the new prime minister, who was both a loyal Gandhian and Nehruvian, but whose authority was limited. Shastri died in 1966 while attending an international conference in Tashkent. The Congress Party was deeply split between clashing personalities. Indira was a natural compromise candidate between the factions. Ram Manohar Lohia, the leader of the socialists, notoriously called Indira a "dumb doll" who could be manipulated with ease. At first she proved pliable as prime minister. But when it became clear her position would amount to little more than providing a rubber stamp for decisions made by others, Indira began to emerge from her chrysalis. She turned into the most formidable and ruthless political figure India has yet seen. She was supposed to behave like a constitutional monarch. But she wanted to be absolute. The contrast with her father's style of governing, which was scrupulously democratic, was sharp. Indira once described her father as a "saint who strayed into politics." Indira, on the other hand, was better known as "Durga," the wife of Shiva, symbolizing feminine power. She gained the epithet after India had defeated Pakistan in the war that resulted in the separation of East Pakistan from West Pakistan in 1971. Indira became prone to hubris. She did not demur when one of her colleagues famously said: "India is Indira."

After Indira had declared an emergency in June 1975 and closed down democracy for nineteen months,* her son Sanjay began to emerge as an even more ruthless operator than his mother. But he lacked her political cunning. In contrast to Rajiv, his professional and soft-spoken older brother, Sanjay was essentially a thug. Although Sanjay held no formal position in government, his power was close to total. Even Indira was afraid of Sanjay, who spoke rudely to her in front of others and whose circle gradually became the power center around which anyone with ambition would gravitate. On one occasion, Sanjay was reported to have slapped his mother around the face six times at a dinner party.[7] The story was unsubstantiated. One close family friend dismissed it as impossible since "not even God could slap Indira around the face six times."[8] But the fact that the story was in circulation revealed much about the relationship between mother and son. Indira permitted Sanjay to devise and take charge of the most draconian social programs India has witnessed.

---

*Indira shut down India's independent media, imprisoned up to 100,000 political opponents, and bypassed almost all the procedures of constitutional government during the state of emergency. It was India's only real modern taste of autocracy.

He oversaw the mass clearance of slums in New Delhi and elsewhere in which millions were brutally evicted from their homes. Sanjay also devised an unpleasant population scheme in which hundreds of thousands of men were sterilized, many of them forcibly. It was a relief to some when Sanjay killed himself in a plane accident (he was an amateur pilot) in 1980. Some mourned him deeply.

Rajiv, who succeeded his assassinated mother in 1984, brought with him a completely different set of hangers-on and advisers, many of whom were childhood friends from Doon School, India's equivalent of Britain's Eton College. His manner was seen as modern and breezy. As prime minister, Rajiv was also famed for his gentle courtesy, and he displayed respect for the rules of democracy. In many of his personality traits, particularly his temperament, Rajiv was his grandfather's grandson rather than his mother's son. When Rajiv was killed in 1991 his children, Rahul and Priyanka, were too young for a dynastic succession to be plausible. And it was too soon for Rajiv to have indicated whether he harbored political ambitions for his children. So the mantle fell on Sonia, whom, as we have seen, retreated into mourning for several years after her husband's death. Eventually Sonia agreed to become regent. Now Rahul, Sonia's handsome son, who, like his father, was also educated at Cambridge University,* and who became a member of parliament in 2004, is emerging as the next heir to the dynasty.

This, then, is a brief genealogy of the Congress Party's first family. But what has it given India? Is it possible any longer to separate the Congress Party from the Nehru-Gandhi dynasty? In spite of Gandhi's grip on the freedom movement, it was Nehru, through his control of the Congress Party, who exercised the most influence on the formative character of India after independence in 1947. Others, such as

---

*Unlike his father, Rajiv, Rahul did complete his Cambridge M Phil degree (the equivalent of a master's), which was in development studies. Nehru was a formidable reader and possessed an acute intellect. Rajiv was not a reader of books. Neither, it seems, is Rahul. Indira also showed impatience with study. She did not complete her degree at Oxford University. Sonia did not attend university.

Ambedkar, who chaired the committee that framed the 1950 constitution, and Vallabhbhai Patel, who, as home minister, skillfully incorporated the five hundred or so princely states into India and
ensured the continuity of the colonial civil service, also played important roles. But Gandhi was assassinated in 1948. Patel, whose
sympathies with orthodox Hinduism clashed with Nehru's strictly
secular vision for the country, died in 1950. And Ambedkar resigned
from Nehru's cabinet in 1951. Nehru still had thirteen years left at
the top.

Nehru left three clear stamps on India that endure today: democracy, secularism, and socialism (a fourth, foreign policy nonalignment during the cold war, is no longer strictly relevant). Each of these
is often still prefixed with the word *Nehruvian* in recognition of
Nehru's role in pushing for their acceptance as part of modern India's
creed. The first, in spite of Indira Gandhi's experiment with dictatorship, is alive and well. The second, secularism, has taken some body
blows in the last fifteen years but remains intact. The third, socialism,
is dead as an official ideology but continues to live on in various
ways, not least in the Congress Party's continuing love affair with an
unreformed state.

It is often taken for granted that a country as diverse and plural as
India is naturally democratic. But it was not a foregone conclusion
that India would embrace democracy in the form that it has. Mohandas Gandhi wanted to restore India to a semimythical past in which
it would be governed by a confederation of village councils. But he
was murdered before the country's constitutional convention got under way. Some argued that the electoral franchise should be restricted
to literate adults, who made up just 16 percent of the population at
independence. Others wanted the vote confined to men. A number of
extreme Hindu nationalists questioned whether religious minorities
should have the vote. India's Communist Party, meanwhile, wanted
a dictatorship of the (virtually nonexistent) proletariat. The party
called off its struggle against Nehru's "bourgeois democracy" in
1951.

Nehru was never in any doubt that India should have a Westminster-style parliamentary system in which every adult would have the vote. His view, which was strongly supported by Ambedkar, prevailed. In retrospect the decision appeared to be a natural outgrowth of the position of the freedom movement, which claimed the same rights for Indians that were available to the British. But at the time, Nehru's position was more precarious. Through charisma and force of intellect Nehru persuaded India to take a unique leap of faith into full democracy at a time when most of the developing world was embracing its opposite.

Ironically, Nehru had much less success instilling a culture of democracy inside the Congress Party. The factional character of the Congress Party had—and continues to have—consequences for the way broader democracy evolved in the country. India began its journey into independence with only one genuine national party, which claimed to represent all of India's castes, religions, languages, and races. In practice, however, the Congress Party was overwhelmingly dominated by the rural and urban elites who were drawn principally from the upper castes. Although the Congress Party was open to all, and although senior office holders were elected by a ballot of the members, the system was hijacked on the ground by local notables. This culture persists in the Congress Party today. In the 1980s Rajiv Gandhi was presented with a report on the Congress Party's state of health which estimated that 60 percent of the party's membership was bogus.[9] Bigwigs were inventing membership lists to tighten their grip on their local party machines.

Nehru controlled the national party from New Delhi. But in the provinces where Nehru's policies of land redistribution and agricultural reforms were meant to be carried out, the party was in the grip of the traditional landowning elites. A large share of public subsidies were captured by local elites since, in most of India, the Congress Party and the state amounted to one and the same thing. "Those who could not afford to pay found themselves at the bottom of the list in the allocation of access to 'public goods.'"[10] An internal Congress

Party report compiled in 1963 in the aftermath of a series of by-election defeats could equally have been written in 2006. It said: "The pivot around which Congress activity revolves is the personality through whom preferment can be obtained and not the aims and purposes of the party."[11] In rhetoric, Congress was democratic and radical. In practice, it was plutocratic and conservative.

The electoral symbol of the Congress Party is the hand.* "The hand of Congress is always with the poor," says the slogan. But as the party's tenure in office wore on, the poor began to realize that the hand of the Congress Party was as often to be found in the till, taking what supposedly belonged to them. Gradually, the party's delicately maintained coalition of communities and castes began to break up and form their own constituent parties. The disintegration of cross-caste and cross-religious support for the Congress Party was not linear. When there was a national crisis, such as the war with Pakistan in 1971 or the assassination of Indira Gandhi in 1984,[†] the Congress Party vote shot back up to the levels it had regularly enjoyed under Nehru, at somewhere between 42 and 48 percent. The last time the Congress Party received a national vote on any scale was in 1991 following the assassination of Rajiv, when it got the support of 36 percent of the vote. Since then, the Congress Party vote share has remained between 25 and 29 percent.

On each occasion the Congress Party squandered its thundering majorities by an inability to live up to the radical and pious rhetoric in which it had imprisoned itself. In 1971, opponents of Indira said, "Remove Indira." Indira countered by saying, "Remove Poverty." Neither

---

*Each party has a visual symbol that enables illiterate voters to know where to place their mark. The Congress Party has the hand, the BJP has the lotus, Samajwadi has the bicycle, and so on.

†Indira was shot dead by her two Sikh bodyguards. A few weeks earlier Indira had ordered the Indian army to storm the Golden Temple in the town of Amritsar. The temple, which is the most sacred place for Sikhs, had been under the control of separatist Sikh militants. When Indira was killed, thousands of Sikhs were murdered in the following riots. Rajiv said: "When a great tree falls, the ground shakes."

was removed. Indira did remove democracy in 1975 after the high court in Allahabad declared her 1971 election illegal on a minor technicality. Rather than resign, Indira suspended elections. It was only because Indira had been advised by admirers that she would sweep the polls that she agreed to restore democracy in 1977. For the first time in its history, the Congress Party was defeated. In addition to large sections of the lower castes, Muslims also voted against the Congress Party in large numbers in 1977 because so many of them had fallen victim to Sanjay's slum clearance and sterilization programs.

Likewise, in 1984, the youthful Rajiv began his term amid the kind of optimism that often greets the advent of a new generation. But Rajiv's inexperience and the corruption of many around him led to an acceleration of the breakup of the Congress Party by the next election in 1989 (the second time it was defeated). The 1991 Congress Party government was led by Narasimha Rao, an old-time Congressman. It lasted the full five years and took radical steps to turn India's economy around. But it ran out of reformist steam halfway through. It was thrown out in 1996. Economic reform was barely mentioned on the campaign trail.[12]

The Congress Party was only able to return to national office in 2004. As recently as 1999, it was still blind to the logic of striking up alliances with other parties in order to regain power. At its annual meeting the Congress Party proclaimed it would govern alone or not at all. The resolution said: "[The conference] affirms that the party considers the present difficulties in forming one-party governments a transient phase in the evolution of our polity."[13] It was because of such hubris—and the superior tone in which it was rendered—that the Congress Party had fallen to a low point in its fortunes. It was also a serious misreading of the direction in which Indian politics was heading. By 2003 the party had woken up to the reality of an India that was likely to remain politically fragmented for the foreseeable future. At its annual conclave in the Himalayan hill station of Simla, Sonia Gandhi agreed to set up an alternative coalition-in-waiting. Her decision, which reversed fifty years of Congress Party tradition, helped bring the party back into office in 2004 with barely a quarter of the national vote.

The second of Nehru's legacies was secularism. As with the decision to give the vote to all Indians, Nehru's influence on the creation of a secular state for independent India should not be underestimated. The Congress Party began life as a party that included all shades of opinion, from Marxist to Hindu nationalist. Many on the Hindu Right were bitterly opposed to what they saw as Nehru's contempt for the traditions of orthodox Hinduism. But the assassination of Gandhi by a Hindu nationalist in January 1948 provided unexpected assistance to Nehru. It forced Vallabhbhai Patel, Nehru's right-wing home minister, to crack down on the RSS, which had held spontaneous street parties up and down the country to celebrate the death of India's greatest freedom fighter. Hundreds of RSS leaders and activists were imprisoned.

"The light has gone out of our lives," said Nehru of Gandhi's death. Nehru skillfully traded on Gandhi's memory to push (most of) his secular agenda through the constitutional convention. It was not a definition that would be recognized in France or Turkey, which interpret *secular* to mean the state should dissociate religion from all aspects of public life. India's version is less militant. The Indian state quite happily promotes all religions, rather than disdaining all equally. Nehru permitted each religious community to retain its own civil laws, or "personal codes," which would govern marriages, divorces, births, deaths, and inheritances. It was probably not Nehru's ideal since it sat uneasily with the principle of equality before the law, which is also enshrined in the constitution. But in the wake of the horrors of India's partition it seemed a necessary concession to the millions of Muslims who had ignored Pakistan and remained behind. Although it was reformed in a liberal direction, retaining separate family legal codes appeased the Hindu orthodox who preferred a Hindu code for Hindus to a uniform secular civil code that would have undermined their hold on tradition.

Yet by accepting the consensus that Indians should be at least partly defined according to the religion of their birth, Nehru inadvertently helped sow the seeds of the communal battles that continue to bedevil India today. The 1950 constitution enshrines both the rights of the individual and the rights of groups, whether religious or linguistic. According to one constitutional article, the state cannot alter laws that govern any religious group without the assent of three-quarters of its membership. This makes it very difficult for Indian governments to interfere with traditional practices, however objectionable. For example, there is little the state can do to tackle polygamy, which the Muslim personal law permits to Muslims. In practice only about 2 percent of Muslim men have more than one wife. But the fact they are permitted to have multiple wives is a stick with which the Hindu nationalists can beat the Congress Party and Muslims in general. So too is the Indian state's continued subsidy for Indian Muslims who go on the *hadj* to Mecca, even though in practice it amounts to a tiny amount of money. The Indian state also provides large subsidies to Hindu temples and trusts.

The decision to classify Indians by their religion in respect to many of their rights also left a questionable political mark on the Congress Party, which the party has yet to transcend: the temptation always to appeal to identity "vote banks." Rather than speak to voters in a language that unites them, the Congress Party got into the habit of customizing its message for each "community." It is not hard to see why this created a backlash, particularly among upper-caste Hindus who resented the alleged mollycoddling of conservative Islam. The Congress Party sometimes appeared to choose Muslim candidates by the length of their beards. It became equally prone to the manipulation of caste to suit local electoral arithmetic.

The adoption of separate legal codes was also a decision that (unintentionally) put strict limits on the evolution of liberalism in India. When a religious group objects to a book, a film, or a piece of art because it allegedly offends their beliefs, New Delhi is quick to ban it. Salman Rushdie's novel *Satanic Verses* was banned in the late 1980s by Rajiv Gandhi because it allegedly insulted the prophet Mohammed. A few years later Rushdie's novel *The Moor's Last Sigh* was also banned because it lampooned Bal Thackeray, a Hindu nationalist leader in Mumbai. Barely a month goes by in India without some book or film being banned or censored. In the India of today, the rights of everyone to freedom of expression are junior to the rights of priests and mullahs to protest on behalf of communities that have neither elected nor appointed them. India is certainly a plural country. But pluralism is not the same thing as liberalism.

The contradictions of India are also the contradictions of the Congress Party. In 1985 Rajiv Gandhi was advised to step in and appease the orthodox Muslim community after the Indian Supreme Court ruled in favor of an impoverished Muslim woman called Shah Bano in a divorce case. From the point of view of the Muslim orthodox, the court had interfered with the Muslim civil code. It ordered Shah Bano's husband to pay his former wife a small monthly alimony. The conservative mullahs were outraged, which worried the Congress Party's electoral strategists. In an extraordinary maneuver, Rajiv Gandhi enacted legislation that deprived Shah Bano of her monthly payments in order to reassure the mullahs that they remained in control of Muslim personal law. Rajiv's move was an unexpected gift for the ascendant BJP, which could point to a Congress Party that would go to any lengths for votes. The inevitable Hindu backlash proved equally worrying to Rajiv's electoral advisers. So Rajiv was persuaded to appease the Hindu right wing. In a decision that was to reshape the contours of Indian politics, Rajiv in 1986 unlocked the gates to the Babri Masjid in the holy town of Ayodhya (because of the controversy, activists had until then been denied access to the site). His ill-advised move set the ball rolling that culminated in the destruction of the mosque in 1992.

The chain of events that Rajiv had set in motion illustrated the peculiar mix of "naivety and cynicism"[14] that had long since come to characterize the Congress Party. The party no longer appeared to believe in anything. In one swoop, Rajiv had alienated liberal Muslims and everyone else by depriving an impoverished Muslim woman of the little alimony she had, then he alienated all Muslims by opening the Ayodhya mosque to Hindu fanatics, and finally he appalled Indians of many descriptions by signaling that neither he nor his party appeared to possess any impulse other than a hunger for votes. Much like the pursuit of happiness, which is best conducted obliquely, naked pursuit of power for its own sake can be self-defeating. It is little wonder, then, that Rajiv's historic parliamentary majority of 1984 was reduced to a rump opposition the next time voters had an opportunity to air their views. Rajiv's battered reputation was restored only after his tragic assassination.

It is hard to imagine Rajiv's grandfather making such chronic tactical errors. Yet, with hindsight, Nehru's generation could be accused of committing a strategic blunder that continues to undercut supporters of Indian liberalism today. Because the principle of equality before the law was diluted by retaining "personal codes," Indian liberalism was encumbered with a handicap it has yet to escape (to be fair to Nehru, he was a democrat who had to give in to the conservative majority on these questions). Because she is a relative political novice and a foreigner, it is not surprising that Sonia Gandhi appears to be as much influenced by the Congress Party's electoral tacticians as her husband was during the 1980s. In 2004, the Congress Party won just 9 out of 80 parliamentary seats in Uttar Pradesh, the home of Ayodhya. In the past the party had regularly won more than half the state's seats. Among the Congress Party's candidates were orthodox Muslims belonging to the hard-line Islamic school of Deoband, which we shall visit in the next chapter.

During the Gujarat state elections of 2002, Sonia felt unable to take a strong stand against the aggressive Hindu nationalism of Narendra Modi's BJP following the anti-Muslim pogroms that had taken place earlier in the year. This was surprising because Sonia evidently felt passionately about the issue. The speech she gave to India's parliament following the killings was widely considered to be her best and to mark her growing confidence as an opposition leader. Toward the end of the speech, Sonia fixed her gaze on the government benches of BJP ministers and accused them of turning Gujarat into "the land of Godse not Gandhi." Gandhi was from Gujarat. Godse killed him.

I spent much time in Gujarat before the election talking to despondent Gujarati Muslims. True to its character, the Congress Party bent to the prevailing winds, which were howling with saffron rage. Sonia was advised to appoint Shankersingh Vaghela, a former member of the RSS, to lead the Congress Party campaign. In a state where almost 10 percent of the population is Muslim, only 5 of the party's 203 candidates were Muslim. Sonia spent much of the campaign visiting Hindu temples. She was advised not to visit the widow of Ehsan Jaffri, a retired Congress Party politician who, as a prominent Muslim, had been butchered—along with the neighbors he was sheltering—in the riots earlier that year.

Having interacted with Sonia Gandhi, I have little doubt she is sincere in her support of secularism. But she often appears to be a prisoner of the Congress Party's network of advisers, courtiers, and carpetbaggers whose efforts have helped to destroy her party's credibility in large tracts of India over the last generation. Unsurprisingly, the BJP won the 2002 Gujarat polls by a landslide. In declining to take a principled stand, the Congress Party machine had learned nothing from Rajiv's mistakes. Sonia bore some of the responsibility. As one commentator remarked, "If you have an A-team, why would you vote for the B-team?"

Nehru's third legacy was socialism. In chapter one, we looked at the failures of India's "import substitution" model and the reasons that *swadeshi,* or self-reliance, was ultimately abandoned in 1991. But it is worth stressing two things. Indian-style socialism, in which the supposedly altruistic workings of an elite bureaucracy act as a substitute for social reform on the ground, lives on in the habitual tendencies of the Congress Party today. The Indian state was partly a creation of Nehru. But Nehru's motivations were ideological and, as we have seen, they were in tune with broader international fashion at the time. Sixty years later, the persistence of an unreformed state can no longer be attributed to ideology. We have to look deeper to discover why India's state is still permitted to operate in its traditional form. Some of the reasons are to be found in the habits and character of the Congress Party.

The inefficiencies of Nehru's state contributed a great deal to India's relatively poor economic performance in the decades after independence. But much more of the blame for India's economic failures should be directed at Indira Gandhi, whose policies led the country to the precipice of bankruptcy. It was Indira who tarnished the neutrality of the civil service when she called for a "committed" bureaucracy that would be openly socialist. This led to a sharp increase in corruption since it dissolved the conventions of neutrality and impartiality that had until then acted as a restraint on the behavior of public servants. It also made it easier for politicians to transfer civil servants on a whim or a fancy.

It was also Indira who nationalized India's banking and insurance sectors in 1969. Many people think of finance as an esoteric subject that is of little consequence to their everyday lives. But the way a country regulates and allocates its capital is a critical influence on the nature of its economy. Finance is to the economy what blood circulation is to the body. In the name of the poor, Indira handed control of finance to an unreformed civil service. But most of the poor continued to go to usurious private moneylenders. Very few of India's farmers possess a formal title to their land. So they lack the collateral even to qualify for a loan. In a survey in 2002, a majority of Indian farmers said they trusted the moneylenders more than they trusted the public bodies that provide electricity and water.[15] They could have said the same of public sector banks. For those lucky enough to qualify for a loan, it takes on average thirty-three weeks to be cleared. And the bribe to get clearance costs on average 10 to 20 percent of the loan. The ultimate cost of servicing a loan is often higher than the usurious rates charged by moneylenders.[16]

Similarly, by imposing a thicket of restrictions on how much banks could lend to whom and when, Indira Gandhi drastically raised the cost of capital for everyone. If you ration something, you increase its price. As a result, India's interest rates have traditionally been far higher than those in other emerging markets. This partly explains why India's rate of investment (and economic growth) has traditionally been lower. Sonia Gandhi's Congress Party opposes any drastic changes to a banking system that was largely created by her mother-in-law. Shortly after it came to office in 2004, Manmohan Singh's government ruled out any drastic reform of banks, including privatization. On some estimates, reform of the financial sector could add two percentage points a year to India's economic growth.[17]

By the same token, Sonia's party also opposes any radical change in the nature of the Indian state. When he became prime minister in 2004, Manmohan said reform of the bureaucracy would be the government's first priority. In his first televised address,[18] the prime minister said: "No objective in the development agenda can be met if we do not reform the instruments in our hand with which we have to work—namely the government and public institutions." What was the use of pouring more water into a leaking bucket? It soon became clear Manmohan did not have the power to make the changes he wanted. With the exception of the right-to-information law, India's bureaucracy continues to work as it always has. In some respects, its role has even expanded under Manmohan's government. We have seen many examples of how policies designed to help the poor often bypass them altogether. India probably has more experience than any other democracy of poverty-reduction programs that largely failed to achieve their purpose. Yet the Congress Party in the early twenty-first century remains as addicted to programs that are entrusted entirely to the bureaucracy as it was in the 1950s. It is hard to believe that the party could be unaware of the record over the last few decades of India's bureaucracy in siphoning off money. It is true that India's persistent rural poverty cannot be addressed without effective state intervention. But trying to effect change through an unreformed and unaccountable state can sometimes be worse than doing nothing at all.

Albert Einstein once said insanity was "doing the same thing over and over again and expecting different results." The most spectacular example of the Congress Party's continued faith in an unreformed state is the Rural Employment Guarantee Act that India's parliament passed in 2005. Much of the law was designed by Aruna Roy, whom we met earlier, and Jean Dréze, an impressive Belgian-born economist, now an Indian citizen. Their influence on Sonia Gandhi, who continues, in turn, to shape the decisions of Manmohan's government from behind the scenes, ensured that the law was pushed through. It is the flagship legislation of the Congress Party–led coalition. The law, which is designed to cover the entire country by 2009, is probably India's most ambitious attempt so far to alleviate poverty through direct state intervention. The intentions of its framers cannot be faulted. Their aim is to make life better for India's rural poor. Yet there is little, other than the legislation's magnitude and its cost, that would distinguish it from previous efforts that failed.

The law is also important because it distinguishes India's approach to poverty very clearly from that of neighboring China, which has preferred to create jobs indirectly by stimulating high (public and private) investment in the economy. Manmohan's government has not followed this path. The law gives one hundred days of manual labor in the countryside to anyone who wants it. Since the payment is at the minimum wage, which varies from as little as Rs 50 a day in some states to Rs 80 in others (between $1 and $2), it is assumed that only the really desperate will take the jobs. In the jargon, the program is "self-selecting." Payment can be in a mixture of cash and food. The work is almost entirely physical. It consists of the type of manual labor India's poor have been requisitioned to do for thousands of years: filling in potholes, digging up landfills, mending river embankments, and clearing irrigation channels.

Judging by the results of previous schemes, notably the food-for-work program, which has successfully prevented famine in postcolonial India, the quality of the work is not the priority. All of it can be done more efficiently and projects built to last much longer with modern machines. Unskilled and hungry laborers cannot build good roads with their bare hands. Potholes are filled in only to be washed away by the monsoon the following year. River embankments crumble at the first flush of rainfall. Irrigation channels silt up within weeks. If, as expected, the program spreads across the whole country, it will eventually cost India up to 2 percent of its gross domestic product and up to 10 percent of its annual budget.[19] Yet it promises no investment in upgrading the skills of the people it is designed to help. Nor does it invest in genuine rural infrastructure, such as all-weather roads, proper electricity supply, or new agricultural technologies. Such investments would stimulate greater economic activity, which would be much likelier to create lasting employment for the rural poor.

This assessment has not even mentioned the "leakage" and corruption that is likely to afflict the program as it unfolds in the coming years. When the law was proposed in 2004, it was dismissed by many Indian and international economists as an expensive way of doing nothing to address the perennial condition of India's poor— their consignment to manual labor at miserably low levels of productivity. Yet India's parliament passed the bill unanimously. Many believed the parliament's rare consensus was prompted by the opportunity for all parties to siphon off a new source of public funds. One Indian commentator even suggested the law should be renamed the Corruption Guarantee Act.[20]

Nor has the Congress Party–led government made any attempt to improve the performance of state-owned companies, whose losses give large swaths of the public sector a net negative value—an extraordinary measure of their inefficiency. There are respectable arguments for retaining some enterprises, including much of India's oil sector, in state ownership. But there are no respectable arguments for packing the boards of such enterprises with politicians lacking in business experience, as the Congress Party has done since 2004 (as did its Hindu nationalist predecessor). A seat on the board of a public enterprise can bring powers of patronage to allocate jobs and to win friends and influence. It also brings perks and status.

I once had a long conversation with the head of police for New Delhi about the number of cars that evaded normal traffic restrictions by putting a red or a blue light on the roof. New Delhi suffers from a permanent epidemic of VIPs. He told me that a majority of the car owners were not authorized to use VIP flashing lights. But his police, who are invariably junior in social status to the occupants of the car, felt unable to prevent it. The same system of discrimination can be observed at the dozens of road security checkpoints surrounding the capital. It is always the rickshaws, motorbikes, and freight trucks that get stopped by the police. The expensive cars are waved through. Few ordinary police constables would feel confident enough to challenge their social superiors.

In his excellent book *The Burden of Democracy,* Pratap Bhanu Mehta quotes Alexis de Tocqueville's observations on the existence of professional values in early America. To a nineteenth-century European, the relationship in America between master and servant was something new. "Within the terms of the contract one is servant and the other is master; beyond that they are two citizens and two men," wrote de Tocqueville. But in a traditional society such as India's, the ties between master and servant apply in all contexts. In India, "your *sahib* [master] remains a *sahib* whether in office or not," says Mehta.[21] What is unusual about India is the durability of feudal social ties in the context of a full democracy. It is a tension that is most visible in the Congress Party.

The Congress Party's love affair with the state is no longer strictly about socialism, to which few Congress Party members nowadays pay much lip service. It goes deeper than ideology. It is partly about status. And partly it is also about preferential access to a whole range of public goods, from free first-class plane and rail tickets, the opportunity to jump queues, the ability to pull strings, and the availability of free services for which the poor have to pay. Corruption, as we have seen, afflicts important public services in India such as food distribution. But it is also deeply integrated into the transactions of daily life.

I once bought a ticket to watch a big international cricket game between India and England at New Delhi's Ferozshah Kotla stadium. I was with two Indian friends. We had paid Rs 5,000 ($120) per ticket. We were denied entry to the ground, along with thousands of other valid ticket holders. The Delhi and District Cricket board, whose president, Arun Jaitley, was India's law minister at the time, had printed thousands of complimentary tickets for VIPs in a ground with a capacity of just 26,000. Mounted police charged an angry crowd that had been shut out of the cricket grounds to clear the way so that VIPs in white Ambassador cars who had not paid for their tickets could gain entry to the grounds. I wrote a letter to Jaitley complaining about our treatment, demanding a refund, and asking for an explanation. Thousands of Indians had paid a large sum of money for tickets to the game. Some had traveled by train overnight to see it. Jaitley's private secretary telephoned the following morning to convey his "profound apologies." He also offered me a complimentary ticket for the next big game. But the next game was between India and Zimbabwe—not the same thing at all. I turned him down.

Two years later, India was scheduled to play Pakistan in an exciting and diplomatically symbolic encounter in New Delhi. Both Pervez Musharraf, Pakistan's president, and Manmohan Singh were to attend the match. Having failed to get tickets by the normal commercial route, I had given up hope of attending the game. Then I received a telephone call from Jaitley. "I have not withdrawn my offer of a complimentary ticket for you," he said. Shamelessly, I accepted his offer. I also grabbed one for my wife. By this stage, I was more inured to New Delhi's ways. Once again thousands of others were stranded outside holding valid tickets. I learned later that Jaitley had been flooded with requests for free tickets from judges, cabinet ministers, and senior civil servants. Even Sonia Gandhi's family, including her children, Rahul and Priyanka, had requested and received free tickets. Of all the requests, only one, from Gursharan Kaur, Manmohan Singh's wife, had enclosed a check for the correct amount. This, unfortunately, is how New Delhi operates: if you are rich and important, you rarely pay. If you are poor, you usually pay through the nose, and there is no guarantee you will get what you pay for.

As for the Rural Employment Guarantee Act, it is difficult to accept at face value the Congress Party's claim that it is a good faith attempt to eliminate poverty in India once and for all. It is hard to see how a scheme that requires the poor to provide twelve hours or more of backbreaking physical labor each day for just $1 or $2 will transform their conditions. If you wander around India's provincial capitals, you see perfectly cropped gardens surrounding the large public buildings and official residences. Often you will see gangs of twenty or thirty laborers, squatting in rows on their haunches, moving gradually forward in a line, plucking the lawns with their bare hands. Inside the buildings, there will be dozens of sweepers, keeping their bodies at all times below yours, rearranging the dust in a posture of time-honored submission. Occasionally, you pause and ask yourself: Is this about employment? Or is it about reminding the sweepers and those for whom they sweep who possesses status in society and who does not?

•    •    •

It took several months of perseverance to get an appointment with Sonia Gandhi. For understandable reasons, Sonia has always been reluctant to speak on the record to the media. Her every word is scrutinized by her enemies for signs that she is not as Indian as she claims to be. Once Sonia told an interviewer, "Everything I have loved and lost has been in India." It would be hard to doubt her sincerity. But still the questions about her national loyalties persist. Naturally, Sonia is even more reluctant to speak to foreign journalists, in case her decision would be misconstrued as bias in favor of non-Indians.

I once met a group of Italian journalists who had flown to India specially to interview their former compatriot. I did not have the heart to tell them that they would be at the very bottom of her list. However, they did eventually get a two-minute introduction to Sonia Gandhi. They spoke to her in Italian. She replied in English.

During Sonia Gandhi's years of mourning between the death of Rajiv in 1991 and her acceptance of Congress Party leadership in 1998, even her smallest gesture would be interpreted and reinterpreted for signs of her intentions. A recent biographer, Yusuf Ahmed, said that Sonia Gandhi's "every utterance would make politicians and journalists draw meanings and construct parallels even where none was intended."[22] After Sonia became leader, it became important to be aware of who was supposedly close to Sonia and who was not. "Madam wishes it" was the stock phrase of the favored courtiers. A number of senior Congress Party leaders found this level of adulation unacceptable. "Coteries do not serve the party," said Jitendra Prasad,[23] who challenged Sonia for the leadership in 1999. "They encircle the leadership, insulate it from the workers, and block channels of communication. They misrepresent all discussions and differences as proof of disloyalty [to the family]." Prasad's bid for the leadership failed. Some of his supporters were beaten up by Sonia loyalists.

It is hard to believe Sonia Gandhi would sponsor or approve of such blind sycophancy. But the system is far bigger and older than she. Even her biographer, who has worked for the Congress Party but tries with some success to maintain an objective tone through most of his book, succumbs to an overblown assessment of Sonia Gandhi's talents. Opponents often criticize her for speaking in a wooden manner. They also complain that her Hindi is heavily accented. Her defenders compensate by likening her to a great modern orator. Sonia's biographer wrote: "Her cadences were balanced with an element of the bellicose, the pauses perfect, equipoise was flashed in abundance, and her words fell like seeds on a fertile and awaiting soil." Even Nehru, a great orator, might have been embarrassed by this.

Nehru would also have flinched at the great outpourings of public adulation Congress Party officials constantly offer up to Sonia. I once saw a Congress Party billboard in Chennai, with a large sepia-touched picture of Sonia Gandhi. "Our pride is Mother India," read the large caption. "Our guide is Mother Sonia." Shortly after the Congress Party returned to power in 2004, the party held a large rally in Delhi's Talkatora stadium to celebrate what would have been Rajiv's sixtieth birthday, had he still been alive. Delhi was flooded with billboards wishing Rajiv a happy birthday. For days, newspapers were dominated by brassy advertisements congratulating Rajiv and praising Sonia. "The Uttar Pradesh Congress Party wishes Rajiv Many Happy Returns!" said one double-page spread. "The Ministry of Rural Development [under a Congress Party minister] wishes felicitations to Rajiv on his sixtieth birthday," said another. The praise for Sonia's children is equally saccharine. At the convention in Delhi to celebrate Rajiv's birthday, one seasoned and widely respected cabinet minister took the microphone and started chanting: "Let Rahul and Priyanka take leadership positions!" A visibly embarrassed Sonia requested that the minister stop speaking. The prime minister, Manmohan, sat patiently and unnoticed in the audience.

My meeting with Sonia took place three months before the 2004 election, when most people were expecting another defeat for the Congress Party. I was with a senior colleague, whose visit to New Delhi helped secure the appointment. We waited for a short while in a small anteroom at Sonia Gandhi's official residence at 10 Janpath Road, a traditional Lutyens bungalow in central New Delhi. Then the door opened and Sonia Gandhi popped her head around. "Please come in," she said. I was surprised to see that Sonia was entirely alone. She took us into her study and we sat down on the sofa. "Can I pour you some tea?" she asked. In spite of myself, I could not help feeling awkward. It felt like Queen Elizabeth was offering to massage my feet. But Sonia appeared even more awkward in the situation. I looked around the room. It had been Rajiv's study before he died. Nothing, whether it was the décor, the gifts from foreign visitors, or the books in the cabinets, appeared to have been altered. A garland of flowers hung around a large picture of Rajiv on the wall. Afterward, my colleague said the room reminded him of the rooms of Miss Havisham, the character in the Dickens novel, *Great Expectations,* whose clocks were stopped at the exact time her fiancé died.

Strictly speaking, the one-hour interview was off the record. We wrote nothing in the newspaper. But enough time has elapsed to overlook this formality. And there was nothing that Sonia said that would cause her retrospective embarrassment. With hindsight Sonia's views seem prescient. At the time they appeared naïve. We asked whether her election campaign's focus on rural poverty would be enough to counter the BJP's "India Shining" campaign, which was dominating the airwaves and headlines. She spoke haltingly and shyly and kept asking us for the right word (we were talking in English) and thanking us when we offered one. But her meaning was clear. "If you travel around India, you see darkness and poverty in so many places," she said. "India is shining in the cities. But it is not shining in the villages, which is where most Indians live. I want the Congress Party to speak for them. Certainly I cannot predict that we will win. But I think the opinion polls are wrong. I travel around India all the time, and the message I have connects with the people I meet. What they say to me also confirms my views." She talked about the need to give the poor a greater stake in India's economic boom. And she denied that her party was opposed to further economic reform. The slogan the Congress Party later adopted was "Reform with a Human Face."

The conversation took a sharp change in direction when we asked Sonia how it felt to be the object of so much vituperation from the governing BJP. She had borne many deeply personal insults. Did she sometimes feel like packing it all in? Sonia took her time to answer. "You know politics does not come easily to me," she said. "I do not enjoy it. I do not even think I am very good at it. Politics killed my mother-in-law and it killed my husband. But when I saw what they were doing to India's secular culture, I felt I could no longer stand by and watch it happen without doing something. Secularism is the most important legacy of my family. I had to stand up and defend it. I could not watch them tear it apart." Sonia's eyes were brimming with tears. She was not sobbing. But there was intense sadness in her face. "What they say about me reflects upon them. I have gotten used to it. It doesn't matter at all." We both murmured our genuine sympathy. "Do you know what happened in Gujarat?" she asked. We said we did. "This was not India."

Three months later I saw Sonia again, although this time from the thick of a crowd of 50,000 people at a large rally in a park on the outer periphery of Chennai. There were just two days to go before the fourth and final phase of India's general election.* And it was only five days before the tally from all the phases would be counted and declared. There were two unusual elements to the rally. The first was that the Congress Party flag was just one among six different party flags. This was the party's first ever election in which it had struck an alliance with other parties. Sonia was also just one among several leaders on the platform, although clearly the most well known. Since we were in a Tamil-speaking part of the country, Sonia spoke in English, not Hindi. She paused every two minutes to allow a very theatrical translator to convert her words into Tamil. He took twice as long as Sonia and ended each rendition with a flourish. The second unusual aspect to the rally was Sonia's expression. She seemed relaxed and happy. She even laughed a few times, mostly when her Tamil interpreter was giving his animated translations. I wondered whether she had sensed the tide was turning against the BJP. Perhaps she was just getting better at doing public rallies.

There was a third unusual detail to the rally. One of the other parties represented on the podium was the Dravida Munnettra

*India's elections are staggered to enable the paramilitary forces to concentrate on different areas of potential instability, rather than spread themselves too thin for a one-phase poll. In contrast, the result is known within an hour or two of the counting since India's voting system is fully electronic and is collated by computer. It makes a pleasant contrast to Florida in 2000.

Kazhagam, a Tamil nationalist party, which had in the past expressed sympathies with the brutal "Tamil Tiger" separatist movement in the nearby island nation of Sri Lanka. It was a Tamil nationalist suicide bomber—a young woman called Dhanu—who had detonated the bomb that killed Rajiv and several others, including herself, in 1991. Rajiv had gotten India embroiled in the Sri Lankan conflict in 1987 by agreeing to send a peacekeeping force to the island. But it quickly turned into a partisan military presence and was involved in numerous clashes with the Tamil Tigers. Following Rajiv's assassination, the Congress Party had refused to have any dealings with the DMK because of its taint by association with Rajiv's killers. But Sonia had eventually agreed that electoral pragmatism should prevail. The Congress Party–led alliance won all forty of Tamil Nadu's parliamentary seats in the 2004 election. Most of the seats were won by the DMK.

Earlier on the day of the rally I had visited Sriperumbudur, the spot about thirty miles from Chennai where Rajiv had been killed. The site had been turned into a memorial. A plaque described how Rajiv was killed by Dhanu. The young woman was wearing a sari and there were flowers tied to her hair. She had bent down to touch the feet of Rajiv in a gesture of honor and submission. Then she had detonated the explosives that were strapped to her body beneath the sari. "So too on another occasion, another assassin bent to touch the feet of the Mahatma," said the plaque. During the rally that evening in 2004, Sonia mentioned the killing of her husband. In a phrase she had used before, Sonia said: "I stand here on the soil that is mingled with the blood of my husband. And I can assert that there would be no greater honor for me than to share his fate for the sake of our country." Not for the first time I reflected that for Sonia the political is very personal.

•    •    •

There is much clear blue water dividing the Congress Party from the BJP. One of the most overlooked distinguishing features is the Congress Party's flexibility. The BJP, on occasions, dilutes its message for tactical reasons. But everybody knows what it believes in. It is often a struggle, on the other hand, to work out what it is the Congress Party believes in nowadays. This is both a weakness and a strength. It is a weakness because it is more difficult for the Congress Party to marshal party workers behind a clearly defined cause, other than adulation of the Nehru-Gandhi dynasty. But it can also be an advantage because it gives the party room to experiment with different strategies in the states that it governs. In some states, such as Andhra Pradesh, in India's south, the Congress Party rules in the traditional style, promising much to the poor, while lining the pockets of the well connected. But in other states, the party is led by reformist chief ministers who have tried to change the way the game is played.

One of the Congress Party's most impressive local leaders is Sheila Dikshit, who is chief minister of New Delhi, the equivalent of mayor. New Delhi is one of the world's largest cities, with a population of 15 million. It adds one million people every three years. It is India's largest or second largest city, depending on where you draw the boundary. The other is Mumbai, which, to illustrate the point, is governed by one of the most inept Congress Party administrations in the country. Partly as a result of the contrasting qualities of the two cities, New Delhi has overtaken Mumbai as a magnet for new investment in the last few years. New Delhi is also the wealthiest part of India with an average personal income double the national average. In the 1990s few Indians would have hesitated if asked where they would prefer to live. Their answer would have been Mumbai. Now the answers would probably be more evenly split. Some credit should go to Sheila Dikshit.

Like Sonia Gandhi, Dikshit is a widow. Her husband, an IAS officer, died young. Like her leader, Dikshit is also part of a dynasty. Her father-in-law was a Congress Party member and her son, Sandeep Dikshit, is a member of the national parliament for a New Delhi constituency. This has become increasingly normal in the Congress Party. Dynasty is not confined to the Nehru-Gandhis. Often when a senior

Congress Party member retires or dies one of his offspring inherits the constituency. The Congress Party has also helped normalize dynastic behavior in much broader areas of Indian society. Inder Malhotra, a former editor of the *Times of India* and a biographer of south Asia's dynastic families, says that only two senior positions in Indian public life—the governor of the central bank and the army chief of staff—are untainted by nepotism. Many people who attack the Nehru-Gandhi dynasty are living in glass houses, says Malhotra. He talks of the "yawning gap between the words and deeds of the chattering classes that are most active in deploring the cult of dynasties." He continues: "Most such people go to great lengths to promote their own progeny in all walks of life."[24]

But in other respects Dikshit is unusual for a Congress Party politician. She talks candidly about the corruption afflicting her administration and complains loudly about the limitations of politics. I asked her why in so many parts of New Delhi rubbish is left to fester on the streets in the summer heat. "It is a question I struggle with every day," she said. "We have thousands of sanitation workers in New Delhi who often don't turn up to work and there's nothing I can do about it. I have tried to introduce mechanization but they resist it because they think it threatens their jobs. You have to introduce change slowly in India. You have to take circuitous routes."

She has similar problems reforming New Delhi's water services. In spite of having a relatively good water supply of more than fifty-three gallons a day per person, most of New Delhi receives little or no water. The poor often have to pay private water truckers—the so-called "water mafia"—to get their supply. The water bills that New Delhi's residents pay do not even cover 10 percent of the cost of delivery. Naturally there are no funds to extend access to the slums. Since most of the supply goes to the middle class, the poor are effectively subsidizing the water supply to the rich. New Delhi's water board has fifteen times as many employees per kilometer of water pipe than the average for a city in an industrialized country. These employees form a powerful vested interest against change.

When Dikshit asked the World Bank to advise her on a plan to contract out water distribution to a private company, she was accused of fleecing the poor. The World Bank was also accused of interfering with what it characterized as a flawed bidding process in order to ensure that PricewaterhouseCoopers, the U.S. consulting firm, won the advisory contract over a number of local firms. Clearly the World Bank had breached its own guidelines, which was both inept and politically naïve, considering the strength of feeling against the Bretton Woods institution. But it seemed overblown to accuse Dikshit of "caving in to the forces of neo-liberalism."[25] When Dikshit increased water bills quite independently of the World Bank controversy, there were similar accusations. In a pattern that is familiar to India, the protests were carried out in the name of the poor, in spite of the fact that the poor would appear to be the victims of the status quo.

Dikshit's troubles show how difficult it is to reform the state in India. Yet it is still possible, even in New Delhi. In March 2004 Dikshit opened the first eleven-mile stretch of the New Delhi Metro, a mostly underground rail network that, by the time it is completed in 2015, will have 225 stations covering almost every corner of India's sprawling capital. Infrastructure leaps such as this can transform a city. The project, which had extended to almost fifty stations by 2006, was consistently ahead of schedule. And the rail service was clean, efficient, and punctual. It stood as a shining antidote to the often tardy, corrupt, and shoddy infrastructure projects elsewhere in India. The New Delhi Metro is a public-private partnership, partly funded by Japanese and German soft loans and managed at arm's length from day-to-day government interference. Dikshit has gone to great lengths to ensure that the public corporation retains operational independence. "Nobody calls me asking for favors," said E. Sreedharan, managing director of the New Delhi Metro. "I do not have to kowtow to anybody. That is why we are consistently ahead of schedule. This is a model of how you should manage the public sector in India. It is not written in the stars that it should fail." Although the Metro could only have been constructed with the benefit of soft loans and subsidies—as has been the case with almost every single mass transit system built in the developed world—it is expected to help multiply the city's economic boom over the coming years.

Dikshit was also involved in a successful drive to clean up New Delhi's choking air quality by converting all public transport, including motorized rickshaws, to compressed natural gas (CNG)—a big environmental improvement on the diesel engines that were replaced. New Delhi's air particle pollution count has fallen by 30 percent since 1999, when the change was introduced. As with the Metro, Dikshit was just one player in a coalition of interests pushing for the change, including the Center for Science and Environment, an advocacy body, and India's Supreme Court, which delivered the ultimate ruling mandating CNG. But when political leaders in India choose not to get involved in the solution, they inevitably become part of the problem. Dikshit is also unusual in having been reelected for a second five-year term in December 2003, in a country where governments only rarely continue beyond one term.

New Delhi's problems are legion. The city is clogged with dirty slums, very few of which get proper public services. But unlike Mumbai, which has yet to agree on a modern mass transit system, New Delhi has at least taken some steps, however small, to address its problems. As Sanjay Gandhi showed during the state of emergency in the 1970s, not only does simply throwing slum dwellers out of the city violate human rights, but it does not work either. People find a way of coming back in larger numbers. It is estimated that by 2026,[26] New Delhi will be one of a handful of global megacities with a population of thirty million or more. "This is a vast, impossible city," says Dikshit. "In my job you have to run and run in the hope you might stand still." She concedes that the more infrastructure is improved, and the more jobs New Delhi can generate (in addition to the many it has created in recent years), the more people will want to move there. Already India's internal migration flows have shifted from Mumbai in favor of the capital. It is a catch-22. "We have no choice but to make our cities more livable and more attractive, even if that proves self-defeating," says Dikshit.

Congress Party–controlled state governments in other parts of India are not as fortunate as New Delhi, whose electorate is overwhelmingly urban. In 2004 the mostly rural voters of Andhra Pradesh ejected their state government. The Congress Party–controlled government of Karnataka, of which Bangalore is the capital, was forced into an uneasy coalition with a local party. In January 2006 the Congress Party was ejected when its local coalition partner joined forces with the opposition BJP to form a new coalition in Karnataka. The Congress Party just clung to power in Maharashtra, of which Mumbai is capital. In all three cases, politicians interpreted the results as a sign of electoral impatience with the growing gap between rural and urban living standards. The new state governments put most urban infrastructure projects on the back burner. In the case of Bangalore, India's software capital, the state government's indifference to the city's growing congestion problems is beginning to result in the diversion of new IT investments to other cities such as New Delhi, Pune, Chennai, and Chandigarh.

In Hyderabad, the perceived rural backlash is even greater. Y. S. Reddy, the Congress Party chief minister of Andhra Pradesh, came to power in May 2004 (Andhra Pradesh's state election was held at the same time as national polls), having promised free electricity to all farmers. He unseated the Telugu Desam Party, a local-language party led by Chandrababu Naidu, who had been widely feted in the local and international media as "Mr. IT" for his successful efforts in attracting software investment to the city. Google's India headquarters is in Hyderabad. Other companies, including Microsoft and Sun Microsystems, have large research centers there. Naidu had even befriended Bill Clinton, who had visited Hyderabad on his presidential trip to India in 2000. Naidu was also a regular at the annual conference of global economic leaders in Davos, Switzerland. He was a poster child of economic reformers. Much of Naidu's reputation was overdone, and he did very little in office to improve opportunities for the state's farmers, or to reduce notorious levels of corruption in his own party. He was also a hate figure among those opposed to reform—again, with some exaggeration, since there was little he could do about the four straight years of drought Andhra Pradesh had suffered before the election. Thousands of farmers in the state had committed suicide because they were unable to service their debts when their crops failed.

Naidu's defeat was interpreted as a sign that Hyderabad's booming successes had come at the expense of the poor in the thousands of villages spread out across this large state. But the electoral picture was more complicated than that. Although the Congress Party ran a campaign on behalf of the rural poor, the secret to its success was an alliance with a local party that wants to break off a chunk of Andhra Pradesh to create a separate state. The Congress Party's vote share fell. But because of the electoral pact, it swept to power with a two-thirds majority. The Congress Party also struck a thinly concealed deal with a local group of Maoist insurgents, called the Naxalites, who control large tracts of the state. The Naxalites, named after the town of Naxalbari in the state of West Bengal, where they first launched their Maoist insurgency in the 1960s, had come within a whisker of assassinating Chandrababu Naidu in a bomb attack in 2003. During the 2004 campaign the Naxalites targeted and killed several candidates in Naidu's party. But they left the Congress Party alone. Shortly after the election, they got their reward. Y. S. Reddy, the new Congress Party chief minister, declared a unilateral cease-fire with the rebels and promised peace talks. Within a year the process had collapsed, as almost all observers had predicted it would. But the Naxalites, now known as the Communist Party of India (Maoist-Leninist), used the interlude profitably to regroup and rearm. "The Naxalites are playing a long game with pauses and strategic retreats," said Jayaprakash Narayan, who runs Lok Satta, a widely respected think tank in Hyderabad. "The Congress Party was playing a very short-term game to win the election."

Nor was Reddy's promise of free electricity to farmers all that it seemed. Under Naidu, farmers had paid only a fraction of the true cost of the power they received—about 8 percent. And only the richest farmers, who possessed electricity connections, had benefited from the subsidy. They had used the electricity to pump water from the ground, pushing the water table farther and farther from the reach of farmers who could afford neither electricity-driven nor diesel-fueled water pumps. Waiving the remaining small electricity bill has only exacerbated the tough conditions for the poorer farmers. Reddy, the chief minister, is himself a rich farmer with no fewer than thirty electricity connections on his farm. The cost of free power to farmers adds up to more than the state's spending on primary health care and education combined. Reddy's election campaign was a textbook example of the Congress Party's skill at using the smoke-screen of pro-poor rhetoric to achieve more crude objectives.

A few months after the election I visited Reddy in his office at the state secretariat in Hyderabad. I asked him what he was doing to provide irrigation to the poor farmers. A large man with an equally large mustache, Reddy was every inch the local satrap. The rooms and corridors outside his office resembled a bustling railway station with dozens of local supplicants awaiting the chance to ask a favor of their chief minister. "Every detail is being taken care of," he replied to my question. And what are the details? I asked. "Everything is possible," he said. What was possible? "Every little detail." Can you provide me with some? "In time, we will fix everything," he said. And so on. At one stage during this singularly uninformative interview, Reddy started scrambling around for a bit of paper. His secretary handed him something. "Yes," he said, reading it. "Sir Arthur Cotton built lots of irrigation for the farmers in this area. He was British. You are British." But what are *you* doing? "We are doing everything possible to ensure irrigation gets to the farmers."

In a slightly more informative interview with Chandrababu Naidu later, the former chief minister alleged that Reddy's election campaign had been funded by building contractors who had been promised large irrigation projects in return. He produced charts and documents to illustrate his allegations. At the time of writing, very few of Reddy's irrigation investments have come on stream. As a seasoned political operator, Naidu could well have been manipulating the facts; I was unable to verify his accusations. And Reddy still has time to deliver. During my interview with Reddy I also asked whether Sonia Gandhi had been involved in his plans. "Madam is very happy," he said. "She approves of everything."

It is a stock phrase of the Congress Party. Its sole remaining organizing principle is the Nehru-Gandhi dynasty. Without the family—and "Madam Sonia's" approval—no Congress Party politician can get very far. But beyond that, the absence of a binding party ideology provides a cover for all sorts of experiments—good and bad—to take place in the many parts of India that the Congress Party continues to rule. At the national level, the Congress Party occupies an awkward position somewhere between the poles of *Mandir* and Mandal, occasionally adopting elements of one or other program, yet remaining unable to dictate the direction of Indian politics.

As for the future of the Nehru-Gandhi family, it is not yet clear how much appetite Rahul and Priyanka have for the hard realities of Indian politics. Nor is it clear how good they are at fending off the sycophants or inuring themselves to the vituperation from which Sonia has suffered in such large doses. Shortly after the 2004 election, a tearful Priyanka, who bears a striking resemblance to her grandmother, Indira, said: "We have never owned our family. We always had to share our parents with the nation." Rahul, who had just been elected a first-time member of parliament, said only this about the BJP's campaign to tarnish his mother: "These guys are a bunch of jokers."

So far Rahul has not played a very prominent role in parliament. Nor has he yet become much involved, as he said he would, in the Congress Party's drive to restore its fortunes in Uttar Pradesh, India's largest state and the home of the Nehru-Gandhi dynasty. Both he and his mother won thundering majorities in their Uttar Pradesh constituencies and drew huge adoring crowds wherever they spoke. But the Congress Party failed to win almost all of the neighboring constituencies. The family magic was confined to a very narrow base.

At some stage in the next five to ten years, it seems likely Rahul will become leader of the Congress Party and possibly even prime minister. His mother, who has signaled ambivalence about her children's future roles in politics—hoping for their success yet fearing for their safety—will presumably retreat into the background. Then the light will shine on Rahul. (Priyanka declined to run for parliament in 2004 but she campaigned for her mother and brother.) Sometime in the future, the light will also start to shine on the next crop of Nehru-Gandhis* as the family moves into a sixth generation.

The story of the Nehru-Gandhis is a long one, stretching back to the late nineteenth century, and it looks set to extend well into the twenty-first century. To many in the villages and in the fields of India, it is the political narrative that best links their feudal past to a democratic present and, it is to be hoped, a more prosperous future. As for the Gandhi dynasty, it shows no signs of losing its appetite for the limelight. Rahul is now at the center of a continuing drama that offers fairy-tale glory and adulation. He has to fend off sycophants wherever he goes. He will also have to try—difficult as it might be—to ignore the possibility of that assassin's bullet.

---

*According to constant Indian media reports, Rahul has a Spanish girlfriend, Veronique, who has only very rarely been photographed with him in public. It is presumed she is Catholic, and, if they were to marry, her religion would entail inevitable political risks for Rahul.

# 6. MANY CRESCENTS

South Asia's Divided Muslims

*I have not done well to the country or to the people, and of the future there is no hope.*

AURANGZEB, the last great Mughal emperor, and the
most controversial, in a deathbed letter to his son
in 1707[1]

I had not realized it was possible. But the mullahs of Deoband, the center of Islamic orthodoxy in south Asia, had managed to circumvent a fatwa (Islamic ruling) out of courtesy to me. They did it so that I could drink a cup of coffee. I was visiting Dar-ul-Uloom—the House of Knowledge—a large Islamic school in the town of Deoband, about ninety miles north of New Delhi. It was early October 2001 and the madrasa was buzzing with anti-American sentiment. The United States was about to start its bombing of the Taliban regime in Afghanistan. The Taliban—deriving from *Talib,* which is Urdu for "student"—belong to the Deoband school of Islam. Although few senior Taliban had visited Deoband, they saw it as their spiritual headquarters. I was sitting on the ground in the study

of Maulana (an honorific given to learned Muslim men) Abdul Kha-
lik Madrasi, vice-chancellor of Deoband, with a group of his students. They were telling me that Christians should make an alliance
with Muslims against the Jews, who were the real troublemakers. It
was Zionists, they said, who had organized the plane attacks on the
Twin Towers in New York a few weeks earlier. It was useless arguing.

The burly Maulana, whose beard almost reached down to his ro-
tund belly, then asked if I wanted a refreshment. I said I would like a
Nescafé, which is the only kind of coffee usually available in north India outside the cities. "No, no," he said sternly. "We have issued a
fatwa forbidding the faithful from buying any American or British
products." I tried in vain to argue that I was not one of the faithful so
the fatwa should not apply to me. They laughed it off. Then I tried
and failed to convince them that Nescafé is owned by Nestlé, which is
a Swiss company. But they had either never heard of Switzerland or
could not see the difference. In much of India the word *Angrezi*—English—simply means "foreign," or "Western." No, they said, wagging their fingers, as if they had caught me pulling a fast one, Nescafé
is Angrezi. Then something occurred to the Maulana, who was a
member of the committee that issues Deobandi fatwas. "I have
thought of a legitimate loophole," the Maulana announced with a
smile. "The fatwa applies only to products bought after September
11. Does anyone here possess Nescafé that is older?" A student raised
his hand. The mildewed sachet of instant coffee that he fetched from
his room considerably predated 9/11. It was one of the most satisfy-
ing coffees I have ever had.

Deoband was founded in the aftermath of the failed Sepoy Mutiny
against the British by rebel Indian regiments in 1857. Known in
India as the First War of Independence, the uprising was brutally quashed by the British. The Indian rebels were vicious in their
methods, killing many of the colonial women and children they
encountered. In revenge the British laid waste to much of north India, burning villages and leaving hundreds strung up from trees along

the main highways. Lacking a clear strategy and credible leadership, the rebel soldiers had placed the aging and wholly titular last Mughal emperor, Bahadur Shah Zafar, at its head. Partly as a result, the British blamed Muslims more than others for the mutiny and targeted symbols of Islam in the reprisals that followed. Parts of Mughal Delhi were destroyed or vandalized. Delhi's great Jama Masjid—the largest mosque in India—became a camping ground for one of the Sikh regiments that had helped the British defeat the rebels. Prominent Muslim nobles and rebels remained in hiding for years. For them, it was a time of despair. The suppression of the Sepoy Mutiny was an emphatic and crushing finale to the era of Islamic dynasties in India.

The response to this defeat by India's Muslim intelligentsia was deeply split. One group, led by Sir Sayyid Ahmad Khan, saw reconciliation as the only practical option. But Sir Sayyid's decision to make an accommodation with the British was also motivated by his fear of what would happen to Muslims in an independent India with a majority Hindu population. Sir Sayyid's expectations of democracy in India were bleak. "It would be like a game of dice, in which one man had four dice and the other man one."[2] In 1875 Sir Sayyid founded the Aligarh Muslim University, which chose English as its medium of instruction and included modern science prominently on its syllabus. Many of Aligarh's graduates went on to join the imperial civil service. Later they would provide much of the vanguard of elite Muslims who led the movement to establish the nation of Pakistan.

The other group, led by two Islamic scholars, Hazrat Nanautavi and Rashid Ahwad Gangoli, saw the failure of the mutiny and its bloody aftermath as a sign that Muslims should return to first principles. Maulana Nanautavi's followers believed the downfall of Indian Islam had been brought about by the sybaritic habits of courtly life under the Mughals. Muslims had also been weakened over the previous two or three centuries by adopting too many customs of the Hindu idol-worshipping majority.[3] The simple Arabian message of the Prophet had been forgotten. Maulana Nanautavi established the school of Dar-Ul-Uloom in Deoband in 1866 to offer despairing Muslims a "shore-less ocean for seekers of knowledge."⁴ It would retreat from the world of unbelievers into a world of certainties.

Very few Deobandis approved of the idea of Pakistan, which was first raised in the 1930s. As a separate nation-state, Pakistan was seen as a divisive prospect since it would artificially split the *Ummah*, or community of believers. Some Deobandis were persuaded to join the Congress Party–led freedom movement in 1919 by Gandhi, who grasped the opportunity presented by the British occupation of the Arabian peninsula following the British victory over the Ottoman Empire in the First World War. There was much Muslim, and particularly Deobandi Muslim, outrage over the presence of the infidel British in the holy lands. Gandhi's endorsement of the Indian Khilafat movement to restore the Muslim caliphate, which had been abolished after Turkey emerged from the Ottoman ruins, instilled in the Congress Party a habit of tactical opportunism toward Indian Muslims that still remains. Little else could explain Gandhi's decision to associate the Indian freedom struggle with a purely religious controversy about the fleeting custody of faraway Mecca and Medina. Believing it was wrong to mix religious faith with politics, Mohammed Ali Jinnah, leader of the Muslim League, who would become Pakistan's first head of state nearly thirty years later, resigned from the Congress Party in disgust. Few Deobandis approved of Jinnah, who drank whisky, ate pork, and was hardly ever seen in a mosque. It was only in the early 1940s that Jinnah swapped his impeccably tailored London suits for an elegant *Sherwani* (tunic) and black cap.

The school of Deoband is a mix of the ramshackle and the splendid, little changed from when it was built. The architecture of the interlocking courtyards and mosque is an unusual combination of classical Islamic and Gothic. I was put up in one of the madrasa's guest rooms and endured an unpleasant night of persecution by cockroaches and mosquitoes. The school has 3,000 students, most of them from poor Muslim families, who are boarded and educated almost entirely for free. Some are sent to Deoband at just five years of age. The boys stay until their teens or twenties. Their day begins with the first *namaaz* at dawn and is punctuated throughout by the call to prayer. Almost the entire syllabus dates to Europe's medieval period. The only science and mathematics taught is "Islamic" and stops with the Ptolemaic system of astronomy rather than the Copernican system that replaced it several hundred years ago. Students are principally taught Arabic, Persian, and Urdu so they can read the Koran and the commentaries in their original language. Much like the regime the Taliban established in most of Afghanistan between 1996 and 2001, Deoband permits little color, music, or celebration, beyond the Islamic festivals.

Yet, unlike the Taliban, or the Deobandis of neighboring Pakistan, who have their own political party, the Jamiat-e-Ulema Islam, which runs the government of Pakistan's North-West Frontier Province with puritanical zeal, India's Deobandis are scrupulously apolitical— at least when it comes to India. "We are good Indian nationalists and good citizens," said the Maulana. Who would they support if India went to war with a Muslim country, such as Pakistan? "We would prefer it not to happen, but we would not betray India," said the students, after some discussion. Were they Indians first, or Muslims first? "We are both," said the Maulana. "There is no contradiction." I mentioned some outrages committed by the Taliban including the destruction earlier that year of the ancient Buddhist statues at Bamiyan in central Afghanistan. My question created a noticeable awkwardness. The Maulana said: "These people in the Taliban are Pathans [an Afghan ethnic group from which the Taliban were principally drawn]. Pathan culture is much more fierce than Indian culture. You would be wrong to confuse the excesses of Pathan culture with Deoband. We do not have a patent on the word *Deoband*."

I related the criticisms of Deoband that I had heard from many nonpracticing Muslims living in India's cities. They said that Deoband and the hundreds of Deobandi madrasas around India, which are often founded and staffed by graduates of Dar-Ul-Uloom, produce students who are poorly equipped to cope with the modern world. Most are unable to get decent employment since the only science, math, and languages they know are confined to an Arabian golden age that has long since passed into history. In today's Indian job market you need modern technical skills, such as computing and up-to-date financial literacy. "Learning Arabic or Persian does not close the mind," they responded. "It opens up a large world of untold riches of which you know nothing." I admitted the point. And what jobs would they go on to do? There was some murmuring. Their answers were unclear. One or two wanted to become Urdu-language broadcasters or interpreters. My guess was that a large proportion would become teachers in madrasas.

But the bulk of the discussion, which alternated between heated and friendly, was about the looming war in Afghanistan, which was the cause of great excitement among the students. They assumed it would result in a Taliban victory. The Maulana, who had a certain rhetorical flair, spoke more than the others. "What do Americans believe in?" he asked. "The believe in nothing. They live for nothing, except themselves. They have no discipline over their lives. In Afghanistan, the Taliban has restored law and order. Do you know that not one graduate of Deoband has ever committed a rape?" It seemed like a bold assertion, since Dar-Ul-Uloom says it has produced 60,000 graduates in the last 140 years. I asked whether he believed all women should wear the burka—the full veil. "Yes, we recommend all women should cover themselves but only for their own safety," he said. "Before the Angrezis came to India, even Hindu women wore the burka." In fact, many Hindu women still cover themselves in the villages of north India. But did this make society stronger? Did it really improve the behavior of men? "All you are taught in your schools in the West is worldly education. There are no ethics in your society. There is only self-indulgence. Do you know why the Taliban are unafraid of the American soldiers?" asked the Maulana. He paused for the punch line. "Because American soldiers are like children. They even eat chocolate." There was much laughter. As it turned out, the United States outsourced much of the eviction of the Taliban to the Northern Alliance.*

•    •    •

After independence in 1947, India's Muslim population lived under a cloud of suspicion. It has never entirely lifted. After partition, which many in India saw as a national "vivisection," the country was in a state of turmoil. India had been wracked by the violence both of partition, in which between half a million and a million people were slaughtered, and the "Great Killings" of Calcutta in August 1946 when Jinnah declared a Direct Action Day, to show the Congress Party the futility of opposing the new nation. When asked about the implicit threat of violence behind Direct Action Day, which left the streets running with blood, Jinnah said: "I am not prepared to discuss ethics."[5] Jinnah had arguably already won Pakistan in 1939 when Lord Linlithgow, the British viceroy, effectively recognized Jinnah's Muslim League as the sole spokesman of all Muslims in British India in return for Jinnah's support for India's participation in the Second World War. The Congress Party had refused to back the war unless it was consulted before war was declared on India's behalf. Linlithgow had announced India's entry into the war without even informing the Congress Party. In retrospect—and even at the time—the viceroy appeared to have made a monumental blunder. Both Nehru and Gandhi were strongly opposed to Nazism and they were fearful of an expansionist Japan. Both would have probably supported the war, if they had been explicitly consulted before its declaration. "How can India fight for democracy if she herself does not have it?" asked Nehru.[6]

*The Northern Alliance consisted of a group of former mujahideen fighters drawn principally from the Tajik Afghan ethnic group and backed by several powers in the late 1990s including the United States, Russia, and Iran. The Taliban were overwhelmingly Pathan.

Even after Linlithgow had snubbed the Congress Party and pushed it into a stance of opposing India's participation in the war, Gandhi asked Indian soldiers to remain at their posts. Nehru, who had needed only a symbolic request from the British to secure his support for India's involvement in the struggle against fascism, said that he would still fight to defend India from the invading Japanese. He would even fight to defend India from the widely expected invasion by the Indian National Army (INA), a group of Indian soldiers who had defected to the Japanese under the leadership of Subhash Chandra Bose, a former Congress Party leader. The INA got bogged down along with its Japanese overlords in the jungles of Burma and never invaded India. Nehru made sure that no officer who had fought under the INA flag during the war was reinstated in the Indian army after independence.[7]

Some Indians trace the creation of Pakistan as far back as 1909 when Lord Minto, the viceroy, established "communal electorates"— reserved constituencies for religious groups—at the same time that he granted limited provincial democracy to propertied Indians. The move, which was presented by the British as a necessary measure to ensure India's largest minority got a fair voice in the debating chambers, helped to embed minority politics in Indian democracy at a very early stage. It ensured there would be a Muslim party that would appeal only to Muslims. That party would have little incentive to speak for, or to, anyone else. "Separate electorates . . . enabled government to work a system of political control which in large part could ignore Congress," according to Francis Robinson, a leading historian of that era.[8] Between 1909 and 1947, the British went out of their way to detach Muslims from the Congress Party. Prominent Muslim members of the party were subjected to particularly close harassment by the authorities. In contrast, Jinnah did not spend a single night in jail. Nehru and Gandhi each spent a decade or so behind bars. I have read many accounts by British writers arguing that Britain was motivated by the noble aim of protecting Muslims from a majority Hindu culture. But over the years Britain did a great

deal to stoke the divisions from which it claimed to be protecting its supposed victims. The generous account of Britain's actions is
hard to sustain in light of the facts. It is clear Britain was hoping to
prolong its rule of India by exacerbating political divisions between
Indians.

But even if the British had originally established the "communal
awards" (separate electorates) in good faith, this effort could not disguise Britain's main purpose as the story unfolded. In 1931 Britain
invited Indian groups to London for a roundtable conference on India's future. Gandhi submitted a list of the Congress Party delegates
he wished to bring with him. The British struck all Muslim names off
the Congress Party list.[9] In 1936 the British held India's first full-
blown provincial elections. The Congress Party won more than half
the vote in the most important state, the United Provinces (later to
become Uttar Pradesh). Jinnah's Muslim League won fewer than half
the Muslim-reserved seats, garnering just 4.4 percent of the vote in
India as a whole.[10]

Some historians, particularly from Pakistan, date the inevitability
of the creation of Pakistan to the aftermath of the provincial elections in 1937 when a triumphant Congress Party refused to enter
into coalition with the Muslim League in the United Provinces. Jinnah's party had won less than a quarter of all seats in the province
and his price of entering into a coalition was that the Congress Party
recognize the Muslim League as the sole spokesman of all Muslims.
This was outrageous, since there were many Muslim members of the
Congress Party and many more who had voted for it. In spite of this,
some people argue that the Congress Party made a tactical error in
spurning the Muslim League's coalition overtures. An opportunity to
defang India's largest communal party was lost. Yet Nehru felt that
if the Congress Party agreed to a coalition with the Muslim League,
it might also have inflamed the Hindu communalists whom he saw
as a growing threat to an independent (and united) India.

What Jinnah lacked in popular support was more than compen-
sated for by the patronage of the British. In December 1939, after

Jawaharlal Nehru and Mahatma Gandhi in conversation, 1946 *(Empics)*

Sonia Gandhi and her son Rahul at the twenty-first anniversary of the death of Indira Gandhi *(Empics)*

Indira, 1979. The most formidable and ruthless leader India has yet seen *(Getty Images)*

Manmohan Singh, India's understated Prime Minister
*(Olivia Arthur)*

An Indian soldier launches a rocket at armed Muslim militants along the
Line of Control, November 2001 *(Getty Images)*

Pakistan's President General Musharraf, September 2001 *(Reuters/Corbis)*

Indian tanks parade on Republic Day, January 26, 2000 *(Reuters/Corbis)*

Indian policemen form a security cordon around supporters of the
Bharatiya Janata Party (BJP) at a political rally *(Emmanuel Dunand/AFP/Getty Images)*

Delhi's new
metro, September
2005 *(Getty Images)*

Muslim women talk on their mobile phones outside a McDonald's restaurant
*(Sohail Akbar)*

Old India: villagers draw water at a well *(Getty Images)*

Bollywood megastar Amitabh Bachchan (far left) dances with Aishwarya Rai, Mumbai's leading lady, and his son Abhishek Bachchan *(Empics)*

One of modern India's young couples *(Olivia Arthur)*

Manmohan Singh and his wife, Gursharan Kaur,
with President George W. Bush and Laura Bush *(Corbis)*

Jinnah had signed on to the war effort, he got his reward. In protest at the British declaration of war on India's behalf, all the Congress Party provincial governments, including that of the United Provinces, resigned. Jinnah celebrated by declaring "Deliverance Day." In March 1940, a few months later, Jinnah proclaimed the "Pakistan Resolution" in Lahore—the first time he had openly called for a separate country. But the Muslim League continued to lack popular support. Right up until the brink of Pakistan's creation, Jinnah's party drew most of its backing from Muslim landowners and urban elites. "What is really the religious or the communal problem is really a dispute among upper-class people for a division of the spoils of office or of representation in the legislature,"[11] said Nehru. Many Indians would agree with M. J. Akbar, Nehru's biographer and an impressive Indian Muslim thinker, who wrote: "Pakistan was a chimera created by an artificially induced hatred."[12] Naturally, few Pakistanis would sign on to this interpretation.

But history turned out the way it did. And so India entered into independence with a large Muslim minority, many of whom went through the conundrum of watching close family members migrate to Pakistan forever. Though their decision to remain in India ought to have put Indian Muslims beyond suspicion, their loyalties were constantly called into question by Hindu communalists and others. Equally, Indian Muslims who migrated to Pakistan from provinces such as Bihar, Uttar Pradesh, and elsewhere are still known in early-twenty-first-century Pakistan as *mohajirs,* or "immigrants." Their status remains decidedly second-class. It is a terrible irony of partition that the Muslims who remained behind in India, and those who left for Pakistan, should have as good a claim as any other to being true Indians and true Pakistanis respectively, given the sacrifices they made. Yet the former are subject to more suspicion about their patriotic loyalties than is any other group in India. And the latter are largely denied access to the power centers of modern Pakistan, not least the Pakistan army. The contradictions of partition have yet to die out.

There was another British legacy that continues to bedevil relations in the subcontinent today and occasionally threatens broader regional stability: the disputed status of Kashmir. Apologists for British imperialism say the epithet of "divide and rule" was unfair. Their view was that in fact "Indians divided, Britain ruled." India, they say, was already deeply divided and the religious divide in particular was not a British invention. There is truth in both points of view. But few would dispute the view that Britain withdrew from India in great haste and with much ineptitude. This is not the book to assess the details of Britain's departure. But there are some aspects to partition that continue to haunt the subcontinent sixty years later.

Under the terms of partition, Lord Mountbatten, the last viceroy, persuaded a reluctant Nehru that the colony's several hundred princely states should decide for themselves one by one which of the two countries they would join. In most cases it was academic, since the maharajah or nizam in question belonged to the same religion as his subjects. But in three cases—those of Junagadh, Hyderabad, and Kashmir—the ruler's loyalties were contradicted by the religion of the majority of his population. In the case of Hyderabad, this divergence was particularly impractical, since the state was geographically nowhere near either East Pakistan (which had been East Bengal, and which in 1971 became Bangladesh), or West Pakistan, which consisted of Sindh, the North-West Frontier Province, Balochistan, and about half of Punjab. At one point in 1948, the Muslim nizam of Hyderabad looked to be on the verge of declaring for Pakistan. Within forty-eight hours Vallabhbhai Patel, India's home minister, had flooded the principality with Indian soldiers. Pakistan protested. But Hyderabad's absorption into India could hardly be reversed. Much the same happened in Junagadh, where a Muslim prince overrode the sympathies of his Hindu subjects and declared for Pakistan. Again the territory was absorbed into India.

The Valley of Kashmir proved more problematic for India. Not only was it a Muslim-majority province that was ruled by a Hindu prince, Maharajah Hari Singh. It also bordered the Pakistani province of Punjab, so its absorption into Pakistan would have been feasible. However, according to the Indians, this would have left India unacceptably exposed, since the state straddles a vital Himalayan high ground of the subcontinent. Kashmir would also be India's only Muslim-majority province, a point of overriding strategic importance for a Congress Party government that wished to burnish its secular credentials. Finally, Nehru had a deep emotional attachment: his family had originally come from Kashmir and he had spent many summer holidays there.

To the growing frustration of both Jinnah and Nehru, the maharajah of Kashmir vacillated hopelessly over which country he should join. They suspected with good reason that he wanted to declare Kashmir's independence from both India and Pakistan. The maharajah finally signed the instrument of accession of Kashmir to India in October 1947 as thousands of Pakistani guerrilla fighters were streaming into the state. The Pakistan "volunteers" were rapidly approaching Srinagar, the capital, when the maharajah formally joined Kashmir to India.[13] Nehru immediately airlifted Indian troops to Srinagar where they managed to defend the city and prevent the mostly Afridi Pakistan tribesmen from going any further. The two sides eventually agreed to a cease-fire, which was brokered by the United Nations. The cease-fire line, which divided the state of Kashmir in two, was known as the Line of Control (LOC). It remains the dividing line today between Indian-administered and Pakistan-administered Kashmir. Although the line is unchanged, the world around it has changed radically. Today, in spite of the latest peace process between India and Pakistan, which began in 2003, and which some believe stands a better chance of success than earlier efforts, the LOC is often referred to as the most dangerous nuclear flashpoint in the world.

The first time I visited Kashmir was in November 2001. I had spent most of the previous two months in Pakistan, along with thousands of other foreign journalists, observing the Pakistan regime's response to the Bush administration's post-9/11 ultimatum. Bush had reportedly told General Pervez Musharraf: "Either you are with us or you are against us." Unsurprisingly, given the power of the United States, General Musharraf quickly decided Pakistan was with the United States in its war on terrorism. He also promised Islamabad's assistance in the ejection of Afghanistan's Taliban regime, which Pakistan had helped bring to power. It was an extremely tense time in Pakistan. I watched General Musharraf's first post-9/11 broadcast to the nation with acute interest. He justified his decision to ally Pakistan with the United States on three grounds. It would protect Pakistan's nuclear assets It would help Pakistan turn its ailing economy around. And it would assist Pakistan's long-running claim to sovereignty over all of Kashmir (again, by ensuring Pakistan maintained good relations with the world's sole superpower). The slogan General Musharraf adopted was "Pakistan First." These two words signaled something crucial: nationalism was more important than religion. Pakistan should come before Islam.

A few weeks later I was taken with a group of foreign journalists to Pakistan's portion of Kashmir, which the Pakistanis call Azad Kashmir—Free Kashmir—and which the Indians call Pakistan-Occupied Kashmir. We visited a small post on the Line of Control overlooking an Indian position about a kilometer away across some green hills. We observed the Indian soldiers through binoculars and they observed us. Everyone waved at each other cheerily. The Pakistani major who was accompanying us was keen to impress on us the importance of holding a referendum in Kashmir. "India should permit a UN-administered plebiscite in Kashmir to allow the people to determine whether they want to be Pakistani or Indian," he said. "If they choose to be Indian then we will accept their choice."

Ironically, considering India's subsequent rejection of any "third-party" involvement in the dispute, it was New Delhi that requested the UN-mediated cease-fire in 1948 which culminated in a Security Council resolution on Kashmir. The resolution called for Pakistan to vacate all of Kashmir before a plebiscite was held. It is inconceivable that Pakistan would vacate Azad Kashmir. So the plebiscite remains a dead letter. In 2004, more than a year after India and Pakistan had embarked on a new peace process, which is still holding, General Musharraf unexpectedly dropped the demand for a plebiscite in Kashmir. It had formed the core of Pakistan's Kashmir policy for more than fifty years.

The week after my visit to Azad Kashmir I found myself having lunch in the officers' mess of the Rajputana Rifles, an Indian regiment stationed very close to the spot on the Pakistan side where I had stood a few days earlier. "Sometimes they shoot at us, sometimes we shoot at them," said the Indian colonel who was my host. "We don't usually hit each other." The real game was—and, to some extent, still is—the infiltration of Pakistan-backed militants (termed "freedom fighters" in Islamabad, "terrorists" in New Delhi) across the Line of Control to the Indian side. It usually happens at night, and the Pakistan army provides covering fire to assist the hazardous nocturnal dash. The Indian colonel claimed he had made many successful "interceptions" of infiltrators. The snows would come soon and, with the change in season, infiltration would decline, he said. The small force of Indian soldiers was dug into trenches overlooking the steep valley from their eagle's nest at an altitude of about 11,000 feet. Already the chill winds of an impending Himalayan winter were whining through the mess. We dined on steaming Mulligatawny soup and hot rotis. It seemed an arduous existence.

There are approximately 450,000 Indian soldiers and paramilitaries stationed in Kashmir. Many of them spend long winters along the high passes of the LOC. Others, who are often just eighteen or nineteen years old, can be seen in position at intervals of about two hundred yards along Kashmir's highways and on its streets sitting in bunkers waiting to be shot at or to shoot first. Their lives are unenviable. But the ubiquity of Indian military uniforms in Kashmir gives the province the unmistakable flavor of being occupied. With Kashmir's population of eight million, the ratio of soldiers to civilians is extremely high. The largest number of European soldiers stationed in

British India was 100,000 in the aftermath of the Sepoy Mutiny when India had a population of more than 200 million. Perhaps this was a measure of how easy it was for the imperialists to divide Indians. Or perhaps today it could be seen as a measure of how difficult it is for India to win the loyalty of Kashmiris.

There was another angle to my visit to Kashmir in November 2001. A couple of weeks earlier, a group of *fidayeen*—trained suicide bombers—had driven through the gates to the compound of the Kashmir legislative assembly in Srinagar and blown up themselves and their vehicle, killing dozens of people. It was a heavily symbolic attack. And it came just a few weeks after 9/11. The people of Kashmir were also in ferment over a campaign by Islamist radicals to change the way Muslims behaved in public. In contrast to Pakistan, where the burka is widely worn, most Kashmiri women are unveiled. The Kashmiri style of Islam draws on rich strands of Sufi mysticism, which bears little resemblance to the orthodox Deobandi, or Talibanized, Islam that is drilled into most of the militants. A number of unveiled Kashmiri women had been agonizingly disfigured in the previous weeks when militants threw acid in their faces. Almost every Kashmiri to whom I spoke disliked the Islamist radicals and blamed Pakistan for their presence. But they also bitterly resented the India security forces, whose intrusion in their lives often resulted in human rights abuses, including rape, torture, and extrajudicial killings. "We are stuck between a rock and a hard place," said one Kashmiri lawyer. A plague, they seemed to be saying, on both your houses.

By 2001 the character of the Kashmiri separatist movement had drastically altered since the early days of the insurgency in 1989. The province had been mostly quiescent between 1948 and 1989. But in 1987 New Delhi had blatantly rigged the state assembly election to ensure that a pro-India party would take office. Resentment at Delhi's heavy-handed and corrupt meddling in the state triggered an insurgency for an independent Kashmir. In the first few years, the uprising had little to do with Islam and was not yet fully controlled by

Pakistan. But gradually during the 1990s the indigenous Jammu and Kashmir Liberation Front, which sought independence for Kashmir from both India and Pakistan, was supplanted by other groups that had infiltrated the province and that wanted Kashmir to become part of Pakistan. Many of the groups were dominated by radical Islamists from the Pakistan side of Kashmir, from Pakistan Punjab and the North-West Frontier Province. There were even some militants from Afghanistan, Saudi Arabia, Chechnya, and other parts of the Islamic world. In short, the Kashmiri separatist movement lost its independence early on. The uprising was taken over by Pakistan, which was prepared to give free rein to *jihadi* (holy war) fighters from outside Kashmir if they would in turn assist Islamabad in its mission to undermine India's hold on the province. From Pakistan's point of view, the timing of the Kashmir insurgency, which took both Islamabad and Delhi by surprise, was highly propitious. It coincided with the withdrawal of Soviet forces from Afghanistan in 1989, leaving in their wake thousands of victorious foreign mujahideen fighters looking for a new cause. Pakistan's notorious Inter-Services Intelligence (ISI)—the equivalent of the CIA—recycled many of the Afghan jihadists to Kashmir during the 1990s and since.

A few weeks after my first visit to Kashmir in 2001, the world's attention suddenly shifted away from Afghanistan to India and Pakistan. The Taliban had already crumbled after the Northern Alliance took Kabul. The Americans were beginning to realize that they might not find Osama Bin Laden in the Tora Bora mountain range on the Afghan-Pakistan border, which they were bombing intensively. In a replay of the *fidayeen* attack on the Srinagar assembly two months earlier, suicide terrorists attacked India's parliament in New Delhi on December 13, 2001. Four men, strapped with explosives, burst through the gates to the outer rim of India's circular parliament complex and detonated the white Ambassador car they were driving. The attackers, who killed fourteen people, were stopped by security guards a few yards short of the parliamentary chamber. Parliament was in session. A couple of seconds later and the car would have demolished part of the chamber and likely taken much of the Indian cabinet with it. I got to the scene within half an hour. Already the streets had been cleared. There was an ominous atmosphere. Previously lackadaisical checkpoint guards were waving guns in people's faces. The whole city was echoing with the sounds of screeching sirens and helicopters overhead. The Indians traced the attack to a Kashmiri militant group based in Pakistan called the Lashkar-e-Toiba—the Army of the Pure. Atal Behari Vajpayee, India's prime minister, held Pakistan accountable and demanded the immediate extradition to India of twenty alleged terrorists harbored by Pakistan. Vajpayee also demanded the immediate cessation of militant infiltration across the LOC and the closure of alleged Pakistan-backed terrorist training camps in Azad Kashmir. General Musharraf angrily denied any involvement. It looked as though the two neighbors were preparing for another round of high-octane antagonism. It would get worse than that.

My parents were visiting India that Christmas and we took them to Ranthambore, a famous tiger reserve in the state of Rajasthan. As it happened we did not see any tigers. But on our journey to the tiger reserve we did catch glimpses of one of the largest military mobilizations in modern history. Vajpayee had ordered the relocation of most of India's 1.2 million–strong army to the international border with Pakistan. The states of Rajasthan, Gujarat, and Punjab are on the Pakistan border. We got stuck at Jaipur railway station in Rajasthan. It soon became apparent why our train to Ranthambore had been delayed. For two hours we sat on the platform watching train after train pass northward through the station carrying tanks, heavy artillery, armored personnel carriers, and thousands of soldiers. Watching India's rusting military hardware chug past us reminded me of what I had read about the preparations for the First World War. Mobilization had followed the dictates of the European railway timetables. India's mobilization, which was later dubbed "coercive diplomacy," was following the stately pace of the Indian railways. Somehow this made events seem even more troubling. It was an unusual beginning to our Christmas break. And it ruined my short holiday since I felt journalistic guilt at being in the wrong place. It was unclear, however, where the right place might be.

As it turned out, nothing happened. Or at least, a great deal nearly happened over the next six months before India stood down from what it had called Operation Parakaram (Valor). There were unsubstantiated but widely reported rumors that both sides had fixed nuclear warheads to nuclear-capable missiles in anticipation that the conflict, which was threatening to break out at any moment, would escalate very rapidly. In the next chapter we will look at the region's precarious nuclear status, which involves China and increasingly, in many respects, the United States. We will also look at America's role in the subcontinent, which proved instrumental in 2002 in averting conflict between India and Pakistan. Twice during the tense standoff, India was on the brink of ordering some kind of cross-border military strike—in January 2002 and then again in late May 2002. Mercifully, it pulled back from the brink. In October 2002 India's railways lumbered back into action, this time to assist the massive demobilization of a very tired and somewhat dispirited Indian army. Perhaps by then Ranthambore's tigers had emerged from their nuclear bunkers.

•    •    •

Somebody once described wars between India and Pakistan as "communal riots with armor"[14] ("communal" meaning religious). It is a catchy phrase. Pakistan is certainly a Muslim country and under its constitution the republic derives its sovereignty from Allah, rather than the people. But India is a diverse and multifaith country with a secular constitution. For all its faults, it would be unfair to describe India's army as "Hindu." India has Muslim and Christian military officers. It has many Sikh regiments. India's parliament elected a Muslim head of state in 2002. General J. J. Singh, who was ap pointed India's army chief of staff in 2005, is a Sikh, as is Manmohan Singh, India's prime minister. India's most powerful woman is a foreign-born Christian.

The phrase "communal riots in armor" might be misleading for another reason. Communal rioting has the connotation of butchery. Comparatively few Indian and Pakistani soldiers have been killed in wars between the two countries since they came into existence. In total, India and Pakistan have been to war three times, in 1947, 1965, and 1971. There was a fourth unofficial war between the two in 1999 when a large group politely known as a "guerrilla force"—in fact a force of Pakistani soldiers dressed in mufti—occupied the strategic heights of Kargil on India's side of the LOC. They were ejected after Indian infantry stormed the mountain in a bloody four-week encounter. Yet for the most part the wars have been very short with only brief moments of intensive engagement. The total casualties of all four conflicts between India and Pakistan amount to fewer than 50,000 killed. There were moments during the First and Second World Wars in Europe when as many men were killed in the space of seventy-two hours. If you expand the definition of war to include what India calls Pakistan's "proxy war" in Kashmir—war conducted through nominally independent militants—the number of deaths rises by between 40,000 and 80,000. It is a large number. But communal riots in India before, during, and after partition have claimed a multiple of this. Neither "armor" nor bullets are the principal cause of communal mortality in the subcontinent.

Yet to many Indians the very existence of Pakistan is seen as a dagger aimed at the heart of India. The Pakistan threat is perceived at a number of levels. First, Pakistan claims Kashmir, which is India's only Muslim-majority province. Pakistan is unlikely to relinquish that claim, since Kashmir is a Muslim-majority province. If the so-called "two-nation" theory (which Jinnah propounded) is wrong, then Pakistan should never have been created. If it is right, then Kashmir should belong to Pakistan, the Pakistanis argue. Given the degree to which Pakistan's military regimes have required national sacrifice in both blood and treasure in pursuit of the Kashmir cause, it would be surprising if Islamabad abandoned its stance.

Second, the creation of Pakistan was seen as an amputation of India's natural geographical and cultural boundaries. It is not only the Hindu nationalists who wish for the day when Pakistan will be reincorporated into Akhand Bharat—greater India. Many Indians, of whatever background, see partition as an unnecessary tragedy that ought, at some unspecified stage in the future, to be peacefully rectified. Naturally, this attitude contributes to Pakistan's own profound insecurities. However, very few Indians would any longer subscribe to Nehru's view that Pakistan was untenable as a nation-state and that it would eventually merge back into India. Indian longing for subcontinental unity remains a vague sentiment. It is not a policy.

Third, and most intractably, Pakistan is seen as posing an existential threat to India's secular identity. No matter how stable relations are between India and Pakistan, in the Indian mind the existence of Pakistan will always have the potential to divide the loyalties of India's Muslim minority, which now accounts for almost 14 percent of the population, or about 150 million people. This, in turn, exacerbates the insecurities of India's Muslims. There is little doubt that Pakistan has on many occasions over the last sixty years sought to stoke this neuralgia. Yet, with the exception of Kashmir, which accounts for much less than 10 percent of India's Muslim population, the expectations of many in Pakistan (and around the world) that India would gradually break up under the weight of its diverse contradictions have been proved wrong. India's Muslims remain firmly ensconced in India, as do most of India's other minorities.* There have been no significant population movements between India and Pakistan since 1947. There have been a few overinflated incidents

---

*India does suffer from a rash of small separatist insurgencies, particularly in its geographically isolated northeastern states that border China, Myanmar, Bangladesh, Bhutan, and Nepal. But these are geographically confined, and most of India's neighbors, particularly China, are thought to have withdrawn the tacit support they once gave to many of the northeastern separatist groups.

wherein Muslim slums in India have flown the Pakistan flag when the two national cricket teams met on the field. But in a different country such displays would fail to register. Most of Britain's Asian community would not pass the notorious "cricket test" set by a right-wing politician in the 1980s in which they were asked to support England when it was playing against their respective country of origin.

The hard-line chauvinists in India and Pakistan have much more in common with each other than they would care to admit. Both mistrust diversity. Both seek through education and culture to regulate and control the role of women in society. They also share a partiality to the use and abuse of history. According to Pakistan's school textbooks, the history of modern Pakistan goes back to the early Muslim incursions into India, when marauders such as Mehmood of Ghazni, an Afghan strongman, conducted raids on north India. Pakistan's medium-range nuclear missiles are called the Ghauri, after Mohammed Ghauri, who became the first Muslim to rule a part of India when he defeated a Hindu Rajput prince, Prithvi Raj Chauhan, in 1192. Likewise India's short-range missiles are called Prithvis (*Prithvi* means "earth" in Sanskrit). Pakistan's schoolbooks stereotype Hindus as "cunning, scheming and deceptive."[15] The textbooks that are used in the 20,000 or so schools operated by the Hindu nationalist RSS in India characterize Muslims as cruel and bloodthirsty. Meanwhile, the emperor Aurangzeb, who was quoted at the start of the chapter, is depicted as a hero by Pakistan and as a villain by India. His great-grandfather, Akbar, who was one of India's most enlightened rulers, is downplayed by both Muslim and Hindu communalists. They are two sides of the same coin.

Someone once said that the rivalry between the Soviet Union and the United States during the cold war was ideological, whereas enmity between India and Pakistan was biological. Whenever I visit Pakistan, I am struck by the very transparent paranoia that the military and diplomatic elites in Islamabad feel toward India. I am equally struck by the absence of these sentiments among ordinary

Pakistanis. The same is broadly true in reverse, although India plays a much larger role in the popular perceptions of Pakistanis than vice versa, partly because of the allure of Bollywood. When ordinary Pakistanis and Indians interact there is usually goodwill and warmth. In April 2004 I flew to Karachi, Pakistan's commercial capital, to attend the first cricket game in years between the two countries. The match was the first in a cricket series on which New Delhi and Islamabad had agreed after the bilateral peace process was launched in 2003. Thousands of Indians were given visas to attend the game. At that point it was the most significant "people-to-people" contact that had been permitted between Indians and Pakistanis since the peace process began. I spent most of the day touring the stadium in search of Indian supporters to ask how they had been treated. Most of them seemed overwhelmed. The boisterous Pakistani crowd were chanting "Akhtar Zindabad, Zindabad, Zindabad!"—Long Live Akhtar! Shoaib Akhtar is Pakistan's fastest bowler. When an Indian batsman played well, the chant of the Pakistan masses switched seamlessly to "India Zindabad, Zindabad, Zindabad!" Every Indian I met said he had been treated like a long-lost brother (the crowd was made up mostly of men). Shopkeepers had refused to accept their cash. Taxi drivers had declined fares. Hotels were waiving bills. And people kept approaching them on the streets to offer sweets and other small gifts. "It is overwhelming," said one among a group of Indian men, dressed in the blue shirts of their national team. "We didn't know what to expect but we feared there would be hostility." India's team won the game and it received a prolonged ovation from the vast Pakistani crowd.

In contrast, at the level of Pakistan's military-bureaucratic establishment, India is a migraine that outweighs all its other headaches put together. The perceived threat from India and the need to secure Kashmir has provided the principal justification for military rule in Pakistan for more than half of the country's history. It explains why Pakistan spends a much larger share of its gross national product on defense than India does. In 2003 India spent 15 percent of its budget on defense compared to 54 percent in Pakistan.[16] Some would describe Pakistan as a home for south Asia's Muslims. Others increasingly see the country as a Central Asian Islamic republic, or even as an extension of the Middle East. A more enduring description for Pakistan's national identity might be "Not India."

Even during periods of warmer relations between Islamabad and New Delhi, the Pakistan establishment routinely uses the perceived threat from India to justify its grip on political power. In October 2005 the region was hit by the most devastating earthquake in living memory, claiming 70,000 lives and making millions homeless. The zone that was the worst affected was on the Pakistan side of Kashmir, although the Indian portion was also hit. There was strong domestic criticism by the Pakistani media of General Musharraf's handling of the emergency. Many believed the Pakistan army had acted too slowly in response to the desperate plight of millions of Kashmiris, which had given the Islamist charities an opportunity to step in and boost their popularity. One ray of light came when India and Pakistan moved (albeit reluctantly) to open up several points along the Line of Control for the delivery of relief aid, mostly from the Indian to the Pakistani side. In the midst of all this, dozens of large billboards suddenly appeared in Islamabad implying that there was a new threat from India. The billboards demanded that India return Kashmir to Pakistan immediately. One said: KASHMIRIS ARE NOT CHILDREN OF A LESSER GOD. It was a reminder of the instinct of Pakistan's military leadership to resort to diversionary propaganda whenever its back is to the wall.

It has become fashionable over the decades to argue that the Kashmir dispute between India and Pakistan is insoluble. From the Indian side, the view is that Pakistan, as long as it is under military rule, will never agree to a peace deal that falls short of full sovereignty over Kashmir. But if a democratic Pakistani government were to conclude a deal that fell short of the country's maximum demands, the army would use this as a pretext to launch another coup. As with General Musharraf's coup in 1999, which followed the decision by Nawaz

Sharif, Pakistan's democratically elected prime minister, to retreat from the Kargil heights on India's side of Kashmir, Pakistan's courts unfailingly uphold the legality of army coups. Pakistan's Supreme Court cites the country's catchall "Doctrine of Necessity" (a body of law developed by judges in Pakistan but which does not appear in the constitution), which says, "That which otherwise is not lawful, necessity makes lawful."[17] In other words, when there is a tank parked outside your courthouse, you tend to go with the flow. Not without reason, Pakistan is alternately perceived by India as either too aggressive or too weak to reach a credible peace settlement.

From the Pakistan side, India is correctly seen as a "status quo" power that will cling to Kashmir but happily leave Pakistan to its much smaller portion of the divided province. India would almost certainly accept a peace agreement in which the LOC were converted from a cease-fire line into an international border. Pakistan almost certainly would not. There are a few Indian irredentists who would like to regain all of Kashmir. But they are on the margins of the debate. Not unfairly, Pakistan's establishment sees India as a country that often agrees to something and then spends years arguing over what it has actually agreed. There are not many diplomatic corps around the world that are as accomplished at semantic nitpicking as India's foreign service. Sometimes this propensity can be self-defeating. In another context, Narayana Murthy, the founder of Infosys, India's largest software company, said that Indian bureaucrats were chronically prone to "MAFA"—mistaking articulation for accomplishment. It is not just the Pakistanis who have felt frustrated by this trait. India's habit of approaching diplomacy in the manner of a clever high-school debater has ruffled the feathers of many governments around the world at one time or another. But short of nuclear war, which would annihilate both sides, there is little Pakistan can do to alter the status quo. It has tried conventional war on several occasions and failed.

Ultimately most observers believe that any credible solution to the Kashmir dispute ought to lie at least partly in the province itself. As the status quo power, India can probably do more to influence the attitudes of Kashmiris in a positive direction than can Pakistan, which, in spite of the peace process, has retained the option of deploying terrorists across the LOC. There have been signs in the last few years that the population of Kashmir would be ready to accept some kind of settlement that would fall short of independence for the province or full merger with Pakistan. It is not because of any sudden affection for India, which has consistently misread the situation in Kashmir and treated its inhabitants with high-handedness and arrogance. This relaxation is probably more to do with the growing sense of fatigue Kashmiris feel about the violence and uncertainty that have dominated their lives for so long. The gradual shift in mind-set might also be related to India's relative economic success in the last few years compared to the more precarious economic scenario in Pakistan.

On my last two trips to Kashmir, this shift has been increasingly visible. Kashmiris more often refer to the militants as "foreigners" and "terrorists." In the past they had talked of "freedom fighters." Kashmir's bewildering array of separatist leaders, who are grouped under an umbrella movement called the All People's Hurriyat Conference, speak with less respect of the militant groups than before. Most of the separatist leaders are vulnerable to assassination at any time. Some of them are the sons, brothers, and nephews of leaders who have been killed by militant groups for having strayed too far from either the pro-Pakistan or the Islamist line. It is not just Kashmiri separatist leaders or the people of Kashmir who believe the militants are out of control. Some of the militant groups have been involved in assassination attempts on General Musharraf. The closest attempt occurred in December 2003 when a remote-controlled bomb blew up a bridge that General Musharraf's car was about to cross. The attempt took place just a couple of miles from Musharraf's official residence in the city of Rawalpindi, the Pakistan army headquarters. Two Kashmiri separatists were arrested. There was also a close shave for Shaukat Aziz, Pakistan's military-appointed prime minister, whose driver and bodyguard were shot dead when Aziz was on the campaign trail in 2004 in the North-West Frontier Province of Pakistan. For General Musharraf and the liberal and modernist sections of Pakistan that sometimes support him, the incidents served as a reminder that Frankenstein can also devour his creator.

The separatist leader in Kashmir who is most vulnerable to assassination is probably Umar Farooq, who is known as the Mirwaiz, the hereditary title of a widely revered Sufi position in Srinagar that has been held in his family for generations. The then teenage but highly articulate Farooq became Mirwaiz in 1990 when his father was assassinated. It is unclear who carried out the killing. In 2004 Farooq's uncle was killed by militants in Srinagar. When I spoke to the Mirwaiz in 2005, I was startled by how much his attitude had shifted since we had first met in 2001. "We, as Kashmiris, belong to many different religions," he said. "We are Muslims, both Shia and Sunni, we are Hindus, and we are Buddhists. Kashmir has a long and tolerant tradition that bears little relation to the Punjabi Sunni Muslim culture that dominates Pakistan." It was the statement of a man who had grown tired of weighing every word before he spoke. The Mirwaiz said that most Kashmiris, including him, had reached the limits of tolerance for violence, from whatever direction it came. "In the past when there was a bomb or an assassination, up to ten different militant groups would claim responsibility," he said. "Now, nobody claims responsibility. That should tell you something about the changes that are occurring."

I was equally struck in 2005 when I visited Abdul Ghani Bhatt, another seasoned Kashmiri separatist leader, at his ancestral village near the town of Baramula about twenty miles from the Line of Control. I was with a colleague and we spotted Bhatt sitting behind a shop window having a cup of tea in the small high street. It was late winter and he was carrying a vessel filled with hot charcoal under his overcoat to keep warm, as is the custom of Kashmiris. I had met Bhatt on many previous occasions and he had come across as one of the most inflexible, albeit charming, spokesmen for Islamabad's point of view. But this time his tone was different. "The whole thing keeps going round and round and people are getting tired," said Bhatt. "India says, 'I am big.' Pakistan says, 'But Islam is even bigger.' It is the usual civilizational debate. Nobody on the ground in Kashmir wants the peace of the graveyard anymore. They want India and Pakistan to pause and be more imaginative." I mentioned Syeed Geelani, the most hard-line Islamist separatist leader in Kashmir, whose Jamaat-e-Islami Party is linked to the most violent militant outfits in the province. Geelani was the most prominent among the remaining separatist leaders who still unequivocally opposed the peace process between India and Pakistan. It would still be dangerous to cross Geelani. "Oh, Geelani is just a malevolent naricissist," said Bhatt. "Don't pay him any attention."

I had, in fact, paid Geelani quite a bit of attention a few weeks earlier when I visited him at his residence in Srinagar. As was often the case, Geelani had been put under house arrest by the Indians. I went to see him with two colleagues, Simon Long of the *Economist* and Amy Waldman of the *New York Times*. The temperature was close to zero. We were seated in a row of three chairs facing the hard-line Islamist leader. "Are you sure you're not too cold, my dears?" Geelani kept asking. Disbelieving our replies, Geelani sent off a young minion to find a blanket. He then instructed the minion to tuck all three of us under the same blanket. It was my most intimate collaboration to date with journalistic competitors. Whenever Geelani said something, his minions would echo the last three or four words in unison. Geelani said: "The Indians kill us mercilessly. They rape our sisters and they rape our daughters." His chorus echoed, "Rape our daughters," before Geelani resumed his monologue. "The Indians have no respect for Kashmiri rights. We are human beings, not animals," he said. "Not animals," they echoed. In spite of his grim words, it was hard for us to keep a straight face. Yet Geelani could not disguise his unhappiness over the peace process on which India and Pakistan had embarked in 2003. He cut a lonely figure.

Later that day we went to the central park in Srinagar where Manmohan Singh was to give his first address as India's prime minister to a rally of Kashmiris. The crowd of several thousand had evidently been corralled into attendance by local pro-India parties. Most of them had been paid a small sum to be there. Security was very tight and there were several helicopters in the sky. But the supposedly organized crowd could not be fully controlled. At various intervals in Manmohan's speech, a section of it would start chanting slogans and the prime minister would have to stop speaking. It was a familiar reception for an Indian politician in a highly dissenting and embittered outpost of the country. But the crowd was not yelling cries of freedom or Pakistan or Islam, as they might have done in the past. They were shouting for jobs. "Remove unemployment," they chanted repeatedly. Perhaps I overinterpreted this very small incident. But it seemed like another indication that the priorities of Kashmiris were changing. After a while Manmohan resumed speaking. The chanting continued.

•   •   •

During my time in India I have constantly been on the alert for any sign that the loyalties of India's Muslim population might be in question. But outside Kashmir (and even there, sentiments are more complex than is often portrayed), I have yet to come across serious evidence of divided loyalties. India's Muslims are a disappointment both to Pakistan, where hawkish types look for signs of oppression of Muslims in India as something that would reaffirm the logic of Pakistan's existence, and to the Hindu communalists whose ideology tells them that it is impossible to be both a true Indian and a devout Muslim. The reality of life for India's Muslims is often more prosaic.

In 2004 the opposition BJP seized upon new data that had been released by India's census bureau. According to New Delhi's demographers, the India's Muslim population had grown by 29 percent between 1991 and 2001, whereas the Hindu population growth rate had been just 22 percent.[18] It provided an opportunity for the Hindu right wing to raise the specter that India was in danger of being swamped by Muslims. It fit with the stereotype that Muslims were a threat to India's balance since they tended to have larger families. Narendra Modi, the chief minister of Gujarat, described the refugee camps that provided shelter to Muslims who had been burned out of their homes in 2002 as "child manufacturing factories."

But the story behind the population data was more complex. India's rate of population growth has slowed sharply among all communities, falling from an average of 2.2 percent in the 1980s to less than 2 percent a year in the 1990s. It is expected to fall to about 1.5 percent by the time of the next census in 2011. During the 1990s, the richer Indian states in the south recorded a more rapid fall in their population growth rates than did the poorer states in the north. The trends were a function of economics, not of religion. Muslims living in the south had a lower rate of population growth than did Hindus living in the north. But since a larger proportion of Muslims live in poorer states, their average growth rate was higher.

The question ought to be why such a large proportion of Muslims live in relative poverty in India. It is an issue that is rarely addressed. Its causes are multiple and varied. But there can be little doubt that the exodus in 1947 of most of India's Muslim intelligentsia to Pakistan was a big factor. A large proportion of India's Muslim civil servants, military officers, and university lecturers left for Pakistan, many of them believing they would have a better chance of preferment in the new state. Poor Muslims barely shifted. In addition, a large proportion of Muslims who remained in India were involved in traditional artisan occupations, such as weaving and basket making, which have suffered economic decline since the 1950s. Some of the poverty is new.

Nevertheless, poverty among India's Muslims has been falling and continues to fall, although at a less rapid rate than the average improvements for India as a whole would indicate. But averages can mislead as much as they inform. Beneath the statistics and the stereotypes, India's Muslim population is as varied and diverse as the rest of India. It is as rare for a Tamil-speaking Muslim to marry a Gujarati-speaking Muslim as it is for their Hindu counterparts to marry outside their communities. Being a Muslim is just one attribute in the complex menu of identities available to most Indians. Nehru once described India as a palimpsest. It was his way of illustrating the large accumulation of histories and cultures that had left their mark on India, none of which had been fully erased. Indians themselves, including Indian Muslims, could be described as palimpsests in miniature.

For example, Muslims in many parts of India are almost as prone to caste classification as are their Hindu counterparts. In Uttar Pradesh, which is home to the largest number of Muslims in India, almost thirty million, Muslim castes are divided into Ashraf and non-Ashraf.[19] Many of the former, who are upper caste, and who have noble-sounding names such as Shaikh, Pathan, Mughal, and Sayyid, claim descent from foreign aristocracy, whether Persian, Arabian, Turkish, or Afghan. They are as disdainful of the lower-caste Muslims, most of whom are descendants of lower-caste Hindus who converted to Islam (ironically to escape caste), as are the upper-caste Hindus toward India's lower castes. The only place in which Ashraf and non-Ashraf rub shoulders on equal terms is in the mosque. Lower-caste Muslims tend to copy the habits and codes of the Ashraf families in their villages by putting their women in purdah—a sign of wealth, because only the rich can afford to remove their women from work in the fields. Meanwhile, the Ashrafs are moving to the cities and in many cases "Westernizing" and abandoning purdah altogether.[20] The long reach of the Hindu caste system might be another reason that more Indian lower castes have not converted to Islam, or to Christianity.*

Another relatively overlooked complexity is the division between India's Sunni and Shia Muslim communities. In cities such as Lucknow, the capital of Uttar Pradesh, where there are large concentrations of both strands of Islam, the principal communal conflicts are between Shia and Sunni Muslims rather than between Muslims and Hindus. For years there was violence surrounding the annual Shia Moharram festival, in which Shia mourn the martyrdom of the Prophet's grandson, Hussain. Being a minority among India's Muslims, Lucknow's Shia community occasionally votes for the Hindu nationalist BJP. It is another example of the "enemy of my enemy" principle in Indian politics. And it suggests limits to which the term *Indian Islam* makes any sense.

One particularly widespread stereotype about India's Sunni Muslims is that they prefer to educate their children in backward madrasas rather than to give them a modern education. Many Muslim children are sent to narrow religious schools, particularly in north India. But this is partly because so many of the government schools around them function only intermittently. According to India's government, on any given day one-third of teachers are absent from government schools. In the state of Bihar, which has a large Muslim population, less than 3 percent of government schools have electricity and less than 20 percent have toilets for their teachers.[21] Only a few schools have separate toilets for girls. Both Hindu and Muslim parents alike keep their daughters away. But where there is a meaningful choice, Muslim parents appear as keen as any others to take advantage of an education for their daughters.

I visited the old city of Hyderabad, which is known as Char Mi-

---

*In most Christian churches in India, especially the Catholic Church, the caste system is almost wholly reproduced with Brahmins as bishops and Dalits as congregation, even though the latter vastly outnumber the former. In some parts of India, Dalits are even allotted a separate cemetery.

nar, after the four minarets that dominate the skyline of this once-Persianized princely capital. The mainly Muslim slums that dominate the strikingly beautiful old city are abysmally served by the government. Many government school teachers are available only for private tuition. So the parents have set up a flourishing network of private schools, staffed by untrained or semitrained teachers, which charge between Rs 500 and Rs 1,500 ($12–$36) a month in fees. The schools all teach in English, which is not available in their government counterparts, which teach either in Telugu, the language of Andhra Pradesh, or Urdu. The private schools overwhelmingly cater to the children of the Muslim working classes— rickshaw-wallahs, vegetable sellers, weavers, and mechanics. Perhaps the most striking dimension to the schools is that there are as many girls as boys in the classrooms. About two-thirds of the schoolchildren of this area of Hyderabad go to private schools in a zone with a population of more than a million.[22] Very few of the girls are veiled.

The schools have incongruous names, such as Oxford Public School, Green Valley, California High, and Windsor Diploma, that belie their makeshift character and humble settings in the tiny back alleys of Char Minar. Although poverty is acute, many of the backstreet alleyways are spotlessly clean. The Muslim slum dwellers of Hyderabad appear to have taken more than just schooling into their hands. At one school, M.A. Ideal, named after its owner, Mohammed Anwar, there was a sign prominently displayed that said: IF LIFE GIVES YOU ROCKS, IT IS YOUR CHOICE WHETHER TO BUILD A BRIDGE OR A WALL. I talked to some of the mothers who were waiting for school to finish. Most were veiled. None of them was literate. And none had received proper schooling except for (oral) training in Arabic schools so they could recite the Koran. They wanted something different for their daughters. "The world has changed since we were children," said Rizwana Begum, whose husband is a rickshaw driver. "We want our daughters to learn English so that they can get jobs. We want our daughters to have the opportunities we didn't have." It was a refrain

I heard often. Begum's husband spends a fifth of his Rs 3,500 in monthly earnings on his children's education.

Inside the classroom, the girls were reciting a rhyme about Jack and Jill. I asked whether they wanted jobs when they were older. All raised their hands. I asked what they wanted to be. Their aspirations varied from doctor to lawyer to astronaut. A couple even wanted to be tennis players. Sania Mirza, a teenage Muslim from Hyderabad, had recently entered the top fifty in the female world tennis rankings and was India's number-one female player. Her poster could be seen everywhere. A Deobandi mullah had issued a fatwa forbidding her from wearing short skirts on the tennis court. Mirza responded by dressing even more provocatively. As the minor controversy unfolded she took to wearing a T-shirt that said: WHATEVER. Outside the Jama Masjid Mosque in Delhi, probably the most concentrated area of urban Muslims in India, Muslim street hawkers responded with equal insouciance. Posters of a scantily clad Sania were on sale outside the hostels for hadj pilgrims. Some of the posters were doctored to make her appear even more scantily clad. I asked the girls what would happen if their husbands did not want them to work. "Then we wouldn't marry them," they said, clapping their hands over their mouths and giggling. They did not seem to be lacking in ambition. Sania Mirza told the Indian media: "It shouldn't matter whether my skirts are six inches or six feet in length as long as I am winning."

Down the road I visited Jamila Amshad, a local Urdu-language poet and a formidable Muslim feminist. She operates a center for slum women. Many are battered wives. "Muslim women have two enemies who have much more in common with each other than they think," said Amshad. "Our main enemy is Hindu communalism. They harbor nothing but ill will toward Muslims. Our other enemy is the Muslim mullahs who think women are just chattels." Amshad is one among a growing number of articulate Muslim women in India who is seeking to overturn central precepts of the Muslim personal law on the statute books. Chief among the women's complaints is the custom of "triple talaq," which permits Muslim husbands to divorce their wives by saying "I divorce you" three times. Amshad reserved particular venom for the All India Muslim Personal Law Board (AIMPLB), which, despite having no statutory position, speaks on behalf of the "Muslim community." The campaign to modernize India's Muslim personal law has yet to achieve success. But it is clear that if Muslim law is to be effectively reformed in India, it is Muslims who must accomplish the change. "Who elected the AIMPLB?" asked Amshad. "By what right do they speak on my behalf? They are not defending Muslims. They are defending patriarchy." On the wall of Amshad's office there was a poster that made me laugh: DO NOT GIVE ME A BANGLE, GIVE ME A PEN. Well-meaning charities often train illiterate slum women to make cheap trinkets.

My visit to Hyderabad coincided with an unrelated event in Lahore, one of Pakistan's largest cities, which was getting much airtime in India. A group of Pakistani women had been badly manhandled when they embarked on a marathon run to highlight the restrictions women face in Pakistan. The run was organized by Asma Jehangir, Pakistan's most courageous and well-known human rights lawyer. The run was broken up by the police before it got under way, since it was considered an un-Islamic activity for women. Some of the women were dragged off by the police and stripped. Jehangir had described the event as an exercise in "Enlightened Moderation," in a deliberate echo of a phrase used by General Musharraf to describe the type of Islam he would prefer to see in Pakistan. But Pakistan's military ruler did nothing to prevent the event from being broken up. I wondered whether Sania Mirza would be hitting forehand winners if she had been born on the Pakistan side of the border.

The condition of India's Muslims is often presented as hopelessly backward. But democracy is as much ingrained within India's Muslim communities as it is in any other. It became a cliché after the plane attacks on the Twin Towers, which were principally carried out by Saudi nationals, to say India had produced no Muslim terrorists because it was a democracy. The cliché was inaccurate. Muslim mafia dons in Mumbai organized a series of terrorist bombings in the city in 1993 in revenge for the riots that followed the destruction of the Babri Masjid in Ayodhya a few months earlier. The blasts killed 300 people. There have been plenty of other bombing incidents that, if the Indian police are to be believed (and very often they should not be), were orchestrated by Pakistan's ISI, the army-dominated intelligence agency. In 2003, dozens of bystanders were killed in Mumbai by a series of car bombs set off by a group describing itself as the Gujarat Muslim Revenge Force. It was an apparent retaliation for the anti-Muslim pogroms that had taken place in Gujarat the previous year.

Yet it is true that only a very small number of Indian Muslims have been recruited to the various global jihads that have occurred in recent decades, including the Kashmir insurgency. In spite of India's proximity to Afghanistan, there were almost no Indian Muslims involved in the jihad against the Soviet occupation of Afghanistan in the 1980s. In contrast, countries as far away as the Philippines and Morocco, which have a fraction of India's Muslim population, were well represented in the ranks of the Afghan mujahideen. Part of this could be attributed to the fact that the Indian government, in contrast to the governments of most Islamic countries, had close relations with the Soviet Union and discouraged Indian involvement. But part of the reason could also be that unlike the citizens of most Islamic countries—Pakistan included—India's Muslims possess a clear right to freedom of speech, expression, worship, and movement. Terrorism is a complex phenomenon: It would be far too simplistic to say it is caused by absence of democracy. But the right to air your grievances peacefully and in public must surely increase the likelihood that you will vent your resentments in a nonviolent manner. Pakistan's population of 150 million is roughly equal to India's Muslim population. They share ethnicity, culture, and religion. Pakistani nationals are frequently linked to international terrorist networks, while Indian Muslims rarely are. Perhaps what really divides India's Muslims from their counterparts in Pakistan is the political system under which they live.

Yet there are concerns that as India's economy continues to grow, many of the country's Muslim communities are becoming more exposed to the type of Islam practiced in the Gulf countries of the Middle East, where the traditions of worship are seen as less tolerant and more orthodox than those in India. This influence is perhaps most visible in the south Indian state of Kerala, where millions of Keralite Muslims have worked and continue to work in the Gulf states, particularly in Saudi Arabia and the United Arab Emirates. I visited "Mini-Gulf," a leafy district about seventy miles south of the Keralan city of Cochin facing the Arabian Sea. The district of Trichur, which includes the Mini-Gulf enclave, is a few miles to the south of Cranganoor, a small town that is reputed to have played host to India's first ever mosque in the eighth century AD. Arabian dhows exploited the seasonal monsoon winds to ply the short route between the Gulf and south India bringing goods and the Word of the Prophet. Nowadays it is Keralite Muslims who cross the waters bringing hefty remittances from employment in the Gulf.

The first thing that I noticed about Abdullah Kutty, a retired Keralan chef who had worked almost thirty years in the Gulf, was that he spoke English with an Arabic accent. Kutty gave me a proud tour of his "dream home," which he had built from his earnings. Like many of his neighbors, who live in large white stucco houses propped up by fake Corinthian columns, Kutty had grown up in a small fisherman's shack, built with bamboo sticks and grass thatch. Now he has an upstairs, a downstairs, spare bedrooms, and a large teak door fronting the entrance. The interior of his home is decorated with the wood of jackfruit trees. One of Kutty's sons owns a hotel and a shop in the Mini-Gulf's booming high street around the corner. Next to the shop is a large new mosque that was built with donations from Kutty and hundreds of other Gulf expatriates. The mosque, which is several times larger than the small place of worship it replaced, is designed according to the prevalent Gulf style. Its minaret booms out the calls to prayer over a much larger radius than before. "We wanted to give something back to the community," said Kutty, who did not otherwise appear to be particularly religious. Kutty said that the effect of exposure to the Gulf had changed other things. Most of the women who had lived there had become more conservative in their dress. "Now the women are considered vulgar if they do not cover all parts of their body, except the face," he said.

Yet the Gulf is having other, less obvious, impacts on Kerala's Muslims. Kutty has two daughters. One of them is a software engineer and has a job in the United Arab Emirates. The other was preparing for university entrance exams. Mrs. Kutty, who is illiterate, said she wished she had had her daughters' opportunities. "Nowadays the girls have to get a good education, otherwise they would never get a job in the Gulf," she said. "All the girls are studying so hard." Since they are educated and financially independent, a small but growing number of the younger women in Mini-Gulf are now deciding for themselves whom they will marry and when. "In our day none of us had any choice," said Mrs. Kutty. If I had driven through the district and simply observed life on the streets, I might have gotten a different impression. In the West, we are trained to see purdah and the veil as signs of women's oppression. But sometimes it is a corollary of women's emergence from the home.

The newfound wealth of this once-impoverished class of Muslims has had other strange effects, which would have been hard to anticipate. Some Muslim families are paying wedding dowries to the families of their sons-in-law, in the form of cash, jewelry, and white goods, such as washing machines. The practice of dowry was once confined to the Hindu upper castes. But it is spreading across India to the lower castes and to other religious communities, including Muslims. The popularization of the dowry could hardly be described as progress. But it is a marker in India of upward mobility. "People are becoming more greedy," said Mr. Kutty.

In the state of Gujarat, which, as we have seen, is perhaps India's least tolerant, Muslims are also changing their dress code. About a year after the 2002 killings, I was invited to a conference called "Vibrant Gujarat," in which Narendra Modi, the chief minister, was showcasing the state's investment opportunities to foreign companies. As had become usual with Modi, whom I had interviewed before, he turned aggressive the moment I asked about the treatment of Gujarati Muslims. He gave a blanket denial that there were any communal problems in Gujarat. "These are lies. You are listening to the propaganda of the pseudosecularists," he said.

Feeling somewhat despondent, I was about to catch a taxi to my hotel, when a senior police officer introduced himself and invited me out to dinner. The officer, whose name I promised to withhold, was in charge of one of the districts of Ahmedabad, Gujarat's commercial capital. My visit coincided with Gujarat's annual festival of Navratri, in which thousands of young women and girls dress up in traditional costumes and compete against each other in pictureseque mass dance competitions. The police official took me to several of the Navratri events. During the evening he talked about what had happened during the riots. I suspected that was the reason he had invited me to join him. "In districts where Muslims were killed on a large scale, the police were collaborating with the rioters," he said. "In districts where there were very few deaths, such as in mine, the senior police official had decided to uphold the law and protect innocent people. If you want to understand riots in India, that is all you need to know." I could not vouch for his accuracy. But later I ran his name past a Muslim group in Ahmedabad, which confirmed his reputation as a professional officer.

The officer took me to one of Ahmedabad's largest private membership clubs, where there must have been at least two thousand young women swirling decorously under the floodlights in a large open ground within its walls. It was a captivating sight. They were wearing colorful skirts, many of which were decorated with sequins that flashed as they twirled. Thousands more were watching the competition in which the girls were progressively eliminated by judges until there was just one winner. The prizes included Hero Honda motorbikes and a Tata Indica vehicle. "If I were a betting man, I would bet that there is not one Muslim here," said the officer. "It is the same in the street parties that are taking place across Gujarat tonight. The Muslims have gone. Ten or twenty years ago both Hindus and Muslims would celebrate each other's festivals. Now that has almost completely stopped in Gujarat." It was a melancholy thought.

The same gradual separation of communities is visible in the clothes Gujarati Muslims now wear. Whereas Muslim women would once wear saris, most now dress in *salwar chameez,* which cover all parts of the body. Likewise, Gujarati Muslim men are likelier to grow beards and don a white cap. "It is a very tragic divorce of two communities which used to be very interlinked and overlapping," said Hanif Lakdawala, a nonpracticing Muslim based in Ahmedabad, who runs a charity for slum women, and whom we briefly met in chapter four. "Now the Muslims of Gujarat are standing out and saying: 'If you want us to be different, we will be different.'" The walls of Lakdawala's small flat in the center of Ahmedabad are decorated with a picture of the god Ganesh, a painting of Jesus, and a scene from the Prophet's life. Lakdawala is married to a Christian from Kerala. They struck me as a quintessentially Indian couple: hospitable, tolerant, and happy for all religions to get at least a passing mention in their lives. Earlier, during my unsatisfactory interview with the chief minister, Narendra Modi had said: "In Indonesia, which is a Muslim country, they have a picture of Ganesh on one of their currency notes. Why can't India's Muslims be more like that?" At the time I did not answer. But it struck me later that Hindus are a minority in Indonesia, just as Muslims are in India. If you were to follow Modi's line of thinking, the accurate parallel would be for India to put an Islamic symbol on one of its notes.

# 7. A TRIANGULAR DANCE

Why India's Relations with the United
States and China Will Shape the World
in the Twenty-first Century

*The likely emergence of China and India as new major global
players—similar to the rise of Germany in the 19th century and
America in the 20th century—will transform the geopolitical
landscape, with impacts potentially as dramatic as those of the
previous two centuries.*

From *Mapping The Global Future*, the 2005 report
of the U.S. National Intelligence Council

Continental shelves shift at a rate that is imperceptible
to nonspecialists. Then one day the tectonic pressure
hits a breaking point. What for decades went unde-
tected by most suddenly becomes apparent to all. Likewise, the ascent and descent of a great power often
happens gradually until some event makes the new situation plain. For Britain, the revealing event might
have been the easy submission of its reputed military
garrison in Singapore to the Japanese in 1942, or
perhaps the ignominious collapse of the planned
Anglo-French-Israeli invasion of Egypt in 1956 when
America withdrew its support for sterling. America's
defining moment might be in 1898, when it showed
its big stick to Spain in Cuba and the Philippines, or
in 1917 when Woodrow Wilson's intervention in the

First World War proved decisive. Some argue the invasion of Iraq in 2003 might in future emerge as a moment of descent for the United States.

For India, the big moment does not seem to have arrived yet, although some nationalists believe it happened in May 1998 when New Delhi ordered the underground testing of five nuclear weapons devices. The 1998 nuclear tests may or may not prove in retrospect to be a staging post on India's march toward becoming a "great power"—a globally significant player. India's rise in the early twenty-first century is very widely expected but it is not yet fully assured. The 1998 tests can certainly be read as a signal of New Delhi's ambitions. But there are questions about what precisely India achieved by becoming an openly declared nuclear weapons state. Two weeks later Pakistan followed suit and tested six nuclear warheads (symbolically detonating one more than India). In the perception of much of the international community, India's conventional military superiority over Pakistan had at a stroke been converted into a level nuclear playing field. China, meanwhile, which had all but arranged Pakistan's nuclear capability, remains many years—and possibly decades—in advance of India's nuclear capabilities.

There is another barometer of the rise of great powers: economic clout, of which military prowess is more a consequence than a cause. It was modern textile production and steam power that propelled Britain's rise in the eighteenth and nineteenth centuries and the internal combustion engine, railroads, and, later on, computers that fueled America's rise. On this measure, India's successes in software and "complex manufacturing" are pushing the country forward as an economic power although at a less rapid rate than neighboring China. If India maintains its current average growth rate of about 7 percent a year, the size of its economy will double every twelve years. India would overtake Japan sometime in the 2020s to become the third largest economy in the world. India's recent economic expansion is sufficiently credible to have prompted a global reassessment of the country's potential. Before I moved to India, I was living in Washington, D.C. Any mention of India by the U.S. administration or by Washington's community of think tanks was usually followed by mention of Pakistan. It was always "India-Pakistan." In the last few years this has changed. As the jargon goes, India is no longer "hyphenated" to Pakistan (although Pakistan remains hyphenated to India). India is now hyphenated to China. It is "China-India." India's recalibration has very little to do with nuclear weapons. By the same token, nobody talks of Pakistan's coming superpower status in the wake of its 1998 nuclear tests.

India and China both possess a third attribute that was lacking in Britain but was present to some extent in the United States—a large population. Possessing a large population is both a strength and a weakness. It is a weakness because the population density of China and India will lead to growing strains on their environment and on their scarce supply of arable land. Unless they seriously modify the nature of their economic growth, this could lead to large-scale environmental crises as the century progresses. But having a large population is also a strength because, if the two Asian giants can sustain their economic growth rates, then weight of numbers will ensure they overtake all other economies, including eventually that of the United States—although that will take several decades longer. However, the disadvantages of having a large population could check and even reverse these advantages if the two countries permit indefinite environmental degradation, which would also impose a large cost on everyone else. Laos and Bolivia can degrade their resources as much as they wish. But if China and India fail to take environmental sustainability into account over the coming decades, they will export their suffering to the rest of the world. We will look briefly in the final chapter at India's current approach to the environment. But it is worth mentioning in passing that the United States, China, and India—the large nation-states to which the twenty-first century is ex-

pected to belong—are today probably the three most important obstacles to an international consensus to tackle global warming.

•   •   •   •

India began independence in 1947 believing itself to be a "moral superpower." It was ahead of other Third World countries in achieving
independence and was the only significant colony to have freed itself
through largely peaceful means. The unique qualities of India's freedom struggle and the deep charisma of Gandhi inspired people
around the world, including Martin Luther King Jr., who applied
Gandhi's form of nonviolent disobedience to the civil rights movement in the United States. India stood tall because it had won by the
power of persuasion and not by the power of the gun. In 1947 India's establishment believed it could project its power around the
world in much the same way. With hindsight this was optimistic.
Britain, for all its faults and pomposities, was a relatively flexible
colonial power compared to the forms of imperialism practiced by
the French, Dutch, Belgians, Germans, and Japanese. Britain was
able to sustain its rule over India only because of the acquiescence,
or at least the tolerance, of most Indians. When it came to a choice
between military suppression or departure, Britain opted to depart—
albeit ineptly and too late. One of the great characteristics of Gandhi
and Nehru was that the two London-trained lawyers understood that
Britain was, in the final analysis, vulnerable to argument. Gandhi
was an uncannily good tactician of the political situation in which he
found himself.[1] As we have seen in looking into some of Gandhi's
economic ideas, what worked in the context of the freedom struggle
did not necessarily translate into good policy for an independent
nation-state.

More than in any other sphere of government, including the economy, Nehru dominated India's foreign policy in the first fifteen years
after independence. Nehru's control was all-encompassing. He held

the post of prime minister and foreign minister until he died. Nehru was the biggest force behind the creation of the Non-Aligned Movement, which was launched in Bandung, Indonesia, in 1955 and which included global statesmen such as Tito of Yugoslavia, Nasser of Egypt, and King Sihanouk of Cambodia. Chou En-lai, the prime minister of China, and second in command to Mao Zedong, was present at the conference, which announced that a large chunk of the developing world would be neutral in the cold war rivalry between the United States and the USSR. China's support for nonalignment was to prove rhetorical and even, from India's point of view, deceitful. Meanwhile, John Foster Dulles, the hard-line U.S. secretary of state, denounced India's moral nonalignment as "immoral."[2] India, in the eyes of Western cold war hawks, was preaching freedom and self-determination to the West while conniving with regimes such as China and Egypt that were snuffing out the freedom of their own people. As time wore on, India moved increasingly closer to the Soviet camp. During the decades of nonalignment, India got most of its armaments from the USSR. It also conducted extensive barter trade with the Soviets, in which the two economies swapped goods rather than trading with cash. Although India was not formally part of the Soviet bloc, ties were extensive and warm at many levels.

Nevertheless, one of the key pillars of Nehru's foreign policy was condemnation of the nuclear arms race between the United States and the USSR. Nehru maintained a constant effort to persuade the superpowers of the merits of nuclear disarmament. His interventions were increasingly ignored. Perhaps because Nehru came to realize global disarmament was an impractical goal, he authorized the creation of an Indian civil nuclear program that could at some stage in the future prove useful for developing nuclear weapons. Nehru never formally endorsed the nuclear weapons enthusiasm of his advisers, most notably Homi Bhabha, India's premier nuclear scientist. But it is hard to imagine that someone as intelligent as Nehru could have been unaware of the new choices he had created.[3]

Another key pillar of Nehru's foreign policy was friendship with

China. Nehru believed close relations between India and China would be the axis around which a postcolonial world order would emerge. *Hindi-Chini Bhai Bhai*—Indians and Chinese are brothers!—was the oft-chanted slogan in Delhi celebrating what was seen as a new era of friendship with China. India's language was idealistic. And it was mostly self-delusion. China's leaders were perplexed by India's limited grasp of realpolitik. Although Beijing was communist, it had a more traditional vision of diplomacy than India did. Relatively soon into the new era, two issues began to bedevil relations: China's suppression of autonomy in Tibet, and a dispute over the correct dividing line on the 2,170-mile border between India and China. In 1959 India gave sanctuary to the young Dalai Lama, who had fled Tibet to escape suppression by the People's Liberation Army. Although India imposed the condition that the Dalai Lama refrain from conducting political activities on Indian soil, where the Buddhist leader is still based (in the Himalayan town of Dharamsala), the decision to grant sanctuary to the Tibetans needled the Chinese.

More ominously, Beijing started to publish maps that redrew many sections of the lengthy Himalayan border between the two countries. Indians called this "cartographic aggression." Nehru, whose idealism had not flagged, found it increasingly hard to read the Chinese. The giant neighbors were rapidly becoming estranged. "It is difficult to know what is in their mind,"[4] said Nehru. "They smile when they say the most callous and ruthless things. Mao [Zedong] told me with a smile that he was not afraid of atomic war. . . . With the Chinese you never know and have to be prepared for unexpected reactions. This may partly be due to their isolation, but it is mainly in the Chinese character I think."

In 1962, Chinese People's Liberation Army troops took their Indian counterparts completely by surprise when they flooded across the Himalayan border and drove back India's ill-equipped military forces. After a short and one-sided military encounter, the Chinese declared a cease-fire along an obscure contour that remains the dividing line between the two in India's northeastern region. The thin slice of territory occupied by their troops lacked any strategic value to the Chinese. Beijing's aim had been to cut New Delhi down to size. It was a humiliation for India. But it was a disaster for Nehru. Political opponents in New Delhi openly mocked Nehru's high-sounding words of nonalignment and peaceful coexistence. Nehru never fully recovered from the shock, visibly aging and shrinking in stature. Within eighteen months Nehru was dead. Shortly after he died in 1964, China exploded the hydrogen bomb. It was a tragic postscript to a life of tireless and often inspiring international statesmanship. With ruthless precision, Beijing ensured that Nehru's fond ideals of Asian brotherhood and nuclear disarmament amounted to nothing. It was a harsh tutorial in the ways of the world.

A third pillar of Nehru's foreign policy was Third World solidarity, particularly when it came to dealings with the United States, which many Indians saw as a neocolonial successor to Britain. Encounters between Nehru and his U.S. counterparts, Presidents Truman and Eisenhower, were notable for their frostiness. In addition to his distaste for American capitalism, Nehru carried traits of upper-class British snobbery toward what he saw as America's brash materialism. On one occasion in New York, Nehru disdained a meeting that had been set up with American businessmen, asking his aides why he should waste his time on millionaires. For their part, the Americans found it as hard to deal with Indian diplomats as with the Chinese. At the time India appeared to believe that the "power of argument" mattered more than the "argument of power."[5] But America was more accustomed to giving than receiving moral lectures. Many in Washington found it irksome that a country that was accepting so much U.S. food aid could be pontificating about how Washington should run the world (or how India would run the world if roles were reversed). "Most American negotiators are so taken aback by what they perceive as Indian arrogance that they find it difficult to engage in lengthy and complicated negotiations with New Delhi,"[6] writes Stephen Cohen, a former U.S. state department official and a leading scholar on India. "Many American officials hate to deal with the Indians compared, say, with Pakistanis, Chinese, or Europeans." Nowadays, however, Americans find an India that better understands the uses of "hard power." In spite of some lingering prickliness, Washington is much keener to engage with New Delhi at greater length and across a range of security and commercial issues.

But American diplomacy could also prove to be counterproductive. Indians were given a reminder in 2005 of the degree to which U.S. leaders had once disliked their country when the U.S. National Security Archives released transcripts of conversations between President Nixon and Henry Kissinger, his secretary of state. The conversations took place in 1971. India was by then clearly within the Soviet sphere of influence. Pakistan was an ally of the United States. China had split from the Soviets and had been coaxed and wooed by Nixon into a rapprochement with the United States. Pakistan's military regime played an instrumental role in helping bring about the U.S.-China détente. When it became clear that India would intervene in the civil war that was raging in East Pakistan, in which the Pakistan army was brutally putting down the Bangladeshi separatist movement, Nixon ordered the nuclear-armed USS *Enterprise* into the Bay of Bengal to deter India from doing so. To Indira Gandhi, India's prime minister, who nonetheless did intervene and whose actions helped create Bangladesh, America's implied threat was redolent of Britain's nineteenth-century "gunboat diplomacy." The situation very nearly developed into a much wider international war. Kissinger said publicly that the United States would not come to India's assistance if China intervened in the conflict, which was a green light for Beijing to do so.

Nevertheless, Indians were still shocked in 2005 to see the kind of language that Nixon and Kissinger had used about their country. "What the Indians need is a mass famine," said Nixon.[7] "They're such bastards," says Kissinger. The latter then calls Indira Gandhi a "bitch." Nixon says: "World opinion is on the Indian side but they are such a treacherous and slippery people." Kissinger says: "I think we've got to tell [the Chinese] that some movement on their part . . .

toward the Indian border could be very significant." Later they agreed to tell the Chinese that "if you are ever going to move, this is the time." Fortunately for India, China did not move. China's intervention probably would have dragged the Soviets and therefore—in turn—the Americans into the conflict. There is no guessing where it might have ended. The incident goes some way to explain India's lingering mistrust of the United States and the paranoia about the United States to which Indira Gandhi was highly prone from then on. India has at times been guilty of preachy moralism. But the United States, at times, could be accused of reckless amoralism.

In a politer phase, Henry Kissinger once said, "India lives in a dangerous neighborhood." This was perhaps an understatement. India watched Pakistan and China move ever closer: they proclaimed their friendship with each other to be as "high as the mountains and as deep as the ocean." Given the circumstances it is unsurprising that New Delhi pushed ahead with the development of nuclear weapons. In the decades after 1962, many in India thought China was attempting to "encircle" India by building close relations with some of India's unfriendlier neighbors, which included Pakistan, Myanmar, and, to some extent, Nepal, even though the latter is the only officially Hindu country in the world (India's constitution being secular). China supported Pakistan's stance on Kashmir whenever it came to a vote on the UN Security Council. The Soviets would invariably support India. After the 1971 crisis in East Pakistan, which had humiliated Islamabad, split the country into two and led to a collapse of Pakistan's second military regime, China became Pakistan's largest arms supplier. It replaced the United States, whose interest in the region had noticeably waned. In the 1980s the United States resumed the flow of preferential arms sales to Pakistan, which offered itself as the front-line state in Washington's drive to reverse the 1979 Soviet invasion of Afghanistan.

Many in Washington's nuclear nonproliferation community, particularly in the State Department, continue to believe that it was deeply irresponsible of India to develop nuclear weapons. But the

United States had at times followed policies in the region that inadvertently raised the likelihood that India would do so. In addition, New Delhi had another, more specifically Indian, reason for going nuclear. This was bound up in India's acute sensitivity to what it saw as modern forms of colonialism. In 1968 the five nuclear powers—the United States, Britain, France, USSR, and China—persuaded most nonnuclear countries to sign the Treaty on the Non-Proliferation of Nuclear Weapons. This enshrined the five as the world's only official nuclear weapons states and promised civil nuclear power assistance to those countries that pledged to forgo nuclear weapons. Countries as diverse as Iran and North Korea signed the treaty. But India did not. And since India did not, Pakistan did not. Indian diplomats brought to bear all their mastery of detail, love of rhetoric, sensitivity about status, and resentments of the West to condemn the treaty as unjust. New Delhi called it "nuclear apartheid." Indira Gandhi stepped up India's clandestine program to develop nuclear devices.

In 1974 Indira Gandhi ordered a series of "Peaceful Nuclear Tests." India's polite fiction was that nuclear devices could be used for civilian purposes such as creating tunnels and building dams. Zulfikar Ali Bhutto, Pakistan's prime minister, responded to India's tests by saying that Pakistan would, if necessary, "eat grass" in its zeal to match India's capabilities. But all Islamabad needed to do was to request help from China, which supplied Pakistan with much of the technology to develop both nuclear warheads and the missile delivery systems. In addition, Pakistan's notorious A. Q. Khan, who later became known as the father of the country's nuclear program, had in the 1970s stolen the blueprints from his Dutch employer that revealed the process by which uranium is enriched into weapons-grade material. By 1987, when India and Pakistan almost came to blows following India's "Brass Tacks" operation—a large-scale military exercise near the Pakistan border, which India says Pakistan misinterpreted as a prelude to war (Islamabad said its interpretation was reasonable)—both were thought to possess rudimentary nuclear devices. It was only a matter of time before they tested them.

Even before the 1998 India-Pakistan nuclear tests, there were growing apprehensions about how easy it would be for one to misread the other in the "fog of war." The fear was mostly directed at Pakistan since New Delhi had unveiled a nuclear doctrine that proclaimed India as a "No First Use" nuclear power. It meant that New Delhi would only use nuclear weapons if its opponent had used them first. Pakistan, on the other hand, had proclaimed itself to be a "First Strike" power. Pakistan's nuclear stance mirrored that of the United States during the cold war, wherein the United States, which had fewer conventional forces stationed in Europe than did the Soviet-led Warsaw Pact, was a "First Strike" power. The Soviets maintained a stance of "No First Use." As the inferior power in terms of conventional military forces, with a ratio of roughly three to two in India's favor, Pakistan was tempted to rattle the nuclear saber every now and then. Many Pakistani strategists believe it is in Islamabad's interests to create doubts among New Delhi's decision makers about how easily and quickly India might cross Pakistan's "nuclear red line" should it initiate conventional military conflict. What would happen in practice is anybody's guess. Whenever tensions between the two countries have risen to high levels in the last two decades, Pakistan has issued veiled warnings to India about the risks of nuclear escalation.

•    •    •

May 2002 was arguably the most dangerous moment in the extensive history of dangerous moments between India and Pakistan. India, as we saw in the last chapter, had deployed most of its army along the Pakistan border following the failed suicide attack on its parliament in New Delhi the previous December. After an initial

IN SPITE OF THE GODS     268

scare in January, when India had been on the verge of ordering some kind of military operation across the Line of Control in Kashmir, tensions had subsided. Under pressure from the Bush administration, which, among other things, feared that a conflict between India and Pakistan would compromise its operations in Afghanistan, General Musharraf had in January 2002 given a national broadcast in which he pledged to crack down on what he called Pakistan's "state-within-a-state" of Islamist groups. But the crackdown was more apparent than real. Groups such as Lashkar-e-Toiba, which India had specifically blamed for the attack on its parliament, simply changed names and shifted their headquarters from Pakistan's province of Punjab to Azad Kashmir, the Pakistan-held section of Kashmir. Once the snows started to melt in late March, terrorist infiltration across the LOC into India's portion of Kashmir resumed at even higher levels than previous years. The situation was drifting back to square one.

Then in mid-May an Islamist terrorist group carried out a particularly bloody attack on the residential quarters of an Indian army regiment in Kaluchak, a town in Jammu and Kashmir. The suicide terrorists butchered thirty-four people, including the wives and children of Indian soldiers. India's army, which had been twiddling its thumbs on the border for months, pushed hard for New Delhi to retaliate quickly. Atal Behari Vajpayee, India's prime minister, flew to Kashmir and delivered a speech to Indian soldiers at an army camp very close to the LOC. Vajpayee spoke of an impending "decisive battle" to overcome the forces of terrorism. There was open talk in India of a "punitive strike" across the LOC on Pakistan army positions and the terrorist training camps they were allegedly protecting. The mercury shot back up. The world's eyes were on General Musharraf to see how he would respond. I flew to Islamabad to interview Pakistan's leader. Conflict was expected to break out at any moment. A few days earlier General Musharraf had ordered the testing of Pakistan's long-range nuclear-capable ballistic missiles in an unsubtle hint of what Pakistan might do if India crossed the LOC or the international border. Pakistan officials, who had honed the language of nuclear threat over many years, had hinted to journalists that Islamabad would consider the nuclear option if India launched a military strike. At the UN, Pakistan's ambassador said: "If India reserves the right to use conventional weapons, how can Pakistan—a weaker power—be expected to rule out all means of deterrence?"[8] Immediately before my interview, Pakistan's leader gave another national broadcast. He was dressed in full uniform and his voice and expression were deeply somber. It seemed as though he was priming Pakistan for conflict. But General Musharraf's address included a coded and conditional pledge that Pakistan would suspend infiltration across the LOC if India stood down. He could not explicitly promise to halt terrorist infiltration, since a specific pledge would be tantamount to an admission that the Pakistan army had been sponsoring it all along—a position Islamabad continues to deny.

"As you know the enemy's forces are deployed on our borders,"[9] General Musharraf told the nation. "The enemy has brought forward its army, navy and air force. They are being faced by the Pakistan army, navy, and the air force and they are serving as a bulwark. The entire nation is with the armed forces and will shed the last drop of its blood but would not allow any harm to come to the motherland. Tension is at its height. . . . We do not want war. But if war is thrust upon us, we would respond with full might, and give a befitting reply. I would now like to convey a message to the world community, Pakistan does not want war. Pakistan will not be the one to initiate war. We want peace in the region. Let me also assure the world community that Pakistan is doing nothing across the Line of Control and Pakistan will never allow the export of terrorism anywhere in the world from within Pakistan.* Now I want to give a message to my Kashmiri brothers and sisters. Kashmir resides in the

---

*General Musharraf's language was precise. According to Pakistan, Azad Kashmir is not technically part of sovereign Pakistan since Islamabad believes the whole of Kashmir is in dispute under UN law. It is also worth noting the tenses he used. "Pakistan *is* doing nothing across the Line of Control." If General Musharraf had said "has been" or "will not be," it would have conveyed something different.

heart of every Pakistani. Pakistan will always fulfill its duty of providing moral, political, and diplomatic support to the cause of Kashmir. Pakistan will always support the Kashmiri struggle for liberation."

Having watched this somewhat unnerving broadcast, I, and my Pakistani colleague, Farhan Bokhari, drove to General Musharraf's official military residence in the town of Rawalpindi, a few miles from Islamabad. We were shown into a stately living room. A few moments later, General Musharraf appeared. He had changed his outfit. In place of the military regalia, he was dressed in an open-necked shirt and casual slacks. He was smiling and relaxed enough to crack a few jokes. The broadcast had been aimed at many audiences: the Indians, the Americans, and a cross section of Pakistanis, including the Kashmiri militant groups and the army. So it had contained a number of contradictory messages. But our one-hour interview was for a Western audience. General Musharraf modified his demeanor. I asked him about the threat of nuclear weapons. "Pakistan is a deterrence country and is very capable of guarding its honor and dignity,"[10] he said. "But I would not like to discuss the nuclear issue. It would be very irresponsible for a statesman to discuss nuclear weapons. There's a lot of tension and war hysteria going on. Nobody wants to go to war. There is no walking over here by any side. I am sure the Indians know this. Sanity demands an avoidance of war but at the same time in pursuit of peace you can't compromise on honor or dignity. One has to strike a balance between maintaining honor and dignity and going for peace."

For a Western audience, General Musharraf altered his vocabulary. Instead of responding with "full might," Pakistan would maintain its "honor and dignity." But the meaning was similar. In coded language, General Musharraf repeatedly conveyed two messages: Pakistan considered nuclear weapons to be a military option; and Pakistan would resume its support for cross-border terrorism unless India agreed to talks about the status of Kashmir. The two points were linked. I asked him about the apparent pledge he had made in the television broadcast to put a complete stop to terrorism. I also asked whether he was using the so-called nuclear bluff to force India to the negotiating table. He put me straight about the pledge on terrorism. "I said nothing was happening along the Line of Control *now*. Whether India accepts it or not, they cannot be the accusers and judges both. . . . I am a realist. There are very serious problems between the two countries which are a cause of tensions which have given rise to three wars here. Other than wars, there are battles going on every second day. People are dying on the borders, along the Line of Control. Why should we not address these problems? This is no bluff. This is realism. Unfortunately we don't see the same realism across the border." At the end of the interview, General Musharraf gave us each his customary gift, a mantelpiece clock embossed with the Pakistan national flag. I am now owner of three identical Pakistan national clocks, each of which tells a different time.

I hitched a lift back to New Delhi on a British government plane. Jack Straw, Britain's foreign minister, was in the region to try to dissuade both countries from embarking on a conflict. A few days later, Richard Armitage, the U.S. deputy secretary of state, traveled the same route. A former soldier himself, Armitage emerged from his meeting with General Musharraf smiling broadly. Later that day Armitage traveled to New Delhi carrying with him a pledge that Pakistan would "permanently" put an end to terrorist infiltration of the LOC. Pakistan's beefed-up pledge was enough for Delhi to put an end to the crisis. The following week, Donald Rumsfeld, the U.S. defense secretary, visited both capitals to put a seal on the new situation. Not for the first time, it was the Americans, assisted by the British, who pulled India and Pakistan's chestnuts out of the fire. Washington had even persuaded China to have a quiet word in General Musharraf's ear. The becalming role that Washington played in 2002, which took skill and persistence, made a pleasant contrast with the high-wire games Nixon and Kissinger had indulged in thirty years earlier.

•  •  •

India was not a leading player in the cold war (in spite of its close ties to Moscow). But the collapse of the Soviet Union opened up new possibilities that New Delhi has done much to exploit. The gradual improvement in relations between the United States and India in the last ten to fifteen years has been matched by a gradual cooling of relations between the United States and China. The logic of diplomacy in today's unipolar world is far more fluid than it was during the cold war. Over the same period India also started to mend fences with China, although New Delhi and Beijing have yet to agree on where exactly those fences should be delineated. Mindful perhaps of its own (admittedly low-level) separatist problems in the country's northwestern province of Xinjiang, Beijing has also watered down criticisms of India's position on Kashmir. Some of China's separatist groups are thought to have links with Islamist groups that are sponsored by Pakistan, even though there is no suggestion that Islamabad has facilitated these links. China was given another reason in 2004 to become more evenhanded toward India and Pakistan when it was revealed that A. Q. Khan, the hero of Pakistan's nuclear program, had sold nuclear secrets during the 1980s and 1990s to any country that was prepared to pay. Since much of the technology that A. Q. Khan sold originally came from China, the revelations were embarrassing to Beijing. Buyers in A. Q. Khan's "international nuclear Wal-Mart" included Libya, North Korea, probably Iran, and possibly Saudi Arabia. In addition, strategists in Beijing reportedly concluded it would be counterproductive to back a rapid expansion of Pakistan's nuclear arsenal because that would spark a nuclear arms race with India, which would bring India more rapidly up to nuclear parity with China.[11]

But there are two even more important reasons that China wanted better relations with India and why it is likely to push for further improvements over the coming years. First, India is a much more hard-nosed neighbor now than it was during the years of nonalignment. India's May 1998 nuclear tests forced China to sit up and take notice of a different India, one that had all but abandoned the diplomatic philosophy of Gandhi and Nehru. In the early 1990s, New Delhi asked Beijing to declare that China's nuclear weapons were "No First Use" vis-à-vis India. Beijing said there was no point in proclaiming a nuclear stance toward a country that did not possess nuclear weapons.[12]

A few days before the 1998 tests, George Fernandes, India's defense minister, stated publicly that China was the biggest threat to India's security. After the tests took place, Atal Behari Vajpayee wrote to President Bill Clinton stating that China, and not Pakistan, was the prime motivator in India's decision to go nuclear. Since China had provided Pakistan with most of its nuclear know-how, India's claim had some credibility. In public, Vajpayee said: "Millions of Indians have viewed this occasion as the beginning of the rise of a strong and self-confident India. I fully share this assessment and this dream. India has never considered military might as the ultimate measure of national strength. It is a necessary component of overall national strength. I would, therefore, say that the greatest meaning of the tests is that they have given India *shakti* [elemental power], they have given India strength, they have given India self-confidence."[13]

China condemned the tests. But its protests were not emotional. In June 2001, India became one of the first countries to endorse the Bush administration's plans of Theater Missile Defense—or "Star Wars II." China condemned the concept as dangerously destabilizing to the established global nuclear order. Washington's plans to build a space-based shield against nuclear weapons have since run into technical and financial difficulties. And the terrorist attacks of 9/11 also made Star Wars II seem irrelevant to the principal security challenges facing the United States. But India's unequivocal stance was not lost on Beijing. China remained critical of India and still insists, somewhat quixotically, that India should roll back its nuclear program and scrap its nuclear weapons. But there is also a wary tone of respect to China's admonitions, one that had been glaringly absent in previous decades.

The second reason for the thawing of tensions between India and China is economic. China embarked on economic reform in 1978. So it has a thirteen-year head start on India, which only began in 1991. Partly because of this, China has roughly double India's per capita income and more than four times India's level of exports. But in the last few years India's economy has begun to accelerate. In 2000, trade between India and China was less than $2 billion. By 2006 it was almost $20 billion. Although this is a small proportion of China's overall trade with the world, India is now China's fastest-growing trade partner, and vice versa. Much of the new trade flows have been driven by China's almost limitless appetite for commodities, including iron ore and steel, which India is supplying in ever larger quantities. But India has also been selling vehicle components to foreign multinationals based in China and providing software design for the next generation of high-tech automobiles. Today the monetary value of the software embedded in a vehicle exceeds the value of its hardware. India's software companies have also set up shop directly in China in large numbers. India's facility both with the English language and with information technology is not matched by China. Many of the foreign multinationals based in China, whose investments account for half of China's exports, use the Shanghai or Hong Kong offices of India's IT companies to supply their software and provide them with systems maintenance. India's competitive pharmaceutical sector has also set up production sites in China.

It was not expected to turn out like this. When China joined the World Trade Organization in 2000, Indian companies were terrified their domestic market would be flooded by cheap Chinese goods. The Indian media buzzed with stories of Chinese umbrellas, batteries, and fireworks that were pricing their local competitors out of business. But India has achieved a modest trade surplus with China for several consecutive years. This has drastically changed Indian perceptions of China; from being a commercial threat it has become a potential partner. So strong is global demand for both Chinese goods and Indian services that the two countries have in many respects ceased to see each other as conventional competitors. "People in India used to say it was China and not India, then they said it was China against India, but if you look at any number of sectors the real story is China *and* India," said N. Srinivasan, head of the Confederation of Indian Industry.[14] "The economies of India and China are complementary."

Assuming that neither country's economy goes off the rails in the next five to ten years—which is, admittedly, a sizable assumption—the growth in the volume of trade between India and China will make it one of the most important trading relationships in the world. Eventually, demography suggests it will be the world's largest trading relationship. Both countries have placed trade and economics at the heart of their new diplomacy. Nowadays, negotiations to create "free trade agreements" dominate much of the time of diplomats in both countries. China is ahead of India, but the latter is catching up. Both countries have concluded trade agreements with the Association of South East Asian Nations. And India is hoping to emulate China's growing trade relations with South America. At the global level, China, India, Brazil, and South Africa lead the G20, a block of twenty developing countries that has become a weighty player at world trade liberalization talks in Geneva. There is also a proposal for a bilateral trade deal between India and China, although this would take years to negotiate.

Does all this mean China and India have entered on a genuine era of friendship? Proponents of free trade are fond of the saying "When countries start trading goods, they stop trading blows." This might be an overstatement. But clearly, as economic links strengthen and as more and more Indians visit China and vice versa, disagreements over the exact position of the international boundary or the precise status of the Dalai Lama become progressively easier to manage. The two countries have held fifteen rounds of negotiations on the border dispute and claim to be within spitting distance of a final settlement. At a summit in New Delhi in 2005, India recognized China's sovereignty over Tibet. In exchange, China recognized India's sovereignty over the Himalayan state of Sikkim, a small (nominally independent) kingdom that New Delhi formally annexed in the 1970s. At the close of the summit between Wen Jiabao, China's prime minister, and Manmohan Singh, India's prime minister, Manmohan said: "Together India and China can reshape the world." It was a bold statement. By implication Manmohan was also warning that if India and China were again to mismanage their relations, they would both be handicapped in their objective of creating a "multipolar" world. Talk of "multipolarity" is a polite way of hoping for a world in which there are stronger limits on the scope of the United States to impose its will on others. It is a goal shared by China and India.

There is a different saying (this time Chinese): "No mountain can accommodate two tigers." Whether strong trading ties between India and China will remove the threat of conflict between the two, as some Western commentators believe is true at all times and of all countries, is a more questionable assumption. Which wisdom will prove more accurate over time is hard to know. But for the time being, the mountain is teeming with easy pickings. At the very least, stronger trading ties between India and China cannot hurt. The two countries have developed a very different mind-set compared to the outlook that led to war in 1962. India is no longer so idealistic. It talks much less of Third World solidarity and much more about its own national interests. Although it has not stated so openly, most observers assume China will require peaceful relations with India if it is to achieve its ambition of becoming a global power.

Tectonic plates are gradually shifting. It is an intriguing phase of international relations that is likely to last for a decade or two before China becomes a genuine political force on the global stage. There are potential obstacles to the parallel rise of India, which we shall look at in the final chapter. But the odds are fairly strong that India will circumvent most of them, not least because the United States now explicitly desires the rise of India.

• • •

In March 2005 the Bush administration did something none of its predecessors had done. It announced it would play midwife to the birth of a new world power. The country was India. Specifically, the U.S. spokesman said that the United States wanted "to help India become a major world power in the 21st century. We understand fully the implications, including military implications, of that statement."[15] The Bush administration's declaration coincided with the publication of a CIA report that identified India as the key global "swing state"[16] of the twenty-first century. The CIA also predicted that India would become the world's fourth most powerful country by 2012, as measured by a combination of economic, military, and technological strength.[17] The view was that building a strong partnership with India, which U.S. officials had repeatedly described as a "natural ally,"[18] would assist in the prolongation of American power in the coming decades. This unprecedented statement was unusual not only for its originality but also for its candor. What was behind it?

Bush administration officials offer any number of explanations for their pro-India enthusiasms. The most often cited is that India is by far the largest democracy in the world. When George W. Bush came to office, he offered Robert Blackwill, a senior adviser,* any ambassadorial posting he wanted. Blackwill, who had been a senior arms negotiator during the cold war, instantly chose India. Bush said to Blackwill: "A billion people and it's a democracy. Ain't that something?"[19] Second, in spite of India's nuclear tests, which had triggered U.S. sanctions on the export of sensitive, or "dual-use," technology to India, the Bush administration was impressed by India's "responsible stewardship" of its nuclear arsenal. In contrast to Pakistan, which had been passing on the technology to anyone who had the cash, India was considered to have a good system of export controls. Third, the almost two million people of Indian origin based in the United States had become a strong new voice in U.S. politics. Indian Americans are the richest ethnic group in the United States, with a per capita income of more than $50,000. India also provides the highest number of foreign students in the United States and accounts for the largest share of the annual H1B visas for foreign technical workers, principally software engineers. India was also emerging as a potentially vast new market for American products, albeit not as large as China's market.

Although U.S. officials rarely mention China in this context, it is the real motivation for Washington's decision to sponsor India's great power ambitions. Because of its sheer size and the nature of its political system, India is seen as the only country that could counterbalance China's rise as a global power. America has watched China's emergence with growing anxiety. American companies have made the most of China's economic openness. But the expected loosening of the Chinese Communist Party's grip on the country's political system that was expected to come as a result of China's economic liberalization has not taken place. Nor has China watered down its objective of incorporating what it sees as the renegade province of Taiwan into the motherland. On the contrary, China's national as-

---

*Blackwill was one of the so-called Vulcans, led by Condoleezza Rice, who provided foreign policy advice to the 2000 Bush presidential campaign.

sembly passed a law in 2005 authorizing military action against Taiwan should it declare formal independence from China. Taiwan is a military ally of the United States. A series of Pentagon reports have also voiced increasingly strident apprehensions about China's rapidly mounting defense expenditures, which some U.S. sources estimate are far higher than Beijing's official budget numbers. There is also concern in the United States, and elsewhere, about China's stated ambitions of developing a "blue water" (far-reaching) navy that would project its power into the Indian Ocean and beyond.

Outside advisers to the Bush administration and former officials are more explicit about linking America's strategy on India to its strategy on China. Ashley Tellis, an Indian-born analyst at the Carnegie Endowment in Washington, was Robert Blackwill's nuclear and military adviser in New Delhi between 2001 and 2003. Among many others, he and Blackwill argued successfully that the United States should recognize India's nuclear weapons status. In an influential paper in 2005, Tellis wrote: "There is a real fear that China might some day turn its rising economic and military power against America. In this context the United States needs to look at a re-ordering of their relationship with India which today is not only a key ally in the war against terror but a counterbalance in Asia against China's dominance."[20] Blackwill, who had left the administration a few months earlier, said: "Why should the United States want to check India's missile capability in ways that could lead to China's permanent nuclear dominance over democratic India?"[21]

Their argument won out. In July 2005 Manmohan Singh, India's prime minister, visited Washington and was offered a nuclear deal that went way beyond New Delhi's expectations. The United States offered to accept India's nuclear weapons status, reinstate the export of nuclear fuel for India's civil nuclear program, and lift all remaining restrictions on the export of sensitive technologies to India. In return, India would tighten export controls to prevent the sale of "dual-use" technology to other countries, accept international monitoring of its civil nuclear plants, and erect more credible walls between its civilian and military sectors—particularly in the space program, where India is believed to have transferred satellite launch technology to its ballistic missile scientists. In other words, India would become the first, and possibly the last, country to be accepted informally into the club of five official nuclear states. Formal international recognition would be beyond reach since that would involve tearing up the nonproliferation treaty. Manmohan was accorded the maximum honor due to a global statesman on the visit. India's prime minister received a nineteen-gun salute. President Bush gave Manmohan an official state banquet at the White House, only the fifth Bush had hosted in four years. And Manmohan was invited to give an address to the joint houses of Congress on Capitol Hill. In March 2006, George Bush paid a return visit to India. To the surprise even of those who had been lobbying the U.S. administration to treat India generously, Bush agreed to pretty much everything the Indians wanted. India would be given access to civil nuclear fuel supplies in exchange for agreeing to put most—but not all—of its civil nuclear plants under international safeguards. Many in Washington and among America's partners in the 44-member Nuclear Suppliers' Group, which includes skeptics such as Australia and Japan, wondered why the U.S. had agreed to a deal that would enable India to benefit from all the advantages of belonging to the nonproliferation treaty without paying the full cost. The answer is simple if one ignores Bush's stated reasons for agreeing to the deal (to reward India's nonproliferation record and strengthen the international nonproliferation regime) and looks instead at the administration's underlying motive: the deal would give India the fuel and cover to accelerate its nuclear weapons program and counterbalance that of China. By this more accurate barometer, the deal made perfect sense.

In the annals of American diplomacy, the two U.S.-India summits stand out as highly unusual events. Perhaps in retrospect, they will be seen as comprising an ascending moment for India.

There were many critics of the deal in America, particularly on Capitol Hill, where approval was essential if it was to go ahead.

Some said a deal would act as a green light for other aspiring nuclear states to follow India's example. Its timing could not have been more awkward. The U.S.-India summits coincided with a heightened phase of concern about Iran's alleged clandestine nuclear weapons program, which Washington wanted stopped at almost any cost. It also coincided with the apparently fruitless talks over Pyongyang's nuclear ambitions between the regime in North Korea and a six-nation group led by the United States, which included China. Others said the deal would provoke an arms race between India and Pakistan, which would inevitably involve China. Ultimately, they said, the Bush administration had signaled that counterbalancing China was more important to America than repairing the rule-based international system to prevent the spread of weapons of mass destruction.

The process of providing India with the benefits of being a nuclear power without formally recognizing it as one (which, among others, would require China's agreement) is likely to be lengthy and uncertain and will probably entail changes to the deal that President Bush unveiled in July 2005. But even if the deal was watered down by congressional opponents at home and America's four nuclear partners abroad, it would be unlikely to upset the U.S. strategy of building up India as a great power. Unrelated to the 2005 nuclear deal, U.S. and Indian military forces have been conducting regular joint exercises since the late 1990s, at sea, in the air, and on land. In 2004 the two countries staged a large joint military maneuver on India's border with China. Beijing said nothing. The two navies have also been conducting joint patrols of the Indian Ocean up to the Straits of Malacca near Singapore to combat piracy and protect vital commercial shipping lanes, particularly the oil tanker route. These and other areas of strategic cooperation between the United States and India, including detailed joint intelligence operations on terrorism, are growing all the time. Barely a week seems to go by without a senior American diplomat, senator, general, or admiral passing through New Delhi.

But the United States cannot take everything for granted in its emerging relationship with India. India is not, like Britain or Japan, a declining power that will happily follow America's lead on most of the important global issues. New Delhi might have learned to curtail some of its traditional Nehruvian moralizing. But sometimes it likes to thumb its nose at the United States for the pure pleasure of it. Much of India's establishment and the country's influential left-wing parties, which prop up Manmohan Singh's coalition majority within parliament without formally participating in government, remain deeply suspicious of the United States, in spite of Washington's increasingly warm and unconditional overtures. Even Jaswant Singh, who, as foreign minister in Atal Behari Vajpayee's government, was the principal architect of the improvement of India's ties with the United States, has given voice to bitterly anti-American sentiments. The former army major, who remains a senior figure in the Hindu nationalist BJP, held a series of intensive negotiations with Strobe Talbott, Bill Clinton's deputy secretary of state, following India's May 1998 tests. Talbott's aim was to persuade India to "cap, roll back and eliminate" its nuclear arsenal. Talbott failed. But the intensive talks with Jaswant, which took place over two years and in many different countries, provided the springboard for the rapid movement in relations during the Bush years. Talbott wrote. "[The Indian government's] strategy was to play for the day when the United States would get over its huffing and puffing and, with a sigh of exhaustion, or a shrug of resignation, accept a nuclear-armed India as a fully responsible and entitled member of the international community."[22]

Jaswant's strategy worked. Yet in spite of the warmth of his relations with Strobe Talbott, Jaswant still lapses into a ferocious anti-Americanism whenever he feels Washington is not according India the respect it deserves. When Colin Powell, secretary of state in the first Bush administration, stepped down in 2004, he recalled Washington's role in helping to prevent a war between India and Pakistan in 2002. Jaswant had been Powell's counterpart. To most people who read Powell's account, it seemed to be uncontroversial. Powell said he had arranged telephone calls between George Bush and Atal

Behari Vajpayee. In addition, he claimed to have set up a conversation between General Musharraf and Vajpayee and suggested one or two things Vajpayee might say. Powell also said that if conflict had broken out, it could have escalated into a nuclear exchange.

An incandescent Jaswant called a press conference in New Delhi to rebut Powell's account. Nobody was expecting such wounded pride. "General Powell's claim that he played a role in Mr. Vajpayee's peace initiative—even to the extent of setting up an elocution lesson—is entirely fabricated," said Singh. "There was never any nuclear dimension at all. It is all very much a part of their [the Americans'] imagination, as was the existence of weapons of mass destruction in Iraq." He continued: "Mr. Powell said: 'We set it up.' So are we to understand the State Department is now acting as a telephone exchange? The U.S. bureaucracy is always three steps ahead of India in obfuscation and finding reasons not to do a thing. The Americans are world champions at bureaucracy. The State Department, the Pentagon, the FBI, the CIA, don't know what each other is doing. The Americans do not know how to assert great power status. They are caught in a web of their own creation."

Jaswant's impassioned rebuttal, which strayed into subjects unrelated to Colin Powell's reminiscences, illustrated something fundamental about India's character that the Americans and others are continually required to relearn. Foreign diplomats sometimes barely get past the opening remarks if their Indian counterparts do not feel satisfied they will be treated with exceptional respect. At times, India's diplomats appear to mind more about etiquette than they do about substance. India wants constantly to be reminded how important it is, and to be complimented on the profundity of its civilization. I have met many Indian diplomats, including Jaswant, and I agree with the following description. It was written by Stephen Cohen, the Brookings Institution scholar who is also an Indophile. "Whether a realist or an idealist, almost every member of the Indian strategic community thinks that India's inherent greatness as a power is itself a valuable diplomatic asset," he wrote.[23] "India's ambassadors are expected to persuade foreign officials of the wisdom and moral correctness of the Indian position, say, by stating the Indian case, and supplementing political arguments with information about India's great civilization, its cultural and economic accomplishments and its democratic orientation."

It would be tempting to conclude that India is rising in spite of its diplomacy. Any suggestion, for example, that there might be outside or "third-party mediation" in the Kashmir dispute is treated as toxic. Similarly, India's elite bristle at the notion there would be any possibility of nuclear conflict in south Asia. In an interview during the 2002 crisis, I asked Jaswant Singh about the nuclear threat. He peered at me in a headmasterly way. "Just because I am an Asian does not mean I am incapable of being responsible," he said tartly. I also asked him to respond to speculation that the United States hoped India would play a counterbalancing role to an emerging China. "India does not play any roles, Mr. Luce," was the extent of his response. Once, in 2002, the Indian government issued a statement dismissing a trivial observation from the (lone) UN military observer in Kashmir. It was not the content of the observation that offended New Delhi but the fact that it was offered by an outsider. The Indian government's short statement said: "We see no need for obiter dicta [incidental or collateral remarks] on the Jammu and Kashmir issue from any third parties."[24] To me, there was something about these seventeen short words that crystallizes the weaknesses of Indian diplomacy.

There is a strong perception that India's obsession with status can sometimes outweigh the practical calculation of what is in the country's national interests. A good example is the management of nuclear relations with Pakistan. To put it bluntly, New Delhi appears to mind more about what it sees as the implicit assumption that south Asians are less responsible with nuclear weapons than others, than it cares about taking every measure possible to minimize the possibility of nuclear misunderstanding with Pakistan. I have yet to come across an example of a Western strategist arguing that south Asians are inherently less capable than others of managing their nuclear arsenals responsibly. But international observers have real concerns that New Delhi and Islamabad continue to be reluctant to put in place the kind of essential safety measures that became routine between the United States and the USSR after the hair-raising Cuban missile crisis of 1962. "We used to have a joke that the nuclear establishments of the United States and the USSR could swap places for a few weeks and everything would proceed as smoothly as before," said Robert Blackwill. "You could not say that about India and Pakistan."[25]

India's sensitivity to what is sees as the underlying racism of Western military strategists has also given rise to some counterintuitive diplomatic positions. During the height of the 2002 India-Pakistan crisis, Indian diplomats regularly briefed journalists that Pakistan would never use nuclear weapons. Pakistan, meanwhile, was busy disseminating the opposite message. The complacency of Indian diplomats was shared by much of the Indian media. During the most tense moments it was instructive to read Western newspaper accounts of the situation, many of which were alarmist to the point of caricature,* and then to turn to the Indian media, which was at times more concerned with the Indian cricket team's performance than the threat of conflict with Pakistan. Rabid commentaries about the evil Pakistan regime were juxtaposed with reassuring editorials that all would turn out fine in practice. As P. R. Chari, one of India's most thoughtful security analysts, told me at the time: "India wants the world to believe that Pakistan is an irresponsible power that should never be trusted on anything—except on nuclear weapons."

There is no suggestion that India would be irresponsible with its own nuclear arsenal. In fact, I sometimes get the impression that India sees its nuclear status as hypothetical. This is reassuring. But it is also vexing, because it means India is relaxed about the nuclear pos-

---

*"Westerners Flee as Nuclear War Looms" was my favorite headline that appeared in one of the UK newspapers. In fact, not many Westerners fled. And it was a possible cross-LOC military raid that was looming. The threat of nuclear escalation does exist. But the probability remains that it will not happen.

tures of its neighbors, which are of a different nature. As a result, India knows very little about the nuclear assets, policies, and signaling of Pakistan and vice versa. In matters nuclear, ignorance is never bliss. For example, knowledge of which types of military planes are authorized to carry nuclear weapons could prevent a potentially lethal misreading of signals in a conflict. Since India and Pakistan are immediate neighbors, this is highly important. The United States and the USSR had a twenty-minute missile warning time given their distance from each other. For neighboring India and Pakistan, the gap is two minutes. "India and Pakistan are ignorant of the basic grammar of each other's nuclear establishments," said Chari. "This raises the possibility that you could completely misinterpret a stray enemy aircraft as a nuclear attack. In a conflict you don't have time to get on the telephone."

Interestingly, one of Washington's additional motivations in pushing for greater U.S. strategic involvement with India was to help create a more responsible nuclear culture in the region. Ever since both India and Pakistan had refused to sign the nuclear nonproliferation treaty, this had been a constant dilemma. "We call it the clean needle dilemma," said Robert Blackwill. "If you start handing out clean needles to drug users, then you are encouraging them to continue using drugs. But if you don't, they might die of HIV-AIDS."[26] There are signs that the India-Pakistan peace process, which began in 2003, might be leading to a better-managed nuclear environment between the two countries. So far they have agreed on symbolic safeguards. For example, India and Pakistan have set up a telephone hotline between their military commanders. And they have agreed to notify each other of the dates and venues of nuclear missile tests. But a more substantive exchange of nuclear information remains hostage to the successful outcome of the peace process—a scenario that cannot be guaranteed. This is curious sequencing. It is particularly important to put safer nuclear systems in place while there is a possibility of war. But the goal of establishing nuclear safety appears to be lower down on New Delhi's list of priorities than maintaining rigid virtue in its

Kashmir position. Progress in talks over Kashmir has often been torpedoed by the slightest variation in words, the tiniest shift of square brackets. In the last decade or two, India has become a more practical power. But it continues on crucial issues and at crucial moments to believe that words matter more than weapons.

There are a number of other limitations to the continued growth in the relationship between India and the United States. First, as Jaswant Singh stated, India apparently does not wish, on behalf of Washington, to play the role of strategic counterbalance to China. India wants to remain equidistant from both China and the United States, while working for good relations with both. In practice, this would still suit Washington's purposes. All India needs to do is to continue to grow economically and become more assertive in its dealings with the world, and in doing so it would naturally act as a counterbalance to China, whether it intends to do so or not. There is a sneaking suspicion that in practice India does wish to have closer strategic links to the United States than to China but would be loath to admit this publicly, both for fear of provoking a domestic political backlash and for fear of offending China. In fact, the growth over the last few years of military cooperation between India and the United States, and the possibility that India will accept Washington's offer of establishing a coproduction facility in India to build American F-18A fighter aircraft, suggests these links are already in place. In which case, India is managing its China relations with tact.

A more difficult constraint on warmer ties with the United States is India's relations with other countries, including regimes that Washington has classified as "rogue." The most notable example is India's relationship with Iran, which is designated as part of President Bush's "axis of evil" but which is a relatively close diplomatic partner of India. In the aftermath of the July 2005 nuclear deal between India and Washington, New Delhi immediately diluted its earlier support for Iran's nuclear stonewalling. Some saw India's change of stance as an illustration of the timeless maxim that once you join a club you want to close the door to new members. But it is likely that India's new pragmatism was more calculated than that. It was probably an implicit quid pro quo that Washington had requested of New Delhi in exchange for the July 2005 nuclear deal. Even then, however, India's change of position triggered bitter complaints by the country's two Communist parties that New Delhi was becoming slavishly pro-American.* India was also critical of the 2003 American-led invasion of Iraq. Washington made strenuous efforts to persuade India to join the "coalition of the willing," which came close to succeeding. But the strong likelihood of a domestic political backlash caused Vajpayee to pull back at the last moment. Not unreasonably, Vajpayee's senior adviser, Brajesh Mishra, said: "India does not have a dog in this fight." India's parliament passed a unanimous resolution condemning the U.S.-led invasion.

But perhaps the most important limitation to the further strengthening of U.S.-India ties is the anemic growth in trade between the two countries—more specifically, the slow growth of U.S. exports to India. During his time in New Delhi, Robert Blackwill, who has done more, perhaps, than any other U.S. diplomat to boost relations with India, often said that U.S. trade flows to India were "flat as a *chappati* [Indian bread]." Large American investors, particularly in the power-generation sector, allege they have been mistreated by the Indian government. Their most glaring example is the debacle over a 2,400–megawatt Dabhol power plant near Mumbai that was built in the 1990s by Enron, the U.S. energy company that went bankrupt in 2001. The Maharashtra state government refused to buy electricity from the plant claiming it was overpriced. New Delhi then refused to honor the counterguarantees it had pledged for the operation during the contract negotiations. India has a more robust and independent legal system than China. But Americans frequently lecture Indians about the "sanctity of the contract."

*India's main left party, the Communist Party of India (Marxist), is also a bundle of paradoxes. It supported China's decision to go nuclear in 1964. And it opposed India's decision to go nuclear in 1998. Now it appears to support Iran's decision to go nuclear. Its position is essentially America-phobic.

The United States has also complained about the slow movement of Indian liberalization of its retail, insurance, and banking sectors, all of which present juicy targets for American companies. India will move at its own pace. But the United States possesses a strong lever to encourage India to move faster. It can threaten to put restrictions on the U.S. economy's openness to India's software sector, which derives more than 80 percent of its earnings from American customers.[27] "At some stage," said a senior U.S. trade official, "India is going to have to reciprocate the opportunities that America is providing to India." It is unlikely that the U.S. government would of its own accord significantly restrict the access of Indian IT companies to the American market, not least because American companies benefit so much from the reduced costs and more rapid service the Indians provide. But Indian software executives remain nervous about the potential for the United States to succumb to a populist backlash against "offshoring." During the 2004 presidential campaign, Senator John Kerry hinted that he would pursue a more protectionist line on offshoring. He was defeated. But it would be rash of New Delhi to believe that American angst over the outsourcing of jobs to India will not resurface, possibly sooner than it thinks. At which point, New Delhi could be faced with the choice of opening up its domestic market to foreign investors in a more decisive way, or risking the health of the software goose that has laid so many golden eggs.

•    •    •

In my first interview with Manmohan Singh after he had become prime minister in 2004, India's new leader said something that struck home forcefully. Unlike many of his colleagues, Manmohan talks in an understated way. He is not known for his rhetorical flourishes or for his ability to sway the public. His national addresses have been painfully wooden. But Manmohan's judgment is very widely admired. So when he gives a strong opinion that you have not heard before, it is worth taking note. "The quest for energy security is second only in our scheme of things to our quest for food security," said Manmohan, in his almost whispering voice. "India is dependent on imported energy, and what goes on in the world today, the growing instability of supplies, gives rise to new challenges. The producers must come to terms with the fact that instability is not something that is conducive to the interest of either the buyers or the sellers. . . . Energy security is of critical importance [to India]."[28]

To take a small liberty with Manmohan's pronouncement, energy security is actually a bigger headache for India than is food security. In the last twenty-five years India has broken the back of its food supply difficulties and is likely to become a large food exporter in the years ahead. India now produces more than enough food to cater to the nutritional needs of its growing population, even though its system of food distribution to the poor leaves much to be desired. On energy, however, India's internal shortfall is large and growing. At the moment India imports 70 percent of its oil needs, and that figure is expected to rise to 90 percent in the next two decades as the domestic economy expands. Likewise, if the dollars being thrown around in overseas acquisitions are any guide, energy security is also one of the most critical issues facing China.

The energy situations facing India and China are strikingly similar. Both have large reserves of coal, which is mostly dirty and inefficient. Both also have oil but not of a sufficient quantity to give them much comfort. Both countries—particularly China—have built controversial dams to boost their hydroelectric capacity. But the political cost of building dams is high and rising. Both also have ambitions to expand their civil nuclear capacity. But nuclear plants take years to build and involve a huge amount of capital. Even if India were able to expand its nuclear power capacity to achieve New Delhi's ambitious target of 20,000 megawatts by the year 2020 (presumably, now, with the assistance of Washington), this would still account for less than 5 percent of India's overall electricity demand. On gas, India has an advantage over China, having struck significant undersea gas fields in the Bay of Bengal and elsewhere over the last few years. Again, however, India's internal gas supply is dwarfed by its overall demand, which, like oil, will mostly be met from overseas fields.

In the coming years, India and China will both look aggressively for new sources of oil and gas around the world. Competition between the two countries is already intense. China, as would be expected, is several years ahead of India in making overseas energy acquisitions, including stakes in Russian, Latin American, and African oil fields. But India is catching up, having taken stakes in Sudan, Russia, and Venezuela. In both cases, the charge is being led by state-owned energy companies and, contrary to the advice of free market purists, who argue that supplies can more efficiently be tied up in the energy futures market, both countries want to extract the oil or gas directly. China and India's ever-restless quest for energy security involves striking deals with a number of rogue regimes around the world. Most important of all, it involves forging close ties to Iran. Journalists in Asia have dubbed the India-China race for energy security the "New Great Game," a reference to the old Great Game, which was a race between imperial Britain and czarist Russia in the nineteenth century to gain sway over the vast tracts of central Asia that divided the Raj from Russia's southern boundaries. The New Great Game is less romantic. But its outcome will have as much impact on the shape of world geopolitics as did the Victorian race between London and Moscow.

From the point of view of the Bush administration and whatever administration replaces it in January 2009, the role of Iran in supplying India and China's energy requirements is troubling. Iran's vast supplies of gas and oil are sufficient to take care of much of India's energy demand over the next two or three decades. New Delhi has indicated that it will not cave in to American pressure to seek its supplies elsewhere. The same applies to China. The U.S. Helms-Burton Act, which was passed in the early 1990s, triggers sanctions on companies that trade with Iran and Libya. It is quite possible that New Delhi's hopes of building a gas pipeline from Iran to India will trigger a new era of friction between Washington and New Delhi. But given India's large energy needs, it is doubtful that the United States could come up with an alternative that would compensate India for the loss of gas from Iran. Equally, it is hard to imagine that any U.S. sanctions on India would outweigh the economic benefits of securing a plentiful supply of cheap Iranian gas. Many Indian strategists also believe the pipeline would have a strongly beneficial diplomatic effect on the south Asian region, since it would have to pass through Pakistan, which also has large and growing energy needs. Although the costs of insuring the pipeline against any possible terrorist attack or Pakistani blackmail during a conflict would be high, the economic and diplomatic gains would be greater. The pipeline would earn Pakistan up to $1 billion a year in transit fees, giving Islamabad a strong incentive to pursue stability with India.

Thus, in many respects, India and China find themselves on the same side of the fence and United States on the other side when it comes to energy security. New Delhi and Beijing have even begun to discuss areas of energy cooperation, such as forming an Asian buyer's cartel to match the Middle Eastern seller's cartel and force OPEC to reduce prices. Mani Shankar Aiyar, who was appointed India's petroleum minister in 2004, said that India and China would compete in some areas of energy exploration but cooperate in others. Academics have coined the ugly term *coopetition* to describe such behavior. For example, the need to protect the busy shipping lanes linking the Middle East to Asia is something that unites Beijing and New Delhi. It might also put a different gloss on China's "blue sea" naval ambitions. In some respects, India's petroleum ministry is a growing unofficial rival to India's formal Ministry of External Affairs. Negotiating the construction of vast pipelines from Myanmar, Iran, Bangladesh, and Pakistan to India is much sexier than drafting subordinate clauses in Kashmir statements.

Partly because of its thirst for overseas energy supplies, India is also becoming a giver—as well as a receiver—of foreign aid. Some foreign aid officials see India's external aid program as an absurd waste of resources considering the continuing economic deprivation in large tracts of India. But that might be to mistake the true nature of aid. For most Western countries, including the United States, overseas aid is as much a tool of foreign policy as it is an expression of humanitarian concern. Again, India is a long way behind China in providing aid to other countries. But New Delhi is catching up with Beijing. India now has aid programs in parts of Africa and Afghanistan. India was also a contributor of emergency relief assistance after the tsunami struck Southeast and south Asia in December 2004. The first planeload of aid to arrive in Sri Lanka, one of the most devastated countries, was from India, not the United States. India also extended aid to Thailand, even though India's death toll was much higher than that of Thailand. In a characteristic episode of Indian prickliness, New Delhi even refused foreign emergency aid for its own tsunami victims, who were mostly concentrated in Tamil Nadu. "India would like to be part of the solution not part of the problem," said an Indian diplomatic spokesman. Many foreign aid officials saw this as another instance in which New Delhi put India's national pride above all else, including in this case the welfare of its most stricken citizens. But in the event, India managed the crisis relatively well. Tamil Nadu has one of the most efficient state governments in the country.

There have been domestic political criticisms of India's decision to pursue a more assertive diplomatic role in recent years. But in spite of the noise from the opposition in parliament (for example, against the BJP's nuclear tests in 1998 or against the Congress Party–led government's nuclear deal with Washington in 2005), there has been continuity in policy from government to government over the last ten to fifteen years. India's diplomatic trajectory looks to be enduring, rather than fickle. For example, it is hard to imagine that a future BJP government would undo whatever nuclear deal finally emerges between New Delhi and Washington. Equally, it is hard to imagine that any future Indian government would abandon the country's strategy of gradual economic integration with the world economy (although at a less dramatic pace than China). Across all political parties, with the exception of the Far Left, there is a consensus that India should be aiming for "great power" status, even if this focus on its standing in the world sometimes looks unbalanced—and even narcissistic—against the backdrop of India's continuing social and economic problems.

In today's increasingly communicative world, relations between countries as large as India, China, and the United States take place on many different levels and between many different types of people. Indian and American diplomats might be toasting each other with champagne in one ballroom, while American trade unions lobby against India's IT sector in the conference room next door. China and India join forces at the World Trade Organization in Geneva to push the United States and the European Union to reduce farm subsidies, while exchanging thinly veiled insults with each other at the International Atomic Energy Agency in Vienna. The United States might regard India as the key bulwark against a rising China, while simultaneously keeping Pakistan sweet by selling it fighter jets that could one day be deployed against India.

Naturally, countries such as Japan, Russia, Brazil, South Africa, Germany, France, and Britain will also be important players in the coming decades. But in many respects the world appears to be on a trajectory where relations between the three big powers will outweigh all other ties as the twenty-first century unfolds. The nodal point in the triangle is, of course, the United States. Short of war, however, the United States cannot prevent China from rising as a global power. So America will continue to assist India's rise as a counterbalancing force. India, meanwhile, will want to benefit from America's help without jeopardizing its relations with China. There are many possible moves in this triangular dance. And there will be many opportunities to trip up.

# 8. NEW INDIA, OLD INDIA

## The Many-Layered Character of Indian Modernity

*There is not a thought that is being thought in the West or the East that is not active in some Indian mind.*

E. P. THOMPSON, the late British historian

The employee identification tag hanging around James Paul's neck says 4844. To James's colleagues, the number identifies the twenty-nine-year-old as among the lucky first few thousand people to get a job at Infosys, which is India's best-known software company. James was hired in 1998, when Infosys was starting to win large contracts to sweep Western computer systems for the much-feared millennium Y2K bug. People at Infosys worried the boom might end in the hangover after millennium eve. Instead it accelerated. India's software sector barely skipped a beat when the United States dot-com bubble burst in 2001. By 2006 Infosys had expanded more than tenfold from when James had been hired as part of a workforce of more than 50,000 employees. Likewise James, who heads a unit of 1,500 people at the company's headquarters in Bangalore, and spends at least half his time visiting clients in places like Houston, Paris, and Salt Lake City, has seen his salary grow more than ten times to $50,000 a year—a princely sum given India's low cost of living. But James is not among the most fortunate of Infosys employees. Because of an early equity option scheme for employees, which was diluted shortly before James was hired, anyone at Infosys whose ID tag is 1000 or less became a dollar millionaire. For a company that few people had heard of in 1995, the creation of wealth from nowhere and on this scale was extraordinary. Similar stories could be told of other Indian IT companies. Azim Premji, the founder of Wipro, is among the richest men in the world. "We get more than a million job applications a year," said Nandan Nilekani, chief executive and cofounder of Infosys, who is almost as rich as Premji. "It keeps our human resources department busy."

There is another side to the Indian IT story that is in some ways even more revolutionary than the money. The sector is meritocratic. If a Martian had dropped in on India's top companies in the early 1990s and done a quick census of their white-collar management, it would have found people of male urban upper-caste background and few others. The Martian would get a more variegated picture today (upper castes are still preponderant in IT and other new economy businesses, but much less so than in the more established industries). In its strange way, India is coming to terms with modernity. The practice of meritocracy is not yet entrenched. But it is now at least getting generous lip service. In much of the business world, there are genuine changes taking place. A large chunk of India's top thirty companies are in IT. Until a few years ago, most people had not heard of them. "We cannot afford to follow the traditional 'jobs for the boys' culture," Nilekani told me. "We have to survive in a very competitive global industry. Our only criterion is to select the best people."

The Infosys campus in Bangalore, which is as sculpted and green as any in Silicon Valley, provides day care, in-house supermarkets, gyms, laundry services, and recreational facilities for the families of employees. It has tens of thousands of women on its payroll. Outside each of the buildings there are bicycles for employees to cycle from one part of the forty-acre campus to another. There are clusters of rainbow-colored umbrellas outside each front door. It feels more like a weekend retreat for wealthy anarchists than a thriving global corporation. "At the weekend this place is like a holiday camp," said James. "Then we have all these 'Bring your children to work' days and even 'Bring your parents to work.' But we also work very hard. Perhaps it is because of this environment that we work so hard."

I spent a day sitting with James in his cubicle in the open-plan office that is typical of software companies. Above his desk there is a sign: PARKING FOR JAMES ONLY. ALL OTHERS WILL BE TOWED. He heads the validation unit, which undertakes stress tests on the software systems of client companies. Most of the unit's clients are global telecom companies. In order for Infosys to develop and finesse the internal software systems for their clients, they have to get to know their business inside out. Inevitably, Infosys is moving into consulting, where the fees are a multiple of what you can earn from doing the relatively mechanical tasks of basic software coding. It is not just Western software companies that are suffering from Indian competition. The big consulting firms, such as PricewaterhouseCoopers and Accenture, are also threatened. "To do software well, you have to understand a lot more than just software," says James.

To get hired by Infosys, James had to work especially hard. Born into a lower-middle-class Christian family in the state of Kerala, James was the first member of his family to get a job outside his home state. His parents are schoolteachers. His grandparents were rice farmers. They earned barely enough to make ends meet. James attended a local school. In 1992 he struck it lucky. Or rather, he created his own luck. He applied to the elite Indian Institute of Technology in Mumbai (there are five other IITs) and was accepted. He had to sit three 4-hour entrance examinations. He placed 637th out of the 100,000 people who sat for the tests. "That was the big moment," said James. "I had to explain this to my parents, who didn't really understand just how big an opportunity it was." James's parents took out a loan to pay the tuition fees, which were then Rs 5000 per term (about $120). Now James earns more than that every day. He often flies back to Kerala for the weekend to catch up with his family. Sometimes he stops off in Kerala en route back from the United States. "I show my grandparents pictures of the Eiffel Tower or Niagara Falls and they seem very happy," he said. "But they can't really locate any of these tourist sights. They just get the impression I'm doing well." Naturally, he sends them some of his earnings. James's younger brother works at CNBC, the U.S. business television channel, in Mumbai.

A growing number of James's coworkers are also from modest backgrounds. Their good fortune has created a very far-reaching change in values. James's wife, Sindhu, is a Hindu from the upper-caste Nair community in Kerala. For both their families the wedding marked a big departure. "Initially there was doubt and hesitation because in our family we usually marry other Jacobite Christians [James's denomination]," he said. "My parents had tried to arrange a marriage to someone within the community. But I didn't really click with the girls they introduced me to. But then they realized me and Sindhu were going to marry anyway, so they accepted it. We had a church wedding in Kerala and then we flew to Bangalore and had a temple wedding there." James said a large proportion of people working at Infosys have intercaste and interreligious marriages. This remains unusual in India. In a detailed poll of middle-class Indians carried out by a news channel, almost three-quarters of Indians said they would not permit their children to marry out of caste. But in the IT sector it has become a regular thing. "Every weekend it seems there is some wedding of an Infosys colleague and often it is an intercommunal marriage," said James. "Nobody raises an eyebrow. It is quite normal." Interestingly, intercaste marriage is not nearly as common among Indian software workers living in the United States.

"Long-distance nationalism"[1] is often much more conservative than its parent.

Like James, Mariam Ram is a Christian from Kerala. But Mariam, who owns her own company, which is based in Chennai, comes from a privileged background. The company, TNQ, typesets, formats, stylizes, and edits some of the world's most complex scientific journals and other nonscientific academic publications. Her biggest client is Reed Elsevier, the Dutch-based publisher. Mariam began from scratch in 1998 with fifteen employees. Now she has more than six hundred. In 2005, TNQ produced 300,000 pages. Her target is one million pages a year. Apart from some of the university publishers in the United States, which still tend to keep their editing in-house, Mariam and her competitors are hoovering up the academic journal work that used to be done in-house in Europe and elsewhere. TNQ edits at about $3 a page, compared to the going rate of at least $10 in Europe.

Some foreigners still think of Indian outsourcing as repetitive work. But Mariam's company requires its employees to have at least a postgraduate degree in the subject field on which they are working. About a tenth of her employees have PhDs. Publications such as *Cell*, *Tetrahydron*, *Semantics Today*, *Medieval History*, and *Polymer* sit on the shelves of the company's main office, which is located in a leafy quarter of Chennai. An elegant and highly articulate woman in her early fifties, Mariam says she can see few threats on the horizon. Finding Anglophone science graduates in Chennai is no problem. "China doesn't have the English language, the Philippines doesn't have science, Ireland is too expensive now—almost all the work is coming to India," she says. "And this is just the thin end of the wedge. There is no law confining us to academic journals. What about newspapers and magazines? I would love to copyedit one of the prestige Western titles."

The business model looks robust. And I suspect India is still at the relatively early stages of the offshoring revolution in services. There are plenty more tasks and functions, both low-skilled and highly skilled, that can be remotely undertaken in places like India for half the price or less of what it costs in the West. But it is the sociological changes in Mariam's world that are potentially more revolutionary. Wherever possible, Mariam hires women. She is also biased in favor of people from lower castes and other minorities. Almost half of Mariam's workforce is female. "Women make much better copy editors," she said. "They are much more conscientious about detail." I talked to many of her female employees and with the exception of one, who had only just started her job, each of the women earned more than their fathers. Most were in their mid-twenties. And the majority of them were the first women in their families to have formal jobs. Unusually in India, some of the married ones had retained their maiden names. Mariam herself is something of an oddity, since she has been married twice. Her second husband, N. Ram, is editor and owner of *The Hindu,* a widely respected newspaper. India being India, N. Ram is also a Marxist. "Very few of my female friends in my generation actually work," said Mariam. "Most of them sit around doing nothing."

The women I spoke to at TNQ left me with two very strong impressions. First, they were obsessed with educating their children up to the highest level, whether they were sons or daughters. And second, they did not mind in the least that I was asking intrusive and often very personal questions. Nosiness is practically a virtue in India. "No, no, it's nice being asked about these things," said Mehroon Tanjore, a young Muslim woman, when I asked whether she would stop at one child. "I think I will discuss it with my husband." Mehroon's mother, who lives in the south Indian temple town of Tanjore, has always worn the burka and is not educated. Her father insisted on keeping her in purdah. But he did not mind his daughter going about unveiled and working with men. Why was that? "I don't know," she said, shaking her head inscrutably from side to side, south India–style, as if the anomaly had not occurred to her. "It's different with me." Mehroon's marriage had been arranged. But she was agnostic about whether she would arrange her son's marriage. "It will be up to him. The most important thing is that he becomes educated," she said. Another woman, Priya Reddy, whose family was originally from the state of Andhra Pradesh, met her Tamil Brahmin husband in a government office. They were both applying for a driver's license. "It was love at first sight," she said. "I think I forgot my license." Her mother is a housewife. Priya hoped her daughter would be a professional. For Mariam, who is something of a mother figure to her employees, the order books might be booming, but she says it is the "romance" of the business that drives her. "This isn't really about money—I don't want to be the richest stiff in the cemetery," she said. "It is about being part of a new India that is opening up opportunities for people who never had them before."

Like Mariam, and many of her employees, James's value system is a million miles from what still prevails in most of village India. Barely a week seems to pass without a gruesome caste-related murder hitting the newspaper headlines. One of the most common causes of caste violence in the villages is when a boy and a girl from different castes try to elope together and get caught. Often, the resulting killing is carried out by men from both families. Sometimes the young lovers are burned; sometimes they are cut up with knives. Although the phenomenon is much worse in north India, there have been incidents of this nature in the state of Karnataka, of which Bangalore is capital. Naturally, such stories disturb James.

Pride of place in James's cubicle at Infosys was given to a picture of the Art of Living Foundation and its guru, Sri Sri Ravi Shankar, whom we met in chapter four. The ashram is about an hour's drive from the Infosys campus. Alok Kejriwal, the Mumbai-based online entrepreneur whom we met in the first chapter, is also a devotee of the Art of Living. James told me that many of his colleagues at Infosys attended Sri Sri Ravi Shankar's night classes. "Mostly it is just meditation and stress reduction," said James. "But it is also the spiritualism. We need to become more Indian, and to improve our self-esteem. For example, I don't see why people drink Coca-Cola when there's beautiful Indian lime juice that they can drink." I understood his point. But I wondered why he had singled out Coca-Cola as the betrayal of Indianness instead of, say, working for a company that operates in English and services Western clients. James looked pensive. Then he said: "Eventually I would like to work for the poor in the villages. We have set up a group at Infosys called 'Good for Nothing,' where we help women in the villages learn how to weave baskets. One day I would like to do this full-time."

Going through my notes of our conversation later, it struck me that James was in many respects representative of the new generation of middle-class Indians I have met—highly skilled, wealthy, cosmopolitan, and comfortable with people of all religious and caste backgrounds. At the same time, he talked a lot about the need to protect Indian culture and its religious heritage from what he saw as the less attractive aspects of global culture—the breakup of families, disrespect of elders, excessive consumerism, abandonment of religious values, and worship of money. Many Indians take as part of their conventional wisdom the view that India's traditional moral values are better than those of the West. It gave a quiet but strongly held underlining to much of what James said. "I believe very strongly that we must protect India's culture and morality," said James. "Because of colonialism we have been made to feel ashamed of our traditions. Now that we are independent we have no excuses anymore. Our fate is in our hands."

•   •   •

Sometimes it seems that in India the modern lifestyle is just another layer on the country's ancient palimpsest. It is simply adding modernity to what it already has. Most Europeans tend to think of modernity as the triumph of a secular way of life: church attendance gradually dwindles and religion becomes a minority pastime confined to worshipers' private lives. Religion turns into a branch of the heritage industry, celebrated more for its architecture and history than for its contemporary relevance. That has certainly been true of most of Europe over the last few generations. In opinion polls today, a majority of Europeans regularly profess either not to believe in God, or else to be agnostic. In Europe the past is the past. But in India, the past is in many ways also the future.

Europe is no longer the universal standard by which other societies measure their progress. For India, the United States offers a more relevant parallel. Neither India nor the United States suffered Europe's history of state-imposed religion, except, in the case of the United States, in the form of a relatively titular Church of England before 1776. Both societies have a tradition of religious communities and sects coexisting and sometimes competing with each other in civil society without benefiting much from state patronage or suffering from state persecution. The absolutist character of the Catholic Church in Europe gave rise to a correspondingly absolutist counterattack, initially in the form of Protestantism, but later in the form of anticlericalism and atheism. India shares few of these impulses because it has a very different history. India's past continues to be visible in its present. On the few occasions in India's history when the state has attempted to proselytize, either the effort has quickly petered out, or else it has provoked a backlash that forced the state to retreat.

For example, in the seventeenth century, the Mughal emperor Aurangzeb imposed the Islamic *jizya,* a poll tax on the heads of unbelievers, which included the majority of the population. This policy went against the relatively ecumenical traditions of Aurganzeb's predecessors. Many of India's Muslim rulers paid respect to India's non-Islamic traditions. For example, Dara Shikoh, Aurangzeb's brother, whom he had killed since he was a rival to the throne, had translated the Upanishads (a series of philosophical tracts on Hinduism) into Persian.[2] Aurangzeb's great-grandfather, Akbar, tried to fuse Islam, Hinduism, and other religions into a new religion, which he called Din Ilahi, but without much success. Hindu nationalists claim 30,000 temples were destroyed by Islamic iconoclasts. But accredited scholars can find verifiable examples[3] for only a fraction of this number. Even then, the temples that were destroyed were usually associated with the outgoing dynasty.[4] It was a tradition for new Hindu dynasties to do precisely the same thing. Turkish Muslim armies left the provocatively erotic temples of Khajuraho* in central India untouched because the Candella dynasty that had built them had already fled.

In fact, Muslim rulers would frequently use Hindu symbols to legitimize their rule in the eyes of the people. For example, Mohammed-bin-Tuglakh, whose dynasty ruled from Delhi, transported water from the Ganges, the holiest river in Hinduism, south to Daulatabad, when he built a new capital[5] in 1327. Contemporary inscriptions never identified the royal house by religion but by language (such as Turkish, Persian, or Afghan). It was also common for Islamic dynasties to repair and provide for the upkeep of prestigious temples. For example, the world-renowned Jaganath Temple at Puri in the state of Orissa was restored during the Mughal era. Because of Aurangzeb's open antipathy to Hinduism and because he tried to stretch his rule too far into south India, he laid the seeds for the breakup of the Moghul empire. One of Aurangzeb's sons even joined a rebellion against his father that was led by Hindu Rajput generals. The space vacated by a declining and enfeebled Mughal empire was gradually inhabited by the British.

Through the Sepoy Mutiny in 1857, the British learned the hard way that imposing its religious bias on India's population could be dangerously counterproductive. That is one reason that fewer than 3 percent of Indians were Christian in 1947 after more than two hundred years of British rule (and most converted to Christianity long before British rule). In contrast, almost a third of Vietnam was Chris-

---

*Much of the Kama Sutra, the classic Hindu manual of sexual positions, is depicted on the exterior of the temples. Other sexual props, including horses, play cameo roles on these unique fourteenth-century stone friezes.

tian when the French left the country in 1954 less than a century after they had colonized it. The British tolerated and in some cases sponsored Christian missionary activity in India in the late eighteenth century and in the first half of the nineteenth century, although with little success. Some Protestant missionary societies believed they could lift India's "idol-worshiping heathens" out of their ignorance en masse.*

After 1857, the British Raj substituted the lukewarm support it gave to missionaries before the Sepoy Mutiny with outright disapproval. Many of the rebels, particularly Brahmin troops from the United Provinces, had allegedly been provoked by rumors that they would have to use a new kind of cartridge that was greased with cow fat. Equivalent rumors about pig fat inflamed Muslim soldiers. The uprising had been preceded by widespread talk in the regiments of official British plans to convert India to Christianity. These were unsubstantiated. But there is little doubt that many of the Protestant missionary groups treated Indians and Indian culture in a way that provoked such resentments. After 1857 the British chose to stress the continuity of their rule within Indian history by reviving many of the ceremonial features of the Mughals and eventually shifting the capital back to Delhi (from Calcutta).

But even among many of the Christian and Muslim communities in today's India, the form of worship is more eclectic and unorthodox than among their coreligionists in most other parts of the world. This has positive and negative implications. On the plus side, the tendency to accept that there are many paths to God derives from India's long-running tradition of tolerance among religions. On the debit side, caste continues to play an important role in dividing Christian congregations (and Muslim communities) along the lines of

---

*Some western Protestant societies still believe India should be converted to Christianity. The methods—which many see as culturally disrespectful—used by various Baptist missionary groups in India's tribal zones and in India's northeastern states remain controversial. With some reason, Verrier Elwin, whom Nehru appointed to take charge of India's Northeast, described Baptists as the "RSS of Christianity."

their members' birth. Somerset Maugham, the British author, once visited what was then the Portuguese colony of Goa (in 1961 Nehru lost patience with the Portuguese and annexed the enclave to India). Maugham made friends with a Catholic priest, whose ancestors had been converted by the Portuguese. "I got the feeling," wrote Maugham, "that even though there were 400 years of Catholicism behind him, he was still at heart a Vedantist [a classical Hindu]."[6] In 2004, Priya and I dropped in for tea at the home of a well-known Goan Catholic author. She had just finished a beautiful restoration of her ancestral home, which was of the classic Brahmin style of the region. I naïvely asked her whether there was any Portuguese blood in the family. "Oh no, that is out of the question," she said. "Our family is Brahmin."

An estimated 70 percent of Indian Christians come from Dalit or Adivasi (tribal) backgrounds.[7] Generally they are not permitted to forget it. This is partly because conversions to Christianity (and Islam) have tended to take place in groups, usually of whole sub-castes, rather than at the individual level. Instead of escaping their caste, they simply add another prefix: "Dalit-Christian," or "Dalit-Muslim." In urban India, such labels matter less. But most of the minorities have not yet entered the urban middle classes. In almost every denomination, the church hierarchy is almost wholly of upper-caste origin. In Tamil Nadu a recent study showed that 63 percent of all Tamil Catholics were Dalit, yet only 3 percent of Tamil Catholic priests were Dalit.[8] Likewise, upper-caste pollution rules dictate that Christian women do not enter the grounds of a church during menstruation or for forty days after giving birth. In many cases, including in Goa, Dalit Catholics have separate churches and separate cemeteries. Somerset Maugham, it seems, had a point.

Many of the progressive trends on caste are to be found within Hinduism in spite of what is happening in the political arena. As India continues to urbanize and as new technology, such as television and the Internet, begin to influence forms of worship, Hinduism is becoming less segmented. In many ways—and for the first time in its history—Hinduism is turning into a unified mass religion. For example, all castes in north India now celebrate Karwa Chauth, in which wives fast for their husbands for one day a year to symbolize their devotion, and Rakhi, in which the sister ties a thread on her brother's wrist to convey her love (both are traditional north Indian upper-caste festivals). Many lower castes are also copying the upper castes by initiating their children into adulthood in ceremonies where they tie a sacred thread on the wrists of their sons before they reach puberty. Brahmins see the initiation as a second birth, which is why upper castes are sometimes referred to as the "twice born." Additionally, there are now many priests who are not Brahmin.

As a result, Hinduism—or at least Hinduism as it is practiced in the cities—is becoming a much more standardized religion. Foreigners often remark on the unique architecture of the traditional Hindu temple. In contrast to most other religions, it lacks a general area in which the congregation can gather. Traditional Hinduism had no real congregation: it was a religion of different castes. The standard Hindu temple has a small inner room, or sanctum sanctorum, in which the god is situated, and which is open only to the eligible castes. But the new temples of the growing urban Hindu cults, such as the Swaminarain sect, or the late-nineteenth-century religious reformist movements of the "Bengal renaissance," such as the Rama-krishna Mission, are built with large open areas where people can worship collectively. Furthermore, simply by switching on their televisions, people can now worship as one large congregation. In the last decade India has seen a mushrooming of the Hindu equivalent of America's "televangelist" cable TV channels. In contrast to the excluding architecture of the temples, India's "God channels" are aggressively inclusive since their main aim is to maximize audience share. Hinduism is also crossing regional boundaries. Festivals such as Divali and Holi, which were traditionally north Indian, are now celebrated across most of the country.

Technology undoubtedly has assisted in the nationalization of Hindu practice. The popular and increasingly pan-Indian Hinduism of today comes from the Puranas, which are the histories of the popular gods such as Shiva, Ram, Krishna, and Vishnu that were written many centuries after most of the classical Hindu texts. Festivals celebrating lesser gods, such as Hanuman and Ganesh* (the monkey god and the half-elephant god), who have grown in popularity over the last century, are spreading across India. Mainstream Hinduism, which Thomas Mann, the Germany author, described as the "all-encompassing labyrinthine flux of the animal, human and the divine,"[9] is growing. In India modernity and religion are marching forward together, sometimes hand in hand. Counterintuitive it may be (particularly for a European), but there is no contradiction.

•   •   •

One of the reasons many of India's educated elites feel ambivalent about modernity is because the new wealth and technology of the last fifteen years appears to have exacerbated some of India's less savory traditions. In large tracts of northern and western India, the so-called "gender gap" between boys and girls has sharply increased. The average ratio of births of girls to boys for India was 945 to 1,000 in 1991. By 2001 it had fallen to 927.[10] In some parts of India, particularly in the southern states, like Kerala, the gender ratio remains healthy at roughly one to one. But in Gujarat and Punjab, in India's northwest and north, the ratio has fallen alarmingly. Gujarat has fewer than 900 girls to 1,000 boys. Punjab has below 800. The average in the West is 1050 girls to 1000 boys.[11] The two states are among the wealthiest in India and have witnessed the most rapid increases in disposable incomes since economic reforms were launched in the early 1990s. But they have recorded the steepest fall in the

*The annual festival, in which a figure of Ganesh is paraded through the streets before being submerged in the sea, is relatively recent having been launched in 1905 by Tilak, a nationalist leader. It began in Maharashtra, and is most popular in Mumbai. But it is spreading to other parts of India.

birth of girls. The poorest states, such as Bihar, have much better gender ratios than the richer ones and have even seen a slight improvement in the last few years. In many parts of India the gender ratio serves as a kind of grotesque barometer of economic progress. Similarly, the practice of dowry has spread most extensively in the wealthier states, with the families of the groom demanding increasingly extortionate compensation for the apparent burden of accepting a new daughter into their family. For many of India's new middle classes, having a daughter is becoming an ever more expensive prospect.

"Are you going to kill your daughter?" says the television advertisement in Gujarat. The aggressive publicity campaign was launched by Amarjeet Singh, the health secretary of Gujarat, who told me this was the most distressing job he had ever done. It has been illegal in India since 2001 to give a "sex determination" test to pregnant mothers. But since it would be impractical to outlaw ultrasound (pregnancy scan), the law is virtually impossible to uphold. There has not yet been one conviction. Yet India has an estimated forty to fifty million "missing girls." A sonograph costs as little as Rs 150. An abortion costs about Rs 10,000. Many more people can now afford to have abortions. "Some of the fall in the gender ratio is because more and more people can now afford to do sex determination tests and then pay for the abortion," says Amarjeet Singh. "So probably we have less infanticide nowadays and more feticide." Yet the gender ratio keeps dropping. Singh shows me a chart of the worst-affected districts in Gujarat. In some parts of the state the ratio is below 800 girls to 1,000 boys. Families in the worst-affected districts are importing girls from other parts of India to serve as brides to several husbands at once—usually the unfortunate woman is shared between three or four brothers. The imported women have no status and are treated as little better than in-house prostitutes. Doubtless their unborn daughters are never born, thus compounding the problem. Singh hopes that Gujarat's gender crisis will gradually fade as people's mind-sets adapt to the modern world. "The solution is to educate women as highly as possible," says Singh. "This will start to happen as people realize daughters have economic value in the modern economy."

Naturally, the problem is worse in the villages. For most villagers the economic opportunities and the social flexibility offered by the urban lifestyle and the new economy remain a distant prospect. In the village, arranged marriages and functional illiteracy remain the norm. India is estimated to have the lowest average age of marriage in the world. Child marriage remains widespread in much of rural India, particularly in the north. According to one estimate, 15 percent of girls in India's poorest five states get married at or below the age of ten.[12] Clearly, almost all of this takes place in the village. Children born in the village are almost twice as likely to die before reaching the age of five as those born in the city.

But as we saw in chapter three, the phenomenon of "Sanskritization," in which the lower castes copy the values and habits of the upper castes, is growing in India. Many of India's upper castes have traditionally regarded daughters as a burden and a cost. So the problem gets worse as other castes, which in the past did not practice dowry, become more upwardly mobile. "It is a lethal combination of old values and new wealth—old wine in new bottles," says Singh. The upwardly mobile lower castes have also become more materialistic. Nowadays it is normal for the groom's family to demand things such as cars, washing machines, and even a U.S. green card as part of their dowries. This explains the odd tendency of newspaper columnists to blame the twin curses of the worsening gender divide and dowry inflation on Western consumer values, even though neither problem exists in the West.

In contrast, most of the educated upper-caste elites in India have largely abandoned the practice of dowry. Their daughters go to university so they have become financially independent. Yet this is not true of all upper castes in all parts of India. For example, the survival chances of unborn daughters in both the Jain and the Marwari communities, who are the traditional business elites of Gujarat and elsewhere, continue to deteriorate. The Jains, who dominate much of Gujarat's merchant trade, are a strictly vegetarian offshoot of Hinduism. Orthodox Jains can be recognized instantly by the white cotton face masks they wear to prevent the possibility of swallowing an insect. In 2001 there were 878 Jain daughters to every 1,000 Jain sons, according to Singh. By 2003 the ratio had fallen to 848. "Just imagine, these people have a religion that says you cannot even harm a fly or a microbe, and yet they are killing off about 15 percent of their daughters," he said. "How to explain this?"

The state of Gujarat is a genuine puzzle. In economic terms it is probably the most globalized part of India. Millions of Gujaratis have family in the United Kingdom, the United States, and other parts of the world. Yet to judge by the gender ratio, which is surely the best measure, the status of women appears to be getting worse. On a more trivial level, the sexes still appear to be segregated as a matter of routine at dinner parties in Gujarat. I have attended several evenings where the men sit down and are served their dinner by the women, who only afterward eat whatever the men have left. I once attended an Indian dinner party in Manila, capital of the Philippines, where my wife, Priya, who is half Gujarati, insisted on joining the men in their separate room. I took this as a cue to join the women. The men took this as a double bonus.

Gujarat, as we saw in chapter four, is also the most Hindu chauvinist state in India. One of the frequently cited reasons for resenting Muslims is because Islam discriminates against women. Yet Gujarat has a worse gender ratio than many Islamic countries, including Pakistan and Bangladesh. It is hard to know what would qualify as a more telling measure of gender discrimination than tolerating mass selective abortion. Renuka Patwa is a midwife in Ahmedabad who left her job at the hospital to work for the Self-Employed Women's Association (SEWA), a large trade union for women. Sewa has more than 600,000 members working in the unorganized sector, where they make incense sticks, bidi cigarettes, and textiles. The union educates its members to value the girl child. Although everyone knows her views, Patwa still gets calls from people asking for referrals to clinics that will perform abortions on female fetuses. "I got a call from a very wealthy Marwari [a business caste originally from Rajasthan] mother-in-law the other day," said Patwa. "After some thought I gave her the number because I knew that the poor daughter-in-law would go through hell if she wasn't allowed to have an abortion. These Marwaris are particularly keen on having sons because they want a son to inherit the business." The couple in question had received a Mercedes and a honeymoon in Switzerland as part of the dowry for the unfortunate young woman who was about to have an abortion.

"It is difficult for me," admitted Patwa, a jolly woman in her late fifties, with an operatic laugh. "I believe in the woman's right to have an abortion. But it is troubling to see the reason most women have abortions. It is the mothers-in-law who are the worst. They were once victims, so now they become culprits." Patwa, whose living room is decorated with cheerful pictures of Krishna playing with *gopis* (cow girls), depicting the celebrated erotic phase of the young god's life, has had direct experience of such prejudice. "In 1972 when I gave birth to my daughter, my mother-in-law came into the hospital room and said, 'You have given birth to a stone.' It was as if I committed a crime. But I did not feel guilty. My husband said: 'I will never disobey my parents.' So I divorced him. I have paid a price because society still does not accept female divorcées. But it was the best thing I have ever done."

Patwa said the situation was improving for the younger generation of educated women, many of whom were beginning to stand up for themselves. But they are clearly outnumbered statistically by the droves of lower castes that are Sanskritizing. "Society still discriminates terribly against women," she said. "Sex discrimination leads directly to sex determination." Patwa poured scorn on traditional moral values. She likened sexuality to a fixed quantity of water. If one channel is shut off, it will find another. "If you repress feelings of sexuality in women, then the woman will not give her husband pleasure," she said. "So the husband will find his pleasure elsewhere. How moral is that?" Meanwhile, the woman's frustrated sexuality would be subliminated into love of her son, said Patwa. This would reinforce her resentment of the daughter-in-law who would eventually take first place in her son's affections. I was not sure how much of this could be proven. But it was worth hearing.

Indian society as a whole seems to be much more at ease with the topic of sex than before. But this is not necessarily an indicator of women's empowerment. Bollywood films, which have always made the most of their world-famous pelvic dance sequences, have become much more risqué in the last decade. Every day the newspapers are plastered with sultry photographs of female "item numbers"—the women who specialize in doing the most revealing dance sequences in a film as a stand-in for the leading actress. Newspapers and magazines also promote the idea that sexual promiscuity is now a normal way of life among the middle classes. This is a dubious measure, in any case, of women's autonomy. But it is patently exaggerated. It is the apparently serious magazines that have led the trend. The polling methodology is usually questionable. Most only canvass one or two hundred people, usually in the cities and usually English-speaking people. But they still generate cover story headlines like: "XXX. Seven out of Ten Delhiites say porn is good for sex."[13] My favorite survey appeared in a leading current affairs magazine in 2005.[14] According to the magazine, only 27 percent of women knew what an orgasm was. In the next box 47 percent of women admitted to having had many orgasms.

Such polls are the stock-in-trade of publications around the world. But in India they also reveal a tendency to mistake the libertine society (however exaggerated) for one that is liberal. Everyone in India has met young women who wear skimpy outfits, go to nightclubs, and have flings with boys, much like their counterparts in the West. But when asked whether they will choose whom they marry, they say they will leave it up to their parents. The sociologist Dipankar Gupta calls this "Westoxification."[15] By this he means a tendency to adopt the brand labels and consumer habits of the West and believe this is what it is to be modern. Perhaps that is all there is to it. Certainly India has far fewer out-of-wedlock teenage pregnancies than do countries such as the United Kingdom and the United States. But the vast gap between the lifestyles and values of India's consuming classes and the rest of the people gives India a social tension that, in Gupta's view, has more in common with Iranian society in the 1970s under the Shah (although Gupta was certainly not predicting a revolution in India).

Bollywood and other branches of the Indian film industry, such as Tamil-language cinema, which is almost as prolific as its Hindi-language counterpart, offer more subtle clues about society's attitudes toward women's sexuality. The typical Bollywood film is a blend of brilliantly choreographed titillation, which goes down very well with much of the male audience, and a resolutely conservative ending, which meets with the approval of their mothers and wives. A much-celebrated hit, *Dil Chahta Hai* (My Heart Wants), shows a young man falling for an older, divorced woman. Much sultriness ensues before she falls ill and dies. The young man ends up with a girl his own age. Because the film depicted a divorcée in a sympathetic light it was celebrated for having broken a taboo.

Or to take another, not-so-classic film, *Girlfriend,* which inexplicably provoked a nationwide boycott by right-wing Hindu groups. A lesbian, who spends her spare time beating up men in amateur kick-boxing sessions, seduces her drunken and unsuspecting best friend. The latter's wholesome fiancé cottons on to the former's preferences and, in confronting her, is almost killed in a furious, muscular assault before he finally prevails. The final scene shows the conventional Hindu couple paying their respects at the lesbian's Christian gravestone. Convincing scripts are not Bollywood's strong point. "Bollywood is expert at having its cake and eating it," says Dev Benegal, an independent filmmaker. "It shows you some flesh but it always ends by disapproving of such behavior."

India expects its actresses to be both sexy and conservative. When a leading actress gets married she is expected to give up her career.

She almost always does. Sometimes, as with Hema Malini or Jaya Bachchan, the stars return to cinema later in their marriage to play matronly roles, as kind but stern mothers-in-law. In a few cases, such as Dimple Kapadia, who married an actor, retired, got divorced, and then returned to the screen as a sex symbol, female stars get a second chance. But these are the exceptions. Mainstream cinema in India owes more to the catwalk than the drama school. The leading stars are first and foremost expected to be beautiful. Next they should dance well and handle the wet sari scenes with appropriate panache. If they can act that is a bonus. But it is not a requirement. They should provoke erotic fantasies without themselves crossing strictly defined lines of acceptable public behavior.

I once visited Mumbai's Film City, a sprawling 517-acre site on the outskirts of the city next to the Rajiv Gandhi national park. Situating the film park next to a jungle was deliberate. No Bollywood film would be complete without one or two dance sequences in the forest or a lovers' duet on a stone bridge overarching a stream. I was taken to watch a scene being shot. A young girl, dressed in a frazzled nightclub outfit, was being harassed by her lover under the shade of a large tree. The shooting over, the young actress headed directly to where I was sitting. "Would you like to interview me?" she asked, with almost unseemly directness.

Shabana Sultan, it turned out, was a twenty-one-year-old Indian who was born and brought up in Tripoli, Libya's capital, where her father was an orthopedic surgeon. Sultan had always dreamed of being a Bollywood actress and this was her first film. "I am not at all nervous," she said. "The camera is my lover." Her father, who never let his daughter out of his sight ("Even the boys are no longer safe in Bollywood," he said) proudly handed over his daughter's portfolio. The file contained a series of pictures of Shabana in different costumes—one in Western evening dress, another in sultry nightclub attire, the next in a sexy wet sari pose, a fourth in more restrained sari mode, and so on. There was not a written word in the file, not even her name. "I don't know why they gave me the part," she said absentmindedly. "There wasn't even an audition." As I left, her father rushed after me clutching a small piece of paper. "This is Shabana's mobile telephone number," he said. "In case you want to continue the interview."

Two recent scandals illustrate what is expected of the mainstream film actress in India. One of Mumbai's biggest stars is Karina Kapoor, whose swaying hips and girlish pout are beloved by audiences up and down the country. Like her costars, she would never kiss on screen. With one or two much-publicized exceptions, kissing remains taboo on screen. So when a nosy fan caught Karina kissing her boyfriend and fellow actor Shahid Kapoor (no relation) at a party in Mumbai and recorded it with a hazy picture on his mobile phone, there was an uproar. Ms. Kapoor denied it was she who had been digitally recorded: "I'm not this kind of a girl. I have an illustrious family name to uphold," she said. More seriously, Kushboo, another actress from the Tamil film industry, provoked even greater public anger in 2005 when she told a magazine interviewer that there was nothing wrong with sex before marriage. Large-scale protests broke out across Tamil Nadu because Tamils thought she had insulted Tamil culture and defamed Tamil women. The beleagured actress, who was briefly taken into custody by the police, had to go into hiding. Until then, Kushboo had been involved in an HIV-AIDS campaign to highlight the merits of safe sex.* She too was compelled to apologize. "Even in films, I never undertook roles that lowered the image of women," she said in a statement. "I have the greatest regard for Tamils, especially Tamil women. If my remarks have hurt anybody's feelings, I tender an apology. I am one among you and will always remain with you."

Bollywood films are not expected to be realistic. Independent filmmakers complain bitterly that the space and financing for films that deal with India's "social reality," or even rural India, have virtually disappeared. Many films ostensibly based in India are actually filmed

*We will look in the final chapter at India's growing HIV-AIDS problem.

in plush resorts in Mauritius or even Switzerland, where the scenery resembles Kashmir. Filmmaker Dev Benegal said: "When we pitch a film about Indian social reality, the financiers say: 'We don't want to do a documentary, we want real acting.'" In the 1950s and 1960s, in the aftermath of India's independence, Bollywood sold the dream of development and modernization and films were often set in rural India, depicting heroes battling against the evils of feudalism. Nowadays Bollywood would more accurately be described as being an arm of the consumer goods sector. The contemporary formula—which has left rural India, in which two-thirds of the nation's people live, on the cutting-room floor—caters to the tastes of India's new consuming classes.

Quite by chance, my tour of Film City coincided with the presence of Amitabh Bachchan, India's most revered film star, whose sixty-second birthday had just been celebrated in dozens of newspaper supplements. I was halfway through an interview with Sanjeevanee Kutty, the civil servant in charge of Film City, when her assistant rushed in: "Mr. Bachchan is ready now," said the assistant. Ready for what? I inquired. "Mr. Bachchan is ready for his interview with you." This qualified as one of Bollywood's improbable little twists. Having no idea that Bachchan was in the vicinity, I had not requested an interview. Had I done so, it would have taken weeks of faxed letters and conversations with public relations agencies to get even the ghost of a chance. Led by Kutty in her official white Ambassador, we piled into a cavalcade of cars and rushed to the shoot. Like most of Bachchan's shoots, it was a commercial. Wherever you are in India, the chances are that if you close your eyes and throw a dart it will land on a billboard or bus siding bearing Bachchan's distinguished grey-bearded visage. Whether it is Pepsi-Cola, Cadbury's chocolate, Parker pens, or Maruti cars, no amount of exposure seems to dilute his brand equity. On this occasion, Bachchan was starring in an advertisement for Dabur, a health-food chain.

Although we were on the edge of the jungle and the temperature was more than 97 degrees Fahrenheit, Bachchan was wearing a balaclava and looking flushed. Behind him a machine was billowing out fog. It was clearly a winter scene. "Are you wearing that [balaclava] for the shoot?" asked Kutty, evidently awkward in the presence of a living legend. "Well obviously, ma'am," replied the megastar, emphasizing "ma'am." My interview was short and to the point. Many independent filmmakers say that Bollywood ignores the realities of India, I said. "Well, yes of course," said Bachchan, with the same edge to his tone. "It's called escapist cinema. Why should somebody pay to see a film with poverty in it when they see poverty in their neighborhood every day. People don't want to be reminded where they live," he said. Would you like to make more films that remind people where they live? "I really don't see the point. Nobody will pay to go and see a film like *On the Waterfront* [the Marlon Brando 1954 classic set in the New York dockyards]." Bachchan put an end to the exchange shortly afterward.

● ● ●

Perhaps the most conspicuous item of consumption in today's India is the wedding, which owes a lot to Bollywood and vice versa. Vandana Mohan, owner of the Wedding Design company and New Delhi's most successful wedding planner, told me the smallest metropolitan middle-class weddings start at $20,000 and climb to more than a hundred thousand dollars. In 2003, Subroto Roy, a prominent industrialist based in Lucknow, spent an estimated $10 million on the joint wedding of his two sons (as a rich industrialist, he paid, although traditionally it is the father of the bride who pays). The event, which almost every Indian politician attended, was stage-managed by Bollywood directors, stage managers, and choreographers.

Alongside the growing cost of weddings, the volume of people invited and the number of receptions, ceremonies, and related gatherings is also climbing. In the past there were three or four receptions. Now there are a minimum of five events and more normally eight,

Mohan said. The "intimate gathering" for only close friends of the two families often exceeds five hundred people. The main reception has upward of a thousand guests. "Sometimes it is hard to take it seriously," says Mohan. "But it is seriously good business."

It is also a boom business for astrologers. Dev Vashishtha, a leading astrologer who charges $120 for a forty-five-minute session, says demand for consultations is growing. "Even Muslims are consulting me," says Vashishtha, who scrutinizes birth charts for suitability of partner and time of the wedding and other aspects. "It is best to get married when Venus is in the ascendant and Jupiter is strong—Jupiter is such a happening planet." The invitation itself is a study in changing values—a kind of designer label one-upmanship between India's rising middle classes. Instead of the simple cardboard box of *mithai* (ceremonial sweets) that traditionally accompanied the card, the sweets now come in crystal bowls, silver-edged plates, or hand-woven baskets. The conventional cardboard invitation has been replaced by expensive fabrics or even handmade paper designed by a leading painter. It has become fashionable among the poshest families to commission M. F. Husain and Satish Gujral, two of India's best-known artists, to design invitations. The guest list often includes people neither the bride nor the bridegroom has met. The point—often misunderstood by foreigners—is for both sets of parents to demonstrate who they can get to attend. The more sumptuous the invitation, the more competitive it will be. For the bigger weddings, some invitations (to relatives and friends) are accompanied by gifts such as Louis Vuitton bags, Revlon cosmetic kits, Bulgari scarves, and Prada accessories. "The days of giving a good old sari are over," says Mohan. "It is not just about how much you spend; it is how much you are seen to be spending."

Then there is the catering. In the last few years, dozens of specialist wedding caterers have sprung up in Delhi, Mumbai, and elsewhere. Hosts no longer confine their offerings to Indian cooking. Many offer "multicuisine," with stalls offering Thai, Moroccan, Japanese, and other exotic fare. "The standard is to have at least seven different cuisines—the more foreign ones the better," says Mo-han. "The fact that everybody heads for the *tandoor* [barbequed] sec-tion is neither here nor there." Equally important is the originality of the décor, the type and variety of candles, the floral arrangements, and so on. Most choose themes for the main party, such as "lounge," "Moulin Rouge," a particular Bollywood film, or even a country. One much-publicized Punjabi wedding in 2004 had South Africa as the motif. The parents of the bride actually transported eight giraffes from Africa to add that authentic touch. "It is as if some kind of madness has gripped India's middle classes," says Mohan, laughing. I presumed that the giraffes were sent back home afterward in a state of high confusion.

•   •   •

But what of India's esoteric traditions: the Hinduism of the Rig Veda, the Bhagavad Gita, and the Upanishads? Have they survived the on-slaught of modern consumer behavior? India has an extraordinary history of subtle abstraction, and a chain of free-wheeling philosoph-ical speculation that stretches back for three thousand years. It may not be the religion of the masses. But if the finer and more subtle di-mensions of India's traditions have survived this long—which I be-lieve they have, with both positive and negative consequences—it seems highly unlikely that they would vanish in today's world. India's most revered texts contain a message that is profoundly asocial—on a literal reading they sometimes appear to recommend an indiffer-ence to the suffering of others. Likewise, there is still a tendency to substitute words for action. Traces of this philosophical aloofness can be found in many aspects of contemporary India.

Writing about the India of more than 2,500 years ago, when the followers of Buddha, Mahavira, and a thousand diverse sects were active, all putting their ideas forward in a climate of relatively per-missive inquiry, A. L. Basham observed: "The intellectual life of India in the seventh and sixth centuries BC was as pullulating and as vigorous as the jungle after rains."[16] Pantheists argued with polytheists, dualists with monists, materialists with spiritualists, and atheists with everyone. The quality of classical Indian grammars, from Pali to Sanskrit, was as sophisticated as any that were ever collated. Those who wish to comment on Hinduism purely as a religion (although some argue it is misleading to describe Hinduism as a religion) should also grapple with its esoteric traditions. I am certainly unqualified to do so. But it is nevertheless hard not to appreciate the complexity of India's philosophical traditions. I was struck by this (not unrepresentative) line from the Upanishads: "The Gods themselves are later than creation, so who knows truly whence it has arisen?"[17] This could be read both as an admission of ignorance about the origins of creation as well as an admission that gods are essentially products of the human imagination.

Some of the texts even contain flashes of nihilism. In the Bhagavad Gita, Krishna, who appears as a charioteer, advises Arjuna, the warrior he is serving, to overcome his doubts about the futility of killing and do his caste duty by going into battle on his chariot. This epic conversation is often cited as an example of the moral code behind caste, since Krishna advises Arjuna that doing one's caste duty is more important than personal considerations. It is also cited as an example of karmic morality: Arjuna can escape the bonds of karma—his past actions—only by acting without regard for the consequences. The emphasis is on intention, not outcome. To a foreigner, what also leaps out from Krishna's words is their bleak consistency. Krishna tells Arjuna: "Thou feels pity when pity has no place. Wise men feel pity neither for what dies nor what lives. . . . I am indifferent to all born things. There is none whom I hate, none whom I love."

Buddha was recorded as having said much the same thing: "Those who love nothing in this world are rich in joy and free from pain."[18] One of the most-cited stories from Buddha's life concerns a young mother who came to Buddha and begged him to restore the life of her young son, who had just died of illness. She would follow him for the rest of her life if he did this. Buddha tells the bereaved mother to go to the nearest town and bring back some mustard seeds from the first household she found that had not suffered a recent loss. The mother leaves her son's corpse with Buddha and goes from house to house in the town. Eventually, as the day wears on, she realizes that there is no household that fits that description. She returns to Buddha as a follower, having accepted the futility of challenging the laws of life and death. Basham contrasts this story with the miracles of Jesus, in which people are raised from the dead and the sick and wounded get up and walk. It is hard to experience the force of many New Testament stories unless you believe they literally happened. Whether or not this small episode from Buddha's life took place, it makes little difference to the force of the message.[19] Basham could equally have contrasted its realist message with the practice of popular Buddhism, in which people walk clockwise around the temple, believing each lap earns them extra merit, all the while chanting the name of an atheist philosopher.

• • •

I was once eating lunch at a large café in the town of Cuddalore in Tamil Nadu when I realized that all the uniformed waiters rushing from table to table were children—some as young as eight or nine. The lunch place was situated about 500 yards from the district courthouse and many of its patrons were lawyers. No one batted an eyelid. Child labor was officially abolished in India many years ago. But large loopholes were provided for cottage industries. And so the employment of children continues in one of India's wealthiest states under the noses of lawyers as they are eating their lunch off large banana leaves.

Tamil Nadu was also the site of a controversial battle over child labor in the 1980s and 1990s when matchstick factories in the town of Sivakasi were revealed to be employing large numbers of children.

The owners of the factories were given small-scale, or cottage industry, status so they benefited from a more lax interpretation of labor laws. Their main competitor, Wimco, was a Swedish company that used modern machine-based methods to manufacture matchsticks using less labor. Wimco complained about the unfair labor practices of its local competitors, who continued to use child labor in their sweatshops. A tussle ensued in which almost everybody, from government officials to social activists, united in opposition to the foreign multinational. The government eventually imposed higher duties on the machines that Wimco imported for its capital-intensive matchstick production. The child labor continued. When it came to the crunch, people from across the spectrum, including the Gandhians, disliked foreign capital more than they disliked child labor.[20]

It is hard to get a precise estimate of the extent of child labor in India because it is so difficult to define. The large estimates of up to forty million[21] children would include youngsters who help out in their parents' shop or who collect water in the morning for household use (often a very long walk). But children who are at least indirectly employed by third parties, such as matchstick makers, bidi cigarette makers, brassware polishers, and middlemen in the carpet industry, probably number about ten million. Another way of estimating child labor is to look at school truancy which, again, totals about forty million. Whatever number you eventually arrive at, it amounts to a lot of young lives.

I have had many conversations with people in India about child illiteracy and child labor, which are very closely related. There is a widespread view that the problem will not disappear until poverty has first disappeared: in other words that it will sort itself out over time. More than a decade ago Myron Weiner, the late American academic, wrote a devastating book entitled *The Child and the State in India*. He pointed out that the consensus among India's elites that child illiteracy and child labor were a consequence and not a cause of poverty was the wrong way around. Most countries, for one reason or another, made education compulsory before they became developed economies. He cited municipalities in Germany that made child education compulsory as early as 1524 under the influence of the Protestant zeal of Martin Luther, who believed all humans should have direct access to the word of God. For the same reasons, Massachusetts in 1647 made child attendance at school compulsory. Japan made it compulsory in 1872 because it wanted to catch up with the West and education was essential to nation building. And the USSR wanted the opportunity to create a socialist "New Man," which it could do through indoctrination in the schools.[22] Much the same applies to China, which has a literacy rate of more than 90 percent, compared to 65 percent in India.

Weiner pointed out that on paper India had done all the right things, having enacted strict laws and incorporated high-sounding principles about child rights in the 1950 constitution. But when it came to implementing these laws, indifference reigned. The same point could be made about statutes outlawing the practice of dowry, untouchability, and child marriage—all of which persist in India on a gargantuan scale. Some problems, such as dowry, are getting worse. Weiner concluded that these laws were "a kind of modern talisman intended to bring results by the magical power of words themselves." Indeed, hundreds of year ago, foreign chroniclers of India (such as Alberuni and Fa Hsien) observed the tendency of Brahmins to prefer words to action, and sometimes to believe they were one and the same thing. Weiner also highlighted the traditional attitudes of the upper-caste elites, who might verbally profess their support for equality of opportunity but who, in practice, behave quite differently. Pratap Bhanu Mehta also puts it succinctly: "The state has internalized the message of the Bhagavad Gita— only intentions matter and not consequences."[23] Hindu philosophy has produced some of the most sophisticated abstractions the world has known. But it has never produced a Martin Luther. Traditionally the lower castes were not permitted to read the classic Hindu texts. This tradition lingers in today's India. How else to explain why a country that made education compulsory two generations ago should tolerate the daily absence of up to forty million children from its schools?

In the autumn of 2004 I visited India's "carpet belt" districts in Uttar Pradesh. There are three districts around the holy town of Varanasi, which together employ roughly 500,000 people and possess 175,000 handlooms,[24] most of them at the cottage industry level. Tens of thousands of children are involved in the production of carpets. Naturally, the region has one of the lowest literacy rates in India. I was accompanied by Dipankar Gupta, the Delhi-based sociologist, who had recommended that I see a project commissioned by Ikea, the Swedish furniture chain store, which buys carpets from the region. Ikea had requested UNICEF, the United Nations Children's Fund, to manage the project. The Swedish company had examined an existing scheme run by a collection of international companies, which is called Rugmark. Any shopper in the West who buys a carpet with the Rugmark label attached to the product is guaranteed it was not made with child labor. As I was to discover, the Rugmark guarantee is at best misleading and at worst fraudulent. There are only a handful of Rugmark inspectors covering tens of thousands of villages. Like all cottage industries, the carpet-making process is highly decentralized and fragmented and so it is physically impossible for the inspectors to verify Rugmark's claim.

We drove down tiny dirt tracks to some of the most cut off villages in the area to observe local "bridge schools," which give former child workers a year of crash education before they are transferred to a mainstream school. Sitting under the shade of a capacious neem tree next to the village pond, the children were learning to count with the aid of carpet knots. At separate village classes, their mothers were being trained in better carpet-making methods (most of the fathers are working in the cities). Defenders of child labor in India's carpet industry use four arguments to justify its continuation. First, the children's parents are too poor to send them to school. Second, the education would be of no use to the children since they could not put it into practice. Third, they work at home with their families so the conditions are reasonable. Finally, children are essential to the intricate process of carpet knotting, since they have nimble fingers. I had always believed the last assertion. But it turns out to be false. UNICEF calls it the "nimble finger myth." In fact, the process of carpet knotting requires strength of which adults obviously have more. "Quality has improved since we moved to full adult labor, which is why I'm very happy working with this scheme," said Fida Hussain, owner of Deluxe Carpets, which supplies Ikea. "The Rugmark scheme is a formality. The buyers don't do their homework."

As for Ikea, its investments are self-interested, which is why UNICEF was convinced the company was committed to the project. By supporting the move to full adult labor in carpet making and by making it worthwhile for families to go along with the project, the company protects itself against possible consumer boycotts or adverse publicity in the West. As important, Ikea also gets more value for its money. Adults work at much higher rates of productivity than do children.* "So often human rights arguments are pitted against arguments of profitability in India and elsewhere," says Gupta, who, in addition to being an academic, carries out "social audits" of foreign and domestic investments in India. "If it is done right, it is usually more profitable to treat people well."

The same argument could be applied on a much larger scale to the most distressing social problems that India continues to face. One of the reasons India finds it so hard to develop a mass labor-intensive manufacturing sector is because such a large proportion of its rural adults are not educated up to a minimum standard. Even for the most basic widget making, the worker needs to be able to read simple instructions. Yet support for the highly inadequate status quo can be found in the most surprising quarters, for example, among Gandhian groups and trade union members. Weiner gives an example of workers in India's large tea plantations who are the most militant defenders of child labor since they want their children to inherit their jobs. I have heard similar

---

*Defenders of child labor in India deploy much the same logic as the nineteenth-century plantation owners in the American South before the abolition of slavery. Free labor turned out to be much more productive than slave labor.

arguments from Gandhian activists, including Aruna Roy, who believe
that in many cases an early apprenticeship in traditional occupations,
such as glassmaking or carpet making, will give the child a much more
relevant skill in life than what the formal education system could offer.
There are some merits to some of the arguments, not least because India's government school system is inadequate. But the notion that children should do what their parents do—and be denied, inadvertently or
otherwise, the skills to make their own choice when they are old
enough—is deeply conservative. At a much higher level of society, it
provides an underpinning to the culture of nepotism that afflicts politics
and administration. Essentially, it is about caste and the maintenance of
hereditary occupations. Weiner called it "social reproduction." He
wrote: "In short, trade unionists, like most parents, employers, teachers
and education officials presume a social order that is guided by the principles of social reproduction."[25]

The rest of the world could learn a lot from India, along the lines of
tolerance, the management of diversity, and the rooting of democracy
in a traditional society. Most people who sample the quality of Indian
food, music, dancing, literature, architecture, and philosophy acquire a
lifelong taste for all things Indian. If world trade were to be conducted
purely in cultural products, then India would have a thumping annual
surplus. But India continues to lack in practice—if not in principle—the
basic condition of genuine citizenship. Equal citizenship is enshrined in
India's constitution. It is expounded by thousands of academics, journalists, activists, and commentators. It is generally presumed to be a reality. But in practice, India falls far short of the claims it makes. India's
caste system and the traditional mentality of its upper castes are changing and may even be in long-term decline. But they have yet to disappear. As we have seen with the continuation of high illiteracy rates, the
low status of women, and the economic valuation of lower-caste children, the persistence of certain traditional attitudes imposes a moral
cost on Indian society. Children of both genders ought to be seen as
priceless. The continuation of such traditions also imposes an economic
cost, which India can ill afford to pay.

# conclusion: HERS TO LOSE

## India's Huge Opportunities and Challenges in the Twenty-first Century

*The only possible idea of India is a nation that is greater than the sum of its parts.*

SHASHI THAROOR, Indian author and
undersecretary-general of the United Nations[1]

I was once offered a chance to ride through the streets of New Delhi on a white horse. To my subsequent regret, I turned it down. My family and I chose instead to arrive at my marriage ceremony in a fleet of white Ambassador cars. The experience was unnerving. Priya was convinced the entire wedding was heading for disaster since her parents had not gotten around to planning anything until a few days earlier. No Hindu priest would marry an Indian to a foreigner, she said. And none of my friends or relatives would have a clue what was going on. Nobody had told me what I was supposed to do during the two-hour ceremony—although I had been given a formal outfit of kurta pajamas to wear. To add to the rising sense of panic, the car that was supposed to fetch Priya from the beauty parlor a couple of hours before the ceremony had failed to arrive. Priya had been forgotten. Armageddon, it seemed, could no longer be prevented.

But we were in India, not England. And what appears on the surface to be chaotic is often just how it should be. The wedding came off beautifully, although it took me about ninety minutes to realize that there was method in the apparent madness that was going on around us. The Hindu priest had arrived. The lotus leaves were in place. The ghee for pouring on the fire was ready and the knot that would bind us together was waiting to be tied. Sitting cross-legged in a small *mandap*—or house of flowers—we were the only still points in the kaleidoscope of color that was swirling around us. In fact, there was one other fixed point that I occasionally used to check my bearings: my relatives, dressed in the sober wedding attire of Anglican England, vaguely wondering whether they were supposed to stand up and start singing. Their collective expression of awkward bemusement gradually dissolved into chatter and laughter as they realized nothing formal would be required of them. It was as good an illustration as any of the "functioning anarchy" that John Kenneth Galbraith, who was U.S. ambassador to New Delhi in the early 1960s, once said of India. In spite of all signs to the contrary, things came together perfectly. Priya, meanwhile, was feeling guilty at ever having doubted her parents.

Whenever events in India appear to be on the verge of falling apart, I often remind myself of our wedding and of Galbraith's very apt description of India. Occasionally I am also reminded of what I was once taught about the behavior of bees. If you were to be transported inside a swarm, it would appear to be anarchic, with individual bees buzzing around in every different direction. But if you stood back and observed the swarm as a whole, it would be going in one direction.

In the last thirty years, India has been through a nineteen-month spell of autocracy; it has lost two leaders of the Nehru-Gandhi family to assassination; it has faced separatist movements in Punjab,

Kashmir, Assam, and elsewhere; and it has switched from a closed economic regime to an open(ish) economy. It has moved from secular government to Hindu nationalist government and back again; it has gone from single-party rule to twenty-four-party rule, from antinuclear to nuclear, from undeclared border wars with Pakistan to a lengthy peace process. It has also moved from virtual bankruptcy to a lengthy boom. By any normal barometer, India appears to be highly unpredictable.

These are India's headlines of the last thirty years. But if you turn to the statistics buried deep in the inside pages you get a strikingly different impression. T. N. Ninan, one of the country's most respected editors, calls India the "one percent society."[2] Whichever indicator you choose, whether it is economic or social, India is improving at a rate of roughly 1 percent a year. For example, India's poverty rate is declining at about 1 percent a year. In 1991 it was 35 percent. By 2000 it was 26 percent.[3] It has probably continued to decline at roughly the same rate since then. Or take India's literacy rate. In 1991 it was 52 percent. By 2001 it was 65 percent. Or life expectancy. In 1991 the average Indian would live to the age of fifty-eight. By 2001 the age had risen to sixty-five years. Roughly the same congruence emerges from India's international rankings. India's human development index, which is compiled by the UN Development Program, went from 0.254 in 1970 to 0.602 in 2005, which translates into an annual improvement of about 1 percent.

To judge by the living conditions of ordinary Indians and not by the drama of national events, the country is moving forward on a remarkably stable trajectory. Many friends of India wish the country would accelerate its rate of progress. An improvement of 1 percent a year is fine if you already have a developed economy. But when almost 300 million people continue to live in absolute poverty, it is painfully slow. India's fragmented political culture makes it very difficult for governments to take decisive action that would convert India into a 2 percent society, like neighboring China. Yet on India's plus side it would take very large scale disaster or war to halt or reverse India's steady progress.

If intentions can be ascribed to nation-states, you could say that India has given a higher priority to stability than it has to efficiency. In many ways, the opposite could be said of China. Myron Weiner, the American academic, said that India moved slowly because it was diverse. That also meant it was relatively stable. If something goes wrong in one part of the country, it does not necessarily spread to other parts of the country as it would in a more homogeneous society like China's. Recall the panicked reaction of China's aging communist leadership in 1989 to the gathering of students in Beijing's Tiananmen Square in support of democracy. Fearing the protests would spread quickly into a national movement, leaders sent in the tanks. India faces a Tiananmen-style sit-down protest in one or other corner of the country for one reason or another every other week. Sometimes the police charge with their *lathis*. Bullets are very rare. "India is like a lorry with twelve wheels," wrote Weiner. "If one or two puncture, it doesn't go into the ditch."[4] To extend Weiner's analogy, China has fewer wheels so it can travel faster. But people far beyond China's borders worry about what would happen if a wheel came off.

What is it that keeps India stable? After independence, many foreign observers predicted the country would not last long in its existing form. Because of its profound social, linguistic, religious, and ethnic diversities, India would inevitably break up into separate nation-states. One authoritative book, *India, the Most Dangerous Decades*,[5] which dwelt on India's separatist threats, was very widely cited. India has not dissolved. Nor does it seem likely to happen. Another widespread expectation was that India would not remain a democracy for long. The assumption then, as now, was that democracy was not compatible with absolute poverty or with majority illiteracy. Again, this view has been belied by events. There are many reasons that these two expectations proved unfounded. Perhaps the most important reason India has remained intact as a country is because it is a democracy. And perhaps the most important reason that India has remained a democracy is because it is so diverse. Far from endangering democracy, India's pluralism makes democracy essential.

A related but more insidious assumption is that China is growing faster than India because it is authoritarian. This is a view that is held by some Western and Asian commentators. I am certainly not alone in having ethical reservations about posing questions to which the only answer is dictatorship. But I also think the debate is misleading. India went through a period of autocracy under Indira Gandhi that turned out to be damaging both to India's social stability and its economic prosperity.* The autocratic tendencies of the Congress Party under Indira Gandhi strengthened the forces of regionalism in Indian politics and stoked separatist insurgencies on its national borders that brought India's national integrity into question. That India remains in one piece owes much to the fact that Indira Gandhi restored India's system of federal democracy, which has provided a peaceful outlet to most of the country's regional tendencies. As for India's plethora of insurgencies, only the Kashmiri struggle poses a serious threat to Indian nationhood. And it is partly sustained by a foreign power.

There is a better answer to those who argue that India suffers from a lack of autocracy: Pakistan. As economist Amartya Sen points out, India's economic growth rate has consistently outperformed that of Pakistan in the last two decades, achieving an average growth rate of 6 percent compared to 3.5 percent in Pakistan. For some of that period, Pakistan has had democracy. Even during periods of free elections, the freedom of Pakistani citizens has been limited. As the joke

*Indira Gandhi's state of emergency was supported by intellectual trendsetters across the Western world, including Robert S. McNamara, president of the World Bank and former defense secretary during the Vietnam War, who believed a spell of autocracy would improve India's rate of investment by reducing populist democratic pressures to raise current spending.

goes, "In Pakistan, freedom of expression is notably stronger than freedom after expression."[6] Because of their ethnic and cultural similarities, Pakistan offers India a much better mirror than China. "The proximate comparison of India with a not always democratic country must be with Pakistan, which somehow does not tend to be the focus of the rosy portrayals of the nondemocratic alternative that India has missed," said Sen.[7]

The contrast between India and China is also selective. Although China has much better economic and social indicators than India, this arguably has little to do with their contrasting political systems. The Indian state of Kerala, which is as democratic as any other in India, has a life expectancy of seventy-four and a literacy rate above 90 percent, compared to seventy years and 90 percent for China. "There is absolutely nothing to indicate that any of China's policies are inconsistent with greater democracy," said Sen. At a more important level, India challenges us to provide a clear definition of what we mean by development, which is usually taken to mean economic prosperity and little else. Should it not also mean giving people meaningful choices in how they express themselves and conduct their lives? If the answer is yes then democracy should be seen as a development goal in itself. On this measure, India is ahead of China. Clearly India will have to find better ways of ensuring that its democracy delivers a fairer economic deal to its people. One way of achieving better governance would be for the Indian state to treat people as citizens with equal rights and not as supplicants on a scale graded according to social status. Viewed from this perspective, India is not democratic enough. As Arun Shourie, the Indian politician, points out: "Governance is not golf: that we are a democracy does not entitle us to a handicap."[8]

To understand why India's decision-making process is slower than China's, one should look at India's more deeply entrenched culture of pluralism. China is also diverse. But it has one script, one official language, and very little religious division. India has eighteen official languages, several different scripts, and deep religious and caste divisions. The highly segmented nature of Indian society makes collective action much more difficult to carry out. Regardless of the political system, it would be difficult for Indian governments to take decisive action. An ethnically homogenous country like Norway that is scrupulously democratic has an efficient and decisive system of government, while dictatorships ruling over diverse tribal countries in Africa and elsewhere are chronically unable to impose consensus on their societies.[9] India's system of government is held back by ethnic divisions in society. It is much harder to build trust between ethnic groups than within them. This makes it far more difficult to undertake collective action. Academics call it the prisoner's dilemma. I prefer the analogy that Indians themselves love to make about the bucket of crabs on the beach. Whenever one crab tries to climb out of the bucket, the others pull it back down because they do not want it to escape.

Some people dispute whether the term *ethnic politics* is appropriate for India, because they do not agree that Indian castes or religious groups are ethnically distinct. The classical Sanskrit word for caste is *varna*. One of the translations for *varna* is "color," which gives a possible indication of the historical beginnings of caste division. One of the principal origins of caste was the gradual incorporation of indigenous Indian tribes into mainstream Indian society by sedentary communities. Each new tribe was allotted a place low down in the system. The battle—often between Hindu nationalists and Christian missionaries—to incorporate India's tribal groups into mainstream society continues up and down the country.

What matters is what people perceive themselves to be. In many ways India's castes behave in a way that is much more similar to tribal or kinship groups than to economic classes. It is virtually impossible to tell which way an Indian will vote by knowing only his socioeconomic status (you are more likely to vote your caste when you cast your vote). This is why so much of Indian politics continues to be absorbed by seemingly petty disputes over social dignity rather than focusing on economic conditions (it is the politics, stupid). It is also why it is so hard in India to build a state that is blind to the identity of its citizens. Most interactions between the individual and the state in India are governed by who you are and whom you know. Some people believe this will fade as India's middle class expands. As we saw in the last chapter, most middle-class Indians are employed in sectors that are subject to global competition, in companies that are increasingly likely to select their employees on the basis of merit and not blood ties. India's middle class still totals between just 200 million and 300 million people, as defined by international standards.[10] It is still hard for India's poor to gain entry to the middle class.

The reforms of 1991 have benefited India. If carried out sequentially, further liberalization would lead to higher growth and bring greater benefits. But India's free market liberalizers cannot simply wish the state away. Nor should they want to. Without a more meritocratic and just state,* India's economy will suffer. To thrive, India's businesses need good infrastructure, a literate and healthy workforce, a sustainable environment, and the promise of law and order. Very little of this can be accomplished by the private sector on its own. The division in India, and elsewhere, is too often between those who believe the state should dominate all aspects life and those who believe it should play virtually no role beyond defense and law and order. As we shall see in the remainder of this concluding chapter, it is in the interests of all people, rich or poor, right wing or left wing, for India to develop a more responsive and modern state.

In what follows, we will look at four critical problems that India faces in the coming years and decades: first, the challenge of lifting 300 million people out of absolute poverty and of providing the remainder with a more secure standard of living; second, overcoming

---

*In addition to the fact that it restricts merit-based selection, there are questions about the justness of India's job reservations system for scheduled castes, tribes, and "Other Backward Castes." According to India's Supreme Court, it is the "creamy layers"—the economically wealthy—among India's socially disadvantaged groups who monopolize the public sector jobs quota.

the dangers of rapid environmental degradation, which, at the human level, is poisoning India's air and water supply and which at the global level will increasingly add to climate change; third, heading off the specter of an HIV-AIDS epidemic, which, if untackled, could derail India's upbeat economic projections; finally, protecting and strengthening India's system of liberal democracy, which, along with the talents of its people, is the most precious asset India possesses. Then we will look at the country's extraordinary potential to rise and rise over the coming decades. But in order to fully exploit its opportunities, India will have to tackle its problems more directly than it has been. Overcoming them would tax the powers and resources of an efficient and forward-thinking state. In the Indian state's present condition, there is a question mark over its ability to achieve these objectives.

•    •    •

In 1900 the world's population was 1.6 billion. By 2050, India is projected to hit 1.6 billion people, overtaking China as the world's most populous nation by 2032. The various United Nations scenarios for India's population plateau range between 1.3 billion people and 1.9 billion people.[11] There is a forecasting margin of error amounting to 600 million people. The more rapidly India can overcome poverty, the more likely its population will stabilize at nearer 1 billion than 2 billion people. Perhaps the key determinant of how quickly India can eradicate mass poverty is whether it can establish a better economic climate for its farmers and create more jobs in manufacturing and services.

India increased its agricultural yields drastically in the 1970s and 1980s. But in the last fifteen years India's yield growth in cereal grains has tapered off. India does not necessarily require another generation of "miracle" rice or wheat to achieve a second green revolution, although new seed technology would help.* At the moment, India's average yield per hectare is roughly half that of neighboring China.[12] India must raise its agricultural productivity if it wants to catch up with China, which means carrying out a series of overdue reforms. This is admittedly easier said than done. But there is little confusion about what those reforms should be; they would include the government permitting the consolidation of rural land holdings by creating a market for voluntary land sales so that the average plot size becomes large enough for mechanization. Families who own just a hectare or two (which accounts for 90 percent of India's farm holdings) can't afford tractors or drip irrigation technology. For some crops it will make sense for farmers to create cooperative farms when there is a guaranteed market for their produce. But most Indian states make it compulsory for farmers to sell their produce to government-appointed middlemen who drive their buying prices down and the selling prices up and pocket much of the difference. India's farmers should be allowed to sell to whom they choose, whether the buyer is foreign or domestic. Liberalizing India's retail sector, which would bring investments in cold storage facilities and new agribusinesses, would also stimulate more rapid change.

But the Indian government must do more than abolish agricultural price controls if it wants to boost rural prosperity. The state must also play a more direct role. The most obvious deficiency is in India's dismal rural infrastructure, both physical and social, necessitating building more all-weather roads linking villages to towns and reforming India's primary and secondary education system to ensure that teachers turn up and do their jobs. The same applies to village health centers, which as often as not are dilapidated hulks stripped (by employees or local residents) of their equipment. Fewer than half of all Indian births are assisted by trained midwives or doctors, com-

---

*India has experimented with genetically modified (GM) cotton with mixed results. There are proposals to permit GM mustard, sorghum, and other crops.

pared to 97 percent in China.[13] The problem is neither money nor technology. It is about the efficiency of government. In order to encourage farmers to grow other crops, New Delhi should overhaul its regressive system of food subsidies to the consumer. As India gets richer, people are spending proportionately more on vegetables and proteins and less on basic cereals. But almost all of India's farm producer subsidies go to wheat and rice farmers. Diversifying the public incentive system to encourage more horticulture, vegetable, fish, and chicken farming, which have greater export potential, would give a large income boost to India's impoverished villagers. Wheat and rice are also heavily water-intensive, and India can ill afford to continue wasting the fickle offerings of its rain gods. Crop diversification would also employ more people. Vegetable farming employs fifteen times more people per hectare than does rice or wheat farming. The government should also deliver reliable electricity and clean water to all its villages. Providing these resources free of charge to select categories of people (mostly the rich farmers), as is the case today, makes it uneconomic to provide them to anyone else. If utilities are allowed to charge customers for what they use, there is an incentive to supply it. There must also be better incentives for farmers to harvest rainwater. More than 70 percent of India's rainfall runs off into the sea.[14] In the cities, charging the poor for water could ensure the poor would actually get it. Giving it to them free means they will continue to get either sewage or nothing. In practice, the poor pay private water suppliers a multiple of what it would cost the state to deliver the same supply.

The other half of India's poverty challenge is to create nonfarm employment for many more people. India's workforce is expanding by roughly ten million people every year. But only about five million new jobs are created every year. Some new employment can be created by reforming agriculture. But not nearly enough. To stray into economic jargon for a moment, India's unreformed farming sector—as it exists now—has a zero or even negative employment elasticity of growth.[15] This means that improvements to agricultural productivity entail less not more labor. The service sector could take up some of the slack, particularly if the country can do more to boost its tourist industry, which remains surprisingly small considering the unparalleled wealth of things there are to see and experience in India. At just 2.5 million foreign visitors in 2005, India had fewer tourists than Dubai or Singapore. Foreigners are put off by India's unreliable transport links and its poor sanitation. Visiting the Taj Mahal is not as enthralling or romantic as it should be when you have to skirt around refuse dumps and dodge beggars and stray dogs to get inside. Building up a tourist industry does not automatically entail the "Disneyfication" of your culture, as some fear. It is hard to believe that a stronger tourist sector, which could provide more formal jobs for the poor in transport, hotels, restaurants, and other services, would subtract from the dignity of Indian culture. Indeed, higher revenues would help better preserve some of India's crumbling monuments.

However, there is no substitute for creating a larger and more labor-intensive manufacturing sector in India. It does not have to be polluting because India possesses the technology and capital to develop in a cleaner fashion than countries that developed earlier. Nor does it have to be socially disruptive. Production, particularly in food processing and textiles, can take place in the small towns of provincial India, especially if the roads are paved and refrigeration is provided. We have already glimpsed some of the skill of which India is capable in the garment and fashion sector, and the precision and value India can add to auto components and pharmaceuticals. But these cutting-edge sectors mostly employ graduates. The rest of India's labor force must be given better education and more vocational training if they are to become employable. India must also remove the obstacles that inhibit investors, both Indian and foreign, from putting more money into the country. Indian managers spend 15 percent of their time dealing with government inspectors,[16] which is almost double that of China. Indian companies also spend far too much time filling in complicated tax forms and dealing with venal customs officers. Although New Delhi has taken steps to simplify its tax code, India arguably has the most complicated tax system in the world.[17] In some parts of India, the system of *octroi*—a tax levied on the passage of goods from one Indian state to another—costs more to administer than it collects. Corruption is the only possible explanation for why it has been kept in place.

Creating better infrastructure, particularly ports, roads, the railway system, and electricity supply, is also indispensable for the development of manufacturing. The infrastructure projects, themselves, would significantly boost employment. India's government is stuck in chronic fiscal deficit, so it needs all the capital it can get from both domestic and foreign private sources to upgrade the country's infrastructure. New Delhi has pledged by 2009 to open up India's banking sector to full competition. Finance houses such as Citibank and Standard Chartered have already picked up significant business from India's growing middle classes. Giving them and India's growing number of impressive and internationally competitive private banks better access to India's poorly managed state-owned rural bank network would significantly boost the country's ability to translate savings into investment, including investment in better infrastructure. New Delhi has also taken steps to partially open up its insurance sector to foreign investors. Less than 10 percent of India's population has life insurance. The more people who can be insured, the more capital there is to invest. India has nothing to fear from further financial liberalization.

Finally, as we saw in chapters one and two, India must reform its labor laws. This would not be an anti-poor effort, as many have argued. If it is impossible to fire someone, you are much less likely to hire him in the first place. India has just 10 million trade union members, of whom only 1.37 million are considered to be active in their unions.[18] In the name of the poor, India's trade unions exercise a veto on reform of the very labor regulations that are partly responsible for keeping most of India's 470 million–strong workforce locked out of the formal economy. India should acknowledge that on this issue the country's trade unions, like its business lobbies, are just another vested interest that speaks for its members, not for the poor.

India's second large challenge is to prevent wholesale environmental degradation. Understandably, Indians see little reason why Western nations should lecture India on protecting its forest cover or reducing carbon dioxide emissions when the West is responsible for most of the world's environmental deterioration. India accounts for only 4 percent of global carbon dioxide emissions[19] but has almost 17 percent of the world's population. Clearly on a per capita basis, the citizens of the United States, Europe, and other rich nations contribute many times the pollution that India does and derive a multiple of the benefits. But that is changing. Many of the richer nations are taking steps to boost energy efficiency and introduce cleaner fuels. As time moves on, India's share of global warming will escalate rapidly. No solution to climate change will be credible without the participation of India and China, led, of course, by the United States, the world's biggest polluter. The West, and particularly the United States, should take a stronger lead in offering India and the rest of the developing world financial incentives to embark on a cleaner path of development. For its part, India must get over its resentment of Western "double standards" and acknowledge that Indians will be disproportionately harmed by the shifts in climate patterns that a majority of scientists are now predicting. India should not cut off its nose to spite its face.

Indians already face acute quality of life issues that are related to its environment. Fewer than 2 percent of Indians own their own vehicles. The comparable figure is 60 percent for the United States.[20] Yet India's cities are already clogged with traffic. For the first time, in 2004, more than a million private vehicles were sold in one year in India. That number will rise sharply. By 2030 India is projected to have 200 million vehicles, public and private, compared to 40 million in 2006.[21] Quite apart from urban air quality, or more mundane issues such as parking space, it is hard to imagine a road-building program that could keep up with Indian vehicle demand. An India with five times as many vehicles as today (and rising) is a vision of purgatory.

There are many areas, such as telecoms, in which mobile phones are booming without fixed line service having improved very much, where India has leapfrogged a stage of development by exploiting new technology. India can leapfrog the classic stage of traffic gridlock by planning now for cleaner and more efficient urban transport systems. India already has some projects, such as the New Delhi Metro, which point the way forward. Every Indian city needs a New Delhi Metro, in spite of the high capital costs and subsidies that are involved in such mass transit projects. Furthermore, India should upgrade its 39,060-mile railways network—the second most extensive in the world—which has the capacity to transport goods and people around the country in a much less polluting and more economically efficient way than roads. At the moment, the opposite is happening. Indian Railways overcharges freight users in order to subsidize passengers, just as India's state power boards do with electricity tariffs. High railway tariffs push freight onto the roads, which clogs them up. Similarly, high electricity charges make it difficult for small businesses to survive, so they have to buy their own highly polluting diesel power generators.

The quality of air and water in India is declining as rapidly as its economy is improving (without being factored in as a cost). It is estimated that one-eighth of India's premature deaths are caused by air pollution.[22] Several hundred thousand children die every year from dirty water. Retreating to the past is not a solution, as some of India's environmental activists seem to believe. In the villages, people die young of respiratory diseases because they lack electricity or access to gas. The climate and the topography of the village make it impractical to burn cow dung, or wood, outdoors. So they light their fire indoors, and gradually they are choked to death. Only about half of India's village households have a power connection. Likewise, most waterborne diseases are caused by lack of modern sanitation. Even if it were technically possible to retreat to a prosperous rural idyll cut off from the modern world, it is too late. India has too many people. The lessons on electricity tariffs also apply to irrigation for India's farmers. As we have seen, it is mostly the rich farmers who can afford to pump water from the ground, leaving everyone else with less water and accelerating the erosion of soil quality by increasing salinity levels. Deforestation is also a factor in erosion. In 1900 a third of India was covered by forest. It is now a sixth.[23] In order to encourage sustainable exploitation of resources, whether it is water, soil, forests, or air, people must be made to pay for what they consume. Businesses that pollute should be fined or closed, which very rarely happens. Corrupt forest officials, who connive with illegal loggers and poachers, should be sacked, although they rarely are. And both water and power should be priced simply and fairly. Many Indians still believe water and electricity should be provided for free or a nominal cost. But somebody, somewhere always pays.

Finally, India should develop a coherent energy strategy, for the sake of both its environment and its economy. Because of the demands of coalition politics, India's energy management is scattered across many different ministries—coal, steel, power, petroleum, hydroelectric, and nuclear. Each one has a different agenda, often oblivious to the others. India needs one ministry of energy. Today India imports 70 percent of its oil. That figure is projected to rise to 90 percent by 2020[24]—unless India were to discover significant new domestic oil fields. Politics makes it almost impossible to build large new dams for hydroelectric power. India's large reserves of coal are very high in ash content, which makes them a particularly dirty form of fossil fuel. As we have seen, the civil nuclear option is costly. But there are other sources of energy. India should move ahead with the controversial gas pipeline from Iran via Pakistan and explore possible pipelines from central Asia through Afghanistan and from Myanmar through Bangladesh. Gas is a relatively clean technology. There are others that can be developed. South Africa has already demonstrated that it is economic to "gasify" dirty coal. India is at least fifteen years behind in exploring the potential of what it could do if it gasified some of its coal reserves in eastern India. As I have argued, India can reduce demand for oil by modernizing its national railway network and by building modern mass transit systems for its cities. There are other more innovative strategies India could adopt. For example, India gets a lot of sun. By giving builders an incentive to install solar paneling in new houses and high-rises, Indians can heat their water and power their air conditioners with natural sunlight. An India that repeats the mistakes of the West is not only a horrific prospect, but it is also self-defeating. India has always believed it has much to teach the world. Perhaps the best lesson India could convey is that you do not have to ruin your natural surroundings or destroy the quality of life of future generations in order to lift your people out of poverty.

India's third challenge is to defeat the HIV-AIDS pandemic. Many influential people in India believe the threat has been exaggerated by the West and that the country ought to focus on solving more long-standing problems like tuberculosis or malnutrition. In one sense they are right. Funding for HIV-AIDS prevention and treatment should not come at the expense of efforts to provide basic health care to India's citizens. There should be no trade-off between the two. But unless India also tackles the AIDS epidemic, it could quickly find its health-care system overwhelmed. It is true that in 2005 less than 1 percent of Indians had contracted HIV. But at 5.1 million people, this made India the second largest sufferer of HIV-AIDS in the world after South Africa, which had 5.3 million infected people.[25] And the present is no guide to the future. One of the most terrifying features of AIDS is the speed with which it spreads. In 1990 less than 1 percent of South Africans had HIV. By 2005 that figure had shot up to 25 percent of the population. The epidemic has mutilated the economic prospects of entire tracts of Africa. America's National Intelligence Council estimates that unless India moves onto a war footing against AIDS, it will have 25 million HIV-infected people by 2010, rising to 40 million people by 2013 (which is only marginally less than the world's total HIV population in 2006).[26] Furthermore, most independent experts believe India's official statistics are an underestimate of the true scale of the problem. Some states, such as Bihar, provide no data. Since there are millions of Bihari males working in cities like New Delhi and Mumbai and then going home to their wives in the village once or twice a year, it is hard to believe the state is not also suffering from the epidemic.

India must overcome one fundamental problem if it is to do better than sub-Saharan Africa in checking the spread of AIDS: it must recognize the unprecedented nature of the threat. In 2005 Richard Feachem, head of the Global Fund to Fight AIDS, Tuberculosis, and Malaria, estimated that India already had the largest number of HIV-infected people in the world, in spite of New Delhi's numbers. India's response to Feachem's statement was not encouraging. In spite of its sensational news value, Feachem's estimate received very little publicity. Meanwhile, the Indian government quibbled with the small print. To some extent India's change of government in 2004 brought a big improvement in official attitudes to the disease. Unlike the BJP-led government it replaced, Manmohan Singh's government was prepared to admit the scale of the problem and discuss sexual behavior at public forums. His Hindu nationalist predecessors alternated between denial and prejudice. It is still common in Hindu nationalist circles to hear people say that homosexuality is a Western import and that Indian women have much higher moral values than foreign women. Apart from the xenophobic undertones, such language adds to the mystification of AIDS as a disease that affects only those who deserve it.

But Manmohan's good intentions alone are not sufficient to inspire confidence that India is doing enough to head off the disease before it becomes a pandemic. For example, New Delhi rejected the advice of the country's Law Commission in 2005 to make homosexuality legal. The statute dates back to the 1880s, when British civil servants labeled homosexuality as unnatural behavior. In its legal treatment of homosexuals, India remains in the same category as Iran

and Saudia Arabia. India is also behind the times in its official attitudes toward contraception. Fewer than half of India's population
has access to regular contraception, compared to more than 80 percent in China.[27] This might also owe something to the influence of
Mohandas Gandhi, who, unlike Nehru, abhorred contraception and
preached abstinence instead. In India, HIV is spread mostly by truck
drivers and migrant workers, who have sex with prostitutes for as little as $US twenty cents.[28] Then they go home and infect their wives.
Such is the ignorance about condoms that one health worker reported a remarkable story. He had demonstrated to prostitutes how
the contraceptive should be used by placing it over his thumb. They
took him literally and put condoms on their thumbs when they had
sex. "Can you beat it?" said the activist.[29] "There's so much to do
and look at the odds we are fighting." There are no reliable estimates
of the number of prostitutes in India. But it is evident prostitution is
a widespread phenomenon.

India's approach to AIDS mirrors other glaring contradictions in
Indian society. Indian drug companies have developed the world's
most cost-effective antiretroviral treatments by improving on the
manufacturing processes of Western-patented triple-therapy dosages.
Cipla, which is based in Mumbai, has done more than any other
company in the world to bring affordable AIDS treatments to millions of sub-Saharan Africans. Yet India is treating only a tiny fraction of its own victims. As with so many problems in India, the
country has the technology and the resources to tackle the problem.
What is lacking is a sense of urgency. A colleague once said to me:
"In Africa poverty is a tragedy, in India it is a scandal."[30] He was not
implying that Africans are less capable of reaching economic modernity than Indians, simply that India began life as a nation with better
institutions and more intellectual capital than its counterparts in
Africa. India knows, through having observed what has happened to
Africa, about the human tragedy of AIDS. It also knows the damage
the disease can do to the economy in terms of crippling the workforce. The Bill and Melinda Gates Foundation has pumped a lot of

money into India to assist in AIDS treatment and prevention. In addition, Bill Clinton, the former U.S. president, has committed his presidential foundation to developing AIDS treatment drugs with Indian pharmaceutical companies and making them available to the poor in Africa, India, and elsewhere. Clinton's advice to India should not be ignored: "I want to be serious here and say that this is not something that you can take casually," said Clinton on a visit to Delhi in 2004.[31] "There is no time to waste and every day you delay you put India's economic future at risk. You have come too far and worked too hard for your future to choose any other course. But if you do not act now millions will die who do not need to die."

The fourth and final challenge that I wish to highlight is the need for India to protect and strengthen its system of liberal democracy. When India achieved independence, many foreigners saw its diversity as a weakness. As we have seen, in some respects India's social divisions do impose a cost on the governance of the nation. But diversity is also India's greatest strength. Nowadays intellectual fashion has swung around to India's point of view. The remarkable project in Europe to build a continental union of many races, nationalities, religions, and languages was born as an idea only a few years after India came into existence as a nation. It has taken many centuries of bloodshed and slaughter—the like of which India has never seen—for Europe to reach this conclusion. India can teach Europe, Southeast Asia, and other parts of the world a great deal about how to keep a multinational and multiethnic entity together without imposing uniformity on its people or denying them basic freedoms. India can still live up to the dreams of Nehru and Gandhi to become a political beacon to the world. But in order to do so, India must guard against a number of threats to its uncompleted project of constitutional liberalism. It must also complete that project.

The most coherent threat to India's liberal democracy is Hindu nationalism. The defeat of the BJP-led government in 2004 and the subsequent outbreak of bitter recrimination with the Hindu nationalist movement persuaded many people that saffron politics was on the decline. This may well prove to be true. But the BJP can still command almost a quarter of the national vote, which, with the exception of the Congress Party (just above a quarter), is more than three times more than any other party. The influence of the movement as a whole in society is arguably greater. The Sangh Parivar (the RSS family of groups) controls India's largest trade union, its largest students' union, and the largest network of daily and weekly publications in India.[32] The movement is attempting to repackage itself to fit in with a rapidly modernizing India. Its image may change. But its basic aim, which is to downgrade the status of India's religious minorities, through peaceful or violent means, remains the same. There are concerns about the loyalties of Kashmiri Muslims. These must be tackled. But attaching a stigma to 150 million Indians is not the solution. It is a recipe for permanent civil war. Readers will have noticed that I have little positive to say about Hindu nationalism. Not only does it preach a violent and vengeful philosophy, but it also tarnishes by association all that is good and tolerant about Hinduism. If the BJP wishes to regain national office it should focus on combating corruption and modernizing India's state. This would clearly differentiate it from the Congress Party, which, apart from the royal touch, remains essentially a party of bureaucracy and patronage. In order to sell its message with any credibility, the BJP would have to sever its ties with the RSS, which remains an unreconstructed enemy of liberalism and a threat to India's national identity. This might be unlikely. But unless the BJP does so, few will believe its claim to be reinventing itself as a moderate party of the center-right.

India also needs to strengthen its system of parliamentary and local democracy. Preventing criminals from standing in elections would be a start.* But India must also find ways of raising the caliber of politicians in general. The quality of debate and scrutiny in India's

*In 2003 India's Supreme Court made it compulsory for election candidates to publish their "criminal antecedents," financial assets, and educational qualifications. This boosted transparency. But it did not result in a reduction of alleged criminals going into politics.

Lok Sabha (parliament) is remarkably poor for a nation that has so many eloquent talkers and sharp intellects. The quality of Indian parliamentarians has declined markedly over the last generation. And this has taken its toll on the quality of public reasoning in India. In the 1950s India's parliament met on average for between 120 and 138 days a year.[33] The average today is between 70 and 80 days a year. This contrasts to the United Kingdom, where the House of Commons meets for 170 days a year, and the United States, where Congress meets for 150 days a year. Indian politicians often profess a passionate commitment to a subject or a cause and then do not bother to show up for the debate, the committee process, or even the final vote. The speaker of India's parliament frequently has to adjourn proceedings because MPs are unable to maintain discipline. India is a paradox. It has an impressive democracy that is peopled, for the most part, by unimpressive politicians. As Anil Ambani, an industrialist who was elected to India's upper chamber in 2004, wrote: "It is time for India's VIPs to follow the people who get no pay for no work." Ambani, who is one of India's most intelligent business leaders, could also set a better example in the company he keeps. Ambani's seat was effectively given to him by the Samajwadi Party of Uttar Pradesh, which, as we saw in chapter four, is one of India's most corrupt.

Finally, India can better protect its internal system of liberal democracy by improving relations with its immediate neighbors, none of which has been able to maintain democracy for long, and most of which are highly prone to instability. The most obvious external threat to India comes from Pakistan, assisted to some extent by China, although Beijing's support for Islamabad has moderated in recent years. At the time of writing, India was in the third year of a peace process with Pakistan. The process shows signs of continuing. People way beyond the shores of the Indian subcontinent will be hoping that the process entrenches itself and becomes irreversible. India can assist this process by shedding its deep-seated neurosis about its neighbor. Pakistan has many flaws. But its existence is a fact with which

India has yet to fully come to terms. As the smaller and less secure nation, Pakistan is more volatile and more prone to initiating conflicts, whether through proxy means, such as terrorism, or by threatening wider conflagration by dropping hints about its nuclear weapons. India must adopt imaginative strategies to encourage a more moderate and less paranoid mind-set in Islamabad. More generous and farsighted statesmanship from New Delhi would help, particularly in addressing the aspirations of the Kashmiri people. Nobody expects or requires India to abandon its sovereignty over Kashmir. But we live in a changing world, where new technology and economic integration are making borders less relevant. It is surely not beyond the intelligence and ingenuity of south Asia's diplomats to devise a fungible and blurred sovereignty for Kashmir that would be accepted by the large majorities of both countries, as well as by Kashmiris themselves.

India also has a history of awkward relations with Bangladesh, which, in spite of the fact it was created by India in 1971, is both fearful and resentful of its large neighbor. There are an estimated ten to fifteen million illegal Bangladeshi immigrants in India. Many more will come if Bangladesh cannot achieve stable long-term economic growth. India must take the largest share of the blame for the fact that trade is so anemic within the South Asian Association for Regional Cooperation (which consists of India, Pakistan, Bangladesh, Nepal, Sri Lanka, the Maldives, and Bhutan). The trade flows between the seven member countries amount to less than 5 percent of their overall trade flow. This is feeble. Since India is by far the largest member country, nothing will change without India's lead. If India wishes to curb worrying signs of Islamic fundamentalism in Bangladesh and Pakistan, which will increasingly spill over into India, it must offer these countries an incentive to maintain social stability by giving their exporters generous access to India's vast domestic market. They would reciprocate. If India also wishes to curb the growing influence in the region of China, which maintains warm relations with Bangladesh, Pakistan, and sometimes even Nepal, then India should try to treat its neighbors as partners, not as irritants. Relations between India and Nepal have always been close. But, true to form, India's diplomats can rarely resist the temptation to patronize their counterparts from the small Himalayan kingdom. Nepal is suffering from a decade-old Maoist rebellion. India too has a Maoist problem with an estimated 10,000 Maoist guerrillas, or Naxalites, operating in the forests and remote areas between Bihar, which borders Nepal, and Andhra Pradesh in India's south. This so-called "red corridor" does not threaten India's national stability. But it destroys law and order in some of India's poorest states. India must tackle its own Maoist problem by providing its poorest districts with a higher quality of governance. But foreign policy should play a larger role. The Naxalites have strong links with Nepal's Maoists. Understandably, India does not want to show any signs of support for the 2005 Nepalese "royal coup" that was launched by King Gyanendra, and which amounted to a public relations victory for the republican Maoists. But India can still help Nepal to defang its Maoist threat by assisting the restoration of democracy in the Hindu kingdom.

Most of this chapter has focused on the challenges India faces in the coming years if it is to continue to ascend the international rankings. They are Herculean. But equally, its advantages are colossal. India never lacks for scale. In spite of the pressures of population density, India's clearest advantage over China and other developing countries is its demographic profile. From 2010, China's dependency ratio—the proportion of the working-age population to the rest—will start to deteriorate. In contrast, India's dependency ratio will continue to improve until the 2040s.[34] In the next twenty years, the proportion of dependents to workers will fall from 60 percent of the population to 50 percent. This will give India's economy a large "demographic dividend." It is commonplace to say a nation's future lies in its youth. But India's future also lies in its youthfulness. The higher the proportion of the population that is of working age, the higher the rate of savings in the economy. A higher savings ratio boosts investment, which lifts economic growth in a virtuous circle that for India stretches almost as far as the eye can see. Already India's savings ratio is improving—from about 18 percent of gross domestic product in 1990 to 26 percent in 2006. This is still well below China's savings rate of more than 40 percent. But China's rate is falling, while India's is rising. India is also improving its economic efficiency. It has achieved between 6 and 8 percent GDP growth with a savings rate of between a fifth and a quarter of national income. Growth in China has been comparatively expensive.

Furthermore, India has accomplished high growth without any of the tools of an autocratic state. No government in a democracy can impose compulsory savings on its population—as happened in much of east Asia—and hope to be reelected. Equally, no government in a democracy is in a position to impose family planning as China has done with its "one-child" policy. India's growth potential is even more striking if you consider how much has been achieved with so little. India lacks the modern infrastructure projects that have helped propel China forward. It also lacks foreign direct investment, which at $5 billion in 2005 was one-tenth the amount that China attracted. And India lacks universal literacy. Yet India's economy is still growing at between 6 and 8 percent a year or more. Imagine what India could achieve if it drastically improved its infrastructure or raised the quality of elementary education.

India also possesses institutional advantages that have convinced some people that the Indian tortoise will eventually overtake the Chinese hare. As India's economy develops, these "soft" advantages, such as an independent judiciary and a free media, are likely to generate ever-greater returns. Many investors are deterred by Indian bureaucracy. But none fear they would be subjected to the arbitrary controls on freedom of speech that Yahoo, Google, or Rupert Murdoch's News Corporation have suffered (and with which they have also acquiesced) in China. India can also draw on a deep well of intellectual capital. One in four business start-ups in the Silicon Valley are launched by nonresident Indians. Almost half of America's annual H1B visas are awarded to Indians. More than one hundred multinational companies have research and development centers in India compared to thirty-three in China.[35]

None of these expectations of India's growing economic strengths can be taken for granted, which is why so much of this chapter has focused on the problems rather than the opportunities that confront India in the coming years. India has in the past demonstrated a tendency to shoot itself in the foot. As the joke goes, "India never misses an opportunity to miss an opportunity." India is also suffering from a premature spirit of triumphalism, believing it is destined to achieve greatness in the twenty-first century without having to do very much to assist the process. Much of the self-confidence of India's elites stems from the country's sheer weight of numbers. They assess India purely in terms of its economic size, rather than comparing the standard of living of its people with that of people in other countries. Surpassing the overall size of Japan's economy is all very well (it is projected to happen sometime in the 2020s on a dollar basis*). But Japan would still have only a tenth of India's population, and virtually no one living in poverty. A nation should surely be judged by how it treats its people, not by how many people it has, or by how many nuclear weapons it has developed. So I will mention one further challenge that India must overcome in the near future: the complacency of its privileged classes. The key to overcoming the first four problems will lie in injecting a much greater sense of urgency into the mind-sets of India's political-bureaucratic elites—which can come only if India's electorate at large is more alert to the country's challenges and can transmit greater pressure through the ballot box to reform the state. India is not on an autopilot to greatness. But it would take an incompetent pilot to crash the plane. As Vijay Kelkar, one of

---

*India is very close to overtaking Japan's GDP by purchasing power parity—a measure of what you can buy if you convert dollars into the local currency.

India's wisest economists, has written, "The 21st century is India's to lose."[36]

• • •

I had just wrestled my way through the bustle and clamor of the crowded railway platform and was looking forward to a night of untroubled sleep. I had booked a berth in the first-class sleeper carriage, which in India still retains much of the feather-bedded comfort of the classic railway experience. It shuts out the noise and the heat. I enjoy the little things, like adjusting the reading lamp or twiddling with the temperature controls. It is an uninterrupted break from the world. The Indian train journey is invariably soporific. There are few more comfortable sensations than fighting a losing battle with sleep as you watch India float past your window.

"What is your name?" asked a voice, on the bunk opposite mine. I turned toward the questioner and saw a young Sikh boy assessing me curiously. I answered the question. "And which country are you from?" Again, I answered. "I wrote a letter to the Queen once," he said. "She still hasn't replied." He told me he had written to advise the Queen that she should visit India more often because lots of good things were happening here. He had also written a letter to President Bush, advising him to pull American forces out of Iraq. Again, he had received no reply. I asked him his age, which was ten, and where he went to school, which was in the city of Allahabad. His father, who was not accompanying him, was a major in the army. His mother, who was on the bunk below (Indian first-class compartments always have four berths) then told him to leave the stranger alone and go to sleep. She switched the main light out. The young boy waited for a few minutes until he was sure his mother was asleep. Then he switched his reading lamp on and trained it on me. He caught me just as I was about to descend into the oblivion of a deep sleep. "Tell me some interesting things," said the cheerful voice. "I have no plans to go to sleep tonight."

I tried many different arguments to convince my young interrogator to turn his light out and go to sleep. But he managed somehow to brush aside all my pleadings, inducements, threats, and protestations without enraging me. His persistence was too artless. "I still don't understand why we can't have a conversation," he said. So I resigned myself to his suggestion of a general knowledge test. I started with simple questions, which he brushed aside easily—the prime minister of India, then the finance minister of India, then India's biggest river, then the capital of Sri Lanka. "I'm not completely stupid," he said. So I moved onto the capitals of Europe, which he found a piece of cake, and then the flora and fauna of India, of which he had far greater knowledge than I, and then the presidents of America, and so on. Eventually after about an hour of swatting flies, he suddenly decided he wanted to scrutinize my career and my educational background. Each of his questions was informed and refined by my previous answer. He was beginning to build my profile. It felt, in fact, more like a criminal profile. Periodically he trained his lamp on me to check that my energy was not flagging.

Finally, I struck a deal with my restless torturer. He would let me go to sleep if I gave him my mobile phone number so that he could call me whenever he wanted to continue the conversation. We shook on it. But he interpreted the deal far too literally. I do not know how long I had been asleep when my pillow started vibrating and brought me awake with a start. The cell phone underneath it was ringing. "I just wanted to check you didn't give me the wrong number," said a familiar voice from the bunk opposite on his own previously undeclared cell phone. I rebuked the boy sharply, only to regret it straightaway. "There's no time to lose," he said, looking crestfallen. "The train arrives in five hours. What shall we talk about?"

So our conversation resumed. Every hour or so the train would stop at one of north India's endless provincial towns. A couple of times we got down on to the platform to buy a cup of milky *chai masala* served in the disposable earthenware cups that are unique to India. I began to feel entertained by his unflagging curiosity and precocious intelligence. There cannot be many ten-year-olds around the world carrying around this amount of information in their heads. In spite of his utter disregard for my sleeping plans, he was courteous to a fault. He was also wily. "Would you like another of my biscuits?" he asked whenever my eyelids appeared to be wavering.

Eventually, having mined me for all the information he possibly could, he announced it was time to sleep. Dawn was already intruding. There was only about an hour of the journey left. "We should really go to sleep now," he said in a tone of mild admonition, gently wobbling his head in the way only Indians can. "Tomorrow we can continue our conversation. Good night." Within seconds he was asleep. But I was well past the point of no return. For some reason I found myself laughing. It began slowly, originating in the abdomen and rumbling its way silently upward. It was that rare kind of laugh that spreads through the body and fills you—for the duration, at least—with a humorous optimism. Someone once said to me: "Remember, India always wins." India has a way of confounding you and still making you laugh about it. My chuckling did not subside until the train had reached Delhi.

# notes

INTRODUCTION

1. http://www.indiayogi.com/content/indsaints/mother.asp.
2. Ramachandra Guha, "Churchill's Indiaspeaks," *The Hindu*'s Sunday magazine, June 5, 2005.
3. André Malraux (from *Tristes Tropiques*) in Pankaj Mishra, ed., *India in Mind* (New York: Vintage Books, 2005), p. 172.
4. Amartya Sen, *The Argumentative Indian, Writings on Indian History, Culture and Identity* (New Delhi: Allen Lane, 2005), p. 152.
5. See Amartya Sen, Introduction to the *The Argumentative Indian*, p. xiv.
6. This story was first told by Arun Shourie in his speech at the annual Dhirubhai Ambani Memorial Lecture in Mumbai, 2003. It has been confirmed for this author by Anil Ambani, Dhirubhai's younger son.
7. M. J. Akbar, *Nehru, the Making of India* (New Delhi: Lotus Collection of Roli Books, 2005), p. 469.

8. Christophe Jaffrelot, *Dr. Ambedkar and Untouchability, Analysing and Fighting Caste* (New Delhi: Permanent Black, 2005), p. 110.

9. Richard Lannoy, *The Speaking Tree, A Study of Indian Culture and Society* (New Delhi: Oxford University Press, 1971), p. 138.

10. See Akbar's *Nehru, the Making of India,* p. 71.

11. Ibid., p. 239.

12. Ibid., p. 242.

## CHAPTER 1

1. Pankaj Mishra, ed., *India in Mind,* p. 303.

2. Lloyd I. Rudolph and Susanne Hoeber Rudolph, *In Pursuit of Lakshmi, The Political Economy of the Indian State* (New Delhi: Orient Longman Limited, 1998), p. 297.

3. Francine R. Frankel, *India's Political Economy, 1947–2004, The Gradual Revolution,* 2d ed. (New Delhi: Oxford University Press, 2005), p. 131.

4. *Lok Sabha Debates,* February 19, 1959, quoted by Frankel, *India's Political Economy.*

5. *Congress Bulletin,* April–May 1969, quoted by F. Frankel, *India's Political Economy.*

6. "Coming to Market," *The Economist,* April 15–21, 2006, p. 69.

7. I am indebted for many of these points to Vijay Kelkar, both in conversation and in his articles. He retired in 2004 as economic adviser to the finance minister.

8. Uma Das Gupta, *Rabindranath Tagore, A Biography* (New Delhi: Oxford University Press, 2004), p. 32.

9. I am indebted to Omkar Goswami, head of Corporate and Economic Research Group, a consulting firm, and former chief economist of the Confederation of Indian Industry, for his studies on Indian agriculture and patterns of rural spending.

10. Tim Dyson, Robert Cassen, and Leela Visaria, eds., *Twenty-first Century India, Population, Economy, Human Development and the Environment* (New Delhi: Oxford University Press, 2004), p. 168.

11. Gurcharan Das, *The Elephant Paradigm* (New Delhi: Penguin Books India, 2002).

12. See Rudolph and Rudolph, *In Pursuit of Lakshmi,* p. 10; or consult any of the U.S. National Intelligence Assessments of recent years.

13. See 2005 Human Development Report of the United Nations Development Program.

14. Credit Lyonnais Securities Asia, "The India Paradox," Spring 2005.

15. "Made in India, the Next Big Manufacturing Story," A McKinsey-CII joint report, October 2005.

16. Rakesh Mohan, "Managing Metros," *Seminar* magazine, January 2006.

17. Ibid.
18. See World Bank's report, *Poverty in India. The Challenge of Uttar Pradesh,* 2003, p. 2.

CHAPTER 2

1. Filippo and Caroline Osella, in C. J. Fuller and Véronique Bénéï, eds., *The Everyday State and Society in Modern India* (New Delhi: Social Science Press, 2000), pp. 149–50.
2. Arun Shourie, *Governance and the Sclerosis That Has Set In* (New Delhi: Rupa & Co., 2004), pp. 3–7.
3. All of these examples are drawn from the *Arthashashtra,* although I was alerted to most of them either in Richard Lannoy's *Speaking Tree* or A. L. Basham's *The Wonder That Was India,* 3rd rev. ed. (London: Picador, 2004).
4. As explained by Thomas R. Trautmann, University of Michigan, in his foreword to the 2004 edition of Basham, *The Wonder That Was India.*
5. Philip Mason, introduction, *The Men Who Ruled India* (New Delhi: Rupa & Co., 1985).
6. Ibid.
7. Nirad C. Chaudhuri, *Autobiography of an Unknown Indian,* introduction (London: Macmillan, 1951).
8. Rudolph and Rudolph, *In Pursuit of Lakshmi,* p. 61.
9. World Bank Report, *State Fiscal Reforms in India,* 2004, p. 21.
10. Bimal Jalan, *The Future of India* (New Delhi: Viking Penguin, 2005), p. 27.
11. Pratap Bhanu Mehta, *The Burden of Democracy* (New Delhi: Penguin Books, 2003), p. 115.
12. Parth J. Shah and Naveen Mandava, in *Law, Liberty and Livelihood, Making a Living on the Street* (New Delhi: Academic Foundation in association with the Centre for Civil Society, 2005), p. 28. They estimate the average bribe is Rs 200 a month.
13. Ibid., p. 25.
14. See the United Nations Development Program's 2005 annual Human Development Report to compare country indices.
15. Ibid. India spends just 0.9 percent of its GDP on public health, compared to China's 2 percent.
16. United Nations, Human Development Report, 2005.
17. To cite a few, see reports by India's Planning Commission, by the government's Centre for Vigilance on Corruption, the many writings by Jean Dréze, a noted economist, or the findings of the Centre for the Study of Developing Societies, a think tank in New Delhi.
18. Mehta, *The Burden of Democracy,* p. 104.
19. Rudolph and Rudolph, *In Pursuit of Lakshmi,* p. 89.

20. Bimal Jalan, *The Future of India,* pp. 107–8.

21. World Bank, *State Fiscal Reforms in India,* 2005, p. 11.

22. This is a detailed estimated provided by the National Institute for Public Finance, a government-sponsored think tank.

23. Amartya Sen, *The Argumentative Indian,* p. 206.

24. McKinsey Report on India, 2001.

25. A smriti-sutra (legal commentaries) that is cited in A. L. Basham, *The Wonder That Was India,* p. 115.

26. An estimate by ICICI Bank, India's largest private sector bank.

27. Craig Jeffrey and Jens Lerche, in Fuller and Benëï, *The Everyday State and Society in Modern India,* p. 100.

28. Rudolph and Rudolph, *In Pursuit of Lakshmi,* p. 1.

CHAPTER 3

1. V. S. Naipaul, *India, A Million Mutinies Now* (New York: Vintage, 1998), p. 517.

2. Richard Lannoy in *The Speaking Tree* lists dozens of subtle differences in meaning of the word *dharma,* pp. 216–22.

3. A. L. Basham, *The Wonder That Was India,* p. 92.

4. Ibid., pp. 143–44.

5. Ibid., p. 67.

6. Ibid., p. 81.

7. Pradipta Chaudhury, "Redressing Disadvantages," *Seminar,* p. 26.

8. I have taken all of these observations about Mahar village life from Neera Burra, whose excellent essay "Buddhism, Conversion and Identity" appears in M. N. Srinivas, ed., *Caste, Its Twentieth Century Avatar* (New Delhi: Penguin India, 1996), pp. 155–69.

9. There are numerous and varying estimates of the average cost of elections in India. Probably the best research comes from Lok Satta, a body that monitors politics, which is based in Hyderabad: http://www.prajanet.org.

10. Data from Public Affairs Centre, a nongovernment think tank based in Bangalore, from its report "Holding a Mirror to the New Lok Sabha," by Dr. Samuel Paul and Professor Vivekananda at http://www.pacindia.org.

11. Most of this data comes from the 2001 census but also from National Sample Surveys that look at the monthly nutritional intake of India's poor. Omkar Gosawami, who heads the Corporate and Economic Research Group, a consulting firm in Delhi, provided me with most of the combined data.

12. Corporate and Economic Research Group.

13. Edward Luce, "Beating Back the Brahmins," *Financial Times,* July 5, 2003.

14. Myron Wiener, in Ashutosh Varshney, ed., *The Indian Paradox* (New Delhi: Sage Publications, 1989), p. 57.

15. From Lucia Michelutti, whose instructive essay "We [Yadavs] Are a Caste of

Politicians: Caste and Modern Politics in a North Indian Town," appears in Dipankar Gupta, ed., *Caste in Question* (New Delhi: Sage Publications India, 2004), pp. 43–72.

16. From an intriguing essay by Anuja Agrawal, "The Bedias Are Rajputs: Caste Consciousness of a Marginal Community," in Gupta, ed., *Caste in Question,* pp. 221–45.

17. Report on the Prevention of Atrocities Against Scheduled Castes, National Human Rights Commission, 2004, p. 114.

18. Valerian Rodrigues, ed., *The Essential Writings of B. R. Ambedkar* (New Delhi: Oxford University Press, 2002), p. 267.

19. A term coined by M. N. Srinivas, the "Father of Indian Sociology."

20. See Kanchan Chandra's superb book, *Why Ethnic Parties Succeed, Patronage and Ethnic Head Counts in India* (New Delhi: Cambridge University Press, 2004), p. 145.

21. Ibid., p. 206.

22. Jean Dréze, quoted in *World Bank's State Fiscal Reforms in India,* p. 8.

23. Quoted in *India Today,* the weekly newsmagazine, August 8, 2005, p. 49.

24. The poll of 15,000 people nationwide was conducted in 2005 by the Centre for the Study of Developing Societies for IBN-CNN news channel.

CHAPTER 4

1. Quoted in Amartya Sen, *The Argumentative Indian,* p. 159.

2. Dr. Tupkary said some of the terms and ideas had been borrowed from Alvin Toffler, the American futurologist, whose books *The Third Wave* and *Future Shock* were widely read in the 1970s and 1980s.

3. Readers interested in the Harappans have much from which to choose. They could start with Romila Thapar's *Early India,* A. Ghosh's *The City in Early Historical India,* F. Braudel, *A History of Early Civilisations,* or A. L. Basham's *The Wonder That Was India.*

4. In an interview with the author, 2004.

5. Natwar Jha and N. S. Rajaram, *The Deciphered Indus Script* (New Delhi: Aditya Prakashan, 2000).

6. Sen, *The Argumentative Indian,* p. 66.

7. Basham, *The Wonder That Was India,* p. 32.

8. Benedict Anderson, *Imagined Communities* (London: Verso Editions, 1983), p. 15.

9. Christophe Jaffrelot, *The Hindu Nationalist Movement and Indian Politics, 1925 to the 1990s* (London: Hurst & Co., 1996).

10. All the Golwalkar quotes are taken from either *Bunch of Thoughts* or *We, or Our Nationhood Defined.*

11. For a detailed and instructive account of the RSS, read Walter K. Andersen

and Shridhar D. Damle, *The Brotherhood in Saffron, The RSS and Hindu Revivalism* (New Delhi: Vistaar Publications, 1987).

12. Sen, *The Argumentative Indian*, p. 48.
13. To name a few, there are compendious reports by Amnesty International, Human Rights Watch, India's National Human Rights Commission, and India's Concerned Citizen's Tribunal. All the reports reach much the same conclusions.
14. From the report "How Has the Gujarat Massacre Affected Minority Women?—The Survivors Speak" in *Untold and Retold Stories of the Hindutva Lab,* edited by John Dayal (New Delhi: Media House, 2002), p. 289.
15. As quoted in an article by the author in the *Financial Times*, April 15, 2002.
16. Neena Vyas in *The Hindu,* October 21, 2002.
17. Amnesty International, Public Statement 183, October 16, 2002.
18. *Sify News,* November 20, 2004.
19. Swapan Dasgupta, "Evangelical Hinduism," *Seminar* magazine, January 2005.

CHAPTER 5
1. Sonia Gandhi, *Rajiv* (New Delhi: Viking, Penguin Books, 1992).
2. Ibid.
3. As quoted in Inder Malhotra's highly enjoyable *Dynasties of India and Beyond* (New Delhi: HarperCollins Publishers, 2003), p. 18.
4. M. J. Akbar's *Nehru, the Making of India,* pp. 24–26.
5. Ibid., p. 23.
6. Ibid., p. 42.
7. Katherine Franks, *Indira: The Life of Indira Nehru Gandhi* (New Delhi: HarperCollins Publishers, 2001), p. 399.
8. Ibid.
9. Frankel, *Political Economy of India,* p. 679.
10. Ibid., p. 203.
11. Ibid., p. 222.
12. According to a survey by the Centre of the Study for Developing Societies, only 12 percent of voters in 1996 had even heard of the phrase *economic reform.*
13. Cited in Yusuf Ahmad, *Sonia Gandhi: Triumph of Will* (New Delhi: Tara-India Research Press, 2005), p. 156.
14. A very apt description I borrow from Frankel, *Political Economy of India,* p. 685.
15. World Bank's State Fiscal Reforms in India, 2005, p. xxii.
16. Priya Basu, *India's Financial Sector Reforms, Recent Reforms, Future Challenges* (New Delhi: Macmillan India, 2005), p. 148.
17. Ibid., introduction.
18. Prime Minister Manmohan Singh's address to the nation, June 24, 2004.

19. This estimate comes variously from the government, from the promoters of the legislation, and from independent economists.

20. Swapan Dasgupta writing in *The Pioneer,* August 14, 2005.

21. Mehta, *Burden of Democracy,* p. 88.

22. Ahmad, *The Triumph of Will,* p. 95.

23. Ibid., p. 245.

24. Malhotra, *Dynasties of India and Beyond,* p. 29.

25. At a press conference given by MKSS and Parivartan in New Delhi, August 2005.

26. Dyson, Cassen, and Visaria, eds., *Twenty-first-Century India, Population, Economy and Human Development,* p. 128.

CHAPTER 6

1. Quoted in M. J. Akbar, *Nehru, the Making of India,* p. 6.

2. Ibid., p. 17.

3. Francis Robinson, *Islam and Muslim History in South Asia* (New Delhi: Oxford University Press, 2000), p. 260.

4. The description provided by the school itself on its Web site: http://www.darululoom-deoband.com.

5. Akbar, *Nehru, the Making of India,* p. 380.

6. Ibid., p. 318.

7. Rudolph and Rudolph, *In Pursuit of Lakshmi,* p. 70.

8. Robinson, *Islam and Muslim History in South Asia,* p. 223.

9. Akbar, *Nehru, the Making of India,* p. 239.

10. Ibid., p. 270.

11. Robinson, *Islam and Muslim History in South Asia,* p. 225.

12. Akbar, *Nehru, the Making of India,* p. 374.

13. There has been some controversy over whether the maharajah signed the papers before or after Nehru airlifted troops to Kashmir, and whether or not he signed the papers under duress, with Indian historians and Pakistani historians naturally taking opposing views.

14. Stephen P. Cohen, *India, Emerging Power* (New Delhi: Oxford University Press, 2001), p. 224.

15. Stephen P. Cohen, *The Idea of Pakistan* (New Delhi: Oxford University Press, 2004), p. 243.

16. Ibid., p. 249.

17. Ibid., p. 58.

18. Census of India, 2001, *The First Report on Religion Data.*

19. Zarina Bhatty in Srinivar, ed., *Caste, Its Twentieth-Century Avatar,* p. 246.

20. Ibid., pp. 256–57.

21. Data from the Administrative Staff College of India (ASCI), Hyderabad.

22. Data from Educare, a Hyderabad-based NGO that researches informal sector—or private—education.

CHAPTER 7

1. I owe much of this insight into Gandhi to conversations with—and the thoughtful writings of—Ramachandra Guha, one of India's leading historians, who is currently writing a biography of Gandhi.

2. Quoted in "US-India Relations Convergence of Interests," *South Asia Monitor* (published by the Washington-based Center for Strategic and International Studies), No. 84 (July 2005).

3. For a comprehensive and authoritative account of India's nuclear weapons program, readers should go to George Perkovich's *India's Nuclear Bomb, The Impact on Global Proliferation* (New Delhi: Oxford University Press, 1999); and also to Ashley Tellis's *India's Emerging Nuclear Posture, Between Recessed Deterrent and Ready Arsenal* (Santa Monica: RAND, 2001).

4. Cohen, *Emerging India,* p. 257, quoting from the memoirs of T. N. Kaul, *Diplomacy in Peace and War.*

5. A phrase I borrowed from C. Raja Mohan, whose book, *Crossing the Rubicon, The Shaping of India's New Foreign Policy* (New Delhi: Viking, Penguin Books India, 2003), gives a balanced argument in favor of India's post–nonalignment foreign policy.

6. Cohen, *India, Emerging Power,* p. 86.

7. National Security Archives, http://www.gwu.edu/~nsarchiv/news/20050629/.

8. http://www.rediff.com/news/2002/may/30war2.htm.

9. http://www.infopak.gov.pk/President_Addresses/presidential_addresses_index.htm.

10. Farhan Bokhari and Edward Luce, "We Want Peace, but with Honour—Musharraf," *Financial Times,* May 28, 2002.

11. James Kynge and Edward Luce, "India and China Let Trade Take the Sting Out of Tensions," *Financial Times,* October 24, 2003.

12. Ibid.

13. Quoted in Perkovich, *India's Nuclear Bomb,* pp. 442–43.

14. Richard McGregor and Edward Luce "A Share of Spoils: Beijing and New Delhi Get Mutual Benefits from Growing Trade," *Financial Times,* February 24, 2005.

15. Institute of Peace and Conflict Studies: http://www.ipcs.org.

16. Ibid.

17. From Ashley Tellis, *India as a New Global Power: An Action Agenda for the United States,* Carnegie Endowment (June 2005).

18. A phrase first used of India by the Bush administration in 2001 and reiterated ever since.

19. These were off-the-record briefings given by Ambassador Blackwill to a small

group of foreign journalists. Since Blackwill is not longer in the Bush admin-istration, I am taking the liberty of putting them on the record.

20. From Tellis, *India as a New Global Power.*
21. Quoted in ibid.
22. Strobe Talbott, *Engaging India: Diplomacy, Democracy and the Bomb* (New Delhi: Viking, Penguin India, 2005), p. 5.
23. Cohen, *India, Emerging Power,* p. 62.
24. From India's Ministry of External Affairs: http://www.mea.gov.in/pressbrief-ing/2001/10/30pb01.htm.
25. From another of Blackwill's briefings to the foreign media in New Delhi.
26. Ibid.
27. Statistics derived from NASSCOM, the Indian software body. Most of the re-maining Indian software earnings come from the United Kingdom and Aus-tralia. http://www.nasscom.org.
28. From transcript of the Manmohan Singh interview with the *Financial Times,* conducted by Quentin Peel and Edward Luce, November 5, 2004.

CHAPTER 8

1. A term coined by Benedict Anderson in his book *Imagined Communities.*
2. Sen, *The Argumentative Indian,* p. 61.
3. Richard Eaton, *Essays on Islam and Indian History* (New Delhi: Oxford Uni-versity Press, 2001), p. 108.
4. Ibid., p. 105–6.
5. Ibid., p. 124.
6. From *India in Mind,* edited by Pankaj Mishra, p. 190.
7. From *Caste: Its Twentieth Century Avatar,* ed. by M. N. Srinivas, essay by J. Thavamangalam, p. 269.
8. Ibid., p. 280.
9. Quoted in Richard Lannoy's *Speaking Tree,* p. 77.
10. Government of India decennial census 2001.
11. Sen, *The Argumentative India,* pp. 225–26.
12. http://www.hindu.com/thehindu/holnus/001200511270311.htm.
13. The *Sunday Brunch* magazine of *Hindustan Times,* May 22, 2005.
14. "Sex and the Single Woman," *India Today* cover story, September 26, 2005, p. 43.
15. Dipankar Gupta, *Mistaken Modernity,* chapter 1.
16. From Basham, *The Wonder That Was India,* p. 251.
17. Lannoy, *Speaking Tree,* p. 330.
18. Ibid., p. 306.
19. Basham, *The Wonder That Was India,* p. 262.
20. Myron Weiner, *The Child and the State in India* (New Delhi: Oxford Univer-sity Press), pp. 23–27.

21. Estimates vary depending on the source. Main sources are government of India and UNICEF.
22. Weiner, *The Child and the State in India,* pp. 127–78.
23. Pratap Bhanu Mehta, *The Burden of Democracy,* p. 126.
24. UNICEF estimates.
25. Weiner, *The Child and the State in India,* p. 201.

CONCLUSION

1. Shashi Tharoor, *India: Midnight to the Millennium* (New York: Arcade, 1997), p. 5.
2. "Weekend Ruminations," *Business Standard,* September 11, 2004.
3. There have been heated disputes about the degree to which poverty has been reduced since 1991. Ninan takes the largest estimate, which is the official figure used by the Indian government and the World Bank. Clearly India's Gini Coefficient—its measure of inequality—has risen since 1991. But that is not inconsistent with a sharply falling poverty ratio. Improvements in other numbers, notably India's human development indicators, corroborate the poverty reduction data.
4. Myron Weiner, *The Indian Paradox,* edited by Ashutosh Varshney, p. 36.
5. Selig Harrison, *India, The Most Dangerous Decades* (Princeton, NJ: Princeton University Press, 1960).
6. Stephen Cohen, *The Idea of Pakistan,* p. 95.
7. Opening speech by Amartya Sen at a New Delhi conference, August 2003, on his book *Development as Freedom.*
8. From a speech given in New Delhi by Arun Shourie in 2003 entitled "The Fate of Reforms."
9. I owe this and several other insights in this section to Pranab Bardhan, a political scientist at Berkeley University, whose comparative writings on India's political economy are always sharp and thought-provoking. Two of his articles are particularly instructive: "Democracy and Distributive Politics in India" and "Crouching Tiger, Lumbering Elephant: A China-India Comparison." Both can be found on the Berkeley Web site.
10. The debate about the size of India's middle class is endless and the varied estimates are huge. Perhaps the best data can be found at the National Council for Applied Economic Research in New Delhi.
11. Dyson, Cassen, and Visaria, eds., *Twenty-First Century India, Population, Economy and Human Development,* p. 76.
12. From *Chindia: The Shape of Things to Come,* a report produced by CLSA, the French investment bank, in June 2005.
13. United Nations Development Program, 2005 Human Development Report.
14. The Centre for Science and Environment, New Delhi.
15. Dyson, Cassen, and Visaria, eds., *Twenty-First Century India, Population, Economy and Human Development,* p. 174.

16. India's Investment Climate, a joint World Bank–CII study, 2005.

17. This is a subjective judgment but it is shared, among others, by the World Bank, see previous note.

18. "India's Economic Future, Moving Beyond State Capitalism," the D.R. Gadgil Memorial Lecture given by Vijay Kelkar, October 26, 2005, p. 50.

19. Estimate given in author interview in December 2005 with Dr. Rajendra Pachauri, chairman of the United Nations Inter-Governmental Panel on Climate Change and head of the Energy Research Institute in New Delhi.

20. Ibid.

21. Dyson, Cassen, and Visaria, eds., *Twenty-First Century India, Population, Economy and Human Development,* p. 190.

22. Pachauri interview.

23. *Looking Back to Think Ahead* (New Delhi: TERI Publications, March 1998).

24. Estimates provided by India's Planning Commission.

25. Global Fund to Fight AIDS, Tuberculosis and Malaria, Geneva.

26. Cited in Jo Johnson, "Road to Ruin," *Financial Times,* August 13, 2005.

27. United Nations Development Program, 2005 Human Development Report.

28. Johnson, "Road to Ruin."

29. Ibid.

30. Martin Wolf, the *Financial Times'* main economics commentator and assistant editor, who worked extensively on India in the 1970s when he was employed by the World Bank.

31. Quoted in Johnson, "Road to Ruin."

32. Cited in Christophe Jaffrelot, ed., *The Sangh Parivar, A Reader* (New Delhi: Oxford University Press, 2005), pp. 4–12.

33. Article by Anil Ambani on the op-ed page of the *Indian Express,* September 4, 2004.

34. Vijay Kelkar, "India's Growth on a Turnpike," paper presented to the Australian National University, April 2004.

35. CLSA, *The Indian Paradox,* Spring 2005.

36. Kelkar, "India's Growth on a Turnpike."

# index